STRUGGLING FOR TIME

STRUGGLING FOR TIME

Environmental Governance and
Agrarian Resistance in Israel/Palestine

NATALIA GUTKOWSKI

STANFORD UNIVERSITY PRESS
Stanford, California

Stanford University Press
Stanford, California

Printed in the United States of America on acid-free, archival-quality paper

Library of Congress Cataloging-in-Publication Data
Names: Gutkowski, Natalia, author.
Title: Struggling for time : environmental governance and agrarian resistance in Israel/Palestine / Natalia Gutkowski.
Description: Stanford, California : Stanford University Press, [2024] | Includes bibliographical references and index.
Identifiers: LCCN 2023026833 (print) | LCCN 2023026834 (ebook) | ISBN 9781503636828 (cloth) | ISBN 9781503637726 (paperback) | ISBN 9781503637733 (ebook)
Subjects: LCSH: Palestinian Arabs—Agriculture—Israel. | Palestinian Arabs—Israel—Social conditions. | Agriculture and state—Israel. | Time—Political aspects—Israel. | Power (Social sciences)—Israel. | Settler colonialism—Israel.
Classification: LCC DS113.7 .G87 2024 (print) | LCC DS113.7 (ebook) | DDC 305.892/7405694—dc23/eng/20230731
LC record available at https://lccn.loc.gov/2023026833
LC ebook record available at https://lccn.loc.gov/2023026834

Cover design: Lindy Kasler
Cover photograph: Shutterstock

For my children
For the children of this land

CONTENTS

ACKNOWLEDGMENTS

A large community took part in the journey that was researching and writing this book. I benefitted from the wisdom and insight of others, from intellectual generosity, engagement, and much support from family and friends across time and space.

My research interlocutors in Israel/Palestine shared their stories, professional trajectories, practices and concerns, aspirations, and critiques. This is a large group of state officials, agriculturalists, agronomists, environmentalists, scientists, planners, and policy advisors. Without their voices and narratives, hard work, time, and kindness in providing me access, this book would not have been. I spent significant time with many of them in public and closed meetings, interviews, and reports; only a fraction of these materials could be integrated into this book. I hope you see that I attend to your work seriously, even when I critique it.

This project was shaped as a book at the Harvard Academy for International and Area Studies. The academy sponsored a stimulating book workshop that provided me with meaningful feedback from Ajantha Subramanian, Samer Alatout, Nadia Abu El-Haj, Matthew Wolf-Meyer, and Gershon Shafir, and their comments and suggestions significantly contributed to this book. Sahana Ghosh was a wonderful colleague supporting this intellectual exchange. Bruce Jackan and Kathleen Hoover helped me make the most of this significant event. Tim Colton and Melani Cammett led the Harvard Academy on a new path.

Beyond the book workshop, Ajantha Subramanian has always had illuminating thoughts on the multiple ways in which land, nature, time, and politics are bound. Under Ajantha's guidance, the Political Ecology/ Political Anthropology Working Group became a stimulating scholarly community at Harvard. This book benefitted immensely from my participation in this community and the friendships I developed there over the years. Thanks to Ekin Kurtic and Dilan Yildrim for their leadership of the working group, and to colleagues and friends whose feedback animated this book: Safa Aburabia, Eda Cakmakci, Xenia Cherkaev, Oren Shlomo, Jasmine Samara, Bethany Kibler, Meghan Morris, Juana Davila Saenz, Nancy A. Khalil, Darja Djorjevic, Chris Gratien, Myriam Amri, Caterina Scaramelli, and Randa Wahbe.

At Harvard's Anthropology Department, Steve Caton has offered close engagements and exciting conversations that guided my thinking on the anthropology of time, ethnographies of water and agriculture, and anthropology of the Middle East. The "Soil, Flesh and Flows in the Middle East" workshop I co-organized with Steve was a fantastic space to look at the material itself and its power in shaping accepted temporalities and expertise in the Middle East. I developed my thoughts on the social history of Palestinian agronomists working for the state for this workshop, and I thank Mandana Limbert for her insightful comments on this piece in its initial form. All the participants and commentators provided illuminating feedback and critique. I thank Omar Tesdell, Emily McKee, Jessica Barnes, Tessa Farmer, Amahl Bishara, Alan Mikhail, Steven Serels, Sam Dolbee, Gökçe Günel, Christine Walley, and Soha Bayoumi. Hilary Rantisi, Slaman Keshavjee, William Granara, and Elizabeth Flanagan supported this event in important ways. At Harvard's Anthropology Department, I also thank the late Mary Steedly, Ieva Jusionyte, John Comaroff, Jean Comaroff, and Michael Herzfeld for their kind advice on ethnographic writing.

The Comparative Inequality and Inclusion Research Cluster at Harvard's Weatherhead Center, under the generous guidance of Michèle Lamont further helped me develop book chapters and think comparatively about state officials from marginalized groups. I thank Anna Skarpelis, Talia Shiff, Merih Angin, Adrien Abecassis, Çetin Çelik, Gökce Yurdakul, Kobe De Keere, Rogério de Souza Medeiros, Shai Dromi, Matthias Koenig, Thomas Kurer, Anne-Marie Livingstone, Charlotte Llyod, Ninive Machado, Ronald Niezen, Bo Yun Park, Silvia Rief, Derek Robey, Paige Sweet, Keye Tersmette, Yossi Harpaz, and Kate Williams.

Sheila Jasanoff's sharp comments on my work and the insights that the STS Circle at Harvard University provided regarding chapter 3, on olive cultivation, were instrumental in the crafting of that chapter. I thank Nina Frahm, Tito Caravalho, Moran Levy, and Gili Vidan for their engagement with my work. Ashawari Chaudhuri became my friend when we met at the STS Circle and has always provided generous and engaged feedback.

At the Edmond J. Safra Center for Ethics at Harvard University I received food for thought across the disciplines on matters of science, ethics, and democracy. I thank Danielle Allen, Eric Beerbohm, Frances Kamm, and Jess Miner for introducing me to an analytical tradition that made me reconsider my assumptions. Tomer Perry, Stephanie Dant, Emily Bromley, Susan Cox, and Joe Hollow provided their support innumerable times. I am grateful to Adriana Alfaro Altamirano and Julie J. Miller for their warm, friendly, and loving support. I am thankful to Zeynep Pamuk, Wendy Salkin, Aleksy Tarasenko-Struc, Beth Truesdale, John Harpham, and Monica Magalhaes for their remarks on my work. In Cambridge, I am thankful to Bryce Ferber, for helping me feel at home at Harvard University. Midge and Hector Merlin and Roberta Apfel and Bennet Simon have been my adoptive families in the Boston area. Your encouragement and love are beyond gratitude.

The period I spent at the Department of Anthropology at the University of California Santa Cruz was crucial to the analytical directions this research has taken. I am profoundly grateful to Andrew Mathews for his close engagement with my work and his advice on walking the scholarly path with joy. I thought with Karen Barad creatively about time, space, and matter. I am grateful for insightful and productive exchanges with Julie Guthman, Lisa Rofel, Nancy Chen, Jude Todd, Jon Daehnke, and Jim Clifford. I am warmly thankful to Emily Reisman, Hatib Negress, Jon Rasmus Nyquist, Gillian Bogart, Oden Lonai, and Maayan Tsadka for many intellectual and friendly exchanges. I am indebted to Zahirah Suahimi-Broder for her sensitive comments. Diana Rothman generously shared her loving home in Santa Cruz and her warm human network during my time there. Paula Marcus, Liron Damir, and Tal Honig created a home away from home for me.

I am thankful to the Land Theme scholars at the Institute for the Social Sciences at Cornell University. Shelly Feldman led the "Land Grabbing and Subject Formation" workshop and the opportunity to reexamine my work through alternative paradigms with the sharp comments of Mustafa Koç, Theresa Selfa, Louise S. Silberling, Alia Gana, and Sedef Arat-Koç.

At the Department of Sociology and Anthropology at Tel Aviv University, I am profoundly grateful to Dan Rabinowitz for introducing me to anthropology, for multiple intellectual insights, and for diverse modes of encouragement and support. My work with Dan instilled the urgency of coupling questions of social inequality and environmental inequality. In the department, I was nourished with rigorous research agendas and an engaged scholarly approach. Yehouda Shenhav and I conducted fundamental exchanges that helped me design this research and sharpen its analysis. Ofra Goldstein-Gidoni offered support and encouragement to take my journey abroad. Khaled Furani provided me with significant advice and thoughtful comments, during different stages of this project.

At the Porter School of Environmental Studies at Tel Aviv University, I benefitted from conversations with Avital Gasith and Hillel Fromm that clarified the necessity of engaging natural sciences and social sciences. At the school, I was fortunate to lead the Lab for Society and the Environment. I thank the lab members for feedback, conversations, and support: Nir Barak, Tamar Neugarten, Noam Zaradez, Galit Samuel, the late Noam Segal, Refaela Babish, and Idit Alhasid. My lab friends Talia Fried, Shula Goulden, and Tamar Novick offered their advice and provided significant scholarly feedback and much friendly nourishment over the years. The lab solidified a friendship and deep collegiality with Liron Shani and Rafi Grosglik, with whom I have been sharing many thoughts and drafts since.

I am profoundly indebted to Laithi Gnaim for teaching me much about al-Battuf through his dedication and care. I thank Ramez Eid for helping me clarify nuanced matters relating to al-Battuf. Abed Kanaaneh and Didi Kaplan have both assisted me in accessing materials regarding al-Battuf that was not available to me otherwise.

Seeking advice from a leading ecologist, Avi Perevolotsky, effectively illuminated the distinctions between various experts' logic in the world of natural resources management and in bureaucratic structures. Our conversations have profoundly enriched me and have undoubtedly simultaneously softened and sharpened my work. Rassem Khamaisi offered his support and perspective on my project and served as a role model for both working within official establishments and efficiently criticizing them.

At the Edmond J. Safra Center for Ethics at Tel Aviv University I thank Shai Lavi for multiple conversations and invaluable feedback, Hagai Boas and David Heyd for insightful comments, Haim Hazzan for challenging my anthropological perceptions, Inna Leykin for her advice, and Michal Rappaport and Eran Shifman for their critiques. Through the center, I met Limor Darash-Samimian, who has provided me invaluable feedback.

I thank the network Transformation in European Societies based at Ludwig Maximilian University in Munich. I am especially indebted to Johannes Moser, Klaus Schriewer, Jacques Picard, Irene Götz, and Nils Jul Nielsen for engaging deeply with my work and offering significant feedback. I thank Daniel Kunzelmann, Anja Kittlitz, Salvador Cayuela Sánchez, Petra Steiger, Miriam Gutekunst, Michel Massmünster, Avital Binah-Pollack, Maya Wallenstein, Elad Ben-Elul, and Andreas Hackl for various collegial exchanges and for teaching me to see anthropology in its plethora of approaches, opportunities, and creativity.

For commenting on late versions of book chapters or offering insights that have significantly benefitted the last stages of this book while I have been located at the Hebrew University in Jerusalem, I thank Irus Braverman, Gabi Kirk, Nora Derbal, Omri Grinberg, Amit Gvariahu, Guy Shalev, Nadeem Karkabi, Miri Lavi-Neeman, Matan Kaminer, Mirjam Lucking, Alexander Koensler, Yael Assor, Muzna Awayed Bishara, Nili Belkind, Glli Hammer, Hodel Ophir, Shahar Shiloah, Basma Fahoum, Nimrod Ben Zeev, Dotan Halevy, Ramez Eid, and Sophia Stamatopolou-Robbins. I am grateful for intellectual support, nourishment, and reassurance in crucial moments from Yael Berda, Naor Ben Yehoyada, Areej Sabbagh-Khoury Gili Drori, Michal Frenkel, Alena Witzlack, Ella Elbaz, Dan Baras, Yael Fisch, Idit Ben Or, Ruthie Wenske Stern, Erez Maggor, Hiba Qawasmi, Raz Chen-Morris, and Yigal Bronner.

Over the years, Dakota Matson and Blaire Byg have helped me refine this text from my third language into a lucid English text. Blaire has been generous to accompany me even through dramatic changes in her life path.

I thank Kate Wahl at Stanford University Press for her support and guidance, as well as Tiffany Mok and Cat Ng Pavel for helping to bring this book to the world. Barbara Armentrout carefully examined that this work is all woven together. Utmost thanks to two anonymous reviewers who paid attention to a variety of details and improved this manuscript significantly. All shortcomings are, of course, mine.

This book is the result of academic engagements that could not have been possible without immense support and love. I am grateful to my friends Mihal Leibel, Aviv Shahrabani, Ruth Bronstein, Lila Noy, Yael Hirsch, Yael Baumgold, Yoav Holan, Zohar Sitner, Fanny Fleishman, Maya Negev, Naama Teschner, and Ruth Lev. Your friendships have nourished me for so many years.

I thank my transatlantic family for helping me conclude this book, which has been a long time in the making. My beloved canine companion Tommy has been a part of this academic journey from my early fieldwork in Galilee, across the Atlantic Ocean, until the last stages of writing this book (which were also his last moments on earth). I cannot adequately thank him for how supportive he was in our shared fifteen years.

My parents Hilda and Silvio, my late grandmother Henia (Saftush), and my sister Ana have supported this project with constant encouragement and love reminding me that what matters in life is to breathe deeply, to look at the sky and the trees growing, to see their roots and ours, and to remember that life is a dance. My grandparents Zaide (Leon), Yoel, and Sara have always been in my mind while I thought of our family's roots, survival stories, and the migration trajectories they had as Jewish refugees as they joined settler colonies across the globe.

My parents-in-law Bob and Leah Dressler provided intergenerational love to my kids while reminding me, in unspoken ways, of life-work balances. Edna, our adopted grandmother, has supported this book not only through her loving childcare but also through her insightful understanding of life. Michael has been my closest ally and my supporting rock, lovingly witnessing and sharing my path. My beautiful early morning bursts of sunshine Shir Hallel and Noam Isaac remind me that playing, singing, hugging, or walking in the Moon Grove is the best thing a woman can do while she struggles for time. In their giggling, they remind me: "Let us live life in the present, let us make a better future."

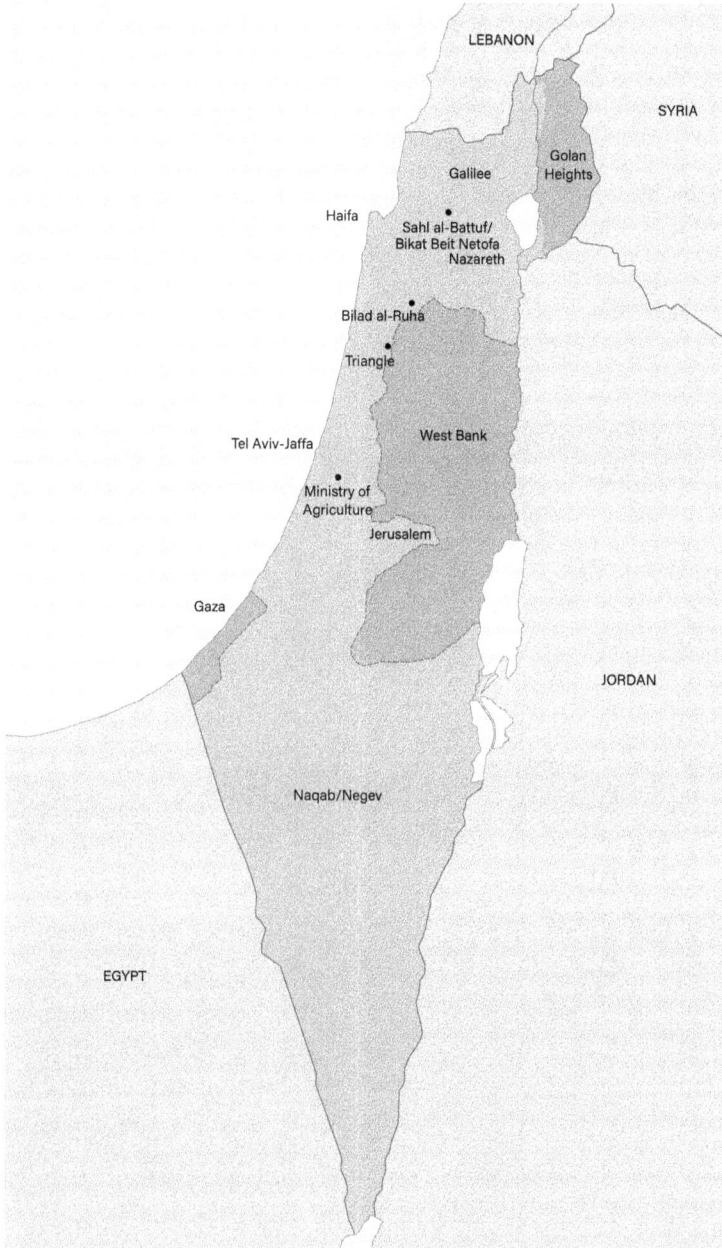

LEBANON

SYRIA

Golan
Heights

Galilee

Haifa

Sahl al-Battuf/
Bikat Beit Netofa
Nazareth

Bilad al-Ruha

Triangle

Tel Aviv-Jaffa

West Bank

Ministry of
Agriculture

Jerusalem

Gaza

JORDAN

Naqab/Negev

EGYPT

Map of fieldwork sites in Israel/Palestine. Map by the author.

Introduction

"Look at all these people sitting here—they have so much time. No one else has as much time as they do," the veteran agricultural economist whispered to me while we listened to the head of the Israeli Ministry of Agriculture's Planning Authority. It was a winter day in February 2014, and we were seated in the ministry headquarters' meeting room in Beit Dagan in the country's center. In this room, thirty-five Jewish-Israeli representatives of governmental and nongovernmental organizations for agriculture and rural areas were deliberating at length over the new Planning Policy for Agriculture and Rural Development. The eighty-year-old economist was frustrated with the bureaucratic process, yet he'd also captured a larger significance of "time-having" in the agrarian environment in Israel/Palestine.[1]

The meeting's participants discussed and regulated various forms of agrarian time as matters of the state. They imagined a historic period and cultural legacy that encompassed biblical ancestry alongside Zionist-created cooperative models and contemporary Israeli innovations in science and technology.[2] They produced an agrarian imaginary, arranging and choosing specific times and peoples that are included in policy while

1

neglecting other forms of understanding the local agrarian landscape and its stories of origin and development.[3]

Absent but present by other means in this meeting and in this policy were Palestinian Arab citizens and their farming villages, towns, and families. They had no representatives in most of the planning process and were only briefly mentioned during the discussions and in the new policy program. When mentioned, Palestinian citizens were referred to in phrases such as "the minorities' villages" or "the traditional Arab agriculture." Often, they were discussed without referring to any collective identity but simply by naming a town that locals know to associate with an ethnic-national identity. Out of the 250-page planning policy, only a five-page section summarized the development and preservation needs of "Arab agriculture."[4]

But even though Palestinian citizens were never explicitly mentioned, their agriculture significantly emerged in policymaking. Planners discussed the importance of preserving societal, cultural, and heritage values that are enlivened through agrarian landscapes. They said that Western countries are adopting policies that support the preservation of "traditional agrarian landscapes" as a part of their cultural heritage and for developing rural areas' tourism. Finally, the policy document stated: "The image of the agrarian landscape is entwined with the biblical tales and the birth of Christianity and embodies an important component of the historical image of the land. The biblical landscape is the backdrop of tourism that wishes to experience the Bible." Then it listed such sites in specific towns scattered across the region of Galilee, where Palestinian smallholders' terraced olive groves and small-scale agriculture characterize the landscape.[5]

The description of contemporary Palestinian agriculture as a "biblical landscape" was repeated in agrarian environments' policy discussions throughout my fieldwork. Struck by this characterization, I sometimes felt on the verge of asking the Palestinian agriculturalists how it feels to have Israeli state servants call your work "biblical agriculture." But I never did. I thought that equating Palestinian practices with biblical times evokes a nineteenth-century orientalist heritage.[6] Then, who is this imaginary of the Palestinian agriculturalist for and why does it persist? What work does the appropriation of Palestinian agrarian time do in the world today?

This contemporary political use of "biblical time" is not a mere gambit—time is deployed in multiple ways in the agrarian environment. At its core, agriculture is the biological engineering of nature. As such, it is imbued with temporal and technical practices that intervene in natural rhythms, compressing or expanding the seasonality and cyclicality of germinating, ripening, harvest, storage, and circulation time. These practices shift time from a natural cycle to an economic, political, and cultural object. Similarly, agrarian imaginaries of the landscape and of the people cultivating it are not arbitrary or natural. Rather, they are engineered and collectively designed as ideas that are materialized through the agrarian environment creating new socioecological worlds in which some win and others lose.[7]

This book focuses on exploring the process in which some groups "have so much time" in the agrarian environment while others are dispossessed of their time. A fundamental argument of this ethnography is that time is central to power and domination in the agrarian environment in Israel/Palestine and beyond. I ask how time is used as a mechanism of colonization for the Israeli state's control over the agrarian environment and how Palestinian agriculture professionals survive and resist daily such uses of power. A settler society, I posit, must necessarily erase native time and claim its own societal time as indigenous to inhabit and colonize the land. In this way, the settler society makes moral claims to justify its settler project. Traveling across both policymaking arenas and agrarian environments in Israel/Palestine, I examine how Jewish and Palestinian citizens, state officials, scientists, planners, and agriculturalists use time as a tool of collective agency, and I show how agriculture is a field uniquely amenable to governance through time.

Producing theory from Israel/Palestine about a struggle for time, I make a twofold and scalable argument: the colonization of time is central to settler colonial societies, and time is a focus of power in agrarian environments' politics during climate change. Contemporary practices of operating time as domination in agrarian environments principally emerge through policies, markets, science, technologies, landscape planning, and bureaucracy; hence, I flesh out how time works as a tool of "slow violence" rather than a prominent, immediate, or spectacular form of violence.[8] By shifting the analysis from the commonly observed space and territory in Israel/Palestine to time, the book offers new insight into the operation of power locally, in settler colonial societies, and in agrarian environments at large.

An understanding of how time becomes power in agrarian governance is particularly urgent given the challenges of climate change and the environmental crisis. Agriculture practitioners are confronting dwindling resources, changing seasons, new ways of modeling change, and multiple ways of predicting, planning, preserving, preparing, securing, anticipating, and speculating for an uncertain future. Governments, corporations, and consumer and producer movements are responding to climate concerns through actions that represent two socioeconomic sides of the same past-present-future anxiety coin. For instance, the passion for heirloom seeds, regenerative agriculture, "slow food," and maintenance of agrarian heritage systems often engages conservation politics, both preserving and re-creating socioecological memory and practice in the present as well as upholding a future potentiality for the use of such seeds, biodiverse systems, and knowledge.[9] On the other hand, the creation of food-tech and climate-smart worlds, as well as the global land rush are motivated by the politics of future global food security along with profit making from the crisis. These are all struggles for time as power in the agrarian environment.[10] To conceptualize such struggles for time, I develop throughout the book the notion of a *time grab* to describe an appropriation process that occurs under agrarian temporal justifications such as care for the agrarian heritage or the agrarian future of a collectivity.

Predictions of climate futures in the Middle East highlight that agriculture will be disproportionally affected by climate change and will likely increase political instability.[11] Yet, agriculture and food politics do not exist in a void. Agri-environmental challenges during climate change are situated within power and domination structures in which resource sovereignty, territory and environmental justice are a great concern for marginalized communities rather than consciously framing their struggles as a climate agenda.[12] Yet, the analysis of these sorts of struggles allows us to trace the reasons, the consequences, and the interventions needed for climate change adaptation in agrarian settings and beyond.

Common portrayals of climate change describe the future of the climate crisis as an eschatological process, resulting in the end of the world as we know it. But colonized communities globally have already known and endured the ending of worlds and see climate change as a continuation of colonial violence and not as an aberration.[13] Then instead of advocating an emergency horizon of "a race against time" as many climate activists propose,[14] fearing dystopic futures but failing to win big-money interests in climate politics, it may be that there are important lessons to learn from the experience of colonized peoples about survival, societal adaptation, resilience, living in ruins and in "the world ends," and struggling for just societies. This line of thought does not deny the need for an immediate response to climate change, but it is an invitation to find alternative futures within different locales, different scales of thinking, and temporalities other than the dystopic and apocalyptic ones. Thus, this book's reflections on settler colonial encounters in agrarian environments in Israel/Palestine and beyond are intended to facilitate an understanding of possible times to come and how temporal images and experiences materialize to control or decolonize.

Settling Time

The societal development in Israel/Palestine is similar to early settler colonial societies such as Canada, Australia, the United States, South Africa, and Argentina. These societies have developed as settler colonial due to a process of immigration, settlement, the displacement and replacement of the indigenous population, spatial segregation, and the formalization and institutionalization of settlers' political and economic privileges vis-à-vis the indigenous population.[15] Often, the emergence or consolidation of settler colonial societies is grounded in a political imagination technique articulating the land as "terra nullius," an unowned empty land, therefore available for colonization.[16]

While these societal characteristics in Israel/Palestine match global settler colonial histories, Jews have been an integral part of the Middle Eastern region for centuries. A Jewish minority lived within the population of Palestine in the early twentieth century.[17] But with the ethnonational basis of the Zionist movement, Jews of Middle Eastern origin

(Mizrahim) have come to occupy a privileged societal status relative to Palestinians although, on internal Jewish terrains, Mizrahim have been marginalized into a lower settler social class. This process shattered the shared multiethnic life of Jews and Arabs in Palestine in the earlier twentieth century, and it allows contextualizing how Jews local to the region have gradually become settlers in a settler colonial process.[18]

The dominant viewpoint among Jewish Israelis is that they are descendants of the ancient indigenous people who returned to their ancestral land to reclaim their traditions and roots and to build a national home for Jews. Consequently, Zionism has been simultaneously a national movement and a settler colonial process assembling Jewish national self-determination on the expense of Palestinians.[19] The Jewish-Zionist return has materialized through ecological and agrarian worldmaking techniques.[20] Yet, the notion of return is not unique to Israel/Palestine and it characterizes other settler societies too. The French settler colonists in Algeria described themselves as the inheritors of the Christian Romans, returning to Northern Africa and liberating it from centuries of Islam. They saw France as the successor of Rome and the settler colonists as resurrecting the ancient granary of Rome in the Maghreb. They became invested in large agro-environmental projects to expand cultivation and forest areas, facilitating land and resource appropriation.[21] Pointing at the political interplay of Jewish return to a land that Jews had sparsely inhabited during previous centuries and populated only in ancient history helps me explain in nuance my book's focus.

I highlight that as space and time are entangled and coproduced,[22] we must understand how an indigenous society not only is removed from its local space but is dispossessed from its time. I point out time as a multilayered tool of power but also as a tool of social agency, collective orientation, and action. By so doing I conceptualize the political dynamic in settler colonial societies beyond its dominant spatial-territorial account highlighting the importance of a temporal analysis and theorization of a settler colonial dynamic. Dominant accounts emphasize that the settler society's central aim is to replace the native society. To achieve replacement, settler societies are centered on *spatial occupation and land appropriation* as a means of establishing a new colonial society.[23] Palestinians have been removed from the land through capital-based land acquisitions prior to 1948, historical and contemporaneous dispossession through legal proceedings, and wartime ethnic cleansing in 1948. These practices shed light on the continuity of Palestinian elimination from space and territory as a recurring dynamic. While Palestinians are eliminated from space, the Israeli society expanded its settlement project altogether.[24] Yet, if we understand that there has been a spatial dispossession process as well as resistance to it, how does it occur in temporal terms?

I argue Israel is *settling time* in a twofold manner. First, Israel is settling social time with Jewish-Israeli cultural, national, and settler colonial significances that aim to reclaim ancestral belonging in the land and erase Palestinian social time. This is exemplified by the governmental practice of articulating Palestinian agriculture as "biblical" agriculture rather than recognizing it as a Palestinian agrarian heritage (notwithstanding that the Bible is also a Palestinian heritage). Second, Israel is settling time as a mediation practice.[25] Settling time is a means of bridging the nonaligning and conflicting "capitalist time" of Israel's industrialized agriculture time and the imagined "biblical time" that Israeli agriculture allegedly stems from and is striving to revive. The political practice of mediation between time conflicts assists the state in morally and politically justifying its existence as a Jewish State.

Palestinian citizens' agriculture has become a central site assisting the state to mediate between conflicting forms of time. Imagining Palestinian agriculture as biblical both erases Palestinian agriculture's collective heritage and disregards the reality of contemporary Palestinians cultivating agriculture and culture. Therefore, Israel's double-time settling techniques are a form of slow violence. According to Rob Nixon, slow violence is a gradual, dispersed, and accumulating form of violence. It is slow because it is non-spectacular, non-immediate, and non-explosive but it inflicts harm personally and collectively.[26]

The settler colonial scholarship defines the recurrence of settler invasion as a "structure" rather than a singular event.[27] Looking at the latter process in temporal terms, the continuous dispossession experience is termed "the ongoing Nakba" (*al-nakba al-mustamirra*), referring to the experience of continuous loss of Palestinian homeland not as a singular event that occurred in the 1948 War, but rather a steady experience that Palestinians have continued to endure ever since. Recent indigenous and Palestine scholarship highlights that settler invasion is not the only structural feature of the settler colonial dynamic. Native struggles for survival, return, and sovereignty are also important structural characteristics.[28] In this book, I highlight mundane Palestinian resistance through time claims, temporal orientation, and agrarian temporal practices, thus resituating Palestinians as active agents of history who use time as a tool of collective agency and social orientation.

While most contemporary scholarly accounts of Palestinian resistance to the settler society's dispossession through agriculture are situated in the Occupied Palestinian Territories (OPT), this literature has neglected the agriculture of Palestinian citizens of Israel for decades.[29] Some of the Palestinian agriculture professionals whom I have talked to consider that "perhaps Israel has finished its land battles with Palestinian citizens and now the struggle is an internal societal struggle, for '48 Arabs to conserve and renew our own agriculture."[30] Such a view is aware of its own societal challenges given the low esteem that Palestinian agriculture in Israel has had, but it also blurs agriculture and Palestinian agriculture as a contemporary form of politics in the Israeli state. This perception obfuscates the ways that Palestinian agriculture in Israel continues to challenge relations between the state and Palestinian citizens, despite its constant dismissal. Native American scholar Gerald Vizenor's term *survivance* will be key in illuminating modes of Palestinian native presence and native existence as resistance over a history of absenting and erasing. Vizenor emphasizes that survivance is the repudiation of essentialized victimhood in native histories via the carrying of traditions and narratives that resist native erasure and produce sovereignty and liberty in the present.[31]

To recognize the nuances of the settler colonial encounter in Israel/ Palestine, I note that Jewish-Zionist history is also a tale of survival, return, and sovereignty. This is due to the history of Jewish persecution and the effects of the Holocaust trauma on Israeli society.[32] The Holocaust has most likely affected the Israeli state's choices regarding modes of violence throughout its state history. Oren Yiftachel conceptualized this trauma's effects as "colonialism of survival."[33] Other settler societies were subject to discrimination and persecution prior to settlement too, yet the Holocaust marks the Jewish-Israeli society as the only settler society that was subject to genocide.[34] But the Zionist narrative of survival followed by the 1948 War and its effect on Palestinians erases the forceful removal of Palestinians from their land and the destruction it inflicted on Palestinian collectivity historically and contemporaneously.[35]

Furthermore, the Jewish-Israeli narrative of return to Israel as an ancestral land does not acknowledge why Palestinians would give up their land after only a few decades of its loss if Jews have craved their land for two thousand years since their deportation from it. The narratives of survival in Israel/Palestine call for an interrogation of the possibilities of articulating different pasts, presents, and futures to reimagine and unmake the settler colonial dynamic.[36] Similarly, the circumvention of historical memory is a shared feature of settler societies that erase their violent pasts and create new national imaginaries, such as the myths of Thanksgiving or Columbus Day in North America.[37]

Despite settler societies' tendency to erase their pasts and create new foundational stories,[38] the discussion of time and its manipulations in settler colonial processes remains scarce. To date, the only systemic exploration of time in settler colonial contexts is Mark Rifkin's pioneering monograph *Beyond Settler Time: Temporal Sovereignty and Indigenous Self-Determination*.[39] Grounded on American fiction and film analysis, Rifkin develops the notion of "settler time" that consigns native peoples to the past and embeds them in the present only to legitimize settler histories and geographies. Engaging with discussions on social change and intersectionality, I expand Rifkin's work by including class dynamics in this process of ethnographically observing "temporal distancing" between settler and native. Such narration of a social story moves beyond the binary of the settler and native and sheds light on the possibility of native benefactors binding the native society to the "time of tradition" based on internal class distinction. Marking class distinction in settler colonial dynamics overcomes the tendency to essentialize identities and to think about the conditions of slippages between distinct societal locations or the alliances that may emerge as Jews and Palestinians are stuck together in this land.[40]

Settler colonial scholarship shows that settlers' narratives use a linear conception of time fueled by ideas of Western modernity, progress, and the need to distance the settler society from its violent past to construct a new present. Indigenous notions of time are structured by a constant relation of the past and the present, building a future image that is grounded on an interpretation of the past, present, and the role of ancestry in the present and future.[41] However, I aim to complicate this narrative by unpacking the stakes in the performance of the past as present for both the settler state and the native subject. Such interrogation allows us to critically observe the settler/native binary by seeing them as contextually defined.[42] It further illustrates that time dispossession is integral to the settler colonial structure, but the ways time is deployed in different societies require analytical nuance.[43]

The settler colonial framework also enables us to observe political processes taking place throughout Israel/Palestine regardless of citizenship status and reveals the logic of control upon which Israel operates.[44] Too often, scholarship on Israel/Palestine attends to the management of Palestinians under Israeli control since 1948 or since 1967 as subject to distinct technologies of domination. This divergent governance view is nurtured by the citizenship status that 1948 Palestinians are subjected to versus military control in the West Bank and Gaza.[45] Alternatively, I illuminate time as a key factor of the Israeli settler colonial agenda, regardless of citizenship status. While this book's ethnographic fieldwork focuses on the encounters of Palestinian citizens of Israel with the state, I insist on making connections to the political reality of the rest of Palestine's population. Such a perspective allows observing governance rationales that extend across the perceived boundaries of the settler colonial regime.[46] Understanding time as a form of power sheds light on possible futures in the land beyond the current moment. It allows us to think about time as a layered concept that functions as a multiplex mechanism of governing from the past to the future.

Timescapes and Agrarian Imaginaries

It is possible to observe layers of time as singular elements: time as duration, time as an imaginary, time as expectation, or time as a cultural or economic concept to manage. This has been the predominant way in which scholars have attended to the modes of time that the Israeli state uses to govern. Some scholars have addressed the Israeli legal uses of time manipulations regarding landholding durations as a tool that facilitates the dispossession of Palestinians from land.[47] Others have explored the wasting and stealing of Palestinian time embodied in the permit regime in the West Bank and the multiple checkpoints where Palestinians need to wait, producing a constant sense of delay and uncertainty.[48] Writings have addressed Israel's state work to instill Jewish Israelis' identification with the nation through repetitive calendric experiences of public events and the anchoring of ancestral belonging in the land through biblical narrations and archeological excavations.[49] Anthropologists have also examined Israeli regimes of preparedness for future threats and the way they ingrain a sense of emergency in the daily lives of Israelis.[50] In parallel, scholars have highlighted the expansive Israeli state work to erase Palestinian collective commemoration, village sites, and cultural and historic records.[51] These rich accounts of time techniques utilized by the Israeli state have created a rich mosaic.

But looking at all these temporal mechanisms as separate instances ignores a crucial aspect of the execution of political power and the political technologies employed by a settler colonial state and society:[52] time is a constitutive power mechanism operated by the settler state. Rather than seeing these instances as distinct cases of governance techniques, these multiple layers of time are a multifaceted mechanism of governance necessary for settler colonial processes. These layers of time are fascinating to follow and conceptualize because they appear in multiple spheres of governance, at times explicitly articulated in formal policies and more often enacted as informal policies. But as opposed to an authority for the management of space such as the Israeli Land Authority, there is no state authority responsible for the management of time. Yet time emerges as a central form of both macro and micro governance that is too often invisible.

Conceptualizing the multiple levels of time together allows us to recognize how different modes of time work in parallel in the political process and in social life. A key tool for conceptualizing this multiplex mechanism is the term *timescape* coined by Barbara Adam.[53] The idea of a timescape emphasizes the nature of time and space as interdependent and multilayered, and it delineates embodied approaches to time. For instance, we might feel the passage of time differently during a period of waiting than we do during the midst of a major crisis. Regarding Israeli agricultural planning, a timescape approach exposes the temporal governance work of the state in multiple ways. It can illustrate the Ministry of Agriculture's perpetually ongoing bureaucratic work; it can be used to explore the state's political fabrication of the "biblical agrarian landscape"; it can also be used as a lens through which to view the rhetoric of progress that is embedded within the Israeli agricultural ministry's discourse of scientific and technological achievements. The timescape approach unveils at least three elements of time in the texture of governance and power. Think of the way a photo of a landscape is composed of various layers and topographic elements—so is the timescape, composed of multiple layers of time, woven into a specific social reality.

Writings on timescapes address this spatiotemporally as situated within capitalist, industrialized, and neoliberal economic regimes.[54] Alternatively, I emphasize that timescapes contain dialectic logics that move between a straightforward capitalist rationale of short-term profit and noncapitalist temporalities that are subsidized by the state and its individuals for the sake of the settler society's continuity and to eliminate political instability. As the Israeli case demonstrates, counter-profit decisions are necessary to maintain the temporal order that justifies the settler society, such as the Israeli state project of regulating Jewish time. Jewish time in Israel has been kept, regulated, and enforced in multiple forms since the state's inception. Jewish time is reckoned through the observance of the Jewish lunar calendar and especially the observance of Saturday as the holy day in the Jewish religion. Counter-profit decisions are exemplified on a regular basis in Israel's regulation of business closures and the banning of public transportation on Saturdays, as well as the prevention of public works on Saturdays. Other instances of observing the Jewish calendar in a counter-profit manner include the closing of cafes and restaurants on the eve and day of the ninth of the Jewish month of Av, observed by religious Jewish subgroups, or the complete business and traffic shutdown of the country's Jewish areas on Yom Kippur (the day of atonement).[55] These performances of Jewish time support the unique character of a "Jewish State" that facilitates a Jewish life.[56]

These practices are not given nor are they shaped only on internal Jewish terrains, but rather they are a political process that emerges in the context of power relations of the settler society. Looking at these different layers of time together, I suggest that the timescape framework better equips us to analyze and understand how different forms of time stretch across one social space and form relations of power. The term *timescape* illustrates how the spheres of time, space, and landscape are interdependent.[57] Throughout this book, I prioritize the analysis of time apart from its intermingled time-space fabric.[58] I highlight how time matters and how it becomes material in the agrarian dynamic. Time colonization reveals the established ways in which evocations such as the "biblical landscape" insidiously appropriate the landscape without ever needing to legally confiscate land.

Examining time as a multilayered form of power in the global agrarian environment illustrates how agrarian modernization projects sponsored by states, colonial forces, or capitalist development mechanisms have always classified people and places, assigning who or what is situated in the past or in the future as a tool in justifying dispossession. Following such discourse to the present moment, speedy technologies that compress time and space erase the previously entwined relations of time, space, and labor. In responding to climate change and rendering land investible for biofuels and renewable energies, land development is often grounded in perceptions of contemporary agrarian "backwardness" versus the "improvement" and futurity that the land withholds through renewable energies on arable lands. Therefore, the emergence of new agrarian production frontiers in the pole and the rise of solar production fields on agrarian land perpetuate the dichotomy between tradition and modernity, shaping the temporal perception of social actors, locations, and forms of production. This recurring pattern in the agrarian timescape signifies power, which I scrutinize in my analysis.[59]

Another concept fundamental to the analysis in this book and to the timescape is the agrarian imaginary. The concept of the imaginary offers a productive interplay and thread between thought, image, and imagination and past, future, and reality. In the context of Israel/Palestine, the political power of the imaginary cannot be underestimated. The facts created on the ground in historic Palestine by the Zionist movement and later the Israeli state provide evidence of the imaginary's power. A hundred and so years ago, the idea of a national home for Jews was a marginal view among Jews in the diaspora and in Palestine, let alone the global community. But when the Zionist imaginary materialized, it created a revolution in Jewish lives globally and in historic Palestine, causing a collective catastrophe for Palestinians. But if imaginaries were so powerful before, they can also be fertile ground to explore the possibilities of new futures. Currently, in Israel/Palestine, imagination is a main tool to counter the collective disappointment about the failure of any "solution."[60] Hence, fleshing out the imaginary as a social practice requires attending to views and speculations of the past and the future of a certain social space and looking at the transcendence of time and space in these collectively fabricated images.

Addressing agrarian imaginaries, I build on political ecologist Diana Davis and STS (science, technology and society studies) scholar Sheila Jasanoff, who attended to the material consequences of social imaginaries in the contexts of the environment, science, and technology.[61] Drawing on their work, I see the agrarian imaginary as a form of world-building based on a shared societal imagination of the condition of the agrarian environment, the circumstances that led it to its condition, views on its ideal state, and the programs set to materialize the imaginary. The agrarian imaginary is anchored in collective views and therefore resides in the minds of social agents and its collective institutions. The agrarian imaginary is enlivened by technological and scientific interventions that are aimed to achieve collective visions and turn aspired futures into realities. Agrarian imaginaries are rooted in sociocultural contexts, and they are supported by changes that societies experience over time. The agrarian imaginary calls us to observe what becomes objects of the social imaginary, who gets to create the imaginary, for whom it works, and what implications an imaginary has as it materializes.

For instance, the image of the Palestinian peasant as a biblical figure was passed from Christian European tourists and settlers to Jewish-Zionist immigrants. In Zionist history, the agrarian imaginary of the Palestinian peasant and shepherd had first a romanticizing aspect, as some Jews at the end of nineteenth-century Palestine aspired to imitate the local shepherds and adopt their knowledge of the land.[62] This romantic imaginary eventually morphed into a denigrating view of traditional Palestinian agriculturalists, which, for close to a century, would become the Zionist movement's way of asserting its superiority over Palestinian agriculture. Contrasting themselves with the image of the traditional Palestinian peasant, Jews in Palestine attempted to demonstrate that they were a modernizing force in the land, capable of feeding a larger population. This book will show yet another shift in the agrarian imaginary of the Palestinian peasant. The contemporary imaginary attempts to convey the Palestinian agriculturalist as an appreciated upholder of the biblical agricultural legacy against the all too modernized Jewish-Israeli agriculture. Evidently, the imaginary of the Palestinian agriculturalist as a steward of the biblical legacy matters to Israeli state politics but the significance of the biblical image keeps changing along the history of the Palestinian–Jewish-Israeli agrarian encounter.

Palestinian-Zionist Agrarian Timescape

The agrarian environment in Israel/Palestine is a productive space to examine the embodiment of time as power in the settler colonial dynamic. For over a century, the countryside in Israel/Palestine has been a site where settler and native narratives and attachments have played out, both for the sake of physical presence and control of the land and its production resources and as a means of anchoring historic patrimony and claims to identity. The rural areas have been a central site where collective stories of self-determination, liberation, dispossession, and power struggles have occurred.[63] Globally, critical agrarian histories are usually told from the perspective of access to the means of production (especially water, land, and forests), labor relations, income, and the reproduction of social class. Locally, some of these themes overlap.

In the late nineteenth century, Palestine was a part of the Ottoman Empire. Arab peasants made up most of the population of Palestine.[64] The country's small size, diverse geographical terrain, and dependence on rain-fed agriculture allowed the development of diverse sources of income utilizing all the topographical elements of the environment. In the fields there were grains, legumes, and vegetables; hills were terraced and planted predominantly with olive trees, while hilly, stony lands were used for grazing; lowlands were used for herding and raising buffalo. Palestinian production was predominantly based on a nonindustrialized mode of cultivation, yet Palestine produced agricultural surpluses and was integrated into the world capitalist economy as an exporter of wheat, barley, sesame, olive oil, soap, maize, and cotton.[65] A significant export industry was citriculture, predominantly located around the port city of Jaffa, making the distance from cultivators to European and Arab markets short.

Yet, major historical accounts and political narratives that emerged with the inception of the British Mandate (1917–1948) in Palestine until recently have described the Palestinian agrarian economy as a primitive one, a subsistence farming society that was completely at odds with modern, capitalist forms of production. Such time-based representation of production advanced a claim that the arrival of Jewish colonization brought significant modernization and progress benefits to Arab agriculture, ignoring former modes of pre-industrial capitalist production and trade in Palestine during the Ottoman Regime.[66] The first mode of temporal orientation in the local agrarian timescape is Jewish agrarian modernization versus Palestinian tradition and de-development. The modernization/tradition binary in Palestine emerged in the context of the settler colonial societal structure and the imperial economic and legal mechanisms that assisted its formation.

A central governance apparatus that characterizes the local agrarian timescape is temporal legality, which is a second orientation mode in the local agrarian timescape. *Temporal legality* is a term I coined to describe all the laws and regulations pertaining to governance through time to control society, space, and time. This aspect of governance is a political legacy Israel inherited from previous powers in Palestine, but Israeli governance developed this system to a level of political mastery. These temporal legalities are fascinating because they reflect the ways that Israel has completely reversed the significance of the land law from its Ottoman multiethnic context aimed to advocate for the cultivation of land to an ethnonational context aiming to appropriate Palestinian peasants' lands for the state and its Jewish settlement project.

The agrarian history of Palestine is marked by the turning point of the Ottoman Land Code (OLC) legislated in 1858. The OLC reform introduced a system of land registration as well as the transformation of land ownership from *Musha'*, communal land held by a Palestinian village, to individual ownership. The OLC allowed anyone who paid taxes to own property both in cities and the countryside, whereas before, land was only leased from the Ottoman state. The land category most relevant for a discussion on temporal legalities is *miri* land.[67] *Miri* was the most common land in Palestine—the land adjacent to the villages. The Ottoman ruler held *miri* land's formal title, which encompassed cultivable land and the empire's source of tax revenue, yet the landholder or cultivator had the full rights to use the land. The ruler had the right to confiscate *miri* land if it was not cultivated for more than three years. The OLC also specified that a person holding and cultivating unregistered land for ten years could request a *miri* title deed, which allowed the government to advance cultivation and land registration for tax purposes.[68] Following the OLC, private ownership in Palestine became expensive, pushing small landowners to sell their land to rich urban families or absentee landlords, turning many smallholders to landlessness or indebtedness. The OLC later played a pivotal role in facilitating the Zionist purchase of land in the pre-state era. [69] Then, World War I brought an end to the Ottoman Empire, and Britain conquered Palestine and received the mandate to rule Palestine from the League of Nations.

One of the British Mandate's greatest impacts on rural Palestinian areas was its misinterpretation of the Musha' communal land management system that prevailed in Palestine. Land designated as Musha' was managed collectively among villagers and redistributed periodically usually in cycles of one, two, or five years serving social and ecological goals.[70] While the Musha' communal land system contestation began with the OLC, the system was not dismantled. But in a classic colonial manner, the British believed that the Musha' traditions of joint property rights and the cyclical land redistribution among village members were inefficient and prevented development. They abolished the Musha' system in the early 1930s. Then, would-be owners had to pay high fees to register their land, which resulted in a greater supply of land available for purchase.[71] This policy accelerated Zionist land purchases, pushing more Palestinian peasants to landlessness while restricting the plots that remained in Palestinian ownership and cultivation. The heightened disruption of the Palestinian peasantry's agrarian life, its economic crisis, and the accelerating pace of Jewish immigration to Palestine during the 1930s created the fertile ground for the Palestinian Great Arab Revolt in 1936–1939 (al-Thawra al- Kubra). The revolt was a Palestinian popular nationalist and anticolonial uprising led by the peasantry against the British Administration and its policies facilitating Jewish immigration and land purchase.[72]

Throughout the British Mandate, the Jewish population in Palestine needed to modernize agriculture not only to support its growing community but to prove to the British government that the land's food production capacity would be sufficient to populate the land with more Jewish immigrants. The Zionist institutions in Palestine were lobbying the British Mandate that the local peasants were not producing efficiently and that they could do it better as bearers of modernization.[73] Development funds were flowing to Jewish agriculture through Jewish philanthropists and Zionist organizations, allowing Jewish agriculturalists to use more intensive methods for agriculture, while Palestinians were not sponsored to do so, except for the Palestinian citrus industry.[74] Hence, Jewish-Zionist agriculture developed since 1900 based on science, technology, and funds invested through the Zionist movement and Jewish philanthropists, while Palestinian agriculture did not benefit from similar sociotechnical instruction or financial investment. Palestinian smallholders' agriculture developed using the resources they had and those they predicted they would have.[75]

Until the 1948 War that resulted in Israeli independence and the Palestinian Nakba (catastrophe), Jews and collective Zionist institutions owned only 7 percent of the land in Palestine. A main challenge for the Israeli state in the following decade was to turn Palestinian land into Israeli land. Then, the temporal legalities from the previous Ottoman and British governments and the cultivation durations that defined ownership were used by the Israeli state as legal mechanisms and logic for appropriating land during and after the 1948 War.

During the 1948 War and in its aftermath, Israel destroyed and depopulated much of the Palestinian countryside. The Nakba resulted in the displacement and exile of approximately 750,000 Palestinians. At least 530 Palestinian villages were destroyed, and over half the displaced Palestinians were villagers.[76] The Israeli army razed entire villages, ensuring that the Palestinians would not be able to return to their homes.[77] A hundred or so Palestinian villages remained in Israel's 1948 borders, with a total population of 160,000 people, all of whom became Palestinian Arab citizens of Israel.[78] In the decade following the war, Israel confiscated 80 percent of the Palestinian land in its 1948 borders.[79]

Wartime regulations and the legislation that came in the war's aftermath enabled the development of a temporal legal system that appropriated Palestinian land and turned it into Israeli land through the work of three regulations. The Emergency Regulations for the Cultivation of Fallow Land and the Use of Unexploited Water Resources (October 11, 1948) allowed the Ministry of Agriculture to declare uncultivated land as "waste land" and ordered these lands to be cultivated. The law was justified by the need to expand agricultural production under war conditions, despite the right of ownership. This regulation authorized the use of any private owner's fallow land for two years and eleven months. The law was extended in January 1949 by the Emergency Regulations—Cultivation of Waste Lands, by which time half a million Palestinian dunums of "waste land" were already under Jewish cultivation. The 1949 regulation allowed the minister of agriculture to control these waste lands for five years.

The greatest interventions in the land regime based on temporal legalities were Israel's seizure of wartime abandoned property and land, the establishment of the Custodian of Abandoned Property, and the final legislation of the Absentee Property Law in 1950. This law was an extended version of wartime regulations and would govern Palestinian property in Israel for decades to come. The absentee property law defined *absentee* temporally—as someone who left their residence in a part of Palestine under hostile control or prior to September 1948.[80]

In 1949 the state transferred one million dunums of absentees' land to the Jewish National Fund (JNF), and later it transferred another million dunums. The JNF is an organization established by the Zionist congress in 1901 and owned "by the Jewish people" as a financial mechanism to collect diaspora Jewish funds to purchase land for Jews in Palestine. But since the establishment of the state, the JNF has become a central quasi-state institution facilitating Palestinian land dispossession and the reproduction of inequality in rural areas until today as it continues investing in agrarian development for Jewish rural communities alone.

The Israeli legal regime in the 1950s–1960s further intervened in land law durations, and Palestinian landowners were required to demonstrate longer periods of cultivation to prove their land ownership.[81] The flexible system of temporal legalities illuminates the ongoing ability of the Israeli state to govern the rural areas and agrarian land through time encoded in the law. Temporal legalities continue to shape rural areas preventing local communities from exercising sovereignty over their land through temporal legal structures.[82]

The de-territorializing of the Palestinians and the transfer of their agricultural means of production (land and water) to the state following the 1948 War is a classic dispossession dynamic as described by Marx.[83] The vast majority of Palestinians in Israel left agriculture, going through a mass coerced retraining and becoming the proletariat strata of the Israeli society.[84]

The loss of the Palestinian home, village life, agriculture, landscape, and collective identity in the land became defining events for both the Palestinians who suddenly became part of an exiled diaspora as well as those Palestinians who were internally displaced and have come to live in fragmented spaces under the control of a military regime.[85] The year 1948 has become not only a central historical event in Palestinian history but also a temporal object of memory for Palestinian diasporic and local communities remembering the life they had prior to the Nakba. Therefore, 1948 is an epicenter of Palestinian temporality from which the Palestinian politics of return (al-ʿawda, Arabic) emerge.

"Return" is the third temporal orientation mode characterizing the local agrarian timescape. Palestinian acts of quotidian return and resistance to the colonizing timescape include both memory work of pilgrimage and family visits to sites of destroyed and depopulated villages, locating the traces of the villages, collecting local plants, and telling stories of life in historic Palestine.[86] In the Palestinian diaspora, in refugee camps, in the Occupied Palestinian Territories, and in Israel proper, hundreds of testimonials about life in historic Palestine have been written, thereby preserving a vivid record of the loss of the Palestinian homeland as a whole and its rural communities specifically.[87] Aside from such memory work, Palestinians reclaim their agrarian traditions by preserving local seeds and local cultivars and returning to farms.[88] Following the fiftieth anniversary of the 1948 Nakba, an annual Return March (masirat al-ʿawda) has been organized by Palestinian organizations on Israeli Independence Day. These marches attract massive popular participation, challenging the state's narrative and making visible the displacement of Palestinian citizens and their aspirations of return.[89] Acknowledgment of the Palestinian return is seen by many as a recognition that the Palestinians have suffered significant injustice in their displacement and have an inalienable right to live in their land.[90] Palestinian return as a temporal mode entails the notion of a possible future of repair and reparation for Palestinians.

While Palestinians experienced massive land dispossession and forced displacement, accounts favoring the Zionist project tend to positively depict its impact on Palestinian agriculture as replacing subsistence farming with large-scale modernization, mechanization, and irrigation by the 1970s and transforming the "fellah to a farmer."[91] These modernization accounts tend to glorify development and explain the gap between Palestinians and Jews as a consequence of a traditional peasant society encountering a modernized society.

Contrastingly, critical and Marxist-oriented scholarship argued that Palestinian de-development is a result of the Zionist quest for land and its perpetual creation of Palestinian economic dependency through the dispossession of production resources such as land and water.[92] Moreover, agricultural modernization has not seen the emergence of technologically advanced industrial activities for Palestinian agriculture or the Palestinian economy.[93] While development and modernization discourse and logic served as a tool to describe the relations between Zionism and the Palestinians, the Palestinians were never subjects of the development and modernization of the Zionist project, as Sherene Seikaly points out.[94]

The settler colonial depopulation of Palestine was coupled with a growing immigration of Jews from North Africa and Middle Eastern countries during the 1950s. The settlement of Mizrahi/Arab Jews in the periphery was meant to both settle the colonial frontier and provide cheap labor to the Jewish state project. The modernization/tradition binary has been used also as an explanatory mechanism to justify the creation of a racialized and subordinated Jewish Mizrahi rural and semi-rural class versus Ashkenazi (East European) Jewry who settled earlier in the cooperative communities of kibbutzim and moshavim. The kibbutzim turned in the 1960s from agriculture to industry, producing noticeable inequality among the Jewish inhabitants of the colonial frontier. In the moshavim, the same bureaucratic apparatus treated differently the veteran Jewish moshavim and the Mizrahi Jewish immigrants, who were often forced to go to the workers' moshavim (*moshav ovdim*), thus creating a new Jewish agrarian proletariat producing farm products for the state industries without owning the means of production.[95]

Yet, while the labor domain is a central focus of the analysis of power relations in the agrarian environment globally,[96] Israel/Palestine has not appeared as a prominent case of labor time exploitation in the growing critical agrarian studies literature.[97] The framing of the local questions in terms of national conflict and the ways that Zionist-Israeli agrarian cooperatives were shaped internally against capitalist terrains have obfuscated the colonial legacies of agrarian development and Marxian structures of labor and value that have been shaping the region.[98] The reading of agrarian labor relations as a mechanism of Palestinian dispossession remained mostly an interest of critical regional scholars.[99] The topic of labor as a settler colonial exploitation apparatus was further marginalized with Patrick Wolfe's formulation that settler colonialism is primarily a contest over land rather than labor. While critical scholars have recently analyzed the central role of Palestinians laboring in Israel's construction sector,[100] I emphasize the importance of the societal negotiations and practice of Palestinian agrarian labor in the settler colonial process of dispossession.

Labor time in agriculture is then the fourth mode of orientation in the local agrarian timescape, and it has been a central exploitation and dispossession mechanism illustrating the production of power relations locally. Globally, the commodification of time under industrial capitalism produced a major shift in the reckoning of time as an oppressive societal process. Peasant societies have been task-oriented, but their work and social exchange were not demarcated but intermingled. [101] The Palestinian shift to hired wage labor in Jewish industrial agrarian operations and the gradual historic process of land alienation positioned Palestinians as the main source of surplus-value agricultural workers.[102] Agrarian labor is exploited to be efficient, fast, compressed in time and space, and restricted to high-demand periodicities rather than long-term employment commitments.

Furthermore, labor time as an exploitation mechanism has shifted forms according to the changing needs of settlement projects. Historically, settler societies often employed natives for the goal of profit-making but turned to forced migration and enslaved work when natives' resistance to work or their extermination by disease or genocide made their exploitation unfeasible, or when the indigenous workforce was not enough to sustain the colonial project.[103] Zionism is distinguished from other settler societies by refusing periodically to use native Palestinian labor when employing Palestinians was (and still is) more profitable.[104] The ethos of Zionism as a Jewish national liberation project glorified agricultural settlement and work. Agriculture was perceived as a way of redeeming Jews from their diasporic lives in Europe, where they had lived mostly as merchants and craftsmen and had been predominantly denied access to land.[105]

But Palestine as an immigration destiny was not chosen by European Jews for its great economic promise, rich resources, or major arable land availability, unlike other settler histories in the "New World." Jews who immigrated to Palestine saw the land as the fulfillment of their ethnoreligious ancestry, a land that Jews prayed for over centuries as Zion. The religious significance of the land and the collective Jewish ethno-nation was redefined by the ideas of modern nationalism that were cultivated in Europe throughout that era. At the end of the nineteenth century, Jews were disappointed by the socioeconomic and political failures of the promises of emancipation, freedom, and equality brought by the era of enlightenment; they were escaping from anti-Semitism and violence in Europe. Thus, Jews envisioned a return to their ancestral promised land.[106]

The Jewish return required the reclamation of a mythical past. Historian Tamar Novick shows how Jewish settlers (and Christians as well) have been literally engaged in producing "the land flowing with milk and honey." Over the past 150 years historians and anthropologists have shown that Jews have returned to shepherding practices, "discovered" indigenous wine cultivars, "found" indigenous wheat varieties, and reclaimed thousand-year-old date trees from seeds.[107] Yet, the ideology of return has always demanded assistance anchored with Palestinians as laborers.

From the onset of Zionist immigration to Palestine in the 1880s until about 1930, the main form of Jewish agrarian production in Palestine was based on a plantation economy supported by Jewish philanthropists. Yet, the new Jewish farmers were city dwellers from Europe and not accustomed to physical labor or the heat and the local conditions in Palestine.[108] Thus, the Jewish colonies soon began employing seasonal Palestinian Arab labor forces mixed with a small Jewish labor force.[109] The Palestinian workforce was cheaper than Jewish workers. The two Jewish immigration waves to Palestine from the early twentieth century (commonly periodized as the Second Aliyah, 1904–1914, and Third Aliyah, 1918–1924) became the backbone of Israeli rural cooperative settlement.[110] Immigrants from the second immigration wave demanded that the first Jewish colonies in Palestine replace the Arab workers with Jewish labor, establishing what they called the primacy of "conquest of labor" and "Hebrew Labor" and institutionalizing it with the JNF's support. Zionism moved from hiring Palestinian peasants for the sake of profit-making in the Jewish plantation economy roughly until the 1930s to excluding Palestinian labor and employing predominantly Jewish workers although it was costlier.[111] Consequently, in this settler colony, there have been times when ideological and political motivations has trumped profit-making, and the articulation "Hebrew Labor" still persists.[112] Yet, the paradoxical relations of Jewish Israeli practices of return are always entangled in negotiations over Palestinian agrarian labor.

After decades of de-development in agriculture and unequal resource allocation for agricultural development, Palestinian agriculture in Israel is vanishing—going from nearly 60 percent of employed Palestinian citizens working in agriculture in 1954 to less than 2 percent in 2015.[113] Of Palestinians employed in agriculture in the 2010s, only 20 percent were self-employed and the remaining 80 percent were dependent on the Jewish sector for their wage employment.[114] Furthermore, the decline of agriculture did not lead the Palestinian villages in Israel to urbanization and industrialization. Rather, it led to semi-urbanization in demography, economy, and employment structure, retaining many ties to ruralism.[115]

In parallel, since the occupation of the West Bank and Gaza in 1967 a proletariat stratum of occupied Palestinian agrarian workers developed. In the 1980s, 25 percent of the agrarian workforce in Israel were Palestinians from the occupied territories.[116] But without worker unions and citizens' legalities, the employment of West Bank and Gaza Palestinians in agriculture grants the Israeli economy labor time flexibility during periods of crisis and of high demand. It allows Israeli employers to lay off surplus labor during recessions and to recruit workers during increased economic activity periods without being restricted to long-term occupational commitments and rights.[117]

Following the first Intifada (Palestinian popular uprising, 1987–1993), the state-imposed closure policies on the Occupied Palestinian Territories caused a shortage of workers for agriculture. At the same time, Israel's neoliberal turn and its doctrine of separation from Palestine began a process of importing Thai migrant workers in agriculture. The employment of Thai migrant workers in the Israeli agricultural sector contributed to higher profitability in this sector but also resulted in the replacement of OPT workers and Palestinian citizen workers by Thai migrants.[118] The temporal conditions of migrant workers living in housing in the agrarian workplace instead of commuting to it assists in labor time exploitation, as these migrant workers are available for long working hours, often exploited in terms of minimum wage and overtime payments. These workers destabilize the Palestinian/Jewish native/settler binary in a few ways. First, the employment of OPT Palestinians and Palestinian citizens on agrarian land they were historically dispossessed from allowed them to maintain a relation to the land through their labor time, but now the hiring of cheaper migrant workers dispossesses Palestinians economically and therefore temporally from connecting to and caring for the land through labor. Second, under citizenship legalities, a few Palestinian citizens of Israel also employ such workers,[119] complicating the local political economy of exploitation through labor time. Third, Thai workers are affected by strict labor migration laws limiting their stay. Thus, they cannot make attachment claims to the land yet blurring the settler/native predicament in agrarian occupation and labor. The role of Thai workers in Israeli agriculture resembles the historical role of "arrivants" in other settler colonies. Arrivants are the non-European migrants that serve the settler society as laboring bodies, forced to migrate by global capitalism.[120] They are essential to the economic building of the settler colony, but locally they do not contribute to a settler population due to

Israeli restrictions on paths to citizenship for non-Jews.[121] Therefore, the employment of the Thai workers is similar to the historical arriving process as migrant workers were employed at a moment when the settler society was not able to further employ OPT Palestinians because of the Intifada and the high cost of employing Palestinians who are Israeli citizens and are eligible for labor law payments.

Production becomes more efficient when machines replace human labor. Israeli agrarian policies support return on investment to agriculturalists who purchase "labor efficient" technology.[122] "Labor efficiency" as a policy discourse refers to refraining from employing migrant Thai farmworkers or contracting West Bank Palestinian workers. Machine labor assists the sociotechnical settler society to become rooted in the land without questioning ancestral claims to belonging.

Following this consideration of the agrarian Palestinian-Zionist labor timescape, I move next to introduce my ethnographic research.

Fieldwork in Governmental Corridors and in the Settler Colonial Encounter

This book focuses on those in power in the context of the settler colonial encounter. It offers a pioneering state system ethnography observing Israeli governance in Israel's 1948 internationally recognized state borders, including its often invisible, professional, scientific Palestinian elite. Grounded in multi-sited fieldwork undertaken mainly in 2012–2015 in policymaking arenas and agrarian sites from Israel/Palestine's center to its north, the book follows the multiple ways that Jewish-Israeli and Palestinian-citizen state officials, scientists, planners, and agriculturalists have been making sense, matter, and meaning of time in the agrarian environment. I conducted additional research in 2019 at Israel's State Archive to further foreground my ethnographic claims for chapter 2. Chapters 3 and 4 also rely on earlier fieldwork, mainly interviews and participant observations that I conducted in 2009–2010 with Palestinian agronomists and NGOs involved in olive agriculture in Israel/Palestine. This monograph then is the result of close to fifteen years of engagement with the local agrarian environment. The main fieldwork this book is based on relies on three years of participant observations in sixty governmental agency meetings mostly at the Ministry of Agriculture's headquarters and the Ministry of Interior's Northern District Planning Committee. I conducted approximately eighty in-depth interviews with Jewish and Palestinian agrarian and environmental actors. I have undertaken expansive content analysis of seventy policy documents. Finally, my photo analysis of agrarian site images has significantly bolstered my critical thinking and evaluation regarding what documents or interlocutors have told me, helping me see interesting and telling gaps and discrepancies.

When I began fieldwork in 2012, time as a political object in agrarian-environmental dynamics was not my focus. Instead, I was interested in the political possibilities that emerged out of the environmental predicament as well as the ways that changes in agri-environmental conditions may lead to changes in social-political relations. I was curious about the significance of new discourses that I began to note in sustainable agriculture policies addressing Palestinian agriculture in appreciative environmental terms. Then, I requested to observe and participate in the new Planning Policy for Agriculture and Rural Development. This policy was seen as a continuation of the Sustainable Agriculture Strategy of the Ministry of Agriculture and Rural Development published in 2010. But the buzzword of the new policy process was "heritage preservation" rather than "sustainability." Both *sustainable agriculture* and *heritage* have strong temporal connotations and global institutions that promote them, but they imply different priorities. As my fieldwork advanced, I realized that many interlocutors were often discussing articulations and practices of time. I examine the implications of such discourses, practices, and politics throughout this book.

During my fieldwork, I understood the importance of social positionality for accessing people and institutions. I appealed to different affiliations depending on whether I was speaking with state officials, Palestinian agriculturalists, or environmental actors. My access to agriculturalists and agriculture officials was assisted either by mentioning that I had formerly worked with the private consultancy that was contracted by the Ministry of Agriculture to write the former Sustainable Agriculture Strategy for the ministry or by sharing that I was a former member of the youth movement Ha-shomer Ha-tzair.[123] Mentioning my former affiliation to this socialist-Zionist movement related to the kibbutzim signaled that I somewhat shared a common language with Israeli rural interlocutors. To Palestinians, especially those who were geographically close to those kibbutzim, my former participation in this movement signaled that I was part of a group that worked favorably with the Palestinian society in Israel through the former Mapam United Workers Party.[124]

Palestinian interviewees, including state employees, agronomists, environmental activists, and agriculturalists, were happy to speak to someone who showed interest in Palestinian agriculture. To my surprise, Palestinian state officials and agriculturalists agreed to have their interviews recorded and to be fully quoted. Some of them also told me they hoped that my research would help to improve the conditions of Palestinian Arab agriculture. Others hoped I would later apply to work in the Ministry of Agriculture and try to affect its policy from within.

My approach to these conversations and the insights I draw from them follow a rationale of an anthropology of the colonial encounter. Reflecting on anthropology's complicity with colonialism, I join other scholars in the task of revealing the structures and processes by which some come to dominate others.[125] As such, this is not a study of Palestinian agriculture per se, but a study invested in understanding the role of the powerful in the settler colonial encounter in agriculture in Israel/Palestine. Reflecting on my privileged position in this encounter as an Ashkenazi Jewish Israeli citizen, I use my social position for entering the Israeli bureaucracy to understand how the Israeli system of control operates.

Seeing societal structures and privileges, I emphasize that most of the Palestinian interlocutors in this ethnography are highly educated professionals, mostly men who have acquired master's degrees or PhDs at Israeli universities or in Europe.[126] These professionals usually belong to the upper middle class of Palestinian society in Israel and benefit from *relative* social mobility, social capital, and symbolic capital that is higher than that of some of the elder Palestinian agriculturalists who were interviewed for this book.

These professionals undertake most of their employment activities in Hebrew. Then, when I attended official state meetings with Palestinian participants who chatted informally in Arabic, I politely joined their conversation, which without my involvement, always sounded like

"Arabrew," a combination of Arabic and Hebrew. I often felt that the Palestinian officials and I were uncomfortable conversing together in Arabic. I was aware of my potential language mistakes, while these professionals were used to speaking Hebrew with Jewish Israelis. But during my time with elder Palestinian agriculturalists and their families usually in their agrarian sites and homes, we mostly conversed in Arabic.

Both Hebrew and Palestinian colloquial Arabic are transcribed with characters understandable to English readers rather than using diacritics and Modern Standard Arabic. All translations in the text are by me. I mostly use the IJMES and Library of Congress transliteration guidelines except when I write interlocutors' names in the way they spell them in English or when I use common spelling in English that does not abide by the guidelines.

In writing this book, I used the interlocutors' real names when we talked about their public capacity as state officials or as public figures in NGOs. All interviewees agreed to be recorded and have their real names used. While historically, the anthropological convention has been to anonymize an ethnography's interlocutors with pseudonyms given the assumption of a power-laden dynamic, this convention is less suitable to the study of social elites and groups involved in professional recognition acts such as publishing and filming their own work or being in positions of state representation in which a pseudonym might work as an "anti-citation."[127]

Naming beyond the individual, articulating the political community at the heart of this study is a contested matter. Palestinian citizens often call themselves '48 Arabs to indicate the year they came under Israeli control (as opposed to '67 Occupied Palestinians). A prominent collective name used by Palestinian citizens is *Arab al-dakhil* (Arabic for "Arabs of the inside" or "Arabs of the interior"), referring to pre-1967 Israel as the core of historic Palestinian territory. The Israeli state invested political efforts in Israelizing this group as well as fragmenting the Palestinian collective in Israel into numerous groups by religion or sectarian affiliation. Therefore, Palestinian citizens are often called by the state "the minorities" or "Arab Israelis," denying their belonging to a Palestinian collective. I call this group "Palestinian Arab citizens" or simply "Palestinians in Israel" to indicate their legal-civic status in the state. I recognize that such a label risks losing other forms of identification and affiliation, but since an inquiry about terms of self-identification was not at the heart of this study, I use the collective political identity commonly used within the group. I highlight this matter to rethink the negotiation and movements between societal categories and affiliations and the sort of alliances and possibilities of self-determination that Palestinian agriculture experts and practitioners whom I have talked with have with their native communities and with the Israeli society.

In my ethnographic commitment to the phrasing used by an interlocutor or an institution, when discussing a place, the text moves between the Arabic name and the Hebrew name or vice versa, according to the interlocutor who is referring to a place. Otherwise, my writing would sound disengaged from the social reality and actors that I describe. I use common English names such as Galilee. For the sake of brevity, I refer to the area in the country's center, known in Arabic as al-muthalath and in Hebrew as Ha-meshulash, as the Triangle region.

I recommend understanding this book as a multi-site project that does not require necessarily a chronological reading of the chapters. Although the short distance between research sites might make it difficult for outsiders to call this ethnography a multi-sited one, in the local context and because book chapters focus on different sites involving sometimes different actors, I suggest such a formulation. Only chapters 3 and 4 would benefit from subsequent chronological reading. I invite readers to read this book in the order they wish, contributing to a polychronic temporal experience that is reflected in the Palestinian voices I bring here.

Chapter Overview

Chapter 1, "Draining the Swamp," discusses the agrarian planning policy of Sahl al-Battuf Plain/Beit Netofa Valley in which multiple threads of time manifest as a multiplex mechanism of power. This valley's agriculture, mostly owned by Palestinian citizens, is considered by ecologists and officials to be a unique traditional agricultural landscape and an endangered wetland habitat due to Israel's wetland drainage history. The maintenance of Palestinian smallholders' agriculture, denigrated in the past by Zionist movement, allowed a unique biodiverse habitat to survive. Thus, the colonial narrative of the land's stewards is overturned. I argue that the Israeli agricultural sustainability policies for al-Battuf encapsulate timescape as governance. These include bureaucratic delays, governing through relations of ecological knowledge and time and a replay of the view of Palestinian agriculturalists as non-modern, but now because the Palestinians wish to develop agriculture and drain the swamp rather than conserve it.

Chapter 2, "Returning to the Seventh Year," discusses the regulation of the biblical commandment of *shmita*—a year of a land "release." The regulatory process of shmita has increased over the last decades, posing bureaucratic challenges to the state by utilizing the Bible as a policy paper. A year of shmita is the most profitable year for the Palestinian agriculturalist, whose agriculture merely survives otherwise. The shmita regulation is compared with the state's neglect of the implications of the qur'anic tradition of inheritance to Palestinian agriculture. I discuss Palestinian agriculturalists' means of surviving the state's policies of dispossession and their entanglements with the shmita system. The recent regulation of shmita embodies settler nation-making through the calendar and reclamation of biblical traditions as a way of claiming Jewish indigeneity. Moreover, shmita sheds light on the cyclical temporality of the settler society and therefore questions the temporal dichotomy between settler and native.

Chapter 3, "Cultivating Time in an Olive Tree," follows the creation of a new olive cultivar, the emergence of water for Jewish olive agriculture, harvest technique changes, the marketing of olive oil as a Jewish traditional product, and the claiming of olive terraces as both biblical and sustainable landscapes. I show how the settler society now reclaims indigeneity and materializes its national ethos through olive agriculture. State scientists are central actors promoting this transformation. Meanwhile, attributing notions of "biblical" landscape to the Palestinian terraced olive agriculture erases the significance of olive agriculture to Palestinian heritage. The latter dynamic ignores the endeavors of Palestinian agronomists who are changing the production modes of Palestinian olive agriculture. By listening to these agronomists, the narrative of the settler state on Palestinian agriculture is contested to show that native modes of being in time are not intrinsically opposed to that of the settler society.

Chapter 4, "Freeing Time like a Palestinian Agronomist," examines the timescapes, practices, and agrarian imaginaries of Palestinian agronomists working for the Israeli state to observe the possibilities of temporal agency and self-determination that their actions entail. Writings on the incorporation of the marginalized or colonized social actor in the state system often describe the minority bureaucrat as put under harsh constraints that leave little room to contest social hierarchies. Palestinian agricultural professionals working for the Israeli state see inequality in agriculture through their work. Although they cannot overcome dispossession through their bureaucratic encounters with state work and may even strengthen the state system during their working hours, they contest the social order through their free-time activities or when they retire. Their initiatives are characterized by a polychronic and nonbinary timescape, embracing Western sociotechnical expertise and science agendas with Palestinian traditional and new societal structures, timescapes, and situatedness. Thus, these agronomists undermine an exclusionary system that has contributed to the demise of Palestinian agriculture. By attending to the free-time activities of these agronomists alongside their temporal agency narratives at work, I reorient the discussion on native professionals' strategies of coping in the state system and point out their mundane modes of resistance, which had been invisible to the research community.

In the concluding chapter, I attend to the narratives of agrarian resistance and survival in Israel/Palestine, and I interrogate the possibilities of imagining different pasts, presents, and futures. The chapter offers a rethinking of the social practices that can be cultivated in the interface of agriculture, environment, and time and reflects on the imaginaries and practices that could be cultivated to unsettle time and agriculture during climate change.

ONE

_____

Draining the Swamp

In the summer of 2012, the Israeli Ministry of Agriculture was at the peak of its announced policy endeavor for sustainable agriculture. After a few years of designing a sustainable development strategy for Israel's agriculture and rural areas, ministry staff was ready for implementation. A marker of policy change was the ministry's choice to fund a program of sustainable agriculture for Palestinian citizens' communities in Sahl al-Battuf (*sahl* means "plain" in Arabic)/Bikat Beit Netofa (*bika* means "valley" in Hebrew) in the heart of lower Galilee.[1]

Sahl al-Battuf is an agricultural terrain of 53,000 dunums.[2] It is currently the largest stretch of agrarian land in Israel proper owned predominantly by Palestinian citizens, most of it by residents of the neighboring towns of Sakhnin and 'Arrabeh and of the smaller villages of 'Uzeir and Bu'eine-Nujeidat. The plain is parceled into 1,500 plots owned by approximately 6,000 landowners, creating a mosaic of agrarian patches, coloring the landscape in joyful and lively colors of soil, vegetation, and growth, especially in springtime.[3] The plain is contoured by escarpments of 350 meters, creating a valley of color against its surrounding hills and the predominant blue sky. This geographical structure forms a basin where a seasonal swamp is created by the heavy winter rains, both hampering agrarian cultivation and creating a wetland habitat that preserves endangered species.

The Ministry of Agriculture's 2012 pilot program aimed to develop a small area of al-Battuf plain called Maslakhit. In the years that followed, a large sustainable development regional plan was created for al-Battuf/ Beit Netofa and advanced by the Ministry of Agriculture in the state's Northern District Committee for Planning in 2013–2018.[4] I talked about the new sustainable development program for al-Battuf/Beit Netofa with a recent appointee at the Ministry of Agriculture, an ecologist who was overseeing the new sustainable agriculture plans. He said: "We did not think of [the Palestinians of al-Battuf] at all, and then they submitted a proposal to the ministry, and we said, 'Wow!' [enthusiastically]. Those little agricultural plots, rain-fed agriculture, they don't use pesticides, a community atmosphere where everyone goes in the afternoon to the valley—it is exactly what we wanted! It is Agriculture That Supports the Environment [naming the newly funded program]."[5] He then detailed with conviction some aspects of the sustainability program: conserving biodiversity, training farmers in sustainable agricultural methods, and holding public meetings with the participation of local stakeholders. He also clarified that it would most likely not include draining the seasonal flood. He hoped that the agriculturalists would not be disappointed regarding the lack of drainage, as they had perceived that as the highlight of a previously failed agrarian development plan.

The ecologist's sentiment about the valley's atmosphere encapsulated a noticeable change in the agrarian imaginary that he, as a representative of Ministry of Agriculture, could see. The *agrarian imaginary* refers to a shared vision and narrative of the condition of the agrarian environment, such as the processes that led it to its condition, views on its ideal state, and often the sociotechnical programs set to materialize the imaginary.[6] Here, the ecologist was enthusiastic about an agrarian imaginary and a timescape (the multilayered landscape of time discussed in the book's introduction) of al-Battuf/Beit Netofa that completely transformed the prevalent Zionist-Israeli view. The Zionist imaginary and timescape involves large, rapidly productive, "modern," monocultural, and "efficient" agricultural fields. Such a model of industrialized agriculture entails science, technology, fertilizers, pesticides, and irrigation. These agricultural resources and techniques enhance growth and compress production time, making agriculture less dependent on natural cycles and constraints. By contrast, the ecologist admired small plots, seasonal water, and smallholders' cultivation. His vision enfolded a specific temporality: a duration of a continuous community cultivating together, assuming long-term land tenure and seasonal agrarian cycles. Moreover, the ecologist recognized agriculture's multifunctional roles aside from food production—preserving landscape and environment, as well as maintaining culture, community, and social values. Also noteworthy in his description was the shift in the agrarian plan for al-Battuf that the Agriculture Ministry advanced. Previously, for over ten years from 1994 to 2005, the Agriculture Ministry had promoted a program to modernize al-Battuf agriculture through drainage infrastructure clearing the seasonal flood alongside agrarian re-parcellation and the construction of two irrigation reservoirs.[7] But now, this new sustainable agriculture program holds a future image of the site without drainage, preserving the wetland and "traditional agriculture" on small plots through agroecological management.

This new plan is an ironic reversal in the ecological standpoints of Zionists and Palestinians. Over the past century, Zionist officials and institutions have historically denigrated traditional Palestinian/Arab agriculture for its lack of efficiency and primitive methods.[8] One of the symbols of Zionism's prominent collective ethos was its project of draining the swamps and turning wetlands and marshes into developed agriculture lands in the period 1920–1950.[9] However, "traditional agriculture" is now suddenly celebrated by the Israeli state, and drainage is avoided. Palestinian citizens are being asked to conserve the wetland, maintain their rain-fed, "traditional" small-scale agriculture and fly the flag for ecological conservation.

Alas, the Palestinian agriculturalists now want to drain the swamp, modernize their agriculture, and benefit from it. As such, al-Battuf residents have promoted alternative agrarian imaginaries. In winter 2013, I traversed al-Battuf by car and by foot with Laithi, who, at that time, was an environmental-social consultant and activist, a resident of Sakhnin who had been involved in initiatives of agricultural development and poverty alleviation in al-Battuf.[10] We saw the fields already drowning, a result of the first heavy rain. Laithi pointed out the fields where landowners, frustrated by the lack of drainage, had invested significant resources in transporting soil to elevate their plots by up to half a meter, decreasing their vulnerability to rain and flood. He told me this practice is helpful in low-rain and low-flood years, and I thought about the investment in transporting soil that the agriculturalists are undertaking manifesting the importance of productive agriculture year-round for these landowners. A few years earlier, Laithi had promoted an initiative to swap land with the state to provide an area for ecological conservation and promote agriculturalists' right to produce intensive and irrigated agriculture in the plain. He presented this initiative in the state's Northern District Planning Committee, but it rejected this initiative, according to Laithi, "as if we are some alien species asking to use state land rather than being people of this land." The practices that agriculturalists use as well as Laithi's proposed plan illustrate how competing agrarian visions and mutual claims of the state and of local agriculturalists are at play in al-Battuf.

This chapter problematizes these competing imaginaries and the timescapes they inhabit as well as the programs and plans aimed to fulfill them. I suggest that the state's transition to promoting sustainability has created a specific timescape that is operated by state agents to govern.[11] I examine the ways different visions for al-Battuf Plain\Beit Netofa are manifested and how the state settles Palestinian agrarian time through the framing of sustainable agriculture. I show that timescape has become the preferred state tool of control and governance, rather than the land confiscation techniques prevalent in the past. State ecologists have become central actors fueling this process, strongly believing that refraining from conservation in al-Battuf will result in irreparable damage for years and generations to come. Contrastingly, many of the al-Battuf agriculturalists and residents prefer drainage and development of modern and intensive agriculture, which they see as their right as citizens of a state that had previously advanced intensive agriculture. The next section will familiarize the reader with Sahl al-Battuf and the contours of its agrarian timescape as portrayed mostly by members of its agrarian community.

Timescape of Sahl al-Battuf

I met Ali 'Antar Waked of Arrabeh in a sunny early summer day in his *'ezba*, the shaded rest area in the field. Ali was in his early fifties, but his skin already showed many sun wrinkles and marks.[12] He is one of the few big cultivators in Sahl-al Battuf. Only a minor group of approximately thirty agriculturalists depend on farming for income in the plain. Ali provided for his family through agriculture; he also has an additional business in earthworks. During our conversations, I felt that he shared with me his intimate knowledge of al-Battuf, its beauty, and its heritage while also at times sounding like a spokesperson for al-Battuf's agriculture, speaking through me and later through journalists about the troubles and difficulties of farming in al-Battuf. He was eager that his claims and hopes for the plain would be heard.[13]

I asked Ali to tell me about farming in the plain and he pointed out the agrarian plots as we passed.

> Do you see how straight the borders of the parcels are? I heard from our elders how they used to do it. They would pull a rope to measure the plot's size and borders, and it is so accurate and well done, even though they were not modern engineers with solid equipment. I truly salute them for their fine work. . . . Until today, people knew what their land borders were even without fencing that marks them. Even when there were land disputes with the state, some traveled to Turkey to bring the official papers showing that their land was registered by the Turkish government [referring to the Ottoman Empire's rule in greater Palestine until 1914] and they are the owners.

Ali was looking at the parcels' margins and seeing the long cultural and political history of al-Battuf, a tie both to his forefathers and to later land disputes with the Israeli state and the Ottoman regime's legal papers. To Ali, these margins are important testimonies of the past; however, for other actors in the region, they have become political-ecological subjects of futurity. State ecologists (whom we will meet later) see in these unplowed margins the habitat that sustains endangered species. Ali emphasized that the plain was cultivated for hundreds or maybe thousands of years, based on the ruins that exist in the plain. The agrarian parcels in al-Battuf are indeed surprising to a viewer who is accustomed to industrialized agriculture. The parcels differ significantly in size between typically smallholders' plots and those of medium holders. Yet, all these plots are small and very narrow, averaging one to five acres per owner. Following the Muslim tradition's inheritance custom, the agricultural plots of al-Battuf have been divided among heirs in each generation, contributing to the narrow and small parcel sizes (image 1). Thus, the current titles to property are small and mostly used for part-time farming to produce goods for domestic consumption and leisure.

The big cultivators like Ali lease farmland from acquaintances or provide produce in return for using the land. It was summertime and Ali slept at night in his *'ezba* to guard his field of ripe watermelons and his neighbors' fields in a rotation they undertake among themselves. In the past, the watermelons of al-Battuf have been a great source of pride as they have been famous for decades in all of Palestine/Israel and even shipped abroad through the port of Acre. But now, according to Ali, they are a source of concern, as marketing was no longer organized by the state as it had been in the 1970s and 1980s. Nowadays, he claims that the Plant Producers' Organization never shows up to support the producers. He needed to find or create his own market and was disappointed with

IMAGE 1. Smallholders' diverse agrarian parcels in Sahl al-Battuf, winter 2013. Photograph by the author.

the lack of state assistance and support for agriculturalists. The producers' organization advised him to find a market for his produce among Arab communities, but the price he received when marketing locally was not good, so he kept searching for additional possibilities. Indeed, finding a market for one's produce is a challenging aspect of an agrarian operation that is small-scale and not organized through a company or a cooperative. Some local smallholders and small producers often overcome market barriers by turning to niche markets or by creating a market by associating their produce with additional social or environmental values.[14] Yet, Ali was midway between al-Battuf smallholders who market mostly domestically and the bigger producers in Israel with ties to marketing cooperatives, chains, and distributors. Other smallholders of al-Battuf sell their produce under shade awnings in the plain, where town and region neighbors come to buy this rainfed and non-industrialized produce, drink coffee, and chat (image 2). For these town members, the plain provides a picturesque and a calm agrarian time, landscape, and a

IMAGE 2. Selling produce under shade awnings in Sahl al-Battuf, summer 2014. Photograph by the author.

sense of community. But Ali was caught in an agrarian market rhythm incongruity, feeling he was left behind by state mechanisms and not in sync with where he wanted to be versus the national market.[15]

Over the time I spent in the plain, I saw that agriculturalists typically cultivated wheat, barley, hay, sesame, clover, vetch, onions, garbanzo beans, peas, okra, squash, and tomatoes, as well as some local species of fakus cucumbers and melons. For decades, the seasonal swamp prohibited year-long agricultural cultivation in the plain. Thus, most of the plain was cultivated for summer cultivars, which instilled a strong sense of seasonality. But in the hillside areas less affected by the swamp, agriculturalists were able to plant seeds for winter cultivars. In the last twenty years, agriculturalists also started planting olives in the plain as well as other fruit trees that require less attention and are adapted to a part-time farming routine. The local wheat and sesame seeds are varieties rarely grown outside of Palestinian communities, so the crop diversity of the valley enables a domestic market for selling agricultural products that are no longer commonly produced in Israel/Palestine and are much appreciated by the Palestinian communities.[16] There are also goats and sheep grazing in the plain, their placid rhythms contributing to a sense of tranquility and ease. I was told by many Palestinian inhabitants of the area that the timescape of al-Battuf provides many locals a sense of relaxation, as well as a sense of ancestral community and belonging.

However, the political time scale of the plain is charged and provokes painful sentiments regarding the changes and turmoil this land has seen. Thus, locals' encounters with the Israeli state were predominantly disruptive. During one of the occasions I spent with Laithi in the plain, we talked about his agrarian parcel, and he softly told me about the significance he sees in bringing his children to play and to cultivate together on his family's land as an intergenerational heritage. But suddenly his tone changed, and he hurled in defiance: "I don't care who is the sovereign here. I care that the land is mine. Until 1948 my grandfather and my uncles had a whole mountain on the southern side of the plain, which was confiscated by the state in 1948. I am attached to it. If I get it back, I don't care who is the sovereign." The year 1948 was a temporal benchmark in Laithi's timescape, one that was repeated by many Palestinian interlocutors, marking the twin birth of the state of Israel and the Palestinian catastrophe and dispossession.[17] Laithi then reiterated that if he received the land back, he would not care who holds the sovereign power—the Turks, the Israelis, or the Palestinians. Laithi distinguished between his right to the land as an intergenerational and native attachment of belonging and state sovereignty as if sovereignty had become an irrelevant or non-urgent issue to Palestinians as a national community. He echoed views I heard more commonly from elderly Palestinians, who saw the land's history as an intergenerational story of conquerors that have been here and have gone while they stayed rooted in the land and connected to it while witnessing the political changes. Indeed, most of the villages surrounding al-Battuf were not uprooted in the aftermath of the 1948 War, as they were listed by the Israeli army as "surrendering" (except 'Eilabun's partial depopulation and return and Mi'ar village's complete destruction).[18] Yet, these communities suffered significant land dispossession due to Israeli land confiscation during the 1948 War and even more in its aftermath, during the military regime imposed on Palestinian citizens from 1949 to 1966. Still, al-Battuf is considered one of the best farmlands remaining in Palestinian citizen proprietors' hands following the state's establishment.[19]

Until the 1970s, agriculture was a main source of income for al-Battuf communities, but agriculture's economic role began to decrease due to a few interlocking factors: a decline in the status of agriculture in the Palestinian society, the increase of labor opportunities outside of Palestinian towns, and ongoing land loss due to major acts of land appropriation by the Israeli state.[20] The next wave of land appropriations affecting al-Battuf communities took place during the 1970s based on the Israeli policy of Judaization of the Galilee. This policy aimed to shift the Palestinian majority demography of Galilee by settling more Jews in small communities designed to divide Palestinian localities spatially and demographically as well as to restrict a potential demand for Palestinian citizens' autonomy. This policy appropriated thousands of dunums of agrarian land from most of the towns around al-Battuf, most significantly Deir Hanna, Sakhnin, and 'Arrabeh.[21] Some of these confiscations took place in the Sakhnin valley north of Sahl al-Battuf and not in al-Battuf proper. Nevertheless, agriculturalists told me that the Judaization of Galilee plan allowed a quasi-state institution. The Jewish

National Fund (JNF/KKL), to settle in the plain through its subsidiary organization Himanuta, which acquired a few hundred dunums in the plain during the 1970s and 1980s. Himanuta undertook its land transactions mostly through landholders who were not able to prove their legal ownership.[22] The Judaization program (Tahweed, Arabic; Yihud Hagalil, Hebrew) also granted half the municipal jurisdiction of al-Battuf plain to the municipal body of the new settlements, the Misgav Regional Council, restricting, until today, independent planning by the Palestinian municipalities. In 1976, the Palestinian citizens' resistance to the massive land confiscation that the Judaization policy entailed culminated in Yawm al-Ard (Land Day) on March 30 with a general strike and marches in Palestinian towns in Israel, protesting the governmental land confiscation.[23] Over the years, Land Day turned into a major commemoration event for Palestinian resistance against the state and its land confiscations. The Palestinian towns surrounding al-Battuf have been a central locus of resistance.[24] Presently, the Palestinian landholders of al-Battuf towns hold only 30 percent of their historical, pre-1948 land.[25]

Despite this charged history, when I was discussing al-Battuf agriculture with Ali Shahawane, head of Sakhnin's agriculturalists committee, he emphasized that although Sahl al-Battuf communities lived a history of land struggles, in al-Battuf proper their struggle had been mostly over land development rather than landholding. Thus, al-Battuf is situated within a longer history of agrarian imaginaries of development in the nexus of water, land, and settlement.

One such imaginary was conceived with the construction of Israel's National Water Carrier (image 3). From 1953 to 1965, the National Water Carrier transported water from the north of the country to the south. It was implemented as a means of fulfilling the Zionist national project "to make the desert bloom" with Jewish settlement and agriculture.[26] The National Water Carrier passes through the center of al-Battuf Plain, bisecting it along 16 kilometers (10 miles). Although the water canal is 4 meters wide (13 feet), 93 meters of land width were expropriated (305 feet), a total of 3,000 dunums. In al-Battuf the water carrier is constructed as an open canal, securitized and fenced with wire on both sides. Israel's Water Authority had encountered the challenge of crossing cultivated land before, but when the land was in Jewish cultivators' hands, a pipe was installed underground at times, above ground in other cases and mostly avoided the most fertile areas.[27]

For al-Battuf agriculturalists, the water carrier is an offensive infrastructure. It serves as a physical reminder of the unequal access to water: a speedy and abundant flow of water designated for Jewish agrarian communities and slow, scarce, and stagnant water for Palestinian agrarian communities in al-Battuf. Another time, Ali 'Antar Waked and I crossed the little road bridge above the Water Carrier, and he told me about his eight-year effort to receive a water quota for irrigation. In Israel, agriculturalists have access to water for agriculture at a reduced price only by belonging to a cooperative water association that creates the irrigation infrastructure and communally pays bills to the water authority. This is a social-economic model that was mainly structured around the rationale of Zionist cooperative settlements such as moshavim or kibbutzim. In the 1960s, the state promoted the creation of Palestinian citizens' water

IMAGE 3. The National Water Carrier in Sahl al-Battuf, summer 2014. For al-Battuf agriculturalists it is an offensive infrastructure symbolizing unequal access to water. Photograph by the author.

associations, but this happened mostly in Israel's central areas, whereas in Galilee there are presently few water quotas for Palestinian agriculturalists. Historically, the social-economic model of a cooperative was not a prominent Palestinian social mode of organization; thus, Palestinian cooperatives did not flourish. However, organizational explanations cannot mask that the low levels of water allocation for Palestinian agriculture are a result of Israel's ongoing race for resource control, a race that is actively dispossessing its Palestinian citizens and OPT Palestinians.[28]

Likewise, Ali and Laithi both told me of past incidents where agriculturalists' attempts to pump water for irrigation from the National Water Carrier resulted in court hearings and criminalization. A few of al-Battuf agriculturalists told me of the shared proverb that the National Water Carrier is like a camel in the desert, carrying water on his back but dying from thirst.

Ali told me how after eight years of bureaucratic work with no results, he finally succeeded in receiving water allocation in 2013 as an outcome of the minister of agriculture's visit to al-Battuf a year earlier. Ali had a sense of collective insult and rage regarding the state of water in the plain; he pointed at the canal and said, "For us water is from Allah, and for Jews there are canals of water and canals of drainage," referring in the same breath to the problem of the annual floods and the lack of irrigation water. If in many other global localities water infrastructures produce a sense of citizenship, here the existing and missing canals are aimed at producing a settler colonial citizenship, clarifying the place of distinct subjects vis-à-vis the state and its infrastructures and resources.[29]

Indeed, the National Water Carrier planners never counted the communities of al-Battuf. During the canal planning in the 1950s, experts saw the Battuf basin as a natural reservoir that could regulate the flow of water from the country's north to south and from rainy to dry years and seasons.[30] Their plan involved flooding the agrarian terrain in al-Battuf and inundating the adjacent topographically low villages with water. The plan evoked much resistance from local communities. This plan for al-Battuf did not materialize, however, and water storage was eventually diverted to Lake Tiberias instead.[31] But "water only from God" without state irrigation or drainage provision remains a central problem for Palestinian agriculturalists until today.[32]

IMAGE 4. Early flood in Sahl al-Battuf, winter 2013. Photograph by the author.

In rainy winters, the eastern side of the plain becomes flooded and creates the *gharaq* (Arabic for the "flooded area"; image 4). With a lot of rain, it even creates a lake landscape. The situation improved somewhat with the failed development plan initiated in the mid-1990s, when early constructors dug a marginal drainage canal. Laithi and other local interlocutors said that the flood landscape serves the Jewish inhabitants of the area, who maintain tourist accommodations on the hills surrounding the valley, enjoying the panoramic landscape of al-Battuf as a lake while the Palestinian agriculturalists suffer agrarian-economic loss. Occurring several times per decade, the swamp causes severe agricultural damage and economic loss because the plain's eastern side has no natural or artificial drainage, aside from the minor "zero canal" dug in 1995.

Thus far, I have introduced the time scale and timescape of al-Battuf plain as seen by the members of its agrarian community. They portrayed a multilayered timescape composed of an intimate appreciation for their ancestors' land work and heritage and a deep sense of connection to the land's past and future. This connection is accompanied by a temporal rhythm of family, community work and encounters, and a deep sense of belonging. They described ambivalently an agriculture that is tied to the seasonality of cultivars and the seasonality of water both as rain and as a swamp. They reiterated the disruptive times of the Israeli state and its impact on the plain as events and conflicts regarding land holding in the plain and nearby lands recurred over the years. They commented on struggles over the temporality of agrarian development and a sense of inconsistency with statewide agrarian markets as well as the slow flow of irrigation and drainage resources.

The problem of time in the plain became stark as I closely listened to the time connotations and images my al-Battuf interlocutors used. I noticed that nowhere else in my fieldwork among Palestinian citizens had I heard so many references to "the Turks." In Palestinian Arabic of the Galilee region, it is a common idiom to refer sarcastically to the Turkish period as a marker of antiquity, especially among people sixty and older. But in al-Battuf people in their thirties and forties referred to the Turkish period too. The Palestinians I met used the Turks not only as a reference to a previous powerful sovereign but also one whose legal-land system was perceived as a more protective one. Later we will also see how referring to the Turks has become a marker of time that tells how the plain was abandoned by the Israeli state, who left the plain.

As I extended my time in the plain and in the settler colonial encounter between al-Battuf communities and the state, I heard about Palestinians repeatedly being told to "come to this state institution and go to that governmental office" as well as many instances of delays and waiting. They waited for decisions over water in the plain for irrigation and for drainage. They waited for government funds for the development of agriculture in the plain. They waited for solutions for the problems of agriculture in the plain. Thus, I saw that waiting is not just a matter of inertia of government and bureaucratic work, but it is also a recurring tool of power imposed on al-Battuf communities.

Timescape of the Bureaucratic Delay

You have no right to know the truth now because the truth might
mean the end of your right to wait. And when the critics started to
argue about the absurdist identity of Godot, you did not understand
what the fuss was about. You were smarter than all the critics and
Beckett himself, for he who has waited twenty years knows Godot.

Mahmoud Darwish, *Journal of an Ordinary Grief* [33]

Sahl al-Battuf has been in limbo of state planning and waiting for implementation since 1994 until today (2023). One of the official reasons
for the multiple delays and waiting periods is the numerous state bodies
that have stakes and jurisdiction over the future of Sahl al-Battuf, such
as the local towns' municipalities, the Misgav Regional Council (of the
Jewish settlements established in the Judaization program), the Ministry
of Agriculture, the Ministry of Environment and its local Environmental
Quality Unit, the Israeli Nature and Park Authority, the Ministry of Interior, the Drainage Authority, the Water Authority, and others.

Until 2005, the Ministry of Agriculture promoted a plan to modernize
agriculture in the plain. According to Israeli state ecologists' surveys,
however, the combination of recurrent floods and small plots characterized by vegetation at the margins has enabled the preservation of a
wetland ecosystem and habitat for endangered species. As a result of
the involvement of these ecologists in state planning, ecological and
landscape conservation arguments have become central to discussions
of the future development of al-Battuf. This has led to an increase in the
bureaucratic red tape needed to act, as a larger number of actors are now
involved in the discussions about the development of al-Battuf.

Scholars studying the state have emphasized how the state often operates in a blurred apparatus where one does not know exactly what "the
state" is, how it functions, and who makes up "the state."[34] This phenomenon is evident in Israel/Palestine at large and in al-Battuf specifically.[35]
In al-Battuf, the blurred apparatus is demonstrated by the role that the
Israeli Nature and Parks Authority (INPA) plays in the planning process
and in community outreach. INPA is a governmental organization responsible for managing nature reserves and parks as well as enforcing
wildlife protection. Although INPA is a state body, it is seen in the public

eye as one of the "Greens"—the term coined for environmental bodies and activists in Israel that are commonly understood as a nongovernmental pressure group. Similarly to other planning procedures in Israel/Palestine in the past twenty years, in al-Battuf the INPA has come to play a primary role in planning politics. However, its interventions are not commonly understood by the agriculturalists as restrictions imposed by "the state" but rather as limitations stemming from environmental activists and ecologists. The blurry role of INPA in this story acts as an "anti-politics machine," masking the work of the state through its action via different state bodies and de-politicizing environmental management and resource allocation.[36] Due to the blurry state apparatus, the first procedures of planning that I will discuss concern disagreements between governmental agencies that clarify how state-making is a struggle between various rationales. Different state actors who participated in the process contributed their minutes to my research and shared with me the description of the events.

Under two different governmental administrations between 1994 and 2005, the Ministry of Agriculture promoted programs to drain the flooded areas and create water reservoirs in al-Battuf—two actions that would have enabled irrigation and the development of modern agriculture in the plain. These plans were endorsed and celebrated by local Palestinian stakeholders, who wished to develop agriculture and benefit from their land assets.

Didi Kaplan, a retired senior ecologist who served as INPA Northern District head ecologist for decades and worked for this state authority for forty years recalled the beginning of INPA's opposition to the drainage plan with a sense of successfully overcoming a tremendous threat. He told me: "In 1995 I returned from a postdoc abroad and had to deal with a stack of paperwork to follow up on everything that was going on in the district while I was gone. I then opened the booklet that discussed Beit Netofa. . . . I saw drainage, irrigation reservoirs, modern agriculture, and the bells commenced tolling. I urged a wake-up call to all of INPA and they understood this is serious." Didi was sure that if he had not noticed this drainage program the Ministry of Agriculture was promoting, Beit Netofa Valley would have been destroyed.[37] At that point, they already dug the "zero canal" in the plain, the first drainageway that was aimed to minimize the rain's flood damage.

Thus, members of the INPA halted the drainage plan, which they claimed would have resulted in tremendous loss of the unique landscape and deterioration of the wetland ecosystem. Their knowledge of the planning process enabled them to use procedural claims to delay the proposed drainage plan. They claimed that this development plan could not be discussed in the district's Planning Committee through the Drainage Law, under which the Ministry of Agriculture had submitted the plan but could only be addressed through the Law of Planning and Construction. This latter law requires inclusion of further environmental considerations and limitations.

By claiming an alternative bureaucratic channel, the ecologists created an alternative ontology and timescape, a radically different view of the situation in al-Battuf/Beit Netofa and its prospect of time, both past and future. The view of the ecologists suggests that there is much more to the plain and to its future than mere ditches and irrigation reservoir infrastructures. The timescape the ecologists promoted was not about developed agriculture but about the future of endangered species and the landscape. Transferring the discussion of al-Battuf's development to the jurisdiction of the Law of Planning and Construction ensured that agriculturalists would not be able to build on their privately owned agrarian land. It also meant that any development of al-Battuf would be much more time-consuming since ecological involvement had to be secured through careful zoning plans. The INPA ecologists were successful in convincing the Planning Committee to require an ecological assessment survey from the Ministry of Agriculture. When the ecological survey was presented to the district's Planning Committee, it was ruled unsatisfactory by the INPA, and so the process was further delayed a few years.

An additional milestone favoring ecological considerations in planning procedures took place in 2005 with the publication of the National Master Plan 35. In this plan, Bikat Beit Netofa was defined as a "landscape zone," meaning that only cautious and moderate development would be permitted. Didi told me that "a final nail was driven into the drainage program's coffin in 2009."[38] Following lobbying and intervention, the head of the Planning Administration, the highest statutory body for planning in Israel, declared that the Ministry of Agriculture should lead an alternative development plan for Beit Netofa. He conveyed that the new plan should offer a novel holistic agricultural and developmental approach that included environmental conservation and that it should be grounded in the Law of Planning and Construction.[39] As Didi, the former INPA ecologist, concluded: "This is how it all began: I can say that I sort of succeeded in creating the delay process until today [November 2014], and I am talking to you about a program [the drainage] that started in 1995 and we are now twenty years later."[40] The process that Didi described is indicative of the political power that environmental bodies have gained in Israel's planning processes since the early 2000s. A noticeable shift in the politics of planning occurred through the activism of environmental bodies. However, this shift was not coupled with greater considerations for social equality. Furthermore, across Israel/Palestine, INPA is involved in different projects of Palestinian dispossession through the zoning of nature reserves and the criminalization of Palestinian shepherds and wild plant harvesting.[41]

This ultimate rejection came fifteen years after the agriculturalists had celebrated the state's decision "to drain the swamp." Yet, once again, no action was taken on the development plan for al-Battuf for several years. It may have taken officials from the Ministry of Agriculture involved in the drainage program a long time to recover from the defeat of the plan that they had worked so hard to advance. Nevertheless, the length of time that it took to propose an alternative program may indicate the low priority of the new plan and its target population: the Palestinian citizens.

In 2011, some two years after the final drainage rejection, the Ministry of Environmental Protection and the INPA launched a formal cooperative effort to develop a new holistic program for sustainable development in Bikat Beit Netofa. Their first official protocol serves as a base for a comprehensive program for the plain that would replace the prior drainage program.[42] Simultaneously, the Ministry of Agriculture, together with the Environmental Protection Ministry, funded a small-scale program led by local partners from the Beit Netofa Basin Environmental Quality Union. The latter is a regional subdivision of the Ministry of Environmental Protection, but here it is completely staffed by Palestinian citizens, inhabitants of the adjacent towns. This program was done in cooperation with the INPA to introduce a pilot project called Agriculture That Supports the Environment, which the Ministry of Agriculture's ecologist referred to in this chapter's introduction. This pilot program intended to bring together a group of fifty agriculturalists working in the Maslakhit area of al-Battuf to introduce them to environmental agriculture methods that could contribute to conservation.

The comprehensive planning layout, approved in the Northern District Committee in March 2014, suggests moderate agricultural development should take place accompanied by policy tools that would contribute to the agriculturalists' welfare and major habitat conservation efforts. This approach is innovative for Israel's agricultural policies insofar as it shifts the focus away from agricultural development and toward environmental conservation as well as development initiatives that are less likely to produce adverse environmental effects. Nevertheless, while planning procedures that promote environmental conservation were already undertaken in statutory planning, more innovative planning measures, such as environmental payment schemes for agriculturalists, have not been implemented. Planners subcontracted for the state have even written: "Although environmental payment schemes have been discussed for twenty-five years, nothing has happened in Beit Netofa Valley. This silence is loud."[43] Thus, al-Battuf agriculturalists are waiting for the state to act for them, but what are the implications of such long-term waiting?

Ali Shawaneh, the head of the Agriculturalists Committee of Sakhnin, explained to me in 2014 that the long policy process has resulted in Palestinian alienation from the land. He said: "How many years can you talk about planning? Can someone announce that he is getting married, and it will take him twenty years to do it? They are postponing until people come to a mental state where they feel that there is no solution, no progress, and then they leave their land."[44] Agriculturalists have left their land due to stagnation and lengthy wait times for development implementation or have leased it to a neighbor able to cultivate a greater area. Agriculturalists are also abandoning their land for other reasons such as the economy of scale, better income in an alternative employment, and the ever-deteriorating image of agricultural work in the view of Palestinians in Israel. Nevertheless, Ali's despair well embodies the ethnographic claims that waiting and agreeing to wait are a means of governmental exertion of power and its acceptance.[45]

Governmental authorities have been stuck in a constant planning cycle for more than twenty years, with almost no implementation aside from the small pilot program in the Maslakhit area started in 2013. However, Maslakhit covers 1 percent of the whole area, and it is used by fifty agriculturalists among a few thousand landowners. Iftah, another senior ecologist of the INPA who participated in a species survey in al-Battuf and in the design of a sustainable agriculture pilot program, told me in the fall of 2014 that once the drainage program was rejected, it was no longer in the INPA's interest to delay development.[46] Consequently, once drainage was ruled out, the INPA has been the only state body working to create alternatives on the ground with partners in al-Battuf basin since 2010. Then whose interest does it serve to work so slowly?

The state apparatus does not work in harmony, and citizens often must wait for state institutions to settle their disputes. Anthropologist Nayanika Mathur showed that in the Indian Himalaya, development work was postponed and citizens had to wait not as a subordination technique but mainly because of contradictions between the timing of procedures and the different long-term aims of diverse state institutions.[47] My observation in al-Battuf echoes her insights, yet there is more behind this prolonged waiting than conflicts between state institutions. Contrary to Mathur's observation, I see the conflicting rationales of ministries as contributing to delays in decision-making, but they also serve as a procedural strategy, masking the work of time, perpetual delays, and inefficiency as tools of governance. Hence, time as a bureaucratic tool can be slowed down and sped up depending on the different strategies and aims those governing institutions employ. The bureaucratic delay then captures how the settler state adopts different institutional mechanisms to deal with the colonized Palestinian citizens.

The next scene might further explain my claim. Following the INPA's retreat from its opposition to the plan, the Ministry of Agriculture claimed that the Ministry of Interior was responsible for creating constant delays in advancing this program. During my fieldwork in 2013–2014, I participated in meetings of the Ministry of Interior's Northern District Planning

Committee where the development plan was discussed. These meetings often seemed like a bad joke about how bureaucratic power is used by officials, only it was reality. The use of bureaucratic procedures and delays as a technique of ruling al-Battuf/Bikat Beit Netofa was manifested time and time again. The head of the Northern Planning Committee was able to find time in official meetings to repeatedly make irrelevant remarks, allegedly jokes, that brought all participants into a state of despair. It was the end of the workday and thirty participants including various state officials, al-Battuf town representatives, and planners contracted by the Ministry of Agriculture were sitting around the Northern District's Planning Committee meeting-room table. INPA's ecologist Iftah Sinai presented Beit Netofa's species survey and with a tone of seriousness explained that this survey took over eight years and these endangered species survived only in this valley. The head of the Planning Committee asked both mockingly and seriously, "Can you make a salad out of these species?" And then, although the ecologist had explained thirty seconds earlier how the combination of small-scale agriculture and unplowed margins enabled the species' survival, the head of the Planning Committee asked, "Why do these species grow only here? Do they have an ID card there? A permanent residence?" Such comments are a small example of meetings that were constantly interrupted in such a spirit. Meeting participants did not know whether to cry, laugh, or scream. Presumably, his naïve or joking comments were critical of the ecological logic and could have contributed to furthering the economic interests of the agriculturalists that local towns' members were worried about. But it was not the case. The head of the District Planning Committee kept making remarks, delaying and prolonging meetings and the whole process as if pushing everyone's limits were his professional mission. My acquaintance from the Ministry of Agriculture who paved the way for me to participate in these meeting told me agitatedly at the end, "This is the last time I agree to come to these meetings without my superior," as if some greater force could have stopped this show of bureaucratic horror.[48]

Additionally, not all the meetings' participants received the materials that were supposed to be discussed in a timely manner. Representatives of the Palestinian towns surrounding al-Battuf basin, for instance, received them only at the last moment. Having less time to prepare for the conversation restricts one's ability to influence it; thus, these representatives made fewer comments, and they were portrayed as disengaged with the process. Using Foucault's argument on how governmental techniques make the state as much as they are deployed by it, development scholarship has shown how "participation" is a means of governance that facilitates forms of governmental contact with marginalized populations. Aside from inviting them to the planning meetings, state planners at that point did not seem to seriously consider Palestinian towns' representatives.[49]

These various layers of the timescape of bureaucratic delay are a demonstration of acting as "the state" according to the settler state logic.[50] According to this logic, there is always a delay actor generating the governmental agency, thereby contributing to the Kafkaesque limbo, stagnation, and the despair of the agriculturalists who see the years passing but nothing happening.[51] Although it is commonly known that bureaucratic procedures take time and Israel's planning system is criticized for this characteristic, the procedures are not exhaustively long. This planning process has taken place during a shift of inverting paradigms in agriculture and planning from productivist to post-productivist sustainable agendas of agriculture. Moreover, this policy change process is situated within the shifting political economy of the settler colonial state that moved from the primacy of agriculture in the 1960s–1980s to industry and the information economy since the 1990s. Thus, new winners and losers are determined among Israeli citizens, and the struggle over the future of al-Battuf has become a site demonstrating this shift. Hence, among governmental bodies in Israel, there is always someone who creates obstacles to the process of planning and implementing in al-Battuf. This is the timescape of bureaucratic delay in al-Battuf. It occurs both in endless meetings on zoning programs and irrigation reservoirs in neon-lit governmental offices and in the abandonment of the agricultural fields. The time of bureaucratic delay is not only about making subjects wait. It is the cultivation of the false hope that "the government is taking care of the situation" but in a timescale that would make any plan irrelevant by the time it is agreed upon.

Similarly, anthropologists studying Palestine's West Bank have observed how West Bank Palestinians are in a temporal mode of a "state/

no-state yet to come." Such a temporal form of anticipation turns West Bank Palestinians into subjects suspended in time. They are prevented from managing their non-sovereign environment through short-term tactical decisions or long-term planning.[52] This situation also exists in al-Battuf, yet the residents of al-Battuf are citizens of the state and not subjects of a colonial military regime. This shared temporal mode of waiting indicates that, regardless of civilian rights, Palestinians' shared status as inferior subjects of a settler colonial regime unifies them as subjects who are deprived of the right to control their own time. When Mahmoud Darwish, the Palestinian national poet I quoted earlier, writes: "You were smarter than all the critics and Beckett himself, for he who has waited twenty years knows Godot," he captures the absurd temporal reality that Palestinians live in.[53]

Hence, the bureaucratic delay encapsulates the *how* of the Israeli state machine: there is always some component to discuss in planning; implementation and action are only ghosts. Here, planning, delays, and the lack of implementation embody a form of governance: planning in the present, gesturing to "the future" without ever taking action to arrive at "the future" or fulfill its goals. The symbolic and declarative role of plans elucidates why, oftentimes, plans are neither approved nor applied and therefore create a timescape of their own.[54] Furthermore, framing the new plan under the primacy of ecological knowledge justified long planning processes that were allegedly designated to assure precautionary ecological principles. In such a way, the ecologists' ability of framing knowledge about time through an ecological timescale deemed conservation as the moral duty of this era.

Ecology as Public Knowledge and as Time

Governments construct public reason, or the forms of knowledge, institutional practices, discourses, and techniques that they then use to justify their policies. Reasoning is situated within political cultures and modes of knowledge and expertise.[55] Hence, two themes are reiterated in official public discourse and in policy documents regarding the importance of the conservation of Bikat Beit Netofa in its "traditional agriculture" mode: first, "it is the last swamp that was not drained"; second, a careful and integrative planning process is required based upon the lessons learned from the environmental history of the draining of a nearby lake, the Huleh Swamp.[56] In the 1950s, Huleh Lake was drained by the Jewish National Fund to create agricultural terrains for the new kibbutzim established in the Upper Galilee, similar to other state-initiated drainage projects.[57] Huleh was partially reflooded in 1994 because it was understood that the Huleh drainage project had heavy ecological costs and the process was not agriculturally beneficial.[58] The Huleh Swamp stands in Israel today as a communal lesson requiring the need for careful, ecologically based decision-making. Therefore, the history of Huleh Swamp drainage justifies current planning procedures that are conceived and framed by state actors as integrative, meticulous, and thoughtful.[59]

However, only this one historic lesson influences policy, while another historic factor is ignored. The vast swamp drainage project that took place in Palestine/Israel during the twentieth century was initiated by the Zionist movement mostly before the establishment of the state. Swamp drainage projects in Palestine were deeply intertwined with malaria control and the politics of Jewish settlement, agricultural modernization, and land improvement. These projects applied a Zionist view of healing to Palestine's landscape, which was conceived as pathological and infested with malaria. Thus, the drainage of swamps in Palestine was not simply a Zionist war against disease, but more of a campaign to create room for Zionist immigration and settlement, to advance the building of a Jewish national home.[60] Drainage, like other infrastructure projects, forms politics by creating coverage decay and maintenance, connections, or disconnections of regions as well as material and economic constructions of differences.[61] Historically, drainage affected the transformation of the local landscape in Palestine/Israel technologically, ecologically, and perceptually by promoting Zionism as a modernized and progressive project, one that the British colonial government would support.[62] Drainage was understood as vital for creating agricultural land but today it is understood that it had heavy ecological costs.

In the 1930s and 1940s, the Zionist movement saw enhancing the production capacities of agriculture in Palestine/Israel as crucial because this would enable it to demand higher Jewish immigration quotas from the British.[63] Drainage was vital for increasing agricultural productivity.

The drainage project created dramatic changes in the land and the significant loss of habitats. Drainage was a project of agricultural modernization in which the Palestinian peasants were not invited to take part.[64] Thus, underdevelopment, exclusion, and settler colonization are the historical reasons that led Beit Netofa Valley to be "the last swamp that was not drained," as policy documents say, but the factors that led this valley to be the last swamp have never been recognized by the state. As the work of Samer Alatout shows, this is a historical context in which water resources functioned to construct a Jewish identity, immigration, and Zionist settlements but rarely to develop Palestinian agriculture.[65] Thus, policy for al-Battuf represents an arrangement of governing through ecological knowledge and selective perspectives of time. These perspectives appear in policy and help to construct the official narratives around the water regime of the al-Battuf swamp, thereby serving the state apparatus.

However, many al-Battuf agriculturalists want to cultivate what is understood as developed and modernized agriculture while officials insist to them that it is modern to conserve. Thus, Didi, the former INPA ecologist, told me, "The agriculturalist lived all his life here [in al-Battuf] and he does not understand how unique this is; he does not have a perspective of all the country to understand how beautiful this landscape is." Didi thought it would be a mistake to drain the swamp and that agriculturalists must be involved in contemporary conservation through agroecology. He posited that it is the mission of our times to educate the agriculturalists about ecological conservation. He presumed that the agriculturalists of al-Battuf lacked a time and environment perspective.

Yet, agriculturalists say that their newly requested role of promoting swamp conservation "for birds and plants," which they find ridiculous, is a contemporary form of governmental control. Munir Hammoudi, an agriculturalist from the al-Battuf area, said at the Israeli Parliament: "They used to confront our demands with the police and the army. Today we are confronted with ecologists, planning committees, 'Greens,' etc. . . . . But we are talking here of human lives, almost a hundred thousand inhabitants. . . . We could also do developed agriculture."[66] Hammoudi identified the environmental agenda as a contemporary form of state surveillance, showing he was very much aware of time and the environment, but as a Palestinian citizen. His claim on "the environment" as a contemporary form of control was shared by other interlocutors as well. Considering that the history of loss of wetland habitats in Israel/Palestine is due to Zionist developmentalism, rather than the work of Palestinian peasants' agriculture, indicates that Hammoudi's rejection of "Green" environmental agendas has strong reasons. The threats to native plants are a part of a settler-nationhood legacy rather than the Palestinian agroecological legacy.[67] Settler colonial projects were always multispecies enterprises involving the settlement of plants as well as animals and people.[68] Furthermore, environmental conservation bodies have had a legacy of participating in native people's dispossession, both in Israel/Palestine and elsewhere.[69]

Furthermore, ecology has become the dominant science affecting the plain and it comes with a time of its own. Over the course of sixteen years, ecologists of the INPA have undertaken eight surveys and studies that mapped the flora and fauna of Beit Netofa. They undertook these surveys with partners from the Society of the Protection of Nature, an NGO that is also regularly represented in the Northern District Planning Committee. They operate in a coalition that serves the rising power of environmental expertise in Israel. With every published survey, a growing body of knowledge and numbers is produced about rare species and endangered species at the site. The species are also presented in the Planning Committee meetings. Thus, the lives of certain living beings are given a political status. Moreover, the ecologists have produced ecological knowledge as an inevitable factor and actor in the political process of planning in al-Battuf.[70] The threat of extinction is a powerful political-discursive tool. It recruits the future risk of species' extinction as a technology of power and produces an ethical time of saving species, suggesting that if the state saved them from extinction, it would stand on a higher moral ground.

The agency of endangered species as a political force has a timescape to it. The ecological production of species futurity is anchored in practices such as slowly walking, locating, and identifying flora and fauna and documenting them in charts that end up as GIS maps of flora and fauna. These GIS maps run on computers that quickly cross-reference to any nongovernmental, governmental, or research institution that is interested in the preservation of these species. Thus, ecological knowledge gains speed over time. Conservationists say that the species survive (sustained over time) in the valley due to the work of the "traditional agriculturalists" and their small plots' margins, meaning that preventing the development of industrial forms of agriculture in the valley is in fact an ecological objective.

The ecological-temporal conception that is produced is not only based on the time needed to gather all the data regarding endangered species, but it is also anchored in two earlier accounts repeatedly quoted in those ecological reports produced by the INPA. These accounts contribute to the ecological temporality construction of al-Battuf and to the creation of the image of the wetland as an inseparable characteristic of this place. These reports quote the fourteenth-century Arab geographer al-Dimashqi and the twelfth-century Jewish philosopher Maimonides, who both referred to the character of the valley as holding water. These accounts fortify the image of the flood as an ancient and pristine "nature" that must be conserved, therefore reinforcing the vision of conserving this landscape as a wetland.

Trying to create alternative knowledge was difficult. In a planning meeting of the small-scale pilot program led by the Environmental Quality Union, Hanadi Hijris, a Palestinian Arab employee of the union worked hard to share her ideas on applicable sustainable development measures for al-Battuf. She anchored her knowledge in a vast literature review that she produced to foster development experience from the Arab world as well as from agrarian development in the Palestinian Authority working with smallholders there. She said:

> In Jordan, they did an impressive process where they involved Bedouins and marginalized farmers in species surveys. They would work together with Bedouins to locate plants, and they would conclude the scientific work in their tents. Whenever plant did not have an Arabic name, only a Latin name, they would involve the public in defining a new plant name in Arabic to create trust with the local community and foster a sense of belonging. . . . Consult the community on where to develop agriculture, where to conserve ecology and where can you develop tourism, always include the community.[71]

Her work was a lively example of efforts to decolonize hegemonic knowledge. Her work was grounded in a time and space that saw al-Battuf as
inseparable from the rest of Palestine and the Arab world.

Yet, her suggestions were rejected by a Jewish-Israeli planner hired
to write the pilot program, experts of the committee, and the Palestinian
Arab director of the union, who felt committed to the experts he thought
would comply with governmental demands that follow European rural
development schemes and the centrality of ecological knowledge.[72] The
dynamic between Hanadi and the experts was a manifestation of how
the Foucauldian notion of subjugated knowledge and epistemic violence
come into action.[73] The knowledge of how to receive funding had to be
framed in hegemonic knowledge structures. Furthermore, the denial of
the Arabness of al-Battuf and the reiteration of European rural development as an inspiration reinforces the Eurocentric orientation of Israeli
institutions and their denial of Israel's Levantine location. This example
emphasizes how this knowledge structure is a political culture anchored
in settler colonial hierarchies and a rejection of Palestinian knowledge.
In a private meeting later, Hanadi shared with me how frustrated and en-
raged she was by the priorities of planning and action for al-Battuf. She
said: "Talking to these other state institutions involved, all with their experts, is like talking to a wall. The plan sets ecological conservation and
agrarian improvement but the aspect of economic development for the
community is totally lacking. . . . I went and interviewed all these special-
ists that headed agrarian development in the West Bank, and they could
have been our instructors with relevant knowledge and action schemes,
but here they could not hear that."[74]

To conclude this section, in al-Battuf, like in other places, knowledge production wields power, silencing other forms of knowledge and
action.[75] Recruiting ecological science's time and selective historical accounts to the process of politics not only makes policy partially informed
but also creates an image of a sustained universality. Indeed, next to the
ecological knowledge base there was no involvement of social scientists
or knowledge that would consider socioeconomic relations in Palestinian
society, social-environmental knowledge, such as ethno-botany, or traditional ecological knowledge.[76]

Constructing "the Other" as Traditional

A powerful tool for reasoning with developed agriculture in Israel while referring to al-Battuf as an exceptional "traditional" case is linked with a colonial heritage of seeing the other as inhabiting another time.[77] Johannes Fabian's critique in his seminal work *Time and the Other* argues that power relations are structured when subjects are seen as nonmodern and non-coeval. Thus, the state treats itself as Westernized and developed and ties its modernity and progressiveness with the willingness to recognize the other as "traditional" and "authentic."[78] This is a time aspect that is prominent in the policy document concerning the official explanation for the unique agricultural state of the Battuf. It posits that the condition of al-Battuf is an outcome of recurrent winter floods as well as a shortage of water sources for summer irrigation as if those were natural and not a result of underdevelopment. The policy also portrays rain-fed traditional farming and no water for irrigation in the summer as a direct outcome of local traditions of inheritance.[79] It is indeed the case that annual seasons and the Muslim inheritance law are contributing factors to the current state of the Battuf. However, rain-induced flooding is an outcome of the lack of drainage in al-Battuf, and the lack of irrigation during the summer is a result not of inherited traditions but rather of unequal water allocation. Fabian would have called this a description of the Other as existing beyond time. This temporal and spatial ordering is anchored in colonial roots of alterity and in uneven distribution of resources.

The agrarian imaginary that al-Battuf evokes and what sort of temporal continuity the establishment is seeking to create were evident in a variety of texts written by the ecologists contracted by the Ministry of Agriculture during the 1990s and early 2000s. The following is a text written by one of these ecologists, Racheli Einav. Although this excerpt appeared in a popular journal rather than a policy document, it illustrates the official imaginary: "Beit Netofa is a closed valley in the lower Galilee. Whoever is there can disconnect and not see the rest of the world. In the valley, it is as if time stood still—there are swamps there and traditional rain-fed cultivars that are harvested with a sickle. . . . It is a real swamp as in the time of the Zionist pioneers, as in the Bible, the last we have that was not yet drained."[80] The text reflects the deep orientalist imaginary embedded in the minds of Israeli officials toward al-Battuf, which evokes nostalgia for the past. It points to the state's priority of conserving de-development as tradition and materializes the image of the fallahin (peasants, Arabic) as a living museum, symbolizing both the early days of Zionism and more importantly, the imagined landscapes of the biblical past.[81]

Another government official, Haim Shenhar, depicted the landscape as biblical in his master's thesis regarding Beit Netofa. Shenhar was the director of the Northern District of Israel's Ministry of Environmental Protection during the 1990s–2000s. He was involved for many years in the initiative to turn the valley into a project conserving "traditional agriculture" and rural tourism instead of advocating drainage. According to Motti Kaplan, a leading planner often contracted by governmental ministries for national and regional master plans:

> The strongest attraction of Israel is the fact that it is the land of the Bible, where one is impressed by the past remains that demonstrate historic heritage. Yet Israel is a modern state, developed in agriculture and based on the economy of scale that creates monocultures. Consequently, Jewish agriculture loses its linkage to the agriculture of the land of the Bible and its landscapes. These continue to exist in the fallahin who cultivate their land extensively, in small parcels and with simple tools. As they go to the field, they are dressed as biblical characters.[82]

Despite Einav's, Shenhar's, and Kaplan's descriptions, in my fieldwork I never saw such biblical figures, but rather men and some veiled women using mobile phones and dressed in the way that many readers of this text likely dress (image 5). The biblical objectification of Palestinians has endured for over a century and a half. The European rediscovery of Palestine in the nineteenth century resulted in a trend of writing about Palestine in relation to the Bible and the Holy Land. Palestinians appeared in nineteenth-century photographs and postcards as decorations and icons of ancient times: images such as the shepherd and his flock, a woman drawing water from a well, or a peasant plowing his field. All

IMAGE 5. Ali 'Antar walking in Sahl al-Battuf, summer 2014. Photograph by the author.

these images have sustained the European imagery of biblical Palestine, and Zionist writing continues that trend.[83] Here too, Beit Netofa is imagined as a site of bringing the past to the present. Thus, Israeli official narratives consign the Palestinians of al-Battuf to the past and embed them in the present to legitimize Zionist settler histories and geographies.[84]

Furthermore, the term *traditional agriculture* that has been used to define the uniqueness of al-Battuf must be reconsidered. The next excerpt, from a conversation with a cultivator in al-Battuf named Muhammad, will help problematize this term. Muhammad and I sat together in Batuf on a sunny spring day in 2014. Muhammad said, "We are doing agriculture here like they did in the days of the Turks."

"What do you mean?" I asked him. Interestingly, right in front of us was a new model combine and tractor, machines commonly associated with current agrarian practices.

"I mean that agriculture here is what it used to be like—we sit here and pray for the rain; we don't have water for irrigation. This is what agriculture is like here," he emphasized. While the state describes the agricultural condition in al-Battuf as the fruit of tradition, Muhammad's emphasis on praying for rain acknowledged the unequal water policies of the state and highlighted the relationship between the identity of land-owners and their given water resources.[85]

During the time I spent in the valley, the agriculturalists used various kinds of new agricultural machinery. They applied pesticides and were well acquainted with contemporary intensive-farming agricultural tech-niques. They also farmed in small plots, which are associated with tra-ditional agriculture. Small plots also exist in the organic farms in Israel, yet there they are deemed modern rather than traditional. Furthermore, even the expert reports from the Ministry of Agriculture lightly criticize the usage of the term *traditional agriculture* to describe Palestinian agri-culture.[86] Nonetheless, policy-wise, the formal term that is consistently applied to the farms of al-Battuf is *traditional agriculture.*

Constructing the Palestinian as "traditional" enables a governmental approach that frames the problem of Palestinian underdevelopment as a result of "traditional" agricultural practices, rather than as a direct prod-uct of the power relations constructed by the state.[87] This form of govern-mental discourse enables stagnation, the long duration of processes, and lack of state intervention because it supposes that "the other" is tradi-tional and will not accept change. The ways in which the agriculturalists have organized in associations to advance the drainage program in the 1990s might imply that this is simply untrue.

Agrarian-Environmental Imaginaries of Justice

From my meetings with various agriculturalists in the valley it became clear that they are interested in modern agricultural development and irrigation. Before the drainage program was rejected, the Ministry of Ag-riculture managed to acquire the signatures of a significant percentage of the landowners in the valley agreeing to give 6 percent of their land for re-parcellation, which was required to execute the plan. Considering the history of Palestinians' land appropriation and confiscation under-taken by the state, reaching this agreement with the owners seems a remarkable achievement after years of distrust. In the early 2000s, the agriculturalists had organized themselves in associations to advance the drainage plan. For the agriculturalists, developed and irrigated agriculture is a matter of equality, of access to resources such as water and an economic and symbolic asset—productive, intensive agriculture. The ideas of conserving plants that do not evoke popular interest or evaluating a dry summer landscape seem absurd. Ali ʿAntar Waked told me: "What sort of a beautiful landscape do they see here? In the center of Israel, by Kfar Saba's orchards you can see green all year long, you can see production. And here, what can you see? No apples or peaches . . . a dry ugly summer. You don't have any beautiful tree to stand by and take a picture with."[88] Highlighting the lack of agricultural production, he experiences this landscape in comparison to Israel's agricultural areas, which are green and productive year-round. His vision is classical political ecology linking ecology and landscape to political economy.[89]

In contrast, Iftah, the INPA senior ecologist, told me:

> I can understand why, in the short term, people might be mad that they lost income due to our efforts to conserve the valley. . . . However, in the long term I believe we are heading in the right direction since modern agricultural development here would have caused salinization to the soil and not only damage on ecological terms. I think that in the drainage program they would have never been able to obtain all the agriculturalists' signatures for re-parcellation, so in the long term, I believe we are right.[90]

Iftah's comment asserts assumptions of past, present, and future beliefs about who is right and just in this process. His analysis assumes different imaginaries of environmental-agrarian development suggested in terms of time; however, it seems that questions about the rightness of the process and its outcomes continue to hover above al-Battuf policy actors and makers.

Anthropological works have noticed that separate time experiences characterize the encounter between a state and an indigenous community.[91] Although various temporalities exist among the multiple actors in al-Battuf, only some matter politically. Thus, Laithi told me, "Every proposed solution to the valley that will not include drainage and irrigation will only be a reproduction of poverty here. It's exactly that: reproducing poverty."[92] The different imaginaries on what is right and just demonstrates additional time-based problems of al-Battuf: the gap between the future intention of these plans with the lived realities of Palestinian citizens.[93] However, what was evident throughout my fieldwork was the strong connection that all sides felt toward al-Battuf/Beit Netofa and preserving its future. However, while the ecological swamp and the survival of nonhuman species have been at the center of the table for the last fifteen years, it seems that the question of human survival is just beginning to arise.

Green Grabbing and the Timescape of Domination

The story of al-Battuf offers an ironic vignette in the Zionist history of agricultural development, particularly the Zionist narratives of the Palestinian peasant. It is a story of the paradigmatic shift from modernist development endeavors to the politics of sustainability. The timescape of sustainable development in al-Battuf is framed as a project that conserves ecological values, but it instead preserves the political construct of a de-developed "traditional agriculture." The current Beit Netofa time is perceived by governmental agents as a Western notion of sustainable development, a model of development that the Palestinians should abide by to prove their environmental citizenship and their embrace of "modern" values. Thus, environmental state bodies expect the Palestinians to devote their land in the valley to environmental conservation. Yet the Palestinians' lived experience of the environment is one of resource dispossession and economic marginalization.[94] These experiences are consistently overlooked by the state, enabling the preservation of the Israeli state's political domination in the new sustainable policy program.

The Israeli officials' sudden appreciation of the Palestinian cultivator seems to be a discursive shift but not a comprehensive one. After all, Palestinian citizens and their environment are still viewed through the biblical imaginaries and orientalist approaches that have prevailed for more than a century. When Palestinian agriculturalists ask for agricultural development, they are looked upon as outside of time, agents of past ideals of landscape and agriculture. Thus, this agro-environmental imaginary of the people and their land transgresses time; it reproduces and extends, lingering in policies from one regime to another and maintaining its hold over institutional modes of governing.[95]

Fellow ethnographers have addressed Israel's theft of Palestinian time through the multiple forms of waiting imposed upon Palestinians, such as waiting for permits and at checkpoints in the West Bank.[96] These observations on Palestinian time theft were drawn from the experiences of Palestinians in the West Bank and Gaza but have not yet been used to examine the experiences of Palestinian citizens of Israel. I suggest that the case of al-Battuf represents Israel's theft of Palestinian citizens' time, highlighting that these practices are not restricted to military colonial control systems but also extend to citizens within the state. Perhaps this is better explained in the words of Ali 'Antar : "In my lifetime I want to see agriculture prospering here." Yet, agricultural planning has gone on and on for twenty-five years now and one wonders whether Ali will retire into a new plan suggested for al-Battuf.

I see the current processes of development plans with no implementation within the ongoing context of Palestinian agrarian colonization, as a contemporary form of dispossession. The Palestinian peasantry was dispossessed from its land in the pre-state days. This was a land grab facilitated by the imposition of a European capitalist economy, both British and Zionist, competing and intervening with a non-capitalist Palestinian economy and advocating these interventions as improvements for Palestinian agrarian economy. In Zionist eyes, these were actions of land redemption that were preparing the land for its Jewish state days. Later, there was the massive land dispossession facilitated by temporal legal mechanisms of the 1948 War "state of emergency" and postwar legislation. For the state, these were acts intended to ensure the cultivation of arable land and the control, development, and settlement of land for the ethno-nation state. This process was coupled by the designation of Palestinians in Israel as a rural proletariat. Then, there were the land appropriations of the 1970s, aiming to solidify a Jewish majority in Galilee, efforts that have failed demographically but succeeded spatially. Nonetheless, these repeated confiscations of Palestinian land have solidified a Palestinian collectivity of resistance.

The story of al-Battuf/Beit Netofa is a direct continuation of these processes. It reflects that we are witnessing a new land dispossession—a green grab, a land appropriation in the name of biodiversity and landscape conservation. This process needs to be understood as the latest stage of a long historical process. It is a more sophisticated land appropriation because it does not entail forced removal from the land, capitalist accumulation, or global interventions like other global green grabs but rather a national superimposition of land management and land use.[97] For the state, this green grabbing is done under the guise of sustainable development, conservation of traditional agriculture, and the integration of Arab citizens into an environmental era.

I have illustrated that this green grab is undertaken through timescape as a tool of domination. It entails the control of duration in planning processes and a discursive shaping of the landscape and agricultural imaginaries as traditional and biblical rather than underdeveloped. It also encompasses a control of the modes of time and knowledge through which al-Battuf is understood. Evidently, controlling time and constructing space are tools of power. In al-Battuf, various actors are engaged in making time and space, but ultimately, it is the state's governing time that dominates power dynamics.

I end this chapter by leaving the door open for agriculturalists' desires for a flourishing agriculture to fulfil themselves in Ali's lifetime. The current stage of planning that has been undertaken since I completed my fieldwork in 2015–2017 offers glimpses of change. The new plan goes beyond the agrarian fields of al-Battuf and incorporates a wider social-economic perspective that better addresses the needs of Palestinian stakeholders. It also includes acts of recognition, such as naming the development plan in both Hebrew and Arabic, as well as mentioning the Muslim heritage of the villages' architecture as a tourist attraction. A radical act for a governmental plan, it also indicates that at the eastern end of the valley there used to be "an important Arab village until 1948, Safuria." Indeed, Safuria was a prospering Palestinian village that was destroyed in the aftermath of the 1948 War, and a Jewish moshav was established over its location.

After a public participation process that included more Palestinian municipality stakeholders, it has finally been decided to partially drain some of the swamp area in accordance with ecological considerations and to provide irrigation to agriculturalists working in the center of the plain, an area that is less likely to interrupt nonhuman species' survival. This development plan is aimed to conserve the local "traditional agriculture" and to protect the endangered species as well as maintain the "traditional agriculture" mosaic landscape. It only took another five years of discussions (from 2013 to 2018) to reach this point. However, to reach the plan's implementation stage, the government needs to approve and allocate funds, implying that the great plan's vision of touristic and agrarian development still has much red tape to cut through. Since the approval of the holistic plan in December 2017 and until November 2021, the plan had not advanced in a national bureaucratic channel that would sponsor the large-scale development program. Nonetheless, minor funding was allocated to provide agricultural instruction services and develop the plain's irrigation plan at Israel's water authority. However, to fulfill the vision of the sustainable development program, significant government funds need to reach Sahl al-Battuf. In May 2023, after four years of failed governments in Israel, the large-scale plan has not been implemented, but the program finally received a promise for funding for 2023–2026 through the governmental decision 550 of October 2021 promoted by the Government of Change coalition.[98] The public announcements in Arabic from the Ministry of Agriculture and the Authority for Economic Development for Minorities about the funds' allocation terms were received on digital platforms with Palestinian contempt, cynicism, and jokes regarding the many years it took to reach this stage. Only a few voices were hopeful.[99] When I recently asked Laithi what he thought about the prospects of program he answered with the Hebrew idiom for "better late than never." Perhaps Laithi did not want to lose his right to wait, or maybe he, like other Palestinians in this land, sustain hope despite their absurd and unjust realities.

TWO

Returning to the Seventh Year

One sunny September day, the Israeli state told an Arab citizen, "One year, my son, all this will be yours—one year." On September 5, 2007, the state of Israel *sold* to Hamadeh Ghanem, a Druze from the village-town Mghar in the Galilee, all the agrarian land cultivated by Jewish cooperative communities in Israel. The deal encompassed 2.5 million dunums of agrarian land.[1] At the deal signing, the purchaser affirmed to the governmental committee that he believed there was one God and that he followed the seven Noahide commandments (the biblical commandments for non-Jews). The chief rabbi of Israel, representatives from the Ministry of Religions, and the head of Israel's Land Authority represented the Israeli state in this unusual deal.[2] Contrary to this unique and rather symbolic ritual, Israel does not commonly sell land to its non-Jewish citizens. Israel nationalized land tenure in the aftermath of the 1948 War, and it mostly prevents its non-Jewish citizens from accessing and leasing state land.[3]

But Ghanem is a retired senior military officer who served in the Israeli army for close to thirty years. He was, therefore, considered a "good Arab" by the state and someone who could be trusted to uphold the performance of such a peculiar legal performance of land sale.[4] As part of the deal, Ghanem would have to return the land to the state after one Hebrew calendar year.[5] The type of land deal that occurred between Ghanem and the Israeli state happens once every seven years and is the result of a highly contested circumvention of Jewish law called *heter me-khira* (a sale permit). This circumvention has existed for 130 years. The sale permit is a religious bypass of the biblical commandment of *shmita* (in Hebrew literally "release"), or the Sabbath of the Land, requiring a collective "land rest" in the Seventh Year.[6] The Bible describes the commandment of shmita:[7]

> When you come into the land that I give you, the land shall keep a Sabbath to the Lord. For six years you shall sow your field, and for six years you shall prune your vineyard and gather in its fruits, but in the seventh year there shall be a Sabbath of solemn rest for the land, a Sabbath to the Lord. You shall not sow your field or prune your vineyard. You shall not reap what grows of itself in your harvest or gather the grapes of your undressed vine. It shall be a year of solemn rest for the land.

According to the biblical commandment, Jews in Israel must allow the land to lie fallow and regenerate in a year of shmita.[8] The seventh year as a rest year is rooted in a sacred temporal order created by God according to the biblical story of creation. God created the world in six days and rested on the seventh day. The name Sabbath—in Hebrew, *Shabbat*—derives from the word *sheva* (seven) or from the word *shavat* (ceased).[9] This commandment is rooted in a cosmology that sees land as belonging to God and humans are allowed to use it only at certain times.

Shmita pertains to a group of Jewish laws that apply only to Jews living in the land of Israel, referring to the biblical map of Israel, which differs from the map of Israel proper. Thus, Jewish Israelis in the southern region of Arabah can continue producing regularly. Shmita also commands landholders to relinquish personal ownership of their fields; whatever produce grows on a Jewish proprietor's land is considered communal property, free for anyone to take.

The modern relevance of practicing shmita emerged with Jewish immigration to Palestine during the onset of Zionism and the establishment of Jewish agrarian colonies in Palestine at the end of the nineteenth century (see table 1).[10] With the understanding that shmita posed a significant challenge to the agrarian colonies' economic survival, a few notable rabbis interpreted Jewish law to allow the use of sale permits in 1888. Their interpretation suggested that by temporarily selling the land to a non-Jew, the prohibitions on Jewish agriculture during the Seventh Year can be circumvented, thereby allowing Jews to live off their agricultural production.[11]

The rabbis defined the sale permit as a temporary alternative to the biblical tradition of shmita, due to the difficult economic conditions at the time. Yet, the temporary became permanent, and the practice of sale permits during the Seventh Year has continued, despite the rabbis' insistence that it is still a transitional work-around. Both then and today, the work-around of the sale permit is needed from the perspectives of Jewish law, religious and nonreligious Jewish agriculturalists, and the state's economy. As one Jewish-Israeli agriculturalist told me, "Fifty percent of Israeli consumers want to eat kosher, so why would you reject them and this shmita process?" Most Jewish Israelis accept the premise that the "Jewish state" is meant to allow a Jewish lifestyle, and they cooperate with many religious influences on civic life in Israel. The state's interest in the sale permit is to provide fresh produce to the population at reasonable prices that cannot be guaranteed if everyone were to cease cultivating the land during the same Hebrew calendar year as the commandment demands. Additionally, agriculture provides support for other industries. Hence, disabling collectively all agriculture for a year is not feasible. Consequently, state mechanisms facilitate shmita subterfuges to settle the settler nation's cyclical religious time with a linear capitalist time.[12]

Ever since its inception, the land sale circumvention has created a fierce internal Jewish polemic, mostly between religious Zionists and the ultra-Orthodox.[13] Ultra-Orthodox rabbis are opposed to the land sale. They argue that selling land to non-Jews and conducting these sorts of limited, dishonest deals are opposed to Jewish law (*halakha*).[14] Yet the practical significance of the state's sale-permit circumvention is that it allows most Jewish-Israeli farmers to obtain kosher certification (satis-

TABLE 1. Shmita in Gregorian and Hebrew calendar years

Shmita in Gregorian calendar years	Shmita in Hebrew calendar years
1881–1882	5642
1888–1889	5649
1895–1896	5656
1901–1902	5663
1908–1909	5670
1916–1917	5677
1923–1930	5684
1930–1931	5691
1937–1938	5698
1944–1945	5705
1951–1952	5712
1958–1959	5719
1965–1966	5726
1972–1973	5733
1979–1980	5740
1986–1987	5747
1993–1994	5754
2000–2001	5761
2007–2008	5768
2014–2015	5775
2021–2022	5782
2028–2029	5789
2035–2036	5796
2042–2043	5803
2049–2050	5810

fying Jewish religious law) and continue their agrarian work with only minor interruption to the agriculture and market routine.

The sale permit is not the only practice that involves Palestinians (and other non-Jews) as problem-solvers of Jewish law in a shmita year.

"The Arab agriculturalists are living from shmita to shmita," said Jamal Medlege, the minorities' referent in the Ministry of Agriculture.[15] He explained that Palestinian citizens who are agriculturalists take the year of shmita as an opportunity to expand operations and use the maximum terrain to increase their production capacity since their produce becomes especially profitable in this year. Other Palestinian agriculturalists told me that Jewish religiously observant groups helped them to receive water allocations and subsidies for the construction of greenhouses during shmita years.

Thus, Palestinian agriculturalists become the main producers for the ultra-Orthodox consumers who oppose the sale permit. Ironic as it is, the shmita Hebrew calendar year has become a cash crop year for Palestinian agriculturalists. Shmita also has created an unlikely hybrid agrarian timescape that enables both Jews and Palestinians to entrench their claim to the land: for Jews through the biblical significance of shmita and for Palestinians through the economic gains of shmita that support Palestinian agrarian practice and their continuing attachment to the land.

While much Hebrew writing has been dedicated to the internal Jewish shmita polemic of the land's sale to a non-Jew, there has not been *any* discussion addressing the actual non-Jews involved in shmita.[16] Hence, this chapter explores two parallel, interlacing themes. First, there are the regulatory and bureaucratic interventions and mediations regarding shmita that manifest how the state is settling time and resolving conflicts in time. Second, there is the entanglement of these interventions with Palestinian agriculture, which is struggling to survive.[17] Conflicts arise from the attempt to regulate a biblical tradition in a time of a capitalist economy and the time of the settler-nation state. In a contrast to the state's extensive mediation and intervention to facilitate shmita, I contemplate the state's laissez-faire attitude regarding the Muslim traditions of inheritance. The examination of these two traditions (shmita and qur'anic inheritance) is instrumental in understanding how tradition as a mechanism of social time is used to sustain a Jewish-biblical agricultural tradition against "modern agronomy." Tradition is also used to reinforce agricultural neglect via the Palestinians' own tradition, which has not been subject to the state's mediating attention until recently. Furthermore, the story of shmita sheds light on the cyclical temporality of the settler society and therefore questions the temporal binary between settler and native that has been defined as a structure in settler colonial scholarship. This literature portrays settler time as a linear and progressive form of time aligning with nation-states and capitalist time frameworks versus the native cyclical form of social time.[18]

This chapter analyzes recent national policies and Israel State Archive's shmita documents and includes fieldwork with Palestinian-citizen state officials and Palestinian agriculturalists in the Triangle area (al-Muthallath/Ha-meshulash). The Triangle is a region in central Israel/Palestine where profitable, intensive agriculture of Palestinian citizens takes place. By attending to the agriculture of this region, I challenge the view that Palestinian agriculture relies on traditional production techniques, and I examine the agricultural timescape that is reflected in these agriculturalists' experiences. The state's work to reclaim shmita solidifies Jewish indigeneity in the land while crystallizing the role of Palestinian agriculture as a facilitator of the observance of Jewish agricultural tradition. However, turning the Bible into a policy paper in a modern state is not an easy endeavor.

The Challenges of Making the Bible an Agrarian Policy Paper

Religious concerns have informed public debates regarding transformations in agriculture, medicine, and the environment locally and globally. Scientific changes in these fields immediately raise theological and ethical concerns regarding humanity's place in the world. But such debates have predominantly been in the background of policy and practice rather than in the forefront.[19] Therefore, it is rather uncommon for self-perceived "Western" states to begin agrarian policy papers with quotations from twenty-five-hundred-year-old texts.[20] But the Ministry of Agriculture's Investment Administration (Minhelet Ha-hashkaot) does just this in the introduction paragraph to their policy brief on shmita agricultural grants. The Investments Administration in the Ministry of Agriculture is a division that commonly invests in new technologies in agriculture. The shmita policy begins with the quote from the Bible's book of Leviticus that details the shmita commandment.[21] The document's author goes on to explain that, due to lessons learned from the previous shmita year, 5768 (the Hebrew year that began in September 2007), the Ministry of Agriculture is preparing for the next shmita a year ahead of time. The interweaving of the bureaucratic document's time with the biblical text's time indicates the emic view (from within the group) of the Israeli bureaucrat and Israeli bureaucracy. The author's natural intermingling of bureaucratic time with biblical time offers a glimpse into the Ministry of Agriculture's process of expanding shmita support over the last two decades.

Despite the Ministry of Agriculture's and the state's more recent attempts to expand their governance over the practice of shmita, this has not always been the case. Since the 1950s, the Chief Rabbinate of Israel and the Ministry of Religions were the central state bodies operating shmita.[22] In 1958, ten years after the founding of the state, the Rabbinate established the Department for Jewish Laws Pertaining to the Land and Agriculture. The Rabbinate's work included providing agricultural cultivation guidelines on shmita years, educating the public about shmita, and collecting agriculturalists' signatures approving the land's sale to a non-Jew. Although Israel's state bodies and quasi-state bodies collectively own the land, the state still requires signatures from each cooperative community or individual who leases the land from the state to perform the land sale "wholeheartedly," according to the requirements of Jewish law.

Yet, according to the Chief Rabbinate's archived letters from the 1950s to the 1970s, there were many difficulties in the initial process of the state institutionalizing shmita. Agriculturalists wrote about their lack of knowledge about how to practice shmita; Jewish agrarian collectivities and individuals complained about the failures of the bureaucratic process of signature collection for the land sale to a non-Jew; and secular constituencies objected to the practice of the symbolic land sale altogether.[23] For instance, a 1958 letter from Kibbutz Nir Oz to the Chief Rabbinate said: "We received your letter regarding our land sale certificate. And we do not understand the method here, if this is a sale of national land to a gentile, is this real, and how can a national institution bearing a national sign sell national land to a gentile and a foreigner. And if this is not a truly sustainable sale, who is being deceived here?"[24] The kibbutz's suspicion of the state's land sale reveals the difficulties of recruiting secular constituents to act together with the state in an "as if" exchange to solve the shmita problem at the time.[25] Anthropologist Michal Kravel-Tovi claims that "as if" exchanges are not a practice of collective lies between the state and its constituents as one might intuitively think, but a dramaturgic performance that serves sociability between the state and its citizens in anchoring state-citizen relations.[26] Shmita land sale as a loophole circumvention is a story of reinforcing state–Jewish citizens' relations, but the story goes beyond such sociality. More than dramaturgic acts between a Jewish Orthodox state bureaucracy and its secular Jewish citizens, shmita regulations reflect the legal and practical arrangement in which the state settles time in its twofold way to mediate conflicts of time and to occupy societal space with Jewish time.

Moreover, shmita exposes the temporal legality mechanism that orders society, space, and time to serve ethnonational settler colonial goals while creating distinct legalities for Jewish citizens and Palestinian citizens. The following quote from a letter from the director of the Ministry of Agriculture's Land Department to the Chief Rabbinate of Israel on June 11, 1959, manifests this distinct legality: "We declare that in any case that a landholder will let us know in writing that he is not cultivating his land due to the shmita year and that he commits to begin cultivating it by the end of shmita year, we will not apply to his land the Emergency Regulations for the Cultivation of Fallow Land."[27] The Land Department director is referring here to the Emergency Regulations for the Cultivation of Fallow Land passed on October 11, 1948. These regulations allowed the minister of agriculture to declare land he deemed "uncultivated" to be "wastelands" (Hebrew, *adamot muvarot*) and order their use. This letter testifies to the fear of Jewish agriculturalists that the state would apply to them the emergency arrangements that it applied to Palestinian land following the 1948 War, ruling that land that is fallow can be appropriated by the state to ensure cultivation. The bulk of these "fallow lands" that the state addressed in its 1948 emergency regulations became over the next decade state property and were appropriated from their Palestinian landholders and annexed to their neighboring Jewish agrarian communities.[28] But the state's differential approach to the category of fallow land is not the only distinct temporal legality that the Israeli state manipulated.

Religious Parliament members advanced an amendment in August 1979 to Israel's 1969 Land Law that supported the sale permit and the practice of shmita.[29] Until then, the practice of shmita violated Israel's land law, which required the registration of every land transaction as well as tax collection from all the parties involved; such bureaucratic measures did not occur with the sale permit, as the state would have had to charge every individual kibbutz or moshav subleasing land from the state for their participation in shmita land sale. Some of these secular Jewish agrarian collectives were already unenthusiastic about the performance of shmita and charging them would not have made political sense. According to the legislators, the purpose of the 1979 amendment was religious; it allowed those who observed shmita to perform it legally. The new law had no objectors in the Israeli Parliament, and it passed rapidly, a month before the beginning of the shmita that came with the Jewish New Year 5740 in September 1979.[30] The legislation reflects the ability of legislators to suspend or advance a socio-legal temporal order according to hegemonic logic and the calendar. The law also crystallized the state's ability to make extraordinary arrangements on a shmita calendar year.

This land law amendment is thought-provoking in the context of colonial governance approaches to fallow lands. In other colonial socio-legal contexts, governments often confiscated local communities' fallow land because it was perceived as inefficient use of the land. Ignoring indigenous communities' moral value of soil futurity for the benefit of the next generations, these colonial governments turned fallow lands into plantations.[31] Consequently, the temporality of capitalist agricultural productivity became a factor of land law and governance.

This was also the case in Palestine during the Ottoman Empire. The Ottoman Land Code (OLC) created in 1858 encouraged the cultivation of fallow lands as the empire's way of tax collection. Lands that were uncultivated for more than a seasonal period were subject to government expropriations unless landholders proved it was for a short agricultural rest.[32] Israel used the OLC Article 78 definitions of *Miri* (Fallow and Uncultivated Land in the 1950s and 1960s) as a central tool for dispossessing Palestinians of their land. These same legal tools were later used to confiscate Palestinian land in the West Bank.[33] Yet for Jews in Israel, the government legislates and supports arrangements for a Jewish fallow year. Hence, the governmental approach to fallow lands distinguishes between the inhabitants of the land. This distinction stems from the state's goal of reinforcing a Jewish settlement timescape of origins in the land while dispossessing Palestinian landholding.

There are other sociocultural and agroecological traditions that implement rest periods for the land as a method to restore soil fertility. However, in these traditions, the frequency of the fallow year is calculated through land restoration considerations rather than a sacred, collectively practiced cyclical calendar. In regional agrarian traditions, such as in Turkey and in the West Bank, generations followed fallow periods, but with the introduction of intensive agronomy techniques, farmers were encouraged to replace fallow cycles with crop rotation, which uses a nitrate cycle in soils as a way of preserving soil fertility.[34]

In Israel, many agriculturalists who seek to apply self-perceived modern agronomic practices use crop rotation rather than a fallow cycle. Yaakov Roth, an ultra-Orthodox shmita advocate, passionately argued that the effects of a fallow year on the soil in agronomic terms are magnificent. His conviction validates traditional agroecological knowledge and methods of land conservation through fallow cycles. His keen view on the agrarian practice of shmita might also be affected by his religious belief as a partial contributor to its perceived success. This belief aligns with the biblical promise given in Leviticus 25:20 that God will provide generously for those who keep shmita in the sixth year: "Hashem [Hebrew, "The Name," referring to God] takes care of us, and he always gives us a miracle in the sixth year so that we need not worry in the seventh."[35]

An environmental-cultural understanding of shmita would emphasize that resting the soil implies care for future generations and long-term preservation of resources.[36] Still, state officials speak about shmita mostly in ethnonational religious terms and agricultural productivity terms, rather than environmental or social terms.[37] In 2008, the codification of shmita into state law entailed the creation of a National Shmita Committee whose role is to adapt aspects of the biblical commandment of agricultural "release" to contemporary agrarian market demands.

Aside from state religious authorities' activities, non-state bodies have been central to the operation of shmita. Religious research and educational institutions such as the Institute for Torah and the Land (Makhon ha-torah ve-ha'aretz) and the Seminary for Jewish Law in Agrarian Settlement (Beit Midrash le-halakha ba-hityashvut) research and provide instruction on shmita agronomy. While these bodies historically worked in collaboration with the Ministry of Religions and the Chief Rabbinate, in the last decade they have expanded their collaborations to include the Ministry of Agriculture.[38] For instance, the religious solidarity fund Keren Hashviis (Fund for the Seventh Year in religious Ashkenazi pronunciation) operating in Israel and the Jewish diaspora has been subsidizing those agriculturalists who cease their agrarian activities in shmita (image 6). Keren Hashviis directs its activity toward a shmita year by fundraising in ultra-Orthodox Jewish communities to support those agriculturalists who disable their operations, and it recruits nonreligious farmers to observe shmita. Keren Hashviis's work illustrates how the marking of the Hebrew calendar's shmita year serves to reinforce a sacred system of time reckoning. By supporting a farmer in Israel in a shmita year, religious diaspora Jews participate in strengthening the temporal order of the sabbath of the land, solidifying ties with Jews of Israel, and expressing sentiments of social particularism and belonging to the land.[39]

The Ministry of Agriculture cooperated with these non-state bodies in an incidental and indistinct manner. A long correspondence in 1994–1996 between the fund's lawyer and the Ministry of Agriculture's legal advisor attempted to solve whether the Ministry of Agriculture had to compensate the fund for the work it had done during shmita 5754 (the Hebrew year that began in September 1993). Keren Hashviis collected the names of shmita-observant agriculturalists for the state to grant them economic support. The fund also instructed agriculturalists on how to cease their agrarian work for a year without damaging the agrarian operation for the long term.[40] The correspondence reveals that in the year of shmita 5754 in the state allocated only the minor sum of five million NIS (new Israeli shekels; approximately US$1.5 million) to support shmita observant agriculturalists and that the Ministry of Agriculture was not a main actor in advocating or guiding shmita practice.[41] The legal advisor of the Ministry of Agriculture was not sure through which channel to pay Keren Hashviis and involved the Israeli deputy attorney general in the

IMAGE 6. "Here Shmita Is Observed" banner, fall 2021. The banner mentions Keren Hashviis as a sponsor of this sign and/or ceased agrarian parcel. Such banners were seen across the country during shmita 2021–2022. Photograph by the author.

resolution. The involvement of a superior state authority and the entire correspondence reflect the messiness of managing a bureaucratic task that is performed once every seven years. Only recently, the Ministry of Agriculture and the fund created a solution to prevent double payments to farmers from both institutions.[42]

Over the years, religious actors and agricultural bodies fiercely criticized the Chief Rabbinate of Israel for its failed management of shmita. The ineffective administration of shmita caused a severe rise in produce prices especially for observant ultra-Orthodox communities while not all Jewish-Israeli agriculturalists were able to benefit from their use of the sale permit. Kosher authorization of municipal and regional rabbinates depreciated the sale permit's kosher-certified Jewish produce and left Jewish agriculturalists in a restricted market condition.[43] The critiques of shmita management led to the passing of a new law in 2008 establishing the state's National Shmita Committee to advance agrarian, technological, and religious solutions for observing shmita (image 7).[44]

Following the 2008 legislation, the Ministry of Religious Services, the

Ministry of Agriculture, the Institute for Torah and the Land, and the National Shmita Committee published a joint agricultural guide for the 2014 shmita year. In this guide, the head of the Agricultural Extension Service of the Ministry of Agriculture, a department responsible for the dissemination of innovative science, knowledge, and best practices to the agriculturalists with a list of prominent rabbis, endorsed this joint venture of shmita. He said, "I had the honor of undertaking experiments in viticulture with the Institute of Torah and the Land, aiming to find scientific and technological ways to observe shmita in vines."[45] It seems that shmita echoes the history of science thesis that argues that European settlers in Palestine/Israel have long enacted techno-mysticism in their attempt *to make* a holy land and enliven the Bible on the ground through scientific and technological methods.[46]

Experiments in adapting viticulture to shmita were not the only agricultural shmita research that the Ministry of Agriculture supported. The ministry has also supported the Jewish cultivation of produce in soil-free containers and hydroponic agricultural tubes in greenhouses that are disconnected from the ground by plastic sheets as another circumvention of the biblical commandment.[47] The state also began subsidizing the

IMAGE 7. Shmita in the lawn of the Israeli Parliament, fall 2021. The sign declares "Gardening work in shmita year is performed according to religious law." Photograph by Maya Negev.

conversion of Jewish cultivators' greenhouses to soil-free greenhouses for shmita in 2007 and 2014.[48] The Institute of Torah and the Land co-developed this agricultural method and advocated it to governmental ministries. In this institute's advocacy documents, soil-free agriculture is promoted as a method that will ensure that Jews need not buy produce in shmita from "haters of Israel" and that "it will prevent the expansion of Arab agriculture on shmita."[49] Such texts appeared during the height of the first Intifada (Palestinian popular uprising) in 1990, but it represents a steady train of thought and imaginary among religious Zionists regarding the implications of Palestinian shmita production.[50] As such, in early 2021 the Institute of Torah and the Land advertised its shmita bypass arrangement with an internet ad illustrating of a box of tomatoes sent from Gaza transforming into missiles landing on the local map on your computer screen. Therefore, not only techno-mysticism is at play with shmita but also techno-nationalism.

In the last two decades, the Ministry of Agriculture's economic subsidization of shmita has significantly expanded. In a matter of two shmita years, there was a significant growth in the budget allocated for direct payments to farmers "to allow subsistence for farmers who disable their operations" (NIS 40 million).[51] The ministry allocated additional NIS 63 million for activities that facilitate shmita and protect both the livelihoods of agriculturalists in a shmita year and the interests of consumers who strictly observe shmita.[52] In shmita 2014, the state allocated NIS 100 million to shmita of which NIS 45 million were allocated for those who disabled their operations. Following the lobbying from the nurseries, the government also began to support fruit tree nurseries with NIS 20 million, as during a shmita year agriculturalists do not plant trees in Israel while the nurseries, regardless, need to sustain themselves.[53] Finally, the ministry has also supported the expansion of greenhouse structures and water allocation for non-Jewish agriculturalists since 2007 (NIS 7 million).[54]

Rasmi Daka of Yama village is one of the major Palestinian agriculturalists from the Triangle area who talked with me about this subsidy. He has his own brand of baby cucumbers sold in Israel and in export markets. When I met him in June 2014, he told me with pride that it was his initiative as a council member of the Organization for Vegetable Cultivators (Irgun Megadlei Hayerakot) "to approach the Minister of Agriculture in 2007 to advance the subsidy for Arab agriculturalists on a shmita year as an act of affirmative action." Rasmi said that the Ministry of Agriculture used to subsidize and support greenhouse development in the 1990s as a national policy, but that has stopped. According to Rasmi, thanks to his initiative, this agricultural development support continues for Arab agriculturalists during a shmita year.[55] Rasmi is the only Palestinian citizen among fifty representatives of growers in the Organization for Vegetable Cultivators council. He was confident that for a big, reputable producer like him, the cultivation during shmita does not imply much of a change of income, but he said that the change is significant for smaller and less stable producers. Indeed, data from the Ministry of Agriculture from the 2007–2008 shmita indicated that shmita enables a 30 percent rise in production among Palestinian communities in Israel and a rise of 25 percent of produce passing from West Bank Palestinian producers into Israel.[56]

A Palestinian employee of the Ministry of Agriculture working as an instructor for vegetable cultivation in the Triangle and Israel's Center District told me that in the shmita year of 2007–2008, he went to speak with Palestinian agriculturalists to tell them of shmita benefits.[57] The incentives they could receive from the ministry were up to a 40 percent return on greenhouse construction and 1,200 cubic meters of water per dunum. These were exceptional subsidies for Palestinian agriculturalists. Although shmita offered a high return on investment, the budget was only partially used. Commonly, Palestinian agriculturalists tend to receive support from family members rather than government subsidies.[58] Furthermore, the state announced its support for Arab agrarian development so late in the year that it was too late for agriculturalists to prepare accordingly.[59] The practice of the Jewish biblical tradition of shmita may potentially result in the best years for the Palestinian agriculturalist in Israel, yet this is another subordination of Palestinian time to Jewish-Zionist time.

In December 2017, the state announced the establishment of a new savings fund similar to an employer-sponsored savings plan. The idea behind it was to allow Jewish agriculturalists who planned to cease agriculture in the upcoming shmita year of 2021–2022 to save up for it and have the state match their contributions to the program.[60] In July 2018, popular Israeli radio stations played ads calling farmers to join the fund. The savings fund implied that the state was directly sponsoring the disabling of productive agricultural activity. Yet, to quit an agricultural operation for a year goes against the capitalist production rationale. The disabling of agrarian production involves the ceasing of tractors and the agrarian workforce, the continued payment for agrarian infrastructure, machinery investments without routine sales, and the halt of food production, income, and gains. For Jewish agriculturalists who cease production in shmita year, quitting annual production is not an economic decision but rather a test of religious devotion linked to the belief in the importance of their spiritual connection to the land.

The announcement of the shmita savings fund was a positive development for only some members of society. The state-sponsored savings benefit does not exist for non-Jewish agriculturalists. I spoke about this discrepancy with Yaakov Roth of Mevo Horon National-Orthodox (Haredi-Leumi) settlement.[61] Roth is a long-time advocate of shmita and a strict observer of the fallow year with his settlement's agrarian cooperative. Roth wrote his own proposal to the Ministry of Agriculture advocating the creation of the shmita savings fund. He suggested that the ministry make this savings fund available to any agriculturalist in Israel, regardless of their religion or their shmita practice. According to Roth, the development of such a mechanism would create an egalitarian education and development fund benefitting all agriculturalists.[62] The Ministries of Agriculture and Finance rejected this suggestion due to budgetary constraints. The ministries developed this unique fund to support shmita farmers in shmita years only; these funds cannot be used to support other forms of agricultural sabbatical, such as taking a leave year to pursue continued agricultural education.[63] The savings fund demonstrates a narrow interpretation of the benefits and benefactors of shmita.

Despite the state's limited interpretation of shmita, the biblical commandment of shmita follows rationales of social equity, soil regeneration, and wealth redistribution. The full-length biblical commandment addresses the needs of the land and the Gentile; it discusses freeing slaves and compensating them for their work as well as caring for the needs of nonhuman creatures.[64] According to the biblical tradition, after seven shmita cycles comes the jubilee year in which all the shmita regulations apply, but also a social reordering: land should be redistributed to address wealth inequality. The jubilee-year land redistribution might be one of the most radical social (perhaps even socialist) visions illustrated in the Bible. Imagine its implications for the reality of Israel/Palestine.

Why then does the state sponsor agriculturalists who keep shmita according to the biblical law? Why is the state involved in a process that, in modern agronomy terms, is somewhat irrational? A simple analysis would see this as primarily a matter of parliamentary coalition interests, responding to the needs of the ultra-Orthodox and religious communities that observe shmita. Yet, the state also sponsors widespread radio commercials and artistic and educational work to explain shmita to the public. I suggest shmita allows the state to signal and enact its unique Jewish social-agricultural character through the politics of biblical time and tradition in the modern state. The state's historical project was to nationalize the land for the development of the settler nation, as a means of achieving territorial control for the Jewish-Zionist society. Now that the state has achieved its land control, it is strengthening that control with moral claims. Therefore, promoting and subsidizing a savings fund for observers of shmita aims to settle government coalition needs and to have the state mediate and materialize the biblical promise for sufficiency in the Seventh Year. It also serves to validate political claims to the land, crystallize Jewish indigeneity and belonging, and prove historical rights that are at stake.

Next, I examine the lived temporalities of Palestinian agriculturalists in the Triangle and their way of surviving a history of dispossession, their dual entanglement with both shmita and the Palestinian-Muslim inheritance tradition.

Living Agricultural Timescape in the Triangle

From the Ministry of Agriculture's corridors and office, it takes less than an hour by car to reach the Palestinian greenhouses in the Triangle area. The Triangle is a cluster of twenty-seven Palestinian villages and cities in Israel located between the West Bank and the coastal region in the foothills of the Nablus/Samarian mountains.[65] With a population of roughly 300,000, the Triangle is second only to Galilee in the size of its Palestinian citizen population. "Triangle" is a geopolitical term that was coined during the British Mandate to indicate an area with a predominantly Arab population. During the 1949 armistice, Israel made a territorial swap with Jordan to control the Triangle region and its northern area of Wadi ʿAra overlooking the coastal plain. Israel's interest in the area was tactical and strategic. At that time, the Triangle area and its 30,000 villagers became Israeli citizens.[66]

Following the establishment of the state, the Triangle villages lost communal and privately owned land during Israel's major acts of land nationalization between 1948–1960, which I discussed as the temporal legalities system of dispossession in "Palestinian-Zionist Agrarian Timescape" in the introduction. Much of the Triangle's land was managed collectively based on the Palestinian *musha'* system of land reallocation, which generally occurred every two years.[67] But *the musha'* system also made it easy for the Israeli state to claim that the Triangle's land is state land in a typical colonial act of using a property law that does not align with the local norms of land use.[68] The state appropriated a great portion of the villages' land through the Absentee Property Law (1950) and the Land Acquisition (Validation of Acts and Compensation) Law (1953).[69] As a result, the land was appropriated by the state predominantly for Jewish settlement and agriculture. Thus, Triangle villages were stripped of their significant land assets. The extent of land appropriation in some of the Triangle villages appears in table 2.[70]

Following the 1948 War, the Triangle villagers were cut off from the West Bank until its occupation in 1967. These relations were severed again with the construction of the Segregation/Separation Barrier in the area in 2003.[71] The proximity of the Triangle area to the West Bank is unique among other Palestinian-populated areas in Israel as it is adjacent to the Palestinian Authority, and some of its towns are located over the Green Line.[72] This location enabled Triangle residents to maintain economic and family ties with West Bank Palestinians prior to the construction of the Barrier.[73]

The Triangle is in Israel's geographic center but on its social periphery. More than half the area's households fall below the income poverty

TABLE 2. Land confiscation in the Triangle during the military regime 1949–1966

Village	Historic village land until 1949, in dunums	Land after state appropriation	Percentage of current to historical levels
Jat	12,000	9,000	70%
Baqa al-Gharbyyie	22,000	7,000	32%
'Ara/ 'Ar'ara	26,000	7,000	27%
Taybe	45,000	13,000	29%
Tira	40,000	8,000	20%

Source: Data adapted from Ian Lustick, *Arabs in the Jewish State: Israel's Control of a National Minority*, Modern Middle East Series, No. 6 (University of Texas Press, 1980), 179.

line. This region's average income, low as it is, is high in comparison to other Palestinian-populated regions in Israel.[74] Arguably, the Triangle's proximity to Israel's central areas explains why incomes are higher there than in the geographic peripheries of the Galilee or the Naqab/Negev regions.

Until the end of the British Mandate, agriculture was the main source of income for the Triangle population. By 2012, the agricultural employment rate in the Triangle had fallen to just over 2 percent. More than half the agricultural workers work outside their hometown, suggesting that they work as hired labor in agriculture rather than being self-employed.[75] Yet, this is a higher-than-average rate of self-employment among Palestinian agriculturalists and is attributable to good conditions for agriculture due to the Triangle's geography, soil quality, and water allocation. Although agricultural employment decreased significantly, there are still some Palestinian agriculturalists who find ways to make a living in agriculture. Thus, the Triangle is the most concentrated region of intensive income-generating Palestinian agriculture in Israel, and most of the farms are family-owned.

Wajeeh and I were in his car on the white dust roads by the agrarian terrains of Baqa al-Gharbiyye and Jat. We contemplated abandoned terrains, deserted and operating greenhouses, piles of unsold cucumbers rotting in the sun, and Palestinian agriculture in Israel at large. Wajeeh is in his fifties. He is among the few Palestinians in Israel who make a living in agriculture, which is supplemented by his business of selling construction infrastructure. He is witty, warm, and humorous, and his daily occupations require ingenuity. Wajeeh is the successful manager of a large vegetable farm in a nearby kibbutz. Despite his jokes and friendliness, he had some harsh things to say about the demise of agriculture in Palestinian society in Israel:

> Once there was agriculture, agriculture that derived from people's hearts. . . . [They] used to work with all the family, no outside workforce, no Thai workers, and no [West] Bank workers. Believe me, it was only the family and they would earn a decent living and eat whatever they had. I will take you to the agrarian terrains and you will see, there is no agriculture anymore. Only a few agriculturalists are holding on by the skin of their teeth because they don't have other choices. . . . Such an agriculturalist cannot become a lawyer or an engineer suddenly, because he is 50 or 60 years old. All these agriculturalists, where will they go? They don't have "where to go"; this is their way to provide.[76]

Wajeeh's comment elucidates a widespread phenomenon: the struggle of smallholders and family farms across the Mediterranean and around the world. Globally, the large-scale abandonment of family farms in rural areas is attributed to the impact of economies of scale, increases in farm productivity, mechanization, urbanization, and global trade. These have rendered small- and medium-sized farms inefficient modes of production that struggle to survive. In many countries, commercial farms have replaced family farms. Agriculture in Israel/Palestine has undoubtedly been subject to many of the same external pressures.[77]

However, the damaging forces of these external factors have unequally impacted Palestinian and Jewish growers in Israel. As I show throughout the book, the institutional mechanisms that have dispossessed Palestinians of basic production resources like land and water, as well as their lack of access to technology and bureaucratic power, have left the remaining Palestinian agriculturalists in a disadvantaged position in comparison to their Jewish counterparts.

Wajeeh's farm was not able to survive as an agrarian family business, but he continued his agrarian practice with passion and expertise for the kibbutz's agriculture on land that had belonged some seventy years ago to an adjacent Palestinian-Arab village. Wajeeh's experience is not singular but rather shared by many Palestinians who have had to shift toward working for more profitable agribusinesses as a means of remaining in agriculture. By concentrating on Wajeeh and his friends' work for profitable intensive agriculture and less on what official discourses call "traditional agriculture," I aim to challenge the common view that Palestinian agriculture relies on traditional production techniques. Alternatively, I examine the timescape, the embodied multilayered experience of time, that is reflected in their story.

I initially met Wajeeh in June 2014 at the small warehouse that served as his office at the kibbutz's agriculture operation. The large welcome sign at the entrance read "Kibbutz Sunny-Vale's Agriculture—Bringing Back the Soul to the Soil" (in Hebrew, "Mahzirim et Haneshama L'adama").[78] A new-age Hebrew slogan seemed an ironic start to a meeting with a Palestinian, and ironies kept emerging throughout our time together. We drank coffee as we sat on a small living room sofa outside the office and looked at a display of tractors. I asked him about his story as an agriculturalist. Like the stories of many Palestinian agriculturalists, his story began with a family farming history, but it took an unusual turn: "I am the son of an agrarian family. My father was also an agriculturalist like they used to be, working small-scale . . . the whole family working together. Unlike the others, I have loved agriculture since I was a child, but everyone else hated it. I loved it and I had a lot of interest in agriculture. But my father did not want me to be an agriculturalist; he said it's a profession with no future." As Wajeeh's statement suggests, Palestinian agriculture in the 1970s–1980s was becoming less popular. Older Palestinian agriculturalists in the area whom I interviewed claimed it was disparaged both because of its low wages and because it damaged men's marriage prospects. Women wanted their husbands to be educated and aspired for their own education as well. In the mid-1970s, agriculture was ranked as the fifth most desirable occupation following doctors, engineers, teachers, and extension officers, but its status continued to deteriorate.[79] Wajeeh eventually combined his experience in agriculture and his studies in automotive mechanics to work with his father for a few years because he did not have sufficient income to continue to study and provide money for his family from the ten dunums of land they had. Since the land and the car repair business were not enough, Wajeeh looked for additional income. He increased his earnings through what was then innovative marketing: selling washed and packed green onions rather than loose, unwashed vegetables.

Wajeeh showed me the different sections of the agrarian operation at the kibbutz: the land where he grew green onions, the women workers washing and packing them, and the area in the fields where workers could eat and rest. Such an area is known as *'ezba* in Arabic and is traditional on Palestinian farms. Wajeeh's *'ezba* was a small tent in the kibbutz's field, remaking and reclaiming the Zionist workspace into a Palestinian resting timescape. I wanted to understand how Wajeeh's operation in the kibbutz worked. He explained that he is the instructor and operator of the vegetable production and that he runs his onion business there as well. The relationship between Wajeeh and the kibbutz seemed complicated. Wajeeh is an experienced agriculturalist; he brings knowledge, expertise, and marketing ability. However, the business runs on the vast land and water resources that are allocated to it, production resources that Wajeeh could not otherwise access. The two parties share the profits of the operation.

Our meeting evolved into an agrarian road trip. We left the kibbutz to explore the Palestinian agriculture in the area. As we drove past a succession of fields, Wajeeh named the owner of each cultivated plot. Most of the people he mentioned were retired or keeping the plot as a side occupation. He lamented how he once used to see many people having lunch together in their *'ezba* in the fields but now hardly anyone was there. The plots we saw were small. I noticed diverse cultivars and drip irrigation pipes. The Triangle area has better irrigation coverage than other Palestinian-populated areas in Israel. This area was granted water from the state through water associations (*agudot*) as early as the late 1950s, when Palestinians' eligibility for agrarian resources such as land, water, and technologies was approved by the military regime.

In the fields we saw olive trees, corn seedlings, hot and sweet peppers, zucchini, and other squash. Some of the plants were in open fields, in low tunnels, or under protective nets, while others were in big greenhouses, operations that required greater investment. According to the Ministry of Agriculture, most of the agricultural terrains in the Triangle practice intensive agriculture using greenhouses, polytunnels, or shade nets. Wajeeh told me that the greenhouses mostly grow vegetables such as cucumbers, tomatoes, and peppers. Strawberries are also grown in low tunnels in the town of Qalansuwa. We passed by a greenhouse advertising itself as a nursery, which is one way to generate income on a small plot of agrarian terrain.

On our drive, Wajeeh told me how the little land his family had was broken in half because of the construction of the Trans-Israel Highway (Hotseh Israel), which left him with a greenhouse covering only five dunums. He did not seem angry or unhappy about it; his expression was matter-of-fact. The Trans-Israel Highway was constructed in the early 2000s to connect Israel's north and south. The highway failed to deliver economic development for the Triangle and exacerbated ethnonational inequality. Much of the traffic that formerly passed through the center of Baqa al-Gharbyyie and brought customers to its shops now uses the highway. Where the highway was routed through agrarian areas near Baqa and Jat, Jewish cooperative agrarian settlements received greater compensation than Palestinian private landowners.[80] This inequity was a classic case of environmental injustice where different modes of land ownership, social-agrarian organizations, and political interventions disadvantaged Palestinian citizens.

As we continued our guided tour and conversation, Wajeeh seemed to accept that Palestinian agriculture in Israel had declined, but he was reluctant to blame Israeli politics—or even to talk about Israeli politics. I asked him if he thought that Palestinian/Arab agriculture still exists. It took him less than a second to respond: "There is no such thing as Arab agriculture anymore, no more families working together in their farms, but we are all dependent on hired labor."

I pushed back and asked, "But are there Arab agriculturalists?"

He said, "Well, of course. I am an Arab agriculturalist and there are others like me, even though there are fewer of us over time." Later he said, "We, the Arabs, have limited agrarian land. Let's not talk about politics of how we don't have land—and how we had—and now we don't have. . . . But there are Arab agrarian terrains, not too many but there

are, and now we don't have agriculturalists to cultivate them." It is possible that Wajeeh refrained from being candid about Israeli politics with
a Jewish-Israeli woman he did not know well. However, his response represents a form of adaptation to the reality of the loss of Palestinian land
and agriculture, combined with a sense of responsibility for the current
state of agriculture. Throughout our time together, he did not blame the
state for a discriminatory agricultural regime but instead chose to focus
his critique on the individual choices of Palestinians. He also expressed
solidarity with the difficulties that all Israeli agriculturalists have, as if
agriculturalists in Israel were one united social class.

It was only later, as I reflected on Wajeeh's role in kibbutz agriculture
and his reluctance to "talk about politics of how we don't have land,"
that I realized that Wajeeh's operation with the kibbutz falls within a
precarious legal situation. His status with the kibbutz operation might be
considered a violation of the 1967 Law of Agricultural Settlements (Hok
Ha-Hityashvut ha-Haklait). This law forbids a *Mityashev* (a Jewish-Israeli
individual who is a member of an agrarian settlement granted land or
water by the state, such as a moshav or kibbutz) to pass land and water
resources that were allocated to this individual or collective entity to
someone else for that person's use. The Ministry of Agriculture justifies
the law as a means of supervising the use of state land. The fact that the
Green Patrol enforcement body supervises the law make it clear that a
principal objective of the law is to conserve the (ethno-) "Nation's Land."[81]
In 2007, the Ministry of Agriculture revised its administration of the law,
as many Jewish moshavim and kibbutzim were subleasing agrarian terrains to improve economies of scale. The ministry created a monitoring
mechanism that enables agriculturalists with land allocated by the state
to ask for a special-use exception permit. If such a request is approved, it
enables various forms of partnerships and subcontractors. If it is not approved, serious fines can be given for subleasing. Since Wajeeh is known
to officials of the Ministry of Agriculture and received work permits for
migrant workers, it is likely that his operation stands within the requirements of the law. However, his story—and the ambiguous legal status
of someone in his position—presents a window into the precarious and
complex positions in which many Palestinian agriculturalists in Israel
have found themselves when they want to continue an agrarian practice

and occupation that is part and parcel of a Palestinian cultural legacy.

The agricultural timescape that Wajeeh has been living in is multilayered. His possibilities within the agrarian occupation were dictated by the circumstances of Palestinian historical land dispossession, which turned him into a successful cultivator on land and water resources that once belonged to his ancestors but that now belong to the kibbutz and that he could not access on his own. Yet Wajeeh's choice to pursue agricultural occupancy allows him to survive a history of land alienation and dispossession and to remake what has become the Zionist space of a kibbutz land into a Palestinian agrarian area. Throughout our time together, Wajeeh reminisced about a prior time in which the family was the primary working unit and expressed melancholy over the market-based work relations of hired labor. After my encounter with him, I wondered if Wajeeh was not also romanticizing what used to be the unpaid labor of women and children in the nostalgic days of Palestinian family farming.

Wajeeh's story is emblematic of other Palestinian agriculturalists' stories in Israel in which capital-intensive, conventional agriculture signifies a dual and contradictory account, symbolic of Palestinian success in the Israeli market. While they identify with a market approach that would frame this sector's success against the challenges common to all agriculturalists in Israel, their own narratives are ones of survival, or, more accurately theorized, survivance.[82] *Survivance* is a term coined by Gerald Vizenor to describe the active role of Native Americans who, by their mere presence, continue a culture they actively inherit and adapt to the present day. Vizenor's term applies also to the Palestinian agriculturalists in the Triangle. Through their occupational-agrarian presence, they continue a culture and reshape it for the present day. They find creative ways to adapt to the present realities in the ethnocratic settler Israeli state, and they sustain a cultural tradition of agriculture and claim to the land. It is an active disruption of the ongoing dispossession and loss of Palestinian agricultural culture, land, and identity.

A Palestinian Smallholder in a Capitalist, Settler-National Time

Wajeeh and I were on the road to meet his friend Sa'id Abu-Nassar, called Abu-Jaber (Jaber's father) by his friends. Wajeeh said, "In a few years you will come here and there won't be agriculture at all. Not too long ago you had in Jat one hundred active agriculturalists and now there are ten. . . . Soon the only one left will be Abu-Jaber. His son works with him and it will pass on. . . . Hardly anyone has their son work with them." Sa'id runs a large, successful agricultural operation that specializes in selling herbs that are certified to have no risk of insects. This is a specific certification for strict kosher produce (in Hebrew, *le'mehadrin*). Strict kosher produce is a profitable niche market serving mostly ultra-Orthodox observant Jews in Israel and abroad. Sa'id sells his produce in the local Israeli market and exports it through the company he founded called Alei Sharon Lemehadrin. The company name, literally "leaves of the Sharon," uses the Hebrew name of this region. The Hebrew name helps the company "pass" in the market, highlighting the conditional inclusion of Palestinians in the Israeli economy.[83]

Sa'id's farm is one of the larger operations in the Triangle. He runs the operation; his wife is the accountant; and his son manages the hired work force. Sa'id's operation is technological, profitable, and conscious of following environmental regulations. He self-built his farm, which consists of several greenhouses, and he operates them with up-to-date computerized systems for irrigation and fertilization. Sa'id works at the top of the profitability chain of crop cultivation, growing vegetables and herbs in greenhouses (image 8).

For Sa'id, agricultural workers are a necessary "means of production" for this agricultural operation; however, hiring them is complex. Given low agricultural profit margins, most agriculturalists think it is too expensive to employ Israeli citizens, who require minimum wages, social security, and retirement payments. Sa'id needs hired workers to do the manual labor of the harvest and leaf-picking. Of the farm's twelve workers, half are Thai migrant workers and half are West Bank Palestinians.[84] This hiring structure indicates that Palestinians in Israel occasionally benefit from upward capitalist mobility that their citizenship status grants them in comparison to the cheap labor of migrant workers and Palestinians of

IMAGE 8. The Palestinian smallholder in a settler national and capitalist economy, summer 2014. Photograph by the author.

the West Bank. This upward mobility allows Sa'id to constitute himself as a higher class in capitalist labor-time terms, where Sa'id gains more profits and enjoys greater free time when he buys the worker's surplus labor time.[85] The process of employing non-Israeli workers is coordinated and legalized through state mechanisms: West Bank Palestinians need to have work permits in Israel from the Civil Administration, a bureaucratic body of the army, or the law will consider them "illegal."[86] Most West Bank workers in agriculture are hired on a seasonal basis, and Israeli agriculture in some regions depends on their work.[87] Sa'id and Wajeeh told me that many West Bank Palestinians prefer to work with Jewish employers to avoid the tension between the two Palestinian communities—a tension born of the forced separation of two communities that were previously united. Thus, despite the geographical proximity of the Triangle to the West Bank, the settler colonial occupation time also defines the labor domain among Palestinians themselves.[88]

Sa'id's use of migrant workers is both unusual and surprising. In 2011, the total quota for Thai agricultural migrant workers was approximately 25,000, of which Palestinian agriculturalists in Israel hired 100 (0.4 percent).[89] The previous year, Israel decided to decrease the quota of agricultural migrant workers, exacerbating the challenges presented by an inadequate agricultural labor supply. Permits to employ a certain number of Thai agricultural migrant workers are allocated by the government. Because most Palestinian plots are small, they do not require an external workforce, and therefore, the state allocates virtually no permits for migrant workers to Palestinian agriculturalists.

When I learned that Palestinian agriculturalists in the Triangle were hiring migrant workers, I was surprised. I had assumed that they would hire employees from their own communities. However, there are compelling economic reasons in a capitalist market economy to hire migrant workers: they usually work more hours and are paid less than Israeli workers' minimum wage requirement.[90] Unlike West Bank Palestinians, they also live on site and are not subject to movement restrictions imposed by the military and the resulting Palestinian time theft regime. Sa'id humorously told me about the Thai workers disappearing one day and then coming back a few days later; they had been lured away by another employer with promises of better pay, but when the promises turned out to be false, they returned to Sa'id.[91] Here too, as in other farm workers' settings, the time and space of migrant workers seemed elsewhere, blurry and inferior to what Sa'id perceived he was offering them.[92] This work dynamic shows that the binary used to describe the power imbalance in labor-time relations among Jews and Palestinians in the labor market is incomplete; everyone knows how to exploit the labor and time of lower social classes.

I have depicted the timescape of Sa'id's operation as an intergenerational and intragenerational intensive and capitalist family farm. It shares many of the challenges of other family farms in a globalized era: locating a profitable niche market, engaging with a globalized market economy of labor and exports, dealing with environmental regulations, and navigating public policies. However, Sa'id's farm is situated in a specific political and cultural context that disproportionately damages

Palestinian agriculture in Israel. Sa'id's land and market management methods for his operation, which I discuss next, highlight the importance of local context.

The Family Farm's Land, Muslim Inheritance, and the State

Although Sa'id has state-allocated hired workers and water quotas, he, like most Palestinian farmers, is not eligible to receive state land. Israel's land policy, created in the state's first two decades, was suited to the goals of the Zionist movement and the settler society's interests and comprised of a high level of state ownership and management, falling short of the nationalization of all land. The state administers 94 percent of all land in Israel and privileges Jewish access to land. Palestinian agriculturalists have lobbied the Minorities Referent in the Ministry of Agriculture to allocate state land to them, but they are relatively powerless. Like other Palestinian agriculturalists, Sa'id owns a certain amount of his own land and must find ways to access other privately owned Palestinian lands to expand his operation.

Arguably, the acquisition of land for agriculture is one of the most labor-intensive parts of Palestinian agriculture operations. Sa'id owns only 20 dunums, but he manages an operation of 135 dunums of greenhouses. He listed twenty neighbors and relatives from whom he leases land to keep up with the demands of an economic agricultural operation. In this regard, Sa'id is no different from dozens of other Palestinian agriculturalists I interviewed: they all had to determine additional sources of land they could lease to make their operation profitable.

Comparing the size of Sa'id's operation to others is telling. According to the Ministry of Agriculture, 80 percent of the agrarian operations in the Triangle are smaller than 30 dunums, which is far from sufficient to make a living.[93] State documents use "30 dunums" as a benchmark for a family farm size. This farm size was the basis of the historic Israeli state system of land allocation for Jewish agriculture called *nahala*. A *nahala* is land designated both for the house of the agriculturalist and the agrarian terrain for cultivation. Family farms in Jewish-Israeli moshavim, in the center of Israel, are allocated approximately 30-40 dunums, while in the peripheries of Galilee and the Negev, a *nahala* is usually between 60-100 dunums per family farm. But the average contemporary size of a Jewish-Israeli family farm is 199 dunums.[94] This figure demonstrates that the original allocation system is far removed from today's market demands. Sa'id's operation is larger than that of most Palestinian agriculturalists in Israel, but it is still smaller than its Jewish counterparts.

Inheritance customs also help to explain why Palestinian plots are often too small to be economically viable. The Muslim law of inheritance works against the capitalist agricultural economy of scale because it requires the division of property among heirs.[95] All the agriculturalists I talked to said that the inheritance tradition presents significant problems for agriculture (I discuss this issue also in chapters 3 and 4).[96] Because the Qur'anic legislation and inheritance were formed historically in the context of a patrilineal society living in an extended family structure in Arabia, inheritance rules were designed to support an extended family. Later, when the immediate family circle of parents, partners, and children took on a more important role in a family's life, laws began to change.[97] Arab countries in the Middle East responded to these new family conditions by enacting personal status laws and codes that included reforms in inheritance. The social purpose of these reforms was to strengthen the inheritance rights of relatives who form the nuclear family, as opposed to the tribal family.[98] Nevertheless, legislation in some modern Muslim states that contested inheritance laws or enabled personal wills was short-lived, although minor changes to inheritance law have persisted.[99] In addition, colonial regimes that intervened in Muslim legal codes typically left inheritance intact.[100]

The Muslim inheritance law has a distributive justice principle: testators are limited to disposing of a maximum of a third of their property in a will, while the remainder of the estate is to be distributed to certain heirs in fixed shares in accordance with the Qur'an. The practice of the law makes it difficult for individuals to distribute their property in a way that is different from what is set out in the Qur'an. Distribution of property during a person's lifetime may work around or challenge the inheritance law, but this might create other personal and familial problems.[101]

In Israel, less than a handful of the Palestinian agriculturalists that I talked to were able to address the impact of inheritance on agriculture in their own families by reaching a de facto agreement not to divide the land in their generation. While such an agreement may resolve the matter between well-intentioned heirs, it runs into legal difficulties with the state. Farmers who work their relatives' land cannot register the land or ask for investment subsidies under their own name. If the state were to decide to invest in the development of Palestinian agriculture, it would be unable to reach out to the users of the land, who may be different from its formal owners.

Further, while Palestinians commonly divide their land with each generation, legal regulations forbid the division of Jewish-Israeli plots in inheritance. The Israel Land Authority decreed that in the agrarian *nahala* only one descendant can inherit the farmland lease (allocated by the state) because the division of a farm will reduce its economic viability.[102] Depicting these two systems of property and inheritance law exemplifies that these two legal issues are linked to economic development, the rule of law, and democracy.[103]

Several Palestinian interviewees wished the state would intervene to change the inheritance tradition, which is "killing Arab agriculture." A discussion I had with Dr. Fathi Abd el-Hadi, a renowned agronomist, also brought forth the issue of inheritance.[104] He claimed that the Ministry of Agriculture does not intervene in the inheritance tradition and its resulting chaos in land registration because it serves the state's politics of de-territorializing the Palestinians. The case he made sounded appealing as he mentioned how other Muslim traditions, such as polygamy, had been banned by the state. Nevertheless, the similarity between Palestinian inheritance customs and those in other Muslim states makes this explanation questionable. Legal scholarship has claimed that the tensions between religious and state issues for Palestinians in Israel in other areas, such as family affairs and individual status, were governed by a multicultural logic, whereas the state accepted the cultural traditions of the local community, which turned out in other ways to be another form of oppression for some Palestinian communities.[105]

When I asked the legal advisor of the Ministry of Agriculture in 2014 about the possibility of establishing an official workaround of land division based upon inheritance and agricultural user rights for Arab landholders, he said that the legal advisor's office never encountered such a request. His response reveals the miscommunications and inefficiencies of the state apparatus. Even though this was a problem attended to by various employees of the ministry, both Jewish and Palestinians, the legal advisor was uninformed of the matter.

In contrasting, the director of the Central District of the Ministry of Agriculture is cognizant of the issue and has shown commitment to solving such problems that she saw as "site specific." Aware of the problem of land registration and inheritance as well as other historical land registration lacunas, she and other officials have tried to lower the bar that demands landholding registration as a condition for state investment in Arab agriculture. They were even able to create a way to work around this issue: if the landowner signs an authorization for another person to cultivate his land, this would allow the cultivator to access certain state subsidies and water allocation.[106] However, this arrangement highlighted the ways in which the legal practices of the state operate via rules that are designed for Jewish-Israeli agricultural cooperatives; this, in turn, creates a difficult legal situation when ministry staff try to create different rules for Palestinian citizens.

Only in March 2015, after decades of restricted access for Palestinians to agricultural subsidy funds from the Ministry of Agriculture, did the ministry finally create a directive that details how a land user can prove user rights to the land even when the land user is not registered by the state as the land owner.[107] In contrast, the regulation of shmita in 1979 land law shows that when the Jewish tradition poses an obstacle to the agricultural economy, the state can actively and quickly negotiate legal and economic mechanisms with the religious Jewish authorities to overcome the legal challenges.

Finally, the challenges that Muslim inheritance tradition have posed to Palestinian agriculture in Israel over many years were met with state reluctance to resolve such time conflicts, as opposed to state intervention and mediation in the case of shmita. The examination of these two customs (shmita and qur'anic inheritance) highlights how religious traditions as a form of a collective timescape can be used by the state either to anchor (Jewish) origins in the land or to reinforce (Palestinian) neglect. These two modes of action highlight how a central task of the state's bureaucracy is to mediate between conflicting forms of social times. However, the state is selective in its interventions. The recent 2015 directive for proving user rights on private land for state subsidy and means of production allocation shows some change is taking place at the Ministry of Agriculture. Whether the new directive will be implemented to maximize Palestinian citizens' use of state resources such as water and infrastructural investments is still in question. As for Sa'id, finding land was a major obstacle for him, but it was not the only one. As our time together evolved, I asked him how he became a producer for the kosher le'mehadrin Orthodox Jewish market. This opened a tale of Sa'id's involvement with kosher certification and shmita year production.

A Palestinian Shmita Agriculturalist

The Hebrew new year that began in September 2014 was a year of shmita. Three months earlier, Wajeeh, Sa'id, their friend Muhammad, and I were sitting together in Sa'id's yard. Sa'id began to discuss his role as a seller in the strict kosher (kosher le'mehadrin) niche market through a year of Jewish shmita. Seven years ago, in the previous shmita, representatives of a company marketing strict kosher produce visited him. This company was committed to strict kosher rules, implying a rigid approach to insect-free produce, and told him that they did not care how much pesticide he used if there were no insects in his produce. They taught him how to work for kosher certification. He told of how they had all gathered in the exact location that we were now sitting in to share food and drinks, a sign of (religious) trust by all parties.

Once Sa'id learned how kosher certification worked and became dissatisfied with the company's payment delays throughout that year, he decided not to cultivate for them anymore. He then founded his own company Alei Sharon Lemehadrin. He was able to increase both the number of greenhouses under his operation and his investments on the farm and expected great profits by the end of shmita. Two months after the 2007 shmita ended, however, he was abruptly notified that his strict kosher certification had been revoked due to claims that insects had been found on his herbs. He started closely monitoring his produce for insects with lab examinations. Although he discovered one instance in which he had used excess pesticide, he never found insects. One day Sa'id met the kashrut supervisor who used to monitor his farm and he asked him for an explanation of the sudden revocation of his kosher status. The supervisor told him that he heard that there were people at the Rabbinate who did not want an Arab to grow le'mehadrin kosher produce on a non-shmita year. Ultra-Orthodox media channels had run advertisements warning buyers that Alei-sharon's produce was un-kosher and should not be purchased.

This period, which he had initially thought would be one of great profit, ended with financial loss; his inability to market his produce through the profitable strict kashrut markets meant that he could not pay for his additional greenhouses and investments. Sa'id did not want to drown in debt, so he invented a solution. He asked one of the religious Jewish marketers working to become the owner of the company that Sa'id had founded and Sa'id would be his agricultural producer. According to Sa'id, the man was initially reluctant but eventually acquiesced. This workaround allowed Sa'id to recover economically and expand the operation by 2014. Despite the drastic reversal in his economic situation, nothing had changed in the operation of greenhouses, except for the name of the owner. The split between needing the Palestinian producer for shmita and then throwing his investment away after shmita is telling regarding the Zionist-Palestinian agrarian labor timescape. The Palestinian producers are an unorganized sector. Therefore, Israeli society can employ Palestinians according to recession and market booms without any commitment to long-term employment responsibilities or union restrictions.[108]

Sa'id seemed content with his agricultural operation in 2014; he said he had overcome many challenges in agriculture in his life and that only death would prevent him from remaining in agriculture. Then he emphasized, "I received this agriculture from my father, and I will pass it on to my son." His comment echoed the significance of Palestinian attachment to land through agriculture as an intergenerational practice and symbol. At the same time, he told me that he was now preparing for the next shmita. The continuity of these comments reverberated in my ears. For Sa'id to continue his agrarian heritage, he now needed to depend on the contemporary reclaiming of Jewish heritage. His adaptability to the conditions imposed on him by the timeframes of the capitalist agrarian market, Palestinian inheritance tradition, and the settler nation struck me. Even more striking was the extensive knowledge that he and his friends possessed about Jewish kashrut—a topic that I, as a secular Jew, knew very little about.

Sa'id's timescape is an interplay between different forms of social time: the capitalist market time of growth and (migrant) labor time regimes, as well as the intergenerational Palestinian family farm's agriculture as a structure that Sa'id was working to sustain in spite of the challenges of acquiring land due to inheritance tradition. His work in the niche market of strict kosher herbs on shmita and beyond also showed his work in the settler state's time. As Sa'id's involvement in the kosher market reveals, shmita has created an unexpected hybrid agrarian timescape that enables both Jews and Palestinians to entrench their claim to the land: for Jews through the biblical significance of shmita and for Palestinians through its economic gains. Moreover, shmita allows Palestinians to persist in agriculture despite a history of agrarian dispossession.

Regardless of the grand opportunities that shmita offers Palestinians in Israel, Wajeeh was not enthusiastic about the 2014–2015 shmita. He claimed:

> Now the Israeli chains are arranging the needed produce with agriculturalists from Jordan. There, it is an easier task for them to just import the agrarian produce for the Haredim [ultra-Orthodox] without taking care of the processes needed in Israel—to achieve more water quotas, get more infrastructures, and take care of the agriculturalists. . . . No special grants and procedures in Jordan, nothing, just make a contract and they will produce. . . . Seven and fourteen years ago you really felt the shmita. Everyone would come here [to the agricultural terrains of the Palestinian towns in Israel] and close deals with the agriculturalists, and you had good prices for everything. But now, you cannot make a living.

The phenomenon that Wajeeh is referring to is not just anecdotal. While the Israeli and Palestinian Ministries of Agriculture had been brokering produce exchanges from the West Bank and Gaza to Israel during shmita years for several decades, the entry of produce from Jordan was new.[109] Perhaps the Israeli blockade of Gaza and its concomitant export restrictions had made the ultra-Orthodox look for new sources of affordable kosher agricultural produce during shmita years. The result of this search was the establishment of new Israeli shmita farms in Jordan, where the biblical restrictions do not apply. By leasing Jordanian land, Israeli agronomists were able to initiate a greenhouse shmita operation on a thousand dunums of Bedouin Jordanian land. Ten Israeli agronomic experts supervised the operation and employed one hundred Jordanian agrarian workers.[110] We may call it the shmita time-land grab in which shmita time is used as a justification, both a driver and a tool in a temporary appropriation process.[111]

The Dialectics of Shmita Time

Hamadeh Ghanem, whom I introduced at the beginning of this chapter, bought the state's land in the 2007 shmita year as a way of helping the state execute the sale permit.[112] When I tried to learn more about his experience as a participant in the sale permit ceremony, Ghanem said that he was happy to serve the Jewish people's religious practice and that he saw that act as a continuation of the alliance between the Jewish people and the Druze. Knowing that agriculture in Mghar, his hometown, is still relatively significant, I asked Ghanem what it meant for him to be a patron of all agrarian land in the context of historical land disputes between Israel and its minority citizens.[113] Ghanem was silent for a moment, and then he said. "This was only a symbolic act. It did not matter in reality. Anyway, it's not like I could do anything with the land that I bought." Then, with some laughter, he said, "The Jews are smart and the lease I signed was very clear and specific on what one is allowed to do or not allowed to do with the land."

The short conversation with Ghanem highlighted that in a settler colonial context, the term *symbolic* in land management and in land exchange agreements is much more important than it might seem. This is demonstrated by the state's effort of finding a "good Arab" who is considered by the ethno-nation a loyal citizen suitable for the sale permit as well as the abundance of Hebrew writing on the politics of the land sale.[114] The continuous regulatory work of expanding agricultural shmita might seem merely a symbolic state effort aimed at solving the interests of ultra-Orthodox communities. However, this chapter has shown that the practice of shmita possesses a political power, deriving from the expansion of the Zionist and religious temporal order. Its power comes from its ability to interweave the biblical story and the contemporary agricultural reality into statecraft involving techno-mysticism and techno-nationalism. Even during 1993 and 2000, years in which the Labor Party was the dominant coalition and less money was allocated to shmita subsidies for agriculturalists, I saw no wavering of the state's commitment to continuing facilitating, sponsoring, and engaging with all the bureaucratic work that shmita demands. By introducing various mechanisms of shmita applications and circumventions, the state has worked to mediate capitalist time's rationale of productivity in agriculture with the cyclical religious rhythm of shmita. Contrastingly, the state did not intervene to settle conflicts in time between Palestinian inheritance tradition and a market economy of scale until 2015. The examination of shmita versus inheritance traditions manifests the anthropological claim that mediating conflicts in time is a central task of a state bureaucracy.[115] But the Israeli regulator demonstrates the significant power of the Israeli state to reorder time and law specifically according to its settler-nation needs. Here, reclaiming religious tradition both for its Jewish religious observers and for the nation using shmita is operated to reclaim Jewish continuity in the land and to indigenize.

Furthermore, while the Israeli state and the Zionist movement denigrated Palestinian agriculture for more than a century for its "primitive and traditional" methods in a typical settler colonial dynamic, Israeli shmita agriculture also manifests an interplay between tradition and its circumventions rather than modern agronomy. Yet, shmita was not practiced for centuries of Jewish history and only reemerged following colonization in Palestine. An examination of shmita's contemporary history allows observing how Israel and Zionism's narrative of agrarian modernity, science, technology, and progress go unchallenged without stopping to contemplate how "tradition" is used in a dialectic manner to dispossess Palestinian society and to crystallize a Jewish settler society.[116] The settler society justifies its own use of "irrational" and "unscientific" practices in modern agronomy knowledge terms. Jewish tradition affects agrarian practice and technology, relying on Jewish and traditional ecological knowledge as part of a dispossession and erasure mechanism organized around religious tradition rather than more common settler societies' mechanisms of capitalist accumulation.

Shmita highlights the importance of delineating the contours of specific settler colonial projects rather than claiming an encompassing trajectory between all settler societies. For instance, observing the role of tradition in both local groups allows us to reconsider the dominant scholarship position that settlers and natives always exist in a temporal dichotomy.[117] Instead, we see that not only do natives live in a cyclical time, but also the settler society's religious traditions summon a cyclical life. The shmita case also highlights that labor and labor time are in fact an exploitation mechanism in a settler colonial society, but it shifts forms according to the changing needs of the settlement project. Here, I critically assess Patrick Wolfe's formulation that settler colonialism is primarily a contest over land rather than labor to show through shmita how the exploitation of native agrarian labor is restricted to high-demand periodicities.[118]

One could claim that the return to shmita stems only from the settler society's work of reclaiming a Jewish past to indigenize. Alternatively, the sociology and anthropology of Jews highlight that "thinking in Jewish" implies living a temporality of repetition, of recurrences, of continuity that significantly differs from linear progressive thinking.[119] Such logic does not pertain only to observant Jews but also to people who are culturally Jewish, and their experiences of time are also anchored by Jewish holidays disregarding religious law. For instance, a foundational verse in Haggadah of Passover is "In every generation, each person must live as if they were among those who went forth from Egypt. Not our ancestors alone were redeemed from suffering, but also we and our families."

So what conclusion can be drawn from the idea that a settler society can also rely on cyclical temporalities? Perhaps the importance of tradition for both groups may allow us to reimagine and redefine the sorts of political communities existing in the local settler colonial condition and the future of this land. Tradition does not dissolve the dichotomy between settler and native, but a new category of time allows for imagining new conceptual and political horizons. For instance, the two traditions revisited are both based on ideas meant to advance social equity. Perhaps in a decolonial future when settlers and natives redistribute power and political privileges of time and space, tradition as a timescape can become an arena of proximity rather than a hierarchy if we are to sincerely acknowledge the nonliberal and nonsecular forces that govern Palestinian and Israeli societies.[120]

Ironically, shmita also created a hybrid timescape for the settler and native in which the native society benefits from the settler's religious time, and it regains and reclaims reconnection to the land and to agriculture through the Jewish calendar. However, such hybridity does not position the two in an equal timescape and ground. Shmita is still a period when Palestinian time is subjected to Jewish calendar time.[121] But during shmita, Jews are highly dependent on Palestinians. Shmita shows that to comply with foundational Jewish observances, a multiethnic society is a necessary societal structure because practicing shmita is almost impossible without Palestinians' presence and their practice of agriculture.

We may also look at how in a different settler-colonial context agrarian Jewish circles are currently using shmita to encourage their community commitment to social justice and land redistribution in the United States, facing agrarian and environmental injustices. Their work critically acknowledges the historical processes that made Jews "White" in America and evokes new sorts of social responsibilities that Jews have in fighting against the colonial and racial system they are in.[122] Although Jewish American culture and Jewish Israeli culture are formed against different political terrains, the mobilization of the shmita tradition as an anticapitalist and a de-colonial tool in the time of climate change allows a new imagination of the political power of religious tradition to encourage societal change.[123]

Regardless of the political power of shmita, it has emerged as a messy bureaucratic task that creates problems for the state system's enforcement, agricultural management, and execution due to its seven-year recurrence. Thus, circumventions of shmita have become commonplace, as a means of overcoming the various challenges that it creates for the state. A kibbutznik told me about the known "wisdom" of the Arab village in the center of Israel that produces 200 tons of vegetables from 10 dunums of land in a shmita year. By telling me this artifice, he hinted that shmita created additional tricks and circumventions of Jewish law such as an impossible triple-production capacity of that Arab village during shmita.

Even the Parliament concluded the 1993–1994 shmita with a reference to the ship that left the Israeli port on a shmita year with Israeli potatoes that were repackaged abroad and then reshipped to Israel. Yet, these subterfuges do not change the fact that from whatever angle one looks at shmita and its polemics, there is always a Palestinian Arab entangled in the Jewish or Zionist practice of expressing belonging to the land.

The story of shmita and its expansion to Israeli agricultural cultivation in Jordan demonstrates that there are land grabs that are performed not only under spatial considerations, ecological justifications, or food availability securitization but also under temporal justifications. In this way, shmita emerges as a new form of agrarian land grabbing, a "time grab."

THREE

Cultivating Time in an Olive Tree

During the last three decades, science, technology, and policy have dramatically changed olive oil agriculture, culture, and the social world surrounding them. One cool November day during the olive harvest in 2013, I found myself in the presence of one aspect of this powerful transformation. I participated in a Ministry of Agriculture field day demonstrating new agricultural technologies for olive agriculture. It took place in the olive groves of Kibbutz Magal, a collective Jewish-Israeli community bordering the Green Line.[1] In the year 2000, with governmental cuts of water allocation for agriculture, the kibbutz replaced its water-intensive cultivars of citrus and cotton with trees local to the region, such as pomegranate, almond, and olive. Magal's olive grove covers a thousand dunums, and it has become one of the larger producers of olive oil in Israel.[2]

I drove slowly along the dirt roads of the kibbutz's olive groves, through the straight rows of tightly packed, silvery-green olive trees on the flat terrain in the center of Israel/Palestine. This olive grove was densely planted and irrigated by drip irrigation. Its soil was clear of any shrubs or vegetation. This grove was a highly industrialized operation. An olive landscape like this one is unusual compared to the region's hilly olive groves. Until the 1990s, olive growing was a typical Palestinian occupation, taking place predominantly on hilly topography terraces in marginal soils. Yet, at the beginning of the twenty-first century, the state sponsored a fifteen-year olive agriculture planting program. The program motivated Jewish Israeli cooperative collectivities such as Magal to plant olive groves. Following the subsidized program in 2016, Palestinian citizens still owned most of the olive lands in the state, accounting for 70 percent of the olive groves in Israel.[3] However, a dunum of industrialized olive groves, prevalent in Jewish agriculture, produces four times more olive oil than a dunum of rain-fed mostly Palestinian olive groves.[4]

I arrived at the machinery demonstration and saw mostly Jewish-Israeli cultivators. People gathered between the trees to watch the operation. The trunk-shaker tractor roared; it reached out a metal arm to grab the base of the trunk and shook the tree. The earth convulsed under my feet. The roots of the olive tree—spread wide like huge fingers under the soil—vibrated in the earth. In five noisy seconds, a rain of olives had fallen (image 9), and the large cloth spread under the tree turned olive green.

IMAGE 9. A mechanized harvester producing a rain of olives, fall 2013. Photograph by the author. The trunk-shaker tractor encircles the tree's base with its metal arm, vigorously shaking both the trunk and the realm of olive cultivation.

I was overwhelmed. So were a few Druze and Palestinian cultivators standing beside me; their laughter, body language, and facial expressions indicated their disorientation. A wave of emotions flooded me; I felt simultaneously amazed by the impact of the machine and suspicious of it. I was trying to digest a harvest system that shakes both the earth and the olive culture. I thought (with no doubt a tinge of romanticism) of previous harvest seasons that I have experienced with Palestinian families entangled for hours between olive branches, of the beauty of handpicking and touching every olive. This new machinery ushered in a novel aesthetic and logic to the olive harvest.[5] It is a logic that privileges one group of agriculturalists over another.

Transforming a crop like the olive tree is significant in Israel/Palestine. Even before the planting program, olives had been the most prevalent trees in the landscape, and they continue to dominate the local groves' terrain. Moreover, the olive tree is a cultural and political symbol mobilized by both groups on this land, making it a particularly crucial object of study.[6]

This chapter examines the recent transformations in olive oil production through science, technology, and policy that have supported the emergence of contemporary Jewish-Zionist olive agriculture while slowly dispossessing Palestinian citizens' agriculture. By following agrarian imaginaries of new industrialized olive cultivars, changes in harvesting techniques, new marketing strategies commodifying olive oil as a biblical/Jewish-tradition product, and the claiming of olive terraces as both cultural-biblical and sustainable landscapes, I trace the politics of time encapsulated in the newly produced world of olive oil agriculture. The new olive timescape simultaneously interlaces olive modernization and profitability for Jewish rural communities while anchoring it as a "biblical and traditional agriculture" for Palestinian smallholders who do not benefit from either modernization efforts or environmental payment schemes. I argue that the transformations in olive agriculture produce a *time grab*, a term I coined to describe an appropriation process that occurs under temporal justifications such as care for the past or the future of a collectivity. The time grab allows the settler society to reclaim indigeneity and belonging and to materialize its national ethos through the timescape it cultivates in olive agriculture.

State scientists are central actors promoting this transformation. Meanwhile, attributing notions of a biblical landscape to the Palestinian method of terraced olive agriculture erases the significance of olive agriculture to Palestinian heritage and indigeneity, and it insists that Palestinians conserve their role as "traditional agriculturists," positioning them in a perceived non-modernized past of olive agriculture.

The latter dynamic ignores the endeavors of Palestinian agronomists who are seeking to change the production modes of Palestinian olive agriculture. By elevating the voices of these agronomists, I question both the official narrative of the settler state on Palestinian agriculture and contest the argument that indigenous "modes of being in time" are intrinsically opposed to those of the settler society. Because the socio-political process of settling olive agriculture was fueled by the introduction of a new olive variety, we will now trace its birth.

The Arrival of a Modern-Zionist Olive Tree

Can a tree become a hero? The compilation of olive cultivar statistics, annual meetings of olive research symposiums, and the Olive Council's annual post-harvest celebrations convinced me that Israel has a new local hero. The Barnea olive variety—designed through a scientific process for industrial cultivation—became a new icon for the Israeli agricultural community during the early 2000s and fueled the process of the Jewish-Israeli reclamation of olive agriculture for olive oil. The industrial turn in olive agriculture was a revolutionary act for olive oil production. Although the olive is one of the oldest domesticated crops and has diverged into many varieties both naturally and with human assistance, the industrial turn in olive agriculture is a recent movement. Barnea variety is its pioneer.

The Barnea cultivar was developed in the late 1960s and 1970s by the research group headed by Professor Shimon Lavee (1931–2016) at the Volcani Agricultural Research Organization of the Ministry of Agriculture (ARO).[7] In the 1960s when the Israeli breeding plan began, the only olive breeding program that existed was at the University of California, Davis, and the variety it produced was ornamental.[8]

The Jewish-Israeli olive community views Professor Lavee as the founding father of modern olive oil agriculture in Israel. Palestinian citizen agronomists spoke of him with much respect as well. European olive oil production powers such as Spain and Italy awarded him various honors for his groundbreaking achievements in olive oil science. These countries established their own breeding programs in the mid-1990s.[9] Lavee was born in Germany in 1931 and gained a Ph.D. from the Hebrew University in 1960. Because he was globally recognized for his olive science achievements, he served as the Israeli representative at the International Olive Council (IOC) for thirty-five years in addition to serving twice as its president, in 2000 and 2008. His position was considered an achievement given the number of Arab states in the IOC unsympathetic to Israel. His career represents, in a structured form, the relationship between science and the state. Throughout his career, he had a double appointment at the Faculty of Agronomy of the Hebrew University and as a researcher at ARO. The latter is a central institute in the history of Zionist agriculture in Israel.[10]

My meetings with Professor Lavee took place in the summer of 2015 at both his home and his university offices in the Department of Agronomy of the Hebrew University in the city of Rehovot. Books and papers on olives surrounded his desk at home as he smoked a pipe made of olive wood and had a small rug decorated with an olive tree under his feet. He told me that in the 1960s and 1970s, the approach of the Israeli agricultural research institutions to the olive sector was "shameful." Little research funding was allotted to olive agriculture, which was considered the "backward, irrelevant, uneconomic, inefficient preserve of the Palestinian peasant."[11] Lavee joked that all his olive research funds in those years came from collaborating with colleagues to "steal" money that was designated for other agricultural research sectors. When I asked Lavee about his motivation to research such a low-status crop, he mentioned first his scientific curiosity for a species that globally lacked the basics of horticultural and agronomic scientific knowledge. Then he explained that without developing efficient cultivating methods, "the state would never grow olives." "The state" meant Jewish agriculture, as most olive groves for olive oil in Israel in the 1960s were owned and attended to by Palestinians.

Israel had left ancient olive trees uncared for or destroyed them to make room for field crops after the 1948 War.[12] The Jewish-Zionist agrar-

CULTIVATING TIME IN AN OLIVE TREE   115

ian communities lacked interest in cultivating the Palestinian olive groves. From a cost-benefit perspective, they saw olive cultivation as unproductive agriculture: it cost more to farm abandoned Palestinian land than the crop was worth. Thus, by 1952, only about a third of displaced Palestinians' olive groves were under cultivation.[13] Hence, from the 1920s to the 1980s, Jews in Mandate Palestine and later in the 1948 state borders cultivated olives for fruit mostly at the kibbutzim of the eastern inland valleys, but they did not produce olive oil.[14] Furthermore, while Palestinian citizens were the main producers of olives for fruit in the 1970s, the Jewish production of olives was subsidized and its marketing monopolized, leaving Palestinian olive producers at a distinct disadvantage.[15] According to the renowned Iraqi-born Jerusalem chef Moshe Basson, famous for cooking with local ingredients, the only Jews who consumed olive oil until the late 1980s were Mizrahi Jewish families who immigrated from Arab countries where olive oil was prevalent such as Syria, Egypt, Morocco, Tunisia, or Algeria. Basson said that olive oil purchase for Jewish Israelis until the late 1980s "depended on ties with Palestinians and Druze or shopping at Arab groceries." It was only in the early 1990s that olive oil appeared on the shelves of Jewish supermarkets.[16] This change occurred following global trends that led to an increased appreciation of olive oil, such as the growing awareness of the culinary and health benefits of the Mediterranean diet. As others have shown, the Mediterranean diet is a social construct promoted by national and international heritage bodies.[17] Additionally, changes in regulations on olive oil production in the European Union made olive oil's global pricing more accessible in comparison with cheaper vegetable oils such as canola and soy oils.[18]

Lavee described the scientific challenge in developing an olive variety that would be profitable and efficient: a cultivar that could take advantage of luxurious irrigation to create a greater yield of fruit and a higher percentage of oil. The local varieties cultivated by the Palestinian agriculturalists did not respond positively to irrigation, as they were "the product of selection over many generations of growth in rain-fed conditions and marginal soils." His research group began to look for new olive cultivars to create the desired tree through hybridization. They started importing trees from all over the world that would possibly be suitable, but this first international endeavor failed.[19] The juvenility period of these trees (juvenility is a horticultural term indicating the time from seed to fruit) was too long; at that time, the average length of olive juvenility was twelve to twenty years. Lavee noted, "I don't know any researcher willing to wait for twenty years to improve the tree's productivity." The research group managed to decrease juvenility to two to three years. Compressing juvenility that much implies a significant change in the life of the tree, its cultivation, its affordability, and productivity. This change also meant that the care work for the tree could be achieved in a short time span rather than a span of generations. The length of the juvenility period has been the principal obstacle hampering the improvement of fruit trees by cross-breeding.[20] Reducing juvenility has been a scientific victory over time, shrinking production time to make the olive cultivar more efficient to suit industrialized agriculture.

Lavee and his research group then continued to look for new cultivars. They found them in the desert plot developed by the British major Claude S. Jarvis in 'Ayn al-Gedeirat (as pronounced in Bedouin Arabic, or 'Ayn al-Qudeirat in standard Arabic transliteration) in the Sinai Peninsula in Egypt. When Major Jarvis was the British governor of Sinai from 1923 to 1936 (image 10), he brought to 'Ayn al-Qudeirat a collection of a thousand olive trees as part of his attempts to improve Bedouin agricultural conditions. Jarvis identified 'Ayn al-Qudeirat as the biblical site of Kadesh Barnea.

According to the Bible, Kadesh Barnea is where Moses's sister Miriam died and was buried during the Israelites' exodus from Egypt (Numbers 20:1). It is also where Moses sent twelve men to check out the Promised Land (Numbers 13:26). Jarvis saw in this site "traces of extensive cultivation and irrigation as well as a fine stone reservoir of great antiquity. . . . Nothing has so far been found in the Wadi that affords any definite clues as to the identity of its builders. From the nature of the construction, it is obvious it is not Roman, and it is possible that the Israelites themselves made it" (image 11).[21] While there still is an archaeological discussion on the accuracy of this narrative,[22] Major Jarvis's biblical inspiration illuminates a Judeo-Christian imaginary and the colonial expansionist legacy that nurtured this site and lingered on into Israeli agrarian imaginaries.

After the 1967 War and Israel's conquest of the Egyptian Sinai Peninsula, Lavee and his team visited the 'Ayn al-Qudeirat site and examined

Major C. S. Jarvis, Governor of Sinai, inspecting a Guard of Honour.

IMAGE 10. Major Claude S. Jarvis, British governor in Sinai 1923–1936. Source: Major C. S. Jarvis, Yesterday and Today in Sinai (William Blackwood & Sons, 1931).

six hundred trees of the Jarvis collection but failed to find the right tree for their "efficient cultivar" mission. They returned to 'Ayn al-Qudeirat six years later, after the 1973 War. This time they selected twenty-two root cuttings that looked potentially suitable. They nurtured the plants for some time and finally chose two new varieties that resulted as suitable for industrialized production. They named them Kadesh and Barnea. The Kadesh cultivar is suitable for olive fruit consumption, and because it contains a low percentage of oil, it is suitable for a low-fat diet. Barnea became the Jewish-Israeli industrialized olive oil hero cultivar. It has an erect growth habit and a sparse canopy physiologically suited to mechanical harvesting. It has high and constant productivity under irrigation, significantly overcoming the olive tree's natural tendency for alternate bearing (biennial bearing). From an economic point of view, alternate bearing causes significant labor, economic, and marketing challenges, because the production quantity is not nearly the same every year and

IMAGE 11. 'Ayn al-Qudeirat oasis and agriculture research station. Source: Matson Photo Collection, Image 23028, Library of Congress.

can drop to a sixth in the "off year." While traditional agrarian knowledge employed summer pruning to decrease the extent of the biennial bearing,[23] providing additional irrigation and nutrition to the new cultivar almost completely overcame the alternate bearing, exemplifying how an abundance of resources provided to the tree can almost overcome natural boundaries. Finally, Barnea also has a higher percentage of oil than the other prevalent local varieties. It was introduced to the market at the beginning of the 1980s.

At first, the Barnea was adopted by less than a handful of kibbutzim agricultural entrepreneurs who were willing to experiment. In the late 1990s and early 2000s, it expanded more rapidly through Israel's Ministry of Agriculture national investment program to increase olive agriculture. Currently, the Barnea variety is used in more than 50 percent of the industrialized olive groves in Israel, reigning in the Israeli market along with other varieties such as the commonly used Palestinian Souri and Nabali cultivars and a few European varieties such as Coratina, Arebquina, and Picholine.[24] Barnea was also widely adopted in Australia, where it constitutes 40 percent of newly planted olive groves.[25]

The variety is not patented and thus it became a pioneer for the later global developments in industrialized olive cultivars. In summary, the modernized-Zionist olive tree is a scientific hybrid, a crossbred variety grounded in some of the earliest horticultural achievements of olive science and enabled by colonial legacies. As in other colonial and imperial botany and agronomy, the Barnea was developed at a time when Israeli territorial expansion allowed agronomic science expansion. A full scholarly analysis of global colonial agronomy and horticulture has yet to be fully conducted, but Barnea is a part of that global history.[26]

The Barnea has been branded through the lens of a Biblical timescape that continues to animate Israeli olive oil making and marketing. Commonly, olive oils are named after their region of cultivation. The Barnea variety is branded as an Israeli cultivar from southern Israel close to the border next to Sinai. But the biblical Kadesh Barnea is not located in Israel proper; it is in the Sinai Peninsula, on Egyptian territory. However, because Kadesh Barnea was in the Biblical map of Israel, the branding of Barnea as an Israeli cultivar allows Israel to materialize the time of the Bible through a new modern variety and appeal to a Zionist temporal ethos of agriculture grounded in science and technology and rooted in the Jewish tradition.[27] Olive agriculture then asserts the national identity on the ground, creating links between the Biblical past and the modern present and solidifying Israel's moral claims to indigeneity. The sociotechnical world around Barnea shifted olive time, intervening in socioecological and natural cycles to create a new olive time that materialized through the olive tree's claims on national time and belonging.[28]

The creation of the Barnea variety exemplifies that scientific knowledge is grounded in political economic structures such as the nation-state. Science is a practice of co-production, founded on social assumptions, identities, and orders, while also embedding them within society.[29] Scientific co-production is well demonstrated in Barnea history as told by Professor Lavee. His story exemplifies that science operates well within a social order in which people know "what counts as science." Lavee emphasized that "the program of olive development was always supported by ARO combining the research on developing industrialized breeds, cultivation methods, irrigation as well as the comprehensive goal of the olive cultivation intensification." However, it was not only science that moved the Zionist tree onward; it was the intersection of science and policy.

Irrigation Flows

If the development of the Barnea cultivar was the first state-funded scientific achievement that enabled the expansion of Zionist olive oil agriculture, then a discovery about irrigation was the second. Scientists from the Gilat Research Center of ARO in the Negev/Naqab region discovered in the early 1990s that saline water from a deep aquifer of the desert was suitable for olive irrigation.[30] This agronomic finding is significant in a period in which global desertification makes it increasingly difficult for rural communities in arid regions to generate income. This insight has already enabled the planting of a million olive trees in Rajasthan in northern India and more recently plantations in arid regions of Argentina. Locally, this discovery led the state to begin drilling for water from the deep aquifer for the benefit of Jewish agriculturalists in the Negev starting in 1995.[31] The Ministry of Agriculture and the Jewish National Fund (JNF) were involved in funding and monitoring the research and its subsequent implementation. The JNF's funding of this research and agrarian research in general highlights again the links between this influential quasi-governmental and nontransparent organization to the creation of disparities in the rural areas in Israel/Palestine. The JNF feeds and nurtures the Jewish populations in Israeli rural areas, providing a lifeline to agrarian settlements that would not have survived without its support.[32]

Water availability or scarcity in Israel/Palestine is a result of an agrarian imaginary that continuously links Israeli agricultural settlements with an unquestioned assumption that the state ought to provide them with water resources.[33] This assumption led to the development of a plan to allocate more water to Israeli olive agriculture in the Negev/Naqab region. Plantations of kibbutzim olive groves in the south of the country expanded even further at the beginning of the 2000s when the Ministry of Agriculture and the Israeli Olive Council (ISROC) announced a program to be undertaken between 2001 and 2016 to increase Israeli olive oil production by incentivizing newly industrialized olive plantations (image 12) and adding irrigation to existing groves.

IMAGE 12. Industrialized desert olive grove by Ashalim in southern Israel/Palestine, fall 2021. Photograph by the author.

Water is yet another example of a resource whose availability and distribution are determined by the identity of the cultivators. In Israel/Palestine water resources are not a given but rather a social fact. Water may emerge from research about its availability or from concerted attempts to access, drill, monitor, control, and assure its proper flow.[34] Moreover, water is a resource whose availability is intimately linked to time and its politics: it either flows with a speedy and efficient rhythm when it is allocated to Jewish agriculturalists, or it gets stuck in the channels of bureaucracy when designated for Palestinian cultivators.[35]

It is not only saline water that benefits Jewish olive agriculture in this way but also reclaimed wastewater, which is the prevalent irrigation water in Jewish-Israeli agriculture but not as common in Palestinian agriculture. Regarding the discriminatory water allocation for Palestinian agriculture in Israel, Dr. Hisham Yunis, a retired Ministry of Agriculture official, wryly commented back in 2009: "If someone wants to start another intifada [uprising], he is welcome to start with this issue." He quickly retracted that statement and explained that although it is not economically beneficial to divert water to the mountainous plots in Galilee, the unequal allocation of wastewater between Jewish and Palestinian agriculturalists must be addressed. As it currently stands, Palestinian water and sewage treatment taxes sponsor the channeling of wastewater to the kibbutzim even though Palestinian agriculturalists have expressed their willingness to irrigate with reclaimed wastewater.[36] Officially, this is due to two main factors. One is a Palestinian-Muslim cultural bias against reclaimed water that is often perceived as impure water. Second, the costs of operating a wastewater treatment plant are high and most Palestinian municipalities are poor and cannot afford to pay the long-term costs of these operations. Such official explanations require problematizing: in neighboring Egypt, where there is a pious Muslim population, drainage water has been used for irrigation for over a century because of water scarcity.[37] Treated wastewater is indeed higher in contaminants than drainage water. Yet, "water good for agriculture" is an agrarian imaginary that can be transformed or manipulated too. Palestinian municipalities in Israel became poor because they govern without significant residential taxes as their constituents were dispossessed of land resources where they could have developed industrial or commercial areas. Therefore, their water is diverted to a nearby Jewish municipality or regional treatment plant for the use of Jewish agriculturalists in an arrangement often defined as temporary.[38] Then, Palestinian municipalities' "failure to manage" a wastewater treatment plant and the state of their stagnant infrastructure are part of a larger trend of assigning all Palestinians to a "failed," "suspended," or "stuck" governance condition, positioning them firmly within an uneven temporality, both distanced from their Jewish counterpart citizens and dependent upon them for sewage treatment.[39]

According to both Jewish and Palestinian-citizen agronomists or olive cultivators, the olive plantation development program resulted in a new industrialized Jewish olive agriculture, while existing groves, mainly Palestinian, were not developed nor allocated water. The development of vast olive groves in Israeli kibbutzim and in Israel at large is striking in comparison to the state of Palestinian citizens' olive sector. The Barnea cultivar and its attendant irrigation systems highlight how historic Zionist institutions such as the JNF, the Jewish Agency, and the regional R & D sponsored by the JNF act as quasi-governmental branches that operate the unequal allocation and flow of development resources for different communities.

The story of the Barnea variety encapsulates the ways that agrarian imaginaries of a desired future for a cultivar materialize a collective vision for the nation and recruit a whole array of material flows toward the fulfillment of that vision.[40] The Zionist olive tree is an emblem of the ideology of modern agriculture in which the new cultivar, like other Zionist agriculture interventions, was created against a "traditional, backward" Palestinian agriculture.[41]

Contesting "Traditional" Palestinian Olive Trees

During the twentieth century, olives, which were always an important part of the local landscape, became a political symbol of Palestinian nationalism, collective memory, and rootedness. In the early stages of the Zionist-Palestinian encounter, the olive tree emerged as the signifier of Palestinian land ownership versus the Zionist pine trees that were planted by JNF to mark purchased Zionist land.[42] Yet, it was not until the 1970s, when olive groves become a tool to resist Israeli confiscation of land, that the olive tree was solidified as the ultimate symbol of Palestinian steadfastness. Olive cultivation is a relatively easy way for Palestinians across the Green Line to prove legal land ownership and thus oppose Israel's confiscation of land.[43]

Olive plots of the Palestinian communities and towns usually surround the built environment. Thus, a continuous landscape of planted olive terrain accompanies the hills in their stone-structured terraces, and more recently have extended to the valleys near Palestinian towns. The size of a single-owner plot often decreases due to inheritance customs over the years, but members of the community or the family still know whose land and trees belong to whom. At the margins of towns, there is a continuous process of both new plantations and land clearing. Thus, an olive grove is both a social-cultural heritage marker and a potential construction area due to pressing land scarcity in Palestinian towns in Israel.

The local varieties of olives that have been cultivated for generations are the Souri and the Nabali. These olive varieties also hold a different political timescape than the Barnea. Souri is in the area of Sour (Tyre) in Lebanon, indicating a political period when Palestine's locale was a part of the Greater Syria political region during the Ottoman Empire. Nabali refers to Nablus in the West Bank.[44] These are olive cultivars of historic Palestine rather than a Zionist biblical timescape. The Souri tree grows to medium size; it is slow growing, and its fruit holds a high content of oil. The Nabali tree is like the Souri and mainly grows in the Palestinian mountain areas of the West Bank. These varieties are suited to the local climate and marginal mountain soils, as in the past, the fertile land of valleys was used for subsistence crops. More recently, as agriculture has declined in the fertile plateaus and valleys, these lands have been planted with olives, which are easier to care for and are useful as "planted flags" marking Palestinian land ownership.[45]

Several Palestinian agronomists with whom I talked during my field-work had radical views on the state of Palestinian olive agriculture, its rain-fed condition, and its low profitability. Since 2000, Israel's Ministry of Agriculture has dedicated funds to improving agrarian roads in Arab communities by connecting the routes from olive groves to the towns and allocated funds to refurbish olive mills in Palestinian towns. But the state of the Palestinian olive industry and its available resources were, according to Dr. Fathi Abd el-Hadi (1962–2016), "nothing nice to see in comparison to Jewish olive agriculture."[46] He was a renowned expert on olive and almond cultivation who had worked for fifteen years for the Ministry of Agriculture before becoming a private consultant both lo-cally and globally. I often met Fathi during my fieldwork in olive oil meet-ings organized by the ISROC, which usually took place in sites in Galilee or at the Faculty of Agronomy at Rehovot. I also met him for lengthy interviews at a kibbutz olive operation's office that he managed at the Jezreel Valley/Marj ibn 'Amer. It was poignant to meet Fathi there—a senior Palestinian expert managing and teaching Jewish-Israeli olive agriculture in an emotionally laden environment. Whereas this fertile agrarian plain marks the Zionist celebratory narrative of the establish-ment of the Jewish/Zionist settlements at the beginning of the twentieth century, for Palestinians, it is a symbol of the massive Palestinian dispos-session during the 1930s and the displacement during the Nakba. Yet, we discussed these matters only indirectly.

Fathi thought that the Palestinian folklore around olive agriculture had "nice elements" but that the Palestinian olive tradition also created habits that were destructive for reaching global standards of quality and profitability. He looked with frustration at conservative habits in Pal-estinian agriculture but was even more frustrated by the state's depri-vation of water to Palestinian agriculture. He saw both as factors that, if changed, could "bring progress" to the Palestinian olive oil industry. Consequently, in 1993, he developed a cooperative association for water allocation in his town of Iksal in Galilee. It took him approximately eight years to receive water allocation from the state. After he finally acquired the water quota for his town, he was able to create a cooperative water association of two hundred town members, all of whom cultivated profitable olive and almond agriculture of which he was immensely proud.

Fathi's view and attempts to modernize Palestinian olive agriculture were pioneering among Palestinians in Israel. He claimed that old olive trees should be uprooted to make space for the planting of new ones, which would be more profitable and efficient. Such views stem from a highly technical-agronomic perception of the tree as a profit-making resource rather than a sociocultural entity.[47] He asked Muslim clergy in his region to help him convince agriculturalists to accept irrigation with treated wastewater, which was not widely accepted in the 1990s. Treated wastewater was perceived as impure and therefore prohibited by Islam.[48] His work with the clergy helped him establish the status of treated wastewater as beneficial for agriculture.

In his private consulting work, he advised mostly big operations of the kibbutzim. In his free time, he consulted with and instructed Palestinian farmers in Israel and in the West Bank. Conversations with him were always an interesting blend of views and ideas. At times, he sounded as though he had assimilated the Zionist development and modernization discourse, applying similar critiques to the view of "the traditional Arab farmer," as his Jewish colleagues did, without acknowledging unequal conditions on the ground. Perhaps it was the result of his many years of work at the Ministry of Agriculture that contributed to this developmentalism and modernization views. As the years passed and he worked more in the private sector, he became more critical of the Israeli state policies and its historical and ongoing neglect of Palestinian agriculture in Israel, especially around water deprivation.

Moghira Younis, a state employee from 'Ara in the Triangle region, and Abdelmajid Hssein, an agronomy expert and a high school teacher from Deir Hanna in the Galilee, had both earned master's degrees in agronomy in Germany in the mid-1990s, where they studied together. Both have been involved part-time in the organic certified production of olive oil for the fair trade Jewish-Arab NGO Sindyanna of Galilee. To achieve significant cultivable land size, they organized their families to avoid dividing land according to Muslim inheritance customs and local Christian religious traditions. While Moghira Younis created an industrialized organic olive operation in 2009, Abdelmajid's operations remained small, improving the family production techniques and focusing on the security provided by the niche market of fair trade NGOs.[49] Yet Abdelmajid, perhaps from his experience as a high school teacher, had a solid intergenerational vision for Palestinian agriculture. He told me that transforming his cultivation into an organic-certified one was his way of keeping agriculture alive as well as preserving his family's land. According to Abdelmajid Hssein, producing organic agriculture and transforming Palestinian agriculture into modern agriculture is a way of earning a dignified living in agriculture instead of abandoning it, a growing tendency among Palestinians in Israel. He repeatedly exclaimed that "if kibbutzniks are receiving the resources to cultivate modern olive agriculture, we [Palestinians in Israel] should receive no less."[50] Abdelmajid Hssein and his colleagues all spoke of agricultural modernization as a way to achieve equality and dignity. He was frustrated with the difficulties of convincing other Palestinians to abandon the local inheritance traditions of agrarian land division, which according to him don't "serve our society anymore." Linking modernized agriculture to equality and to Palestinian societal transformation reflects these agronomists' refusal to accept the settler society's time, which takes for granted a future based on native dispossession and stagnation. Instead, these agronomists envision an alternative future of Palestinian societal change and civic equality in status and resources.[51]

Fathi, Abdelmajid, and Moghira are among the few Palestinian growers and agronomists in Israel that consistently have used industrialized or organic methods to produce olive oil and whose oil has been consistently rated "extra-virgin," receiving the quality certification from the Israeli Olive Board (equivalent to the IOC).[52] There are only ten certified Palestinian citizens' olive oils out of 215 Israeli producers of certified olive oil. However, these innovative operations have not been promoted by the state as agrarian role models in Palestinian citizens' agriculture even though Jewish-Israeli agricultural officials are aware of such endeavors and have worked daily as colleagues of these professionals. Hence, the voices and actions of these agronomists show the agrarian change occurring among the Palestinian professional elite in Israel. However, such change is made invisible, almost nonexistent by a state system that simplifies the view of who is the Palestinian agriculturalist. Such a dynamic reflects the indigenous claim that narrations about societal change are made impossible by the settler society, which repeatedly assigns them to the past.[53]

Despite evident changes in the attitudes of the professional elite of Palestinian agronomists toward olive agriculture in Israel, there remains an institutional tendency to depict the Palestinian society's approach to olive agriculture as traditional and cultural rather than addressing the structures of inequality to which these agriculturalists and agriculture are subjected. For instance, Dr. Arnon Dag, the head of the olive science research panel at ARO told me:

> Olives are so important to the Arab sector. . . . They will continue with [olive cultivation] no matter the government or marketing. . . . It forms their connection to the land and to tradition and their ability to go outdoors with their families on the weekend. Perhaps the system will sometimes burden them with environmental regulations on olive mills and they may get upset with the state at times . . . but I think that if we identify this or that nutrient lacking in their production or discuss the olive oil's quality, it will not matter. The importance that olive agriculture has for them internally is much greater than what the governmental system can give them.[54]

While Dag rightly identified the great socio-ecological and cultural significance that olive cultivation holds for Palestinians, his quote reveals a failure to recognize the deep inequality in the allocation of agricultural resources and the governmental responsibility for it. Moreover, his view and those of other state scientists neglected the fact that the contemporary achievements of industrialized and irrigated Zionist olive agriculture are based on the olive's agrarian environment that was cultivated by Palestinians for centuries.

But interestingly, the relations of the rain-fed olive sector versus the irrigated/scientific one is seen asynchronously in a narrative that glorifies industrialized agriculture. For instance, Professor Lavee reiterated that "without intensive olive agriculture, Israel would have lost its olive industry. The high cost in wages and labor required for the manual hand-picking of traditional olive groves would have been too great to bear eventually." Lavee also claimed that the industrial olive sector benefitted the traditional groves because the large-scale application of integrated pest management practices prevalent in Israel protects both the irrigated and rain-fed trees.

But the modern industrial olive oil economy was made possible by previous production methods and olive varieties, some of which are still grown in the new olive groves today. Furthermore, the Palestinian olive landscape in Israel/Palestine supports the economy of industrialized olives; it creates local imagery that supports the marketing of intensively cultivated olive products.

Contrary to Lavee's claims, however, olive cultivation in the West Bank is economically viable without industrialization because Palestinian agriculturalists are supported by local Palestinian and European NGOs that provide agricultural instruction services for smallholders and channels for reaching socially responsible, environmentally inclined niche markets.[55] Some would claim that such producers do not compete in the free market, but neither do industrialized/modernized Israeli producers who have received governmental support in science, technology, and new plantation subsidies. Alternatively, the knowledge surrounding less-intensive rain-fed olive agriculture is depicted as unscientific and unimportant to sustain.

"Unscientific and Non-commoditized Olives"

As we sat in Fathi's kibbutz office, he told me how in recent years, the global scientific benchmarks for olive oil quality had increased. Olive oil is now standardized as a healthy product rich in polyphenols, antioxidants, and peroxides, requiring chemical and organoleptic analysis. According to these standards, not everything that looks and tastes like olive oil is scientifically considered to be olive oil. The scientization of olive oil means that every phase of production contains practices that affect the product's biochemical quality. It also means that an increasing gap has opened between Palestinian olive oils and international scientific standards.[56]

Even Hadas Lahav, the director of Sindyanna of Galilee fair trade NGO (more on this NGO in chapter 4), a politically left radical with a co-resistance approach,[57] a fluent Arabic speaker who has been working relentlessly for the last thirty years to develop market opportunities for Palestinian agriculture and its olive oil producers, and a close colleague of Fathi had similar thoughts. She told me: "Let's abandon our nostalgia, folklore, and romantic perceptions and admit it: Arab olive oil is damaged and oxygenated." Coming from a radical egalitarian perspective, she was still convinced of global standardization and certification of extra-virgin olive oil and was frustrated by the number of Palestinian producers she had to reject from the fair trade olive oil initiative because of the high acidity of their olive oil.[58] Yet, critical agrarian scholars have highlighted how similar cases of global standardization have always pushed small producers off the market without providing proper alternatives.[59]

Taken together, the Palestinian olive trees, oil, and growers are all seen as "unscientific." A few scientists working in ARO, as well as Palestinian agrarian instructors, told me that it is hard for them to conduct systematic research in cooperation with Palestinian cultivators or to address issues that are relevant for the Palestinian small-household cultivator. Moghira Younis, for instance, has worked for the Israeli Ministry of Agriculture Extension Service since 1995. Moghira's role is grove instructor for the Center District of the Extension Service. The center district has a relatively big constituency of Palestinian agriculturalists, but most of the community he serves and instructs are Jewish agriculturalists. Moghira told me:

During the first and second intifadas some Jewish Extension Service instructors were afraid to provide service for Arab sectors. This enabled me to provide service for both sectors, the Jewish and Arab. It is fascinating to provide instruction for [the Arab] sector, but professionally in terms of the learning process, I would not have advanced if I did not have the Jewish sector. In my work, I relate to both sectors. . . . But the Jewish sector provides the best field site for observations and experiments because it functions as an organized agrarian operation which is orderly and coherent.[60]

His articulation of "Arab sectors" and "Jewish sector" was unusual. *Arab sectors* is a term that results from the historical and ongoing divide-and-rule policy of the Israeli government, an intent to separate the Palestinians into a few Arab minorities instead of one collective group.[61] But Moghira was addressing both Arabs and Jews as a sector in a discursive articulation that placed him as almost distinct from these two groups. Perhaps his categorical distinction reveals the temporal distance that Palestinian agronomists experience as highly educated professionals according to Western science terms, working in a governmental ministry that ostensibly follows such terms and observing the agrarian practices of two separate communities. The quote above indicates how Moghira perceives knowledge that is relevant for agricultural progress as stemming from Western scientific methods used by the "Jewish sector" as if instructing smallholders how to optimize their agricultural assets was not a worthy professional task. In that, the Zionist agrarian imaginary succeeded in convincing leading Palestinian agronomists that small holders' agriculture has no science nor future.

Other Palestinian and Jewish agronomists with whom I talked provided additional explanations as to why so little scientific work is done in collaboration with the Palestinian cultivators in Israel. They said that Palestinian olive agriculturalists usually have little terrain that they can allocate to scientific research. Similar to Moghira's opinions, I heard from other agronomists that Palestinian producers may be less consistent in cultivation methods and unable to provide the scientists the personnel they need to perform research tasks, such as harvesting at specific times to meet research goals. In addition, these senior agronomists admitted that, as in other scientific fields, their research depends on grants and budgets, which typically favor the industrialized olive sector's interests. These comments do not recognize what E. P. Thompson has called "rational time" that Palestinians allocate to their agrarian chores, following a task-based time-division system rather than a scientific one given that olives are not their main source of livelihood.[62]

Increased olive oil standardization has created new problems for Palestinian producers, but some of the problems perceived with Palestinian olives have changed little over the last half century. Governmental agricultural research reports published in the 1960s explored improved technical methods for olive harvest for "the villages" (of Palestinian citizens) and storage of olive fruit between harvest and oil processing. They looked for the ideal time to process the olive in mills to maintain low levels of acidity.[63] Fifty years later—when the ISROC steering committee met in July 2013 to discuss research and improvement possibilities for rain-fed olive groves—some of the same issues were discussed as characteristic problems of rain-fed olive cultivation.

During this meeting, which is emblematic of the unusual equal political participation structure of the ISROC, Palestinian citizens, Jews, and Druze discussed various concerns and ideas about how to improve the state of rain-fed agriculture. Dr. Fathi Abd el-Hadi claimed that rain-fed agriculture fails in all production stages: from cultivation methods to pest treatment, to harvest time and methods, as well as storage of the product. He called for workshops and conferences to instruct rain-fed agriculturalists and the need to organize cooperative marketing of Palestinian villages' olive oil. Moghira also joined Fathi's opinion that knowledge instruction is essential to improve the state of rain-fed agriculture, and various other speakers mentioned the research needed in rain-fed agriculture groves for best practices of pruning, pest management, harvest mechanization of small holdings, and more.

The end of the meeting, however, demonstrated the ongoing tension in the contemporary Israeli agricultural professional establishment between a formal desire to allocate resources on an equal basis and the institutional legacy in government circles to de-develop Palestinian agriculture. Dr. Adi Naali, the head of the ISROC at that time, concluded the meeting by saying that half of rain-fed olive oil production was for self-consumption and the other half went to trade. Consequently, he observed that the willingness of smallholders to invest in professional improvement or production processes was minimal because it would bring little economic benefit. He suggested that it would be important to gather all the professional olive knowledge, translate it into Arabic, and find ways to distribute that knowledge to agriculturalists. He mentioned the possibility raised during the meeting of marketing rain-fed olive oil for its health benefits, but he emphasized that this should be done together with the advancement of all olive oil to improve the economic capacity of the olive oil sector.

Naali's comment regarding the minimal economic benefit of investment in rain-fed olive agriculture is an unusual example of a high-ranking agriculture employee referring to Palestinian agriculturalists in terms of making a rational economic choice. Naali's comment stood out in opposition to the tendency to portray the Palestinians as motivated by tradition, custom, and sentiment rather than by modern economic concerns. This comment echoed the 1960s American economist Theodore Schultz, who showed that traditional agriculture operated rationally and allocated its resources effectively based on well-balanced economic reasoning.[64] Nevertheless, Naali's conclusion of the meeting, which emphasized that rain-fed agriculture must be advanced with the rest of the olive sector, shows that, for an Israeli official, branding and promoting Palestinian rain-fed olive oil on its own terms might still be too radical to contemplate.

Could rain-fed olive oil be marketed on its own terms—outside the international framework of "extra-virgin"? Palestinian interlocutors often told me that they send bottles to friends and relatives in other countries, and it is a much-prized gift. Even in the official Olive Oil Council meeting, Palestinian olive oil's bitter and strong taste was discussed as a marketable trait. Still, the international, seemingly apolitical standards of olive oil now define the ways in which people around the globe experience its taste.[65] Yet, the Palestinian citizens' olive oil is mostly circulated through local economies as well as relations of affect where a bitter taste is both valued and commodified rather than the standardized capitalist market temporality. Contrast it to the Jewish-Israeli industrialized olive oil that gets bar-coded, thus traced, and sold in the market economy. According to the Israeli Olive Oil Council, about half the Palestinian olive oil produced in Israel is traded outside of the bar-coded market. Often, olive oil becomes a good that avoids the state's market and tax economy to retain non-state economic circulation. I am considering this as a counter-tempos, a form of resistance to the Israeli state project of modernizing, scientizing, and commodifying the production of olive oil. However, I do not idealize this alternative mode of circulation. Palestinians in Israel often complain of getting stuck with the previous year's oil because they have no market for their olive oil; thus, their labor loses its value, and their commodity becomes damaged over time. However, these parallel circulation modes reflect that olive oil commoditization does not eradicate local meanings or the social networks revolving around this product.[66]

Even if the unique taste is not enough of a selling point for a broad audience, health benefits might be greater from oil made from rain-fed olives. Dr. Arnon Dag claimed that rain-fed olives have better health qualities than industrialized ones, "if processed correctly." However, at least two types of scientific research are needed to fulfill the promise. The first type must establish the health benefits of rain-fed olive oil compared to modernized olive oil.[67] The second type must work with the Palestinian agriculturalist to realize the health benefits. "Health benefits" then become a black box—a discursive device composed of internal functions and mechanisms that are currently unknown to the state and its scientific and agrarian-knowledge instruction systems. Both types of research require agricultural instruction systems. Nowadays, Israel does not support agricultural extension (instruction) as it once did. As a result, only large-scale Jewish producers have consistent access to scientific and agronomic supervision.

Since the research needs of Palestinian agriculturalists in Israel are not met by the Israeli government, some advocates have looked for help elsewhere. Fathi Abd el-Hadi told me of the efforts to develop research funds for Palestinian olive groves in Israel and in the West Bank through a Palestinian agricultural NGO in Israel, Hawakir (more on this NGO in chapter 4), and through American funds from both USAID's Middle East Research Cooperation (MERC) program and the Near East Foundation, a New York–based NGO. The two American development bodies supported Palestinian olive agriculture as well as collaborative training for Palestinians in Israel, West Bank Palestinians, and Jewish-Israeli agriculturalists. Those research funds were not only a testament to the ethos of olive agriculture as an international symbol of peace but also a recognition that Palestinian agriculturalists in Israel are not equally supported by the state and that they require research and development funds from external bodies. American involvement, however, has a complex role in these interventions as it often places Jewish-Israeli and Palestinian participants as equal parts of an agricultural olive endeavor, obfuscating the power relations and the different access to resources, as well as the distinct political timescapes of the colonized and the colonizer.

Although Palestinian citizens are politically represented in ISROC, their political power is weaker there and the institutional support that led to the development of the Zionist olive is almost entirely missing for Palestinian groves. Abdelmajid Hssein told me, "When the olive sector was solely an Arab cultivation, the state could not care less." Notably, the state did have an interest in developing olive agriculture, but it focused on the cultivars and the farmers who were "responsive." Israel joined the IOC as a founding member in 1958. After the 1948 War, it was in the then-new state's interest to use the remaining Palestinian agricultural assets to enhance agricultural productivity and quality. Since the 1960s, government institutions have provided some instruction services to Palestinians in Israel. Such work included guidance on tree pruning techniques (that rejuvenate old trees and maintain their productivity) and planting seedlings instead of grafting.[68] But that work was concluded long ago.

Dr. Arnon Dag admitted that while there has been an increase in knowledge production for "modern" olive cultivation, the local "traditional" olive sector is losing intergenerational knowledge on best practices for pruning and maintaining a healthy and productive grove. He concluded that because there is no professional development or instruction for the traditional cultivators in Israel, the olive council and scientists "deserve an F grade." Such a comment acknowledges that there is professional knowledge involved in "traditional" olive tree maintenance and that the knowledge is worth saving. Arguably then, the conservation of less-intensive olive agriculture can be supported beyond claims to tradition but rather for the sake of local ecologies and knowledge. Since none of these insights on the development of rain-fed agriculture and traditional knowledge are recorded, we may consider this as an example of the claim that governance is not only about producing knowledge but also about producing ignorance.[69] The temporal distancing of "traditional agriculture" as outdated makes it easier to forget and depreciate.

Mustafa Natour, born in 1936, was one of the first Palestinian employees of the Ministry of Agriculture in the 1960s. In the 1990s he became a senior consultant for the Minister of Agriculture. I met him at his home in Nazareth to discuss his life memories of promoting Palestinian agriculture. Natour told me that it would be technically feasible to provide scientific instruction and knowledge to Palestinian cultivators—if there were the political will to do it. To transform the existing Palestinian groves to be more profitable due to irrigation, specific plans would need to be created for each field site. Such plans should specify groves in which all trees should be replaced with new ones, existing trees should be pruned, or new trees should be added to the grove to increase its density and profitability. Site-specific management and development are possible in technical terms, but perhaps not in political terms. Natour, like his fellow Palestinian agronomists, was interested in a model that would allow Palestinian agriculture to modernize and especially be profitable.

For a technical model, he suggested, we can look at the olive mills' waste management strategy. Indeed, in the early 2000s and until recently, waste from olive mills contaminated water bodies and caused severe damage to sewage treatment plants.[70] A survey and policy program mapped out the possible solutions for more than ninety different olive mills in Galilee, characterizing them and creating management plans for all types of olive mills in geographic clusters.[71] Because the stakes for the pollution of groundwater were high and the risks immediate, there was political will to fix the problem. However, this resulted from the political power and temporal urgency inherent in states of emergency, such as the emergency of water bodies contamination, a power and urgency that traditional groves do not evoke.

Harvest Timescape

The last thirty years of industrialization of olive cultivation have brought labor-saving tools and machines. These turned the olive harvest culture from a time of family gathering, storytelling, and long conversations into a time of harvest efficiency, as large tractors moved across olive groves and a few hired workers ensured the machines worked well. The large operations of olive agribusiness and olive agriculture in kibbutzim and some moshavim cooperatives use mechanized harvesting tractors. Uri Yogev, one of the pioneers of Israeli Negev olive operations and the ISROC manager appointed in 2019 claimed: "Mechanized olive harvesters are a wonderful solution because they can work day and night and harvest the exact quantity that the olive mill can press. It is not only about the cost [of labor]; it is about the accuracy of the rhythm of harvest. These machines free you from being dependent on workers' groups that now have closure [referring to West Bank employees subordinated to Israeli closure policies] and therefore cannot arrive or cannot do it in the right pace."[72] In Yogev's praise of the agrarian machine is the explicit notion that agrarian technologies free Israelis from their temporal labor dependency on Occupied Palestinian employees hired for their skilled cheap labor. During the time I was conducting my fieldwork in 2015, Palestinian agriculturalists rarely used these machines—aside from the few industrialized operations that I mentioned earlier, such as those of Dr. Fathi Abd el-Hadi and Moghira Younis. In January 2023, ISROC produced a video celebrating the recent bountiful harvest season featuring clips of various olive operations' harvests. The video shows mechanized harvesting of all Jewish cultivators, but it also includes one clip of a Druze family manually harvesting.[73]

It is well established that mechanized harvesting saves significant production costs because it saves labor time. Karl Marx highlighted the commodification of time under industrial capitalism and indicated the oppressive characteristics of the process.[74] In a Marxian analysis, E. P. Thompson's seminal article on time and work-discipline claimed that the shift to industrialism brought about a fundamental change in the reckoning of time. He remarked that peasant societies are task-oriented but that work and social exchange are not differentiated but interwoven. Thompson posits that, in contrast, in factories, routine workers were required to work steadily, regulated by mechanical clocks, and thus developed a sharp sense of time.[75] In industrialized harvests, time may not be observed as strictly as in a factory, but it is surveilled. Working hours are counted and used as a measure of the efficiency and profitability of the agrarian operation.

In contrast to the industrial harvest, Palestinian harvesters would manually pick olives with their families. Underneath each olive tree, they would place a large *fallaeh* (cloth or canvas used to collect the falling fruit), climb on ladders, and pick the fruit from the branches, or they would pull out their shirt to hold the fruit they picked. Palestinian agriculturalists in the Galilee often use an *obbeyye* (Arabic; called *kharrata* in the West Bank), a wooden stick approximately two meters long, to bat at the tree branches and shake the olives loose; they then collect the olives from the canvas. In the past, harvesters wore a *qamis* (Arabic for shirt), a garment with additional sleeves or large pockets reaching the feet, to allow them to temporarily hold the collected fruit (image 13).

IMAGE 13. Palestinians harvesting olives with qamis and ladders pre-World War II. Photo by Khalil Raad. Courtesy of the Institute For Palestine Studies.

A small agricultural household might use an affordable plastic rake (image 14) or a metal comb to facilitate a quicker manual harvest that does not damage the tree branches by hitting them but rather combs the fruit off the branches. If the household has available capital for agriculture, it might invest in a small-scale electric machine such as the pneumatic harvester that combs the olives off the branches with its lightly vibrating head.

The harvest season is the most labor-intensive period in olive agriculture. Current olive agronomy and biochemistry indicate that harvest timing is key to olive oil's nutritional value and taste qualities. Thus, an agriculturalist needs to calculate the right time for harvest, estimate how long harvesting will take, plan to store the harvested fruit in ventilated containers rather than plastic sacks, and coordinate with an olive mill for the earliest available time to cold press the fruit. According to Dr. Fathi's observations, many Palestinian agriculturalists miscalculate these times,

IMAGE 14. Abdelmajid Hssein holding a plastic rake in olive harvest in Deir Hanna. Courtesy of Sindyanna of Galilee, a non-profit fair trade association.

and therefore their olive fruit and oil become highly acidic. If one accepts the notion that a better track for Palestinian agriculture is "to modernize it," then this sequence of actions deserves time and knowledge to bring into motion. Yet, there are other questions we may ask about harvest time if we seek alternative explanations to the modernization narrative. For instance, what explains Palestinian households' long-enduring harvest technique of manual picking with ladders and *obbeyyes*?

Palestinian olive groves are mostly rain-fed and predominantly on hilly topography, so they are not well suited for heavy mechanized equipment. However, this is not the only reason why mechanized harvest technologies "skipped" over Palestinian olives. Even households that have olive groves in topographic areas that are friendlier to heavy machinery often do not employ a mechanized harvest. The decreasing availability of land for Palestinian agriculture may also partially contribute to the harvest's technological difference, but this is not the central explanation.

Rather, the agrarian imaginary that fueled the changes to the local olive agriculture may be a better source of explanation for why technological change excludes Palestinian agriculture. The industrialized and mechanized olive agriculture in Israel has been developed via a state-mediated process that seeks to create a fundamentally different paradigm of olive agriculture. This new paradigm of olive agriculture is Jewish-Israeli rather than Palestinian. The new cultivator has access to state-allocated land rather than Palestinian private land. He or she benefits from governmental subsidies for innovations in science and technology, such as olive harvesting machines. One of the olive harvesters is a tractor adapted to olives from the almond harvest, and another harvester was adapted from industrial grapes harvest, through Israeli-Spanish cooperation.[76]

One of the key logics of industrialization is the belief that production becomes more efficient when machines replace human workers. In Israel's state-supported program for the development of olive agriculture, this technological logic has been pushed toward its natural limits for industrial olive groves but not for the small households' groves. Since 2001, the state's olive program brought along the intensification of technologies required mostly by the kibbutzim. A kibbutz agrarian operation has, on average, 600 dunums, but can reach 2,000 dunums of olives. This contrasts with Palestinian households in Israel which own, on average, 5–10 dunums, as well as the moshavim agriculture, which averages 25 dunums and may reach up to 80 dunums.[77]

In 2012, Moghira Younis, in his role as an employee of the Ministry of Agriculture's Extension Service, told me of his discussions in the ministry a few months earlier.[78] The state's agricultural support schemes offered incentives to purchase "labor-efficient" agricultural equipment, sponsoring up to 25–30 percent of the agrarian technology.[79] In Israeli agrarian economics, "labor efficiency" refers to refraining from employing migrant Thai farmworkers or contracting West Bank Palestinian workers. Younis tried to convince the subsidies committee that the ministry should sponsor the pneumatic harvester, a small mechanical device, as it would support small-scale Palestinian agriculture; he asked, "Don't we deserve efficiency as well?" At first, Younis said, the committee did not understand why they should fund a mechanical tool that would not be used for the industrialized (Jewish) olive sector. Nevertheless, in further discussions, the committee approved sponsoring the pneumatic harvester.

In 2018, however, the pneumatic harvester was not on the list of supported technologies. Reading into the funding scheme, I found five olive harvesters that the state sponsored and all except one served large-scale cultivators, implying these are technologies serving mostly Jewish cultivators. The state funds agrarian technologies on condition that they are used on a plot size that is between at least 200 and 1,000 dunums; only one machine subsidy started at the baseline of 75 dunums. This funding scheme illustrates state officials' assumption that a technological shift in olive agriculture can occur only via hyper-productive agricultural operations with significant land resources demanding labor time saving.

Agrarian technology is a key to understanding the production of disparity in agriculture. Formerly, agrarian economists defined the production factors of agriculture as land, water, labor, and capital; today, however, the input of agrarian knowledge and technology (as well as fertilizers and marketing) are equally significant. Furthermore, mechanization, science, and technology are symbols of "modern time," representing the notion of linear progress along with other temporal signifiers of modernity, such as trains or clocks that serve to standardize and commodify time.

Agrarian mechanization in an iconic crop such as the olive tree enacts the recording of time through agriculture as a modernized practice and as a produced landscape. The state sponsorship of agricultural machinery and technology becomes a technique of governance and timekeeping, which becomes especially valuable in a crop that is so symbolic to local cultures and local imaginations of indigeneity and belonging.

Since the discussion of olive harvest technology might risk perpetuating the modernization narrative or one of technological determinism, I wish to withdraw for a moment from the view of technology and science as power to present an alternative view of the matter. The technological shift works to perfectly fulfill the short-term capitalist goals of higher productivity and circulation. However, trees tend to disrupt plans to fully exploit them over the long term. According to Dr. Arnon Dag, the yield of industrialized and irrigated groves drops significantly after fifteen to twenty years. The cause of the sudden decline is not yet understood.[80] In contrast, olive trees cultivated via traditional systems continue to yield fruit for hundreds of years. This is a prime demonstration of the limits of capitalist time. The industrialized olive operation is an economic endeavor, but the act of uprooting trees every twenty years to maintain profits may represent the failure of sustaining this agriculture and trees for generations to come. The uprooting of trees that refuse to continue producing is a materialization of the settler society's constant work to indigenize and its failure to do so. As opposed to longue durée narratives of Palestinians' connection to their olive trees, the settler society's capitalist temporality does not befriend the olive tree's limits. Nevertheless, as a capitalist endeavor, Israeli olive oils are conquering higher bars of productivity and circulation. Facilitating a capitalist-national timescape of olive agriculture opened the floodgates of cultural production and the reclaiming of olive heritage.

Settling Olive Landscape, Heritage, and Sustainability

A salient aspect of the recent development of olive agriculture in Israel is the way it works to interlace the capitalist time of olive profitability for Jewish rural communities with a settler national time. Another strain of policy intervention has been the development of the olive agrarian landscape as a cultural heritage in need of preservation. This perception was promoted by some of the leading planners in Israel who were contracted by the Ministry of Agriculture and the Ministry of Interior's Planning Authority for many years. The concept of landscape as cultural heritage was discursively adopted by the Ministry of Agriculture, the Ministry of Interior, and the Ministry of Environmental Protection. In fact, these planners demonstrated to the state what was already widely agreed upon in UNESCO and in the European Union: agriculture produces not only food, fiber, and pharmaceuticals but also creates a landscape of cultural heritage by provoking a sense of belonging and a unique sense of place and providing economic profits through tourism.[81] The notion of a cultural heritage landscape also invokes the Braudelian sense of the longue durée to suggest that belonging to a particular place is a product of relationships between the environment and the local culture.[82] Landscape preservation policy invokes notions of care for the future based on the conservation of the past. But whose past and future does the state envision through its landscape?

A landscape imaginary consists of images, representations, and stereotypes that, although often inaccurate, possess power and animate political passion.[83] As such, the olive tree is an emblematic and sacred figure to various cultures across the Mediterranean region through Greek mythology, the Hebrew and Christian Bible, and the Qur'an.[84] Locally, the deep-rooted cultural heritage that sparks Israeli society's image of a landscape is the Hebrew Bible. In texts of early Jewish tradition, such as the Bible and the Talmud, the olive tree was both the embodiment of the tie between the Jewish people and place and a sign of peace. The olive branch also appears in the Israeli state emblem created in 1949, indicating its continued symbolic importance in the modern Israeli state. Yet as I showed earlier, there is a discordance between the olive tree's importance as an emblem and the attention it was given as an agrarian product by the Israeli state.

Like the al-Battuf plain, the notion of a biblical landscape offers an arena in which Palestinian olive agriculture, for the first time in a hundred years, can be appreciated by Zionism and the Israeli state. In the 2000s, it seemed as though there was a growing recognition of the contributions of the Palestinian olive landscape. New environmental planning proposals from the Ministry of Agriculture and the Ministry of Environmental Protection offered a potential route for addressing and promoting "traditional agriculture" and olive tree terracing as agriculturally sustainable and central to the maintenance of the cultural heritage landscape.[85] They were inspired both by UNESCO and European agricultural policies, which served as a role model for Israeli sustainable agriculture policy. The following excerpt from the National Agricultural Planning Policy Protocol demonstrates this:

The heritage of agriculture and rural life in the land of Israel is ancestral and there are various types of archeological evidence of its existence from prehistoric times until today. . . . The agrarian tradition in the country extends over three thousand years. The image of the agricultural landscape is grounded in the biblical tales and the birth of Christianity and it is an essential part of the historical imagery of the land. The biblical landscape is the backbone of tourism that wishes to experience the biblical landscape through the existence of vineyards and olive, pomegranate, and fig groves.[86]

The policy document goes on to identify sites that should be conserved because they embody such biblical landscape agriculture, referring to the olive groves cultivated by Palestinian Arab towns and communities in Galilee but without naming the collective identity of these caretakers of the landscape. A policy document like this implies that Israel's "vineyards and olives" are the rightful inheritance of Jews and Christians who may wish to visit their heritage and spend money as tourists. However, there is no attribution of heritage rights and legacy to the ethnic, religious, and national collective that lived in this landscape for centuries and cultivated and developed these terraced olive landscapes to be vibrant and fruitful, manifesting the many ways in which the settler state eliminates the native.[87] These references to the Bible in landscape conservation policy demonstrate the constant work of validating political claims to the land that is at stake.

At the same time, such a narrative erases the meanings of the Palestinian countryside, its history and heritage, and its importance to indigenous collectivity. Repeatedly assigning a biblical significance to this environment negates the continuous life and agrarian culture and work of Palestinians on this land.[88] These olive terraces require continuous hewing of stone and hauling of infill earth. They would have been washed out if they had not been carefully attended to and expanded by the inhabitants of this land for centuries. Hence, this biblical claim is an act of elimination of the Palestinian agrarian environment by the settler society. Unlike the prominent countryside rewriting that took place as a physical demolition of Palestinian village life following the 1948 War, this erasure and appropriation of the vibrant and flourishing agrarian environment are discursive. While the 1948 erasure has been largely discussed by scholars,[89] a discussion about the implications of the current reworking of the landscape is absent. Yet, the vibrant agrarian Palestinian environment, although small-scale is a living testament to the Palestinian citizens' survivance in a state that dispossessed them. Yet, the appropriation of this landscape as biblical enacts symbolic and slow violence.

While the European Union compensates farmers with environmental payment schemes for maintaining the scenic or ecological value of the landscape and its agricultural heritage,[90] such a plan was considered and rejected by the Israeli Ministry of Agriculture. Government subsidies for the olive sector were analyzed and proposed by the Ministry of Agriculture and the Olive Council in a detailed economic analysis that examined the socio-environmental benefits of olive agriculture to Israeli society.[91] ISROC promoted directly paying olive agriculturalists for their contribution to the country's landscape heritage and their external environmental contributions; however, the Finance Ministry opposed this plan. Palestinian agriculturalists could have been major beneficiaries of such environmental payment schemes. Dr. Adi Naali, head of the Olive Council, told me that the Ministry of Finance's representatives preferred to support olive agriculture through indirect subsidies, such as agricultural research and development and import tariffs that protect the price of Israeli-produced oil.[92] Higher customs are helpful, especially for those producers whose oil is traded through bar-coded formal markets. But they are less beneficial for producers whose trade is for personal consumption, family exchange, or gifts—which is the case for at least half the Palestinian-produced oil in Israel. As a result, Palestinian-citizen smallholders' olive terraces are not economically reimbursed by the state. They are economically punished despite their contributions to the environment and cultural heritage.[93]

Conserving the perceived biblical landscape and reclaiming ancient Jewish olive rituals and heritage is a process evident in all forms of cultural production involving olive oil commercial branding. Biblical landscapes are invoked in both private capitalist markets and public state institutions. I observed olive oil bottle labels that appealed to a historical and biblical legacy. For instance, the design of global award-winning Ptora boutique olive oil in 2013 was "Ptora was named after a biblical settlement which was uncovered by archeologists in 2004 near Moshav Sdeh Moshe. The olive groves and vineyards from which our olive oil and Ptora wine are produced were planted on the Tamir farm many years previously, next to the remnants of the ancient settlement. Findings indicate that the area was historically a center for producing wine and olive oil." Ido Tamir, a hip Tel Aviv resident with a master's in business administration acts as the proud manager and entrepreneur leading his family's boutique agrarian rebranding. Ido shared with me that it was his grandfather who planted the olive grove in the 1970s and it was mainly a business decision to invoke the historic sense of place, which has seemed to work well since the farm's re-branding profits have grown significantly.

The state has also invoked ethnic practices to speed up the olive market as a new consumption regime. Here too, culture and identity have become highly commodified products. In the Israeli olive world, culture and identities are used to increase the consumption of locally produced olive oil. As opposed to other Mediterranean consumer cultures, the Jewish Israeli one is not a high per capita consumer of olive oil. Thus, raising the public's awareness of the multiple benefits of olive oil and increasing its local consumption became one of the main missions of ISROC. Various channels of public advertising laud the healthy qualities of olive oil, TV shows feature different uses for olive oil, and scientific works and state-sponsored festivals also help increase consumption efforts. In November 2017, the Authority for the Development of Galilee, the Ministry of Tourism, ISROC, and olive oil producers themselves jointly marked the twenty-third year of the celebration known as the Olive Festival. The festival started as a regional Galilee development initiative during and after olive harvest. It was meant to connect Jews and Palestinians in the Galilee region and to introduce the Jewish public to the olive oil, olive mills, olive folklore, and the producing communities. Thus, the festival has been branded as an opportunity to get acquainted with the "diverse Israeli olive oil industry, including Arab, Druze, Christian, Bedouin and Jewish communities." This festival soon became a tradition in the north of the country. Its annual celebration in November was inspired by traditional olive festivals in Palestinian communities during the late October and November harvest season. However, starting in December 2015, ISROC added a second olive oil festival that follows the Jewish calendar.

ISROC established Hanukkah as the reclaimed holiday of olive oil. In the Gregorian calendar, Hanukkah takes place in the month of December, shortly after the olive harvest. The holiday of Hanukkah celebrates an event from 165 BCE: the rededication of the Second Temple in Jerusalem after the victory of the Maccabean revolt against the Seleucid Empire. Some recent rabbinical writing claimed that prior to the events of the Maccabean revolt, the time of Hanukkah was the Jewish postharvest celebration in the land of Israel. Thus, ISROC introduced to the Israeli public a new festivity: the reclamation of Hanukkah as the Israeli

celebration of olive oil. The public figures who advocated this new festivity, principally ISROC's director Adi Naali, did not intend to increase
nationalist discourse. Rather, in the annual emails from ISROC to olive
producers since the first 2015 Hanukkah initiative, the work of a market
temporality becomes starkly noticeable as ISROC urged producers to
join this new festival to increase the visibility of olive oil to the Israeli
public. ISROC worked to commodify culture and heritage as a selling
tool. The success of its project has been embodied in a steady rise in olive
oil consumption.

While the close links between nurturing values of (Jewish) cultural
heritage and the local environment were used as sales tactics, they were
not used to benefit the smallholding farmers, mostly Palestinian citizens.
The official discourse of the positive environmental effects of olive agriculture was amplified with the appointment of Dr. Adi Naali as ISROC
director in 2011. Naali's doctoral research discussed the sustainability of
small- to medium-scale olive farms in moshavim, cooperative agrarian
communities.[94] Yet, he adopted an approach that highlighted the positive effects of industrialized olive production on the Israeli environment
based on arguable environmental economic calculations.[95] Naali and
others argued that irrigated olive groves that use treated wastewater are
ecologically more beneficial than rain-fed groves since the former absorb
urban waste. Researchers from ARO found that reclaimed wastewater
contains important nutrients that nurture the olive tree and decrease
fertilizer use.[96] Reclaimed wastewater is a nationally allocated resource
that is unavailable to many Palestinian agriculturalists.

It is questionable whether industrialized olive agriculture provides
greater environmental benefits than less intensive groves. Some of the
less intensive rain-fed groves are decades or even centuries old and help
to maintain historical landscapes, protect slopes from soil erosion, fix
carbon dioxide through the trees, and create biodiversity.[97] Studies on
the challenges that climate change and drought pose to the region clarify that local varieties are better adapted to deal with water scarcity.
These studies show that the Israeli industrialized olive variety unintentionally developed agriculture that is less resistant to drought.[98] But the
environmental-economic analysis promotes the benefits of industrialized olive agriculture to Israeli society while downplaying the benefits

of Palestinian olive agriculture.[99] The practice of uprooting and planting industrialized olive groves every twenty years for the sake of profitability sheds light on the unsustainable capitalist temporality that governs industrial olive cultivation. Such practice cannot be seen other than as a practice of a capitalist overextraction.[100] Thus, through environmental discourses, Palestinian olive agriculture has been reduced to a merely idealized landscape: framed as biblical while it is de facto de-developed; preserved as a cultural heritage but not reimbursed for its environmental contribution; controlled by limited governmental allocation mechanisms and appropriated by the settler-state timescape politics.

Both environmental-economic calculations of olive agriculture benefits and conservation are used against the Palestinian citizens' interests while the elements of rain-fed agriculture that contribute to sustainability are ignored. Then, environmental discourses act as another means of dispossession. Rather than enacting a violent spectacle, they operate similarly to the work of science and technology; they utilize educated, globalized discourses and policies as acceptable ways of governing the agrarian environment and enforcing sociopolitical inequality.

The Olive Time Grab

I conclude by asking what it means to create changes in science and technology that move the earth under one's feet. What does it mean to shake the world of olive cultivation so that for some cultivators the olives fall in abundance like rain while others are de-developed to eventually be abandoned? The story of the transformation of olive agriculture reflects an agricultural process that produces what I call a "time grab." A time grab implies an appropriation and alienation of time as a resource. In the olive agriculture story, the appropriation of time interplays with the appropriation of an agrarian practice and landscape. But a time grab can also occur in other arenas. A time grab relates to an appropriation process that occurs under temporal justifications such as care for the past or the future of a collectivity. Thus, articulations such as "the future of olive farming" or "develop efficient farming or we will lose the industry," as well as "conservation of the biblical landscape," are mobilized to justify the appropriation of an agrarian practice. "Time grab" is closely related to concepts such as land grabs and green grabs, describing the global land rush of purchasing land for food, fuel, or "green" goals since the 2008 food crisis, but it is distinct from them in that it captures time as a central focus in resource competition.[101] In a time grab time is used as a justification, as a driver, and as a tool in the appropriation and alienation process. Hence, the development of a new efficient olive variety and labor-efficient harvest technologies—processes that neglected and alienated Palestinian cultivators—under the pretext of preserving the future of Israeli olive farming. In the time grab of olive agriculture, the state claimed Palestinian olive terraces as biblical agricultural landscapes, thereby erasing their contribution to Palestinian heritage. While the state recognizes the need to preserve these terraces as landscapes and cultural assets, it does so only through zoning programs that limit Palestinian cultivators' land-use rights, omitting the social-economic benefits they deserve from their conservation of the landscape. The settler society embedded olive oil marketing in a Jewish calendar and heritage, portraying industrialized agriculture as more sustainable and concerned with the preservation of resources for the future. At the same time, it erased the present and future-oriented environmental contributions of Palestinian olive agriculture. These cumulative effects demonstrate how olive agriculture was time-grabbed and appropriated into a settler nation's produced timescape comprising multiple layers of time.

The timescape materialized through the olive tree enacts both social politics of pasts and futures. These processes move beyond a late or dislocated mid-twentieth-century green revolution in agriculture where modernization through technology, irrigation, and the introduction of high-yielding varieties created a significant increase in crop yields and a disproportionate benefit to large-scale landholdings in the developing world.[102] Rather, here policies of agrarian development and environmental conservation are put together almost simultaneously, and although their land management logics contradict, they both result in preventing economic development from the same group of smallholders, erasing the socio-ecological worlds that Palestinian citizens live in and appropriating their agriculture as a temporal practice rather than a spatial one. As opposed to the green revolution's main rationale as a capitalistic endeavor allegedly aiming to end poverty, here the capitalist and the settler-nation rationale intermingle.

The transformation of olive agriculture illustrates a silent and dispersed mode of dispossession and governance through the timescape and imaginaries of agricultural policies, science, and technology. While previous works on Israeli-Palestinian planting dynamics, such as Irus Braverman's, focused on the role of Palestinian olives and Zionist pines as tools of war,[103] I show that violence enacted through the bodies of two distinct olive trees can also be much subtler. The olive tree is a signifier, a soldier in an unequal land battle, and a medium to convey belonging (image 15).

These processes have a wider reach as they impact all of Israel/ Palestine and olive agriculture globally. In Israel/Palestine, larger dy-

IMAGE 15. The story of two olive trees. Source: Dani Karavan, installation The Good and the Bad Government, in the exhibition Pardes at IVAM. Photographer: Juan García Rosell, Institut Valencià d'Art Modern, Generalitat, Valencià, Spain 2002.

namics of land grabbing have been occurring through olive agriculture since the beginning of the 2000s. In the West Bank, the Israeli military uprooted hundreds of thousands of olive trees, using security justifications.[104] At times, uprooting trees on the roadsides next to Israeli settlements served as a method for confiscating land. West Bank settlers such as the "Hill-Top Youth" vandalize Palestinian olive groves, believing it is their duty to push Palestinians off the land.[105] Anthropologist Anne Meneley has shown that olive oil production and circulation in the West Bank suffered from the Israeli "occupation time" in every single stage of its making.[106] Thus, the top-down and bottom-up West Bank land grabbing through uprooting and sabotaging olive trees shows the power of violent "events" to call attention.[107] Although the techno-scientific dispossession and the olive landscape appropriation are equally insidious, they are also somewhat invisible, indicating the difficulty of making news of slow violence that is dispersed and silent but no less powerful in its erasure.[108]

Globally, the olive tree is entangled in settler colonial processes. It is a tree that migrated with European settlement to the "New World." Hence, the social histories of olive cultivation in Australia, Argentina, and California and their contemporary industrialized transformations are also tied to indigenous dispossession. However, these dynamics have yet to be examined and are ripe for exploration in future scholarship.[109] Olive agriculture in the region is also tied to the struggles of local farmers across the Mediterranean to sustain their relationship with the land and maintain agri-environmental production practices against super-intensive olive cultivation. The latter cultivation method is commonly based on agri-business and capitalist modes of production. These processes will likely create an abandonment of olive worlds and its socio-ecological relations of care unless collective action is taken. The role of smallholders' care of the environment is not only about food production but also the provision of land management, landscape values, and relations to land that cannot be maintained in a world where trees are uprooted every twenty years.[110]

Finally, the purpose of the story on the olive transformation is not the documentation of the wrongs of science, technology, agricultural practice, or its history. Rather, I draw attention to the material as well as ideological power of naturalized agrarian history so that it can be challenged by remedial and oppositional histories, such as those told here by Palestinian agronomists. Hence, I ask how we can ensure that our contemporary food, agriculture, and environment systems honor life and the environments that sustain it. I reflect on how to democratize the production of food and sustain our environment in the twenty-first century as we face the challenges of a changing climate and the consolidation of food production in the hands of a few rather than the hands of many.

FOUR

Freeing Time Like a Palestinian Agronomist

Moghira Younis is an agronomist born in the early 1960s in the town of 'Ara in the Northern Triangle region. We met on a cool Saturday in March 2010, just a few days prior to the Palestinian Arab commemoration of Land Day in Israel/Palestine.[1] I was introduced to him at the inauguration of the fair trade olive grove established on his family's land in a partnership with an Arab-Jewish fair trade NGO, Sindyanna of Galilee.[2] Fair trade endeavors are dedicated to the integration of marginalized producers in developing countries into the Global North market. However, Israel is considered a developed country. Yet, Sindyanna demonstrated to the World Fair Trade Organization that the conditions of Palestinian Arab producers in Israel differ significantly from the production conditions of their Jewish Israeli counterparts and they deserve to be included in this alternative globalization market. Thus, Sindyanna sells Palestinian Arab producers' olive oil in the international fair trade certified marketplace.[3]

Moghira led the partnership between the family-owned agricultural company al-Juthoor (Arabic for "roots") and Sindyanna of Galilee NGO.[4] The NGO and the Younis family created an agricultural development partnership on Younis's lands in southern Bilad al-Ruha (Arabic for Land of the Winds) in the Northern Triangle region (al-Muthalath in Arabic; Ha-Meshulash in Hebrew, or Ramat Menashe). The family-owned company is a partnership of seven Younis households, including some of Moghira's uncles. Moghira's intervention facilitated the consolidation of the family land, instead of parceling out inherited agricultural plots, and the development of the agrarian investment plan.[5] The partnership between the family and the NGO culminated in the creation of this newly established olive grove called Oasis—Organic Olive Grove for Solidarity between Arab and Jewish Societies (image 16). Only later I learned that Moghira had been working as a state employee since 1995 serving as an agricultural extension expert for the Israeli Ministry of Agriculture, where he instructs about groves of olives, pomegranates, and guavas.[6]

Inaugurating a fair trade agricultural project in al-Ruha was at least a twofold celebration contesting the settler colonial structure and process.[7] Much of Palestinian citizens' privately owned land in al-Ruha was confiscated in the aftermath of the 1948 War. Following the war, close to thirty Palestinian villages were razed from that land.[8] Later, additional al-Ruha land was confiscated by the state for military training in the

IMAGE 16. Inauguration of Oasis Olive Grove in Bilad al-Ruha. Courtesy of Sindyanna of Galilee, a non-profit fair trade association.

1960s. For many years the state did not compensate landowners for their land. And not only was the land appropriated but also military training had taken place near Palestinian towns and homes in Wadi 'Ara, endangering inhabitants and houses at the margins of towns near the training zone with wandering bullets. In 2005, after more than seven years of political protest and a few governmental committees and negotiations, the protesters' land claims were accepted. The Committee for the Protection of Bilad al-Ruha was the main body organizing the protest, consisting of town mayors from the Wadi 'Ara area, agriculturalists, and landowners.[9] The struggle regarding the land was evoked in the post-Oslo Peace Agreement military rearrangements. Israel was preparing for the evacuation of military units and firing zones it had used in the West Bank and claimed that these units should resettle into an expanded al-Ruha military zone. The Committee for the Protection of Bilad al-Ruha organized protests to oppose the expansion of the military zone and reclaim their land. Finally, the memorandum of understanding between government representatives and the popular committee achieved the return of 11,500 dunums of agrarian land to its Palestinian-citizen landowners across Wadi 'Ara towns and villages.[10] It also restricted military activity to a well-defined, smaller zone. Thus, the Younis family's reclamation of al-Ruha land with a new olive grove was a true celebration. Their return to their 1960s confiscated land signified a feat that Palestinians have not often accomplished—a return to their decades-long appropriated land. As a moment in the collective consciousness aspiring to return, this event was remarkable because it signified the reversibility of dispossession.

Wadia Yunis, Moghira's uncle and the director of al-Juthoor, greeted the event participants in Arabic on behalf of his family with a great deal of sentiment and pride:

> We in al-Juthoor partnership invest and cultivate in al-Ruha land that until recently was a military training zone. We were forbidden not just to cultivate the land but even to access it. We will not forget that there are still other confiscated lands. We hope that a day will come when we take back these lands and return them to their true owners. These are lands that our fathers and grandfathers planted and watered with their sweat, and it grew wheat. The aroma of its bread

scented our hearts. We remember to this day this nostalgic smell. We all hope that we have put the first building block for a large project that will cover new lands, encouraging other farmers to cultivate the land with fruitful olive trees. By this, the sound of deadly bullets will not be heard in this land anymore. . . . They planted so that we eat, and we plant so that the next generations will eat.[11]

Wadia's speech was emotional and poetic, laden with an intergenerational consciousness, nostalgia, and hope. It elicited a strong sense of return in recalling the past and in evoking the hope that one day the land could return to its owners and repair the past.

Return (al-ʿawda) is a central temporality in Palestinian collective consciousness, mainly thought of and imagined in the context of the return of the Palestinian refugees and the return of the internally displaced to their places of belonging in historic Palestine.[12] Rashid Khalidi claimed that return is perceived by Palestinians as a moral issue recognizing their national peoplehood rather than a specific set of legal rights. Acknowledgment of the Palestinian return is seen as an acceptance of the fact that the Palestinians have suffered significant injustice in their displacement and have a natural right to live in their ancestral land.[13] Nadim Rouhana and Areej Sabbagh-Khoury have characterized the past twenty years as the "return of history" in Palestinian citizens' collective consciousness, referring to the understanding that the 1948 Nakba has completely shaped their collective history and their social-political lives.[14] In May 2019 the High Follow-Up Committee for Arab Affairs and the Association for the Defense of the Rights of the Internally Displaced (ADRID) arranged a mass popular Return march to Bilad al-Ruha on Israel's Independence Day to commemorate the Nakba. Yet, in Oasis Grove, the dispossessed land was not only reclaimed but it was going to be cultivated again with olive trees (image 17), and it had a future of an international market through fair trade alternative globalization circles and Jewish-Palestinian solidarity work.[15]

Other speeches were full of pathos and were delivered mainly in Arabic, a little in Hebrew, and some English for the Italian fair trade NGO partner who helped sponsor the foundation of the new grove. Sindyanna NGO is unusual among local left-leaning organizations in Israel as it dis-

IMAGE 17. Oasis Grove planting ceremony. Photograph by Erez Wagner.

rupts language hegemony.[16] The NGO's Jewish activists are invested in achieving comprehensive Arabic language skills, and their community supporters' events are often held in Arabic without significant translation into Hebrew, an act that challenges the status quo. Speakers were celebrating the reclaiming of land, olive agriculture, and the Arab-Jewish and international solidarity that supports this endeavor. The event was also remarkable for the number of leading women activists who spoke both Palestinian and Jewish, as well as for the two significant speeches delivered by children of the Younis family, which made everyone smile as the future generation spoke about land, belonging, and solidarity. The crowd at the event numbered some seventy people, including representatives of the Younis family and Palestinian and Jewish supporters of the NGO from the Triangle, Galilee, Haifa, and Jerusalem who arrived independently. A busload of supporters also arrived from Tel Aviv. They were excited to plant new olive trees together on a cool spring day.

Collaborative agrarian work involving olive grove harvesting and planting has become a prevalent mode of expressing political solidarity with Palestinians, usually in the Occupied Palestinian Territories.[17] Planting is an embodied practice of rooting in the land and of place-making; it embodies long-term care for the land and is an act of tending for a sustainable future. Planting is a pivotal practice in the nation-making activities of Israelis and Palestinians,[18] but it is usually undertaken separately by the two groups. However, in al-Ruha it was performed together as participants planted Israeli Barnea olive saplings and the Italian Co-ratina cultivar, both designated for industrial cultivation in an act that dissolved the binaries and boundaries between settlers and natives. Moghira observed the event from the side. With his calm and quiet demeanor, he spoke publicly about the technical elements of the new agrarian operation. I was curious about Moghira's position as he discursively focused on the technical as if he was almost a bystander rather than a visionary. At this unusual event, Moghira was a liminal actor.

At that time, I did not recognize the extent to which he and other Palestinian agronomists occupy a particular timescape between their society and the Jewish-Israeli society. His creation of a "native mode of being," becoming and experiencing social significance and social time through intersections of Western science and Palestinian social situatedness, became evident to me only later.[19] An agricultural endeavor like Moghira's partnership with Sindyanna is unique. Yet, as I talked with more Palestinian Arab agronomists who worked for the Ministry of Agriculture, I found that all of them use their professional expertise creatively, initiating personal and public endeavors that contest the status quo of the Ministry of Agriculture's policies and temporalities. These initiatives are characterized by a polychronic and nonbinary timescape, embracing multiple temporalities by bringing together Western socio-technical expertise and science agendas with Palestinian traditional and new societal structures, timescapes, and situatedness.[20]

This chapter examines the timescapes, practices, and agrarian imaginaries of Palestinian agronomists working for the Israeli state to observe the possibilities of self-determination that their actions entail and the challenges encapsulated by such practices. Scholarship on the incorporation of marginalized citizens in the state system that dispossessed them often describes minority group bureaucrats as put under harsh constraints. This literature criticizes turning indigenous or minority groups into disciplined state servants, leaving them little room to contest social hierarchies.[21] Palestinian agricultural professionals working for the Israeli state experience various challenges and see inequality in agriculture through their work. Although they cannot close the gap through their bureaucratic encounters in state work and may even strengthen the state system during their working hours,[22] they contest the social order through their free-time activities or after they retire. Thus, these agronomists undermine an exclusionary system that has contributed to the demise of Palestinian agriculture. In their after-work activities, they show that "free time" is a crucial resource for people, no less than employment, income, or wealth, because it allows them to pursue their goals.[23] Hence, free-time activity offers a glimpse into professionals' mundane and ordinary resistance to power structures that they cannot easily express during work hours. By attending to the free time and retirement activities of these professionals alongside their work narratives, I reorient the discussion on minority and native professionals' strategies of coping in the state system and point out their mundane modes of resistance, which have been invisible to the research community so far.

Through an examination of the views and practices of these agronomists, I highlight a perspective that is often unmentioned in indigenous/settler colonial studies and Middle Eastern studies: the perspective of the native population's scientific experts, as opposed to that of the colonial agrarian-environmental scientific community.[24] As a group, Palestinian Arab scientists and educated professionals are predominantly absent from the historical and ethnographic record of Israel/Palestine, and scholars have only recently begun to address this social stratum.[25] This record has been dominated for decades by Zionist accounts of traditional Arab society versus Zionist modernity and expertise in science, technology, and agronomy.[26] Palestinian agronomists' narrations of their work and after-work activities are thought-provoking because their profession ties them to the core issues of space and time-making in the settler colonial encounter and to broader situated knowledge of native middle and upper rural class in colonial and imperial contexts.[27] Their stories shed light on the possibilities and difficulties of altering existing realities through the position of native scientific experts working for the settler state and their polychronic native mode of "being in time."[28]

Oasis Grove Agricultural Cooperation Endeavor

Since the Oasis Grove agricultural area was too exposed to the wind and sun, the social activities following speeches were held nearby in the small pine forest that the JNF had planted in the past. This pine forest, like many others in Israel/Palestine, is a part of the JNF's afforestation efforts to claim the land as belonging to the Jewish collectivity and block the expansion of Palestinian towns in Israel. Irus Braverman analyzed the opposing tree landscapes of Jewish pines and Palestinian olives as "planted flags" in the landscape.[29] Seeing Palestinian and Jewish families play and cook together in the JNF forest was bittersweet.

After the celebrations, I engaged in a conversation with Moghira to learn about this agricultural operation. He told me that the partnership between the NGO and the family's company al-Juthoor included a sublease of half the family's land, fifty dunums, to the NGO for twenty years. The NGO economically invested in the agricultural operation of developing an organic olive grove from scratch. It included paying one of Moghira's uncles for the preparation of land that was not cultivated for decades, and then using an industrial olive farming technique to plant it, with little distance between trees, and finally buying seedlings of Barnea and Coratina olive varieties—suitable for irrigation and mechanized harvest. Planting the grove with Barnea olive trees, the development of Israeli science in olive agriculture, and the Italian Coratina variety stood out as an uncommon choice among Palestinians in contrast to the prevalent *baladi* (Arabic, local to the land) cultivars, Souri and Nabali.[30] Integrating the industrialized varieties in the al-Ruha reclaimed family land reflected the importance of economic profit and modernized agriculture for Moghira and Sindyanna of Galilee.

Pulling up water and pumping it through irrigation infrastructure to the Oasis Olive Grove on the hill was a costly aspect of the operation. The water was supplied by the quota the Younis family has had through the water cooperative al-Amahl since the 1960s. Dr. Hisham Yunis, a relative of Moghira's and one of the first Palestinian employees of the Ministry of Agriculture, told me that their family's early water allocation quota was the result of good relations with the neighboring kibbutzim of Hashomer Hatzair and their pressure on the military regime to support their good neighbor relations by allocating water quotas to their Arab neighbors. In general, Palestinians in the Triangle area have more agricultural irrigation quotas than in other Palestinian regions in Israel. Most explanations point to the 1960s ties between Triangle residents and the Left Zionist parties of Mapai (Labor Party) and Mapam (United Workers

Party affiliated with Hashomer Hatzair Socialist Movement) as well as the central geographic location of the Triangle in comparison to Palestinian peripheries in the Negev/Naqab and Galilee.[31]

Going back to this operation as explained by Moghira, once the trees produce olives, the fruit is taken to an organic olive mill and is marketed through the fair trade channels that Sindyanna NGO works with globally. The minimum price of the olive oil is agreed upon beforehand as common both in fair trade agreements and in the olive oil market in historic Palestine, thus ensuring the cultivators are paid enough that they can plan investments regardless of market fluctuations.[32] As a part of their agreement, the Younis family was the sole caretaker of the whole agricultural operation, thus ensuring their independence and sovereignty over the agrarian process. Additionally, from the grove's planting in 2010 until 2018, when the NGO began developing additional lands, the NGO has been gathering its supporters every year in the Oasis Olive Grove. The NGO volunteers participate in various agricultural tasks such as weeding, a time-consuming manual task of organic agriculture, or manual harvesting with olive rakes when the trees bear fruit. Additionally, they purchased a chain mower that sustains organic fertilizing of the soil and prevents erosion.

Although the al-Ruha terrain was suitable for a mechanized harvester once the trees began to produce a bounty of fruit, the act of manual harvest is performed as a means of promoting cooperative Jewish-Palestinian work during the harvest season. The manual harvest preserves one of the logics of traditional agriculture, whereas the harvest season is not only the most labor-intensive time of olive cultivation but also a time of community, sociality, collective identity formation, and festivities in the olive groves. Here, combining mechanized and manual harvest in olive growing manifests the harvest timescape as a time for both economic objectives as well as societal exchanges and engagements. In this way, Oasis Grove conserves the labor and harvest rationale of an indigenous peasantry as task-oriented but allowing both social time and labor time.[33] These annual meetings in al-Ruha fostered a socioecological time of Jewish-Palestinian solidarity.

The profits of the olive oil sales through the fair trade market support the payments to the family members who work at the operation, allow the family investment in the development of additional land, and facilitate additional employment opportunities for Palestinian women employed by Sindyanna in their various endeavors, which is a major goal of the NGO.

The fact that the family agreed to sublease their land to an NGO represented by a Jewish CEO, Hadas Lahav, could have raised eyebrows, considering how fragile questions of land ownership are in the context of Jewish-Palestinian land dynamics. NGOs have played questionable roles in dubious land deals in Israel/Palestine over the years.[34] Moghira told me, "I don't think there is a problem with such land leasing agreements when they are signed by lawyers, and one understands the meaning of such lease. I know there are people here that would think that after the agreement term is over, the Jews will not return the . . ." He did not complete his sentence, perhaps contemplating but not expressing all the times that Jewish Israelis have not returned Palestinian land. He continued by saying, "But we do have trust." Moghira knew Hadas Lahav's activity in the olive sector working to enhance Palestinian Arab agrarian production for eighteen years (during our conversation in 2013). The economic benefit from this agrarian operation for his extended family was significant. The family initiated an agricultural endeavor that brought practically fallow, confiscated land into the fair trade market.[35] Considering how many Palestinian families in Israel are either abandoning their small agricultural parcels or are stuck with the olive oil of previous years, having a global market for their produce from the very beginning is an achievement that marked a timescape of progression rather than the market incongruency that other Palestinian interlocutors discussed.[36] For the NGO, on the other hand, this was a means of ensuring accountability for the quality of its olive oil product. Achieving the international standards of organic certification for its olive oil was an issue the NGO had struggled with for years when it worked with several Palestinian smallholders. Here, the two sides of this agrarian operation were pleased with this endeavor.

As Moghira illustrated the story of his endeavor, multiple brush strokes of time had emerged and colored the oasis timescape: a Palestinian family's reclaimed and returned agrarian land and legacy, a fair trade market temporality—repositioning the producer's socio-political conditions while reaching international markets. This grove also encapsulated a sociotechnical vision of futurity using industrialized cultivars, those created by Zionist modernist sociotechnical imaginaries.[37] Hence the al-Juthoor Younis family agrarian company project and its collaboration with Sindyanna of Galilee NGO enlivened and regenerated the Palestinian family's agriculture. This project had significant implications for sustaining the Palestinian family's spatial, temporal, and political continuity and identity.

Pre-1948 Timescape and Imaginaries

Over six years, Moghira's and my paths crossed in Roha land for various agricultural activities organized by the Sindyanna NGO as well as in my fieldwork at the Ministry of Agriculture and olive science meetings in the Faculty of Agronomy of the Hebrew University. In February 2013 we met to converse about the agricultural development initiative in al-Ruha. I was curious to learn about his family's decision to avoid dividing land among heirs, a major contemporary obstacle to Palestinian cultivators. Moghira told me: "There's a problem. It is difficult to find today in Arab families brothers and sisters that have enough land you could amalgamate—I mean, you could find only a few. The Younis family, before '48, had thousands of dunums. If you look from 'Ara to Haifa, these are our lands. Yes, before '48 we had forty thousand dunums, before '48 . . ."

I asked if all the land was appropriated in 1948 or if there were more recent state confiscations.

Moghira said, "Confiscations, land exchanges, elections, all these sorts of things. You," addressing me in the plural for being Jewish Israeli and giving me an ironic smile for this, "you exchange ten dunums for one, right?"

I laughed bitterly.

Moghira continued, "So it is hard for me to believe that people have any land reserve that they can work with and consolidate into a big parcel. Only when I think about the situation here, there is not much to work with, except working maybe as they do in the [West] Bank, consolidating marketing efforts." Moghira's descriptions of time and space had the effect of incorporating pre-1948 Palestinian landholding imaginaries

into agricultural models of the West Bank, thereby creating a continuous Palestinian identity and imaginary in time and space.[38] His reference
to marketing consolidation efforts alluded to contemporary West Bank
endeavors of fair trade cooperative marketing rather than the Zionist
collective models. Indeed, land tenure patterns among Palestinians in
the West Bank and in Israel remain similar, whereas Jewish land tenure
differs significantly. Moghira's timescape highlights that the continuous governmental efforts to discipline and reorder Palestinian political
memory and thought have had little effect.[39] The Palestinian gaze—even
of a long-time employee of the Ministry of Agriculture—refuses to erase
the timescape of pre-1948 Palestine in terms of landholding, as well as
the Palestinian community's spatial, temporal, and political continuity
and identity.

The land ownership figures that Moghira shares of his family's past
holding situate them among the wealthy upper-rural-class inhabitants of
historic Palestine. However, in recent generations, many family members
were schoolteachers, he shared with me. Yet, in British government surveys of land ownership in Palestine during the 1930s, only 0.01 percent of
the population held more than 5,000 dunums. Instead, 91.8 percent of the
population held 0–100 dunums, implying that most of Palestine's population was landless or did not have sufficient land to make ends meet and
thus were employed on other people's land, often as sharecroppers. The
large landowning class in Palestine held estates of 100–1,000 dunums,
and they comprised only 8 percent of the population.[40] These figures illustrate that although the Palestinian peasant became a national signifier for the Palestinians in the context of their struggle for liberation, the
reality of many of those peasants was deep poverty.[41] Nevertheless, Palestinian refugees noted that village life in historic Palestine regardless
of its difficulties and poverty was "a paradise" in comparison to living as
refugees or exiles.[42] But Moghira's timescape was not simply nostalgia
for village life; it also referred to a time when his family was a part of the
elite of Palestine's rural areas.

Moreover, Moghira's timescape was of a Palestinian Arab agrarian
family unit producing together. Moghira told me that the Younis brothers, sisters, and uncles meet in what was his grandmother's home after
the Friday noon prayer, incorporating Muslim prayer time as a marker

for the family dynamic to discuss issues related to al-Juthoor financial investments. They are undertaking a bigger plan to develop more organic agriculture for export—a family-based economic development program integrated into a global market endeavor. Moghira described a model like the Palestinian peasant's family before 1948: a family collective that encompasses the economic aspects of both consumption and production, pooling labor, income, and material aid when needed as well as being a moral unit of solidarity and collective consciousness.[43] Moghira's story was partially unlike that of other Palestinian agronomists in describing an active extended family as an economic production unit. Other interlocutors described mainly family land leasing and family mutual loans for agricultural development.[44] However, Moghira's story was a characteristic Palestinian agronomist story in referring to the land his family had held before 1948. Most of the Palestinian agronomists I interviewed who have worked for the state told their agrarian identity story as based on a family agrarian lineage, which commonly referred to their grandparents' or parents' agrarian work and holdings before 1948. In comparison, although many of the Jewish employees of the Ministry of Agriculture were members or descendants of the cooperative agrarian communities in Israel such as moshavim or kibbutzim, they rarely mentioned the intergenerational aspect of their continuous interest in agriculture.

The link between the family's extensive pre-1948 agrarian holdings and the future of their agriculture was created by the al-Juthoor company, which reclaimed the family's agricultural wealth through the newly established industrialized and socially supported Oasis Grove. Aside from other Palestinian agronomists' enterprises, mainly those who work or have worked in the Ministry of Agriculture, there is no equivalent industrial and organically certified olive grove operation by Palestinians in Israel.[45] As I have shown elsewhere, no state body or non-state organization advanced the organic certification of Palestinian olive oil in Israel aside from Sindyanna. Arguably, achieving organic certification should not have been too difficult for Palestinian producers if they had agricultural extension (instruction) services. Many Palestinian agriculturalists have lamented the decrease over the years in agricultural extension services in Israel and its implications for Palestinian agriculturalists.[46] More extension services might have enabled more of their agricultural produce to reach the market.[47] The agricultural innovation of this endeavor in the sociotechnical and political-economic landscape of Palestinian Arab agriculture in Israel was evident. Moghira's choice to develop a Palestinian industrialized agricultural operation was an act of continuing a family heritage embedded in agriculture and a means of insisting on Western science and technology in the Palestinian family's olive grove. Here too, science and technological systems were embedded in sociocultural imaginations of a promising future considering the past and the present moment.[48] Thus, in Moghira's endeavor, the Palestinian family as an intergenerational and traditional moral and economic unit does not contradict science, technology, and other Western benchmarks of progress. Rather, the Palestinian family's agricultural unit peacefully exists alongside all these temporal and social designations without destroying previous development models.

The stories here illustrate the timescape that prevails in the agrarian imaginary and practice of Moghira's endeavor. His actions are embedded in an inherited social tradition, a political consciousness of historic Palestine that is situated within a contemporary industrialized agrarian operation, a family agribusiness on reclaimed land with the financial and market collaboration of a fair trade Jewish-Palestinian NGO. Given the history of agrarian dispossession and the resulting suspicion between Palestinians and Jewish Israelis as well as the diversion of Palestinians to every occupation but the agrarian one in Israel, this endeavor seems extraordinary. Is this what it takes to be a Palestinian agronomist in the Israeli state system? What sorts of trajectories and mechanisms of coping are put in place to survive this system?

The Scientific-Modern Self

"Write it down that this is what I am telling you," Dr. Hisham Yunis told me fiercely. "We are not socially organized in anything," referring to Palestinian Arab communities' agriculture in Israel. "In my work, I reached in twenty years a transformation of Arab agriculture from extensive and poor to intensive, and I achieved that the agriculturalist would believe me that he is buying fertilizer, not soil." Dr. Yunis was one of the first Palestinian Arab employees of the Ministry of Agriculture, where he worked from the 1960s until his retirement in 2007. He told me that he saw his work in the ministry over the decades as dedicated to the modernization process of Arab agriculture. He said both humorously and ironically that this was "Arab Zionism," using *Zionism* in the sense of patriotism and being a pioneer for his society (or perhaps he assumed that referring to Zionism when speaking to a Jewish Israeli would illustrate his dedication to his society's collective objectives). We were sitting together in his *hakura* (traditional Palestinian domestic garden)[49] in the village/town of 'Ara in the Triangle in February 2013 to discuss Palestinian Arab agriculture. I had met him earlier during my fieldwork in the Ministry of Agriculture's planning meetings.

Dr. Yunis was recruited to the Ministry of Agriculture as a graduate of Kadoorie Agricultural High School, a prestigious agricultural school established during the British Mandate.[50] Kadoorie High School by Mount Tabor became an emblem of Israeli education, attended by leaders of the 1948 Zionist generation such as Yitzhak Rabin, Yigal Alon, and the new Israeli state leadership, a generation seen by Jewish-Israelis until today as the salt of the earth. It was with much pride that Dr. Yunis told me of his education in Kadoorie. Kadoorie also meant social prestige and mobility for its few Palestinian Arab students. Palestinian Arab youth of significant landowning families were accepted to the Zionist agricultural schools such as Kadoorie or Mikveh Israel in the early state days.[51] Some of them ended up working for the Ministry of Agriculture starting in the 1960s. Many of the comments and stories that Dr. Yunis has shared with me were related to his generational location. During our interview in 2013, he was in his mid-seventies. He grew up during the years of the military regime and experienced the repression that Palestinian citizens went through during those years.[52] He was witty, opinionated, and critical of both Jewish-Israeli and Palestinian societies.[53]

Dr. Yunis earned his academic degrees and developed his professional career with the support of the state system. His academic formation was sponsored by the state, and he received stipends for his studies as an employee of the Ministry of Agriculture through an education trajectory that aimed to support higher education for state servants who had no degrees. Scientific education is one of the institutional mechanisms that the state puts in place to create coherence among its employees. He

started his career at the Ministry of Agriculture as an extension instructor for Arab villages in the 1960s in his early twenties. He continued as
a plant protection specialist and completed a Ph.D. in plant pathology
from the Hebrew University in 1990 as well as a postdoc from the University of California, Davis, in 1992. In his last fifteen years of work in
the Ministry of Agriculture, he became the national extension specialist
for vegetables and the cultivation of herbs. The industrial cultivation of
herbs was new in the 1990s, and much work was needed to supervise
various diseases related to it. His trajectory of academic education in the
agrarian sciences is exceptional in comparison to the lack of agronomic
higher education in Palestinian society in Israel for decades.[54]

In contrast to the noticeable rise of Palestinian citizens' participation
and graduation in higher education, the field of agronomy and its related
sciences do not attract Palestinian youth, a fact easily associated with
the social and political processes that led to the demise of Palestinian
agriculture in Israel and the declining status of the agrarian profession.[55]
Over the last century, agriculture for Israeli Jews has been a social value
and a social program that came with much funding and a passion for
agrarian higher education. For Palestinian citizens, the case is reversed.[56]
Even though there are a few Palestinian Arab experts at the top of the
Israeli Ministry of Agriculture,[57] their presence in the agrarian sciences
is the exception rather than the norm. An examination in 2017 of the
leading agricultural research institutions' websites found that 1.2 percent
of the researchers in the Faculty of Agronomy of the Hebrew University
in Rehovoth were Palestinian Arabs and 3.7 percent of the employees of
the Volcani Agricultural Research Organization of the Ministry of Agriculture were Arabs, including all ranks of employees from technicians
to professors. These are very low numbers in comparison to the employment of Palestinian professionals in other state institutions, which was
6.5 percent in 2007 and 12.2 percent by 2019. As Palestinian citizens are
approximately 20 percent of the Israeli population, these numbers indicate significant underrepresentation in the state system.[58] In my visits to
the Faculty of Agronomy at the Hebrew University, the leading local institution training professionals in the fields of agriculture, I noticed that
the Arabic language is not heard, a stark difference from other Israeli
universities' campuses, where Arabic is heard frequently. In contrast, in

the social sciences and humanities departments at Israeli universities, Palestinian scholars are succeeding in promoting a critical agenda and are shifting the sociology of knowledge about Israel/Palestine.[59] But in other highly professional fields of both the public and private sectors such as medicine, private law firms, and technology, this critical rhetoric is not present, as success in these fields often demands that Palestinian individuals depoliticize and assimilate.[60]

Anthropologist Kim TallBear claims that, in North America, indigenous peoples are expanding their governance participation through their growing share in cultures of techno-science. She suggests that through their increasing involvement in biosciences, indigenous people are shifting research priorities, ethics, and the benefits of academic research.[61] However, these dynamics seem to be only partially true in the context of Israel/Palestine. Dr. Yunis's extensive career narrative only somewhat resonates with TallBear's claim. When Dr. Yunis told me about his academic achievements and professional growth process, he contested the prevalent view that Arabs are "traditional" and "conservative," but he did not share radical experiences of shifting institutional agendas. He talked about the best scientific research practices designated to develop professionally and to serve the Ministry of Agriculture's wider scientific challenges. But his public recognition as an established agronomist also afforded him an advising role at the policy table, thus allowing Jamal Medlege, the minorities referent at the Ministry of Agriculture to invite Dr. Yunis to the discussion table when national policy plans were examined. Scientific training thus creates a time of authority. It allowed Dr. Yunis to expand governance participation, not necessarily by contesting policies but by being recognized as a legitimate shareholder where decisions are being made. Edward Said wrote that "for much of its modern history, Palestine and its native people have been subject to denials of a very rigorous sort. . . . The Zionists convinced themselves that these natives did not exist, then made it possible for them to exist only in the most rarefied forms."[62] The authority of Western agronomy science contests the continuous erasure that Palestinians have experienced for generations, at least at the individual professional level.

Moghira Younis voiced a similar professional standpoint, although he is twenty years younger. As opposed to his relative Hisham Yunis, whose training was supported by state channels, Moghira's academic training was undertaken in Germany, where he completed his bachelor's and master's degrees in agronomy, returning to his hometown of 'Ara in 1995. He first worked as an extension specialist serving Bedouin cultivators in the Naqab/Negev township of Rahat in what was back then a new governmental development program for the cultivation of roses in greenhouses. After the economic collapse of the agricultural export of flowers from Israel, Moghira saw the opportunity to develop professionally in grove agricultural production. In 2002 he became a regional extension specialist in the Central District of the Ministry of Agriculture, where he mostly has been working with Jewish cultivators. At that time, he also became the olive extension specialist for Arab agriculturalists in all of Israel proper, responding to a time of political instability and violence in which his Jewish colleagues feared instructing in Arab localities during the second Intifada (Palestinian popular uprising). This appointment illustrates how Palestinian professionals' careers are sometimes shaped by eruptions of spectacular violence, determining their spatiotemporal work mobilities.[63] The settler society's fear of entering a Palestinian Arab locality becomes an indirect spatiotemporal disciplining practice. Palestinian professionals are required to pay the price of settlers' fear through the time they spend driving.[64] Instead of working close to his residence in the Ministry's Center District, Moghira drove north to serve Palestinian Arab olive growers.

The expert native is then not devoid of social situatedness for the state. Yet for him, the professional scientific self sometimes trumps the socially situated one.[65] Moghira's views on the professional benefits he has seen in instructing Jewish agriculturalists versus Palestinian Arab agriculturalists in olive agriculture were strong.[66] Moghira saw Jewish agriculturalists as organized and consistent in their agricultural work and therefore easier to develop scientific research with. Developing research was key to his own professional development.[67] Thinking about his view through a politics of time and coevalness, this perspective resonated with a European gaze on the Middle East as a place of imprecision and tradition. Such views also echoed discourses that Jewish officials have used regarding Palestinian peasants for decades. These science-based time discourses illustrate that the temporal structure of

Western science that emphasizes universality, punctuality, progress, and productivity locates the native science expert in a higher hierarchical position toward their own society. Professionalism becomes a way of class-making. Professional training abroad becomes a site where Palestinian elites temporally distinguish themselves from their own society in agriculture and beyond.[68]

However, a class dynamic is nothing new in the history of rural Palestine. Rather, internal fissures and tensions characterized the rural Palestinian society well before it was subject to European colonization, both British and Zionist. The differentiation between a rural class that owned landholdings and agricultural businesses and trade created a dynamic resembling class struggle in the rural areas in nineteenth-century Palestine.[69] Contemporaneously, the Palestinian experts and scientists I have met are not only descendants of the rural middle and upper classes, but their scientific education and training grant them another resource, creating class distinction among Palestinian agriculture practitioners, as in other spheres where education implies class.[70]

Then, much of the social importance and the benefits of the two Younis family members' scientific expertise stem from their ability to claim expert authority and status within the agrarian establishment. Both have been invited to take part in various decision-making processes in their agricultural professional fields.[71] Yet, their academic-scientific training does not seem to transform scientific inquiry in ways that serve Palestinian Arab agriculture at large. It might be that, like other minority bureaucrats, they are cautious about how much they can push an institution to change, or they have much to lose in trying to shift priorities. After all, the Israeli establishment has been a hostile environment for members of their communities for decades. Moreover, claiming they have not been successful in expanding the benefits of science to encompass Palestinian agriculturalists in Israel does not undermine the importance of diversifying science and state institutions. But the question of the bureaucratic structure and its knowledge backbone is of no less importance. Is it legitimate for a Palestinian Arab employee of the Ministry of Agriculture to shift the institute's agenda and the culture of science itself? It might be the case that the answer is no, as many agrarian endeavors undertaken by Palestinian workers in the Ministry of Agriculture take place in their free time.

De-politicizing State Work

Dr. Hisham Yunis mentioned in our conversation that he felt that the Ministry of Agriculture was at no time a particularly discriminatory state office, but rather a ministry that never developed a clear policy toward Arab agriculture. He believed that what he and other extension service officials did and initiated would happen. It was a personal narrative of entrepreneurship that undermined the role of the state institution in the social history of Palestinian dispossession and surveillance.[72] He was proud of his past endeavors to bring more technology to Palestinian Arab agriculture and villages. In many ways, his personal narrative aligned with the state's account of the contribution of the Israeli state to the Palestinian peasant. His narrative resonated with the Zionist account of "transforming the fellah to a farmer," delivering modernization and ceasing subsistence farming.[73] His blurring of the role of the Ministry of Agriculture in historical dispossession began hinting at the techniques needed to survive in the system.

Mustafa Natour, born in 1936, was a colleague of Dr. Hisham Yunis from his generation in the Ministry of Agriculture. He was also educated at the Kadoorie Agricultural High School and started working at the Ministry of Agriculture in 1961 as an instructor for vegetable cultivation in the Hadera district, later became an instructor in the Nazareth district, and then a manager of the Nazareth district. In the early years of his work, he attended to mainly Palestinian Arab growers. From the mid-1980s until his early retirement in 1997, he was an economist working nationally with all growers through the Department of the Agrarian Production Economy. He became a senior advisor to the first Palestinian deputy minister of agriculture Walid Sadik in 1992–1994 during the term of Prime Minister Yitzhak Rabin, considered by many Palestinian citizens the golden age of Palestinian citizen–state relations.[74]

I met Mustafa in his home in Nazareth in 2013, and we kept corresponding over the years. Mustafa said similar things: that a comprehensive development policy regarding Arab agriculture was absent and that comprehensive plans were never implemented but there was freedom to act. He talked humbly about his achievements at the ministry, emphasizing that they were collective efforts and related to accomplishments aimed at modernizing Palestinian agriculture during the 1960s–1970s. Among the ones he mentioned were instructing Palestinian agriculturalists in the Triangle to change from rain-fed agriculture to irrigated agriculture, instilling the use of new cultivars appropriate for irrigation, instructing about the efficient use of pesticides and fertilizers, and increasing the correct use of manual and mechanical agricultural tools. He proudly talked about instructing agriculturalists to cultivate high-yield wheat varieties. In Galilee, he and his colleagues disseminated the cultivation of sugar beets, tomatoes for industry, and onions for export and seeds, as well as assisting in organizing the marketing and the transportation of products from many smallholders to markets. According to Mustafa, these were efforts of significant socioeconomic contribution and were undertaken in rain-fed conditions, thus demonstrating dedicated agrarian development work adapted both to rationales of water allocation and water scarcity, or more commonly for Palestinians, water deprivation.

His successes can be seen as the work of a local Green Revolution in agriculture, transferring technologies and knowledge to Palestinian agriculturalists and turning from subsistence farming to industrialized modes of agriculture. Viewing these efforts today with the changing climate in mind, one may question their sustainability given the loss of knowledge and know-how of agriculture that is well adapted to the local climate and resilient in the face of droughts. Rain-fed smallholders' agriculture was not sufficiently appreciated at the time as the agrarian modernization fervor seemed central in professionals' views, but in the last twenty years, agroecology has repositioned the importance of conserving such modes of agriculture in the face of future agri-food-system threats such as extreme droughts predicted for the Middle East.[75]

Yet, as I have shown throughout this book, discrimination in the allocation of production resources such as water and land are the defining experience of Palestinian agriculturalists and experts. Thus, despite the successes of his agrarian development efforts, Natour said that he had not been able to change the distortion of agrarian water allocation dominating Arab agriculture or to overcome the bureaucratic barriers to advance the drainage of al-Battuf. He also shared that when he was a consultant to Deputy Agriculture Minister Walid Sadik, they were unable to fulfill Sadik's great passion for the development of Arab agriculture, mainly due to competition and politics between the deputy minister (Mapam Party) and the minister (Mapai Party). After a year and a half as a consultant, he returned to his professional unit at the Ministry of Agriculture, and soon after, he retired.

Natour's and Yunis's statements indicate the role of specifically motivated people in large, bureaucratic state institutions as actors and agents. But these statements also imply that the "laissez-faire" policy that the Palestinian Arab agricultural experts saw was, in fact, a tool in a policy of abandonment and a comparative de-development toward Palestinian agriculture that was prevalent for decades. By *de-development*, I refer to a term coined by Sara Roy addressing a process that weakens the ability of an economy to grow by preventing it from accessing and utilizing critical inputs needed to promote internal growth. Water, scientific knowledge, technologies, and agrarian land are some of the examples that I have illustrated throughout the book as resources withheld from Palestinian agriculture.[76] "No-policy" then becomes an intentional abandonment project and a comparative de-development policy when contrasted to the great investment project that the agricultural and rural Zionist countryside was for the Israeli state. The Palestinians were at no point developmental subjects for the Zionist movement and state.[77]

Mustafa said that when there were disputes about what was going on, everyone used to blame the agriculturalists for the situation, a phenomenon that I saw in my fieldwork too when Palestinian agriculturalists were accused of their conservative character and unwillingness to accept change. Mustafa detailed an example of no-policy with the case of the recent investments in olive agriculture that took place after he retired. He said calmly:

A couple of years ago they decided to invest in water-efficient cultivars here such as olives and almonds. They said the state would sponsor 25 percent of the investment, including the preparation of land for planting, the water infrastructure, the purchase of saplings . . . everything. But they put two conditions on the subsidy scheme: each sponsored operation requires the agriculturalist to invest a minimum of 25,000 NIS per unit and the developer must have a veteran tax revenue account. But 99 percent of Arab agriculturalists do not have enough land to enable this sum of investment. The land was appropriated or divided upon inheritance. Moreover, the Tax Authority does not want the headache of starting to work with an agriculturalist whose financial activity is smaller than 50,000–60,000 NIS. So, they decided on policy conditions that immediately remove the Arab agriculturalists from the subsidy game. They need to acknowledge it and enable subsidy conditions that will be suitable for Arab agriculture too.

Mustafa described agrarian neglect as a lack of recognition of difference and as a fixable matter rather than an intentional policy. He saw the de-development currently happening, but his articulation of it was not belligerent.

My excavation through the Ministry of Agriculture's policy plans from the 1980s until recent years revealed how de-development is expressed through the policy paper. While there was often a policy goal of "developing Arab agriculture" or "developing minority agriculture" in the Ministry of Agriculture's planning goals, this goal was typically devoid of meaning as the policy had no detailed plan in the Planning Authority's documents in contrast to detailed plans for the allocation of resources for Jewish-Israeli cooperative agriculture. For instance, in 1996 the plan stated that one of its goals was "to promote the agrarian-rural Arab farms that have known many years of relative backwardness," but the rest of the document said nothing regarding the fulfillment of this objective.[78]

In another instance I asked Moghira Younis how he felt working in the Ministry of Agriculture, and he said, "It is just a workplace to provide income. It is not the army or the police.[79] It's like any other governmental institution where Arabs work. It is like being a teacher or a doctor. My Jewish colleagues treat this as plain work and not any Zionism or anything like this." Moghira's comparative view of the agrarian field as equivalent to a presumably universal school education or the medical profession as purely civic occupations without any struggle behind them depoliticized and denationalized the charged significance of agriculture in Israel/Palestine. He preferred to put aside that agriculture and the rural areas have been central objects of colonization and dispossession. His statement was remarkable—as if there was almost no space nor time for the political implications of agricultural work but only the present tense of existing and working in a neutral context. The present seemed to offer a safer space for a Palestinian agronomist. In a similar vein, the medical profession holds a "shared fiction ethos of neutrality" as Guy Shalev notes, that allows Palestinian Arab citizens to increasingly integrate at Israeli medical institutions. Nonetheless, the ethos of what is neutral versus what is politicized is not equally shared among Palestinian and Jewish citizens. Rather, the neutrality ticket is a survival scheme for Palestinian doctors.[80] Likewise, to be at ease at work, Moghira needed to de-politicize his workplace and make its significance universal, devoid of space and time of conflict and power. That was his way of enacting survivance in agriculture, manifesting Gerald Vizenor's claim that for native people survivance is about renouncing dominance, tragedy, or victimhood but simply surviving in society.[81] Similarly, developers and designers working on Palestinian housing in the West Bank make the barriers they encounter technical or devoid of politics, although they clearly work within a complete political domination matrix, as Kareem Rabie shows.[82] Political pragmatism and repression of the control system seem necessary to survive labor worlds in the settler colonial condition.

In another moment of the conversation, Moghira said that sometimes at his work and in the Israeli public space, people use Zionist arguments and discourse to justify why the state needs to support agriculture in the periphery near the country's borders, but for Moghira this seemed to be only a rhetorical tool to use for pragmatic reasons and nothing more. I pushed back on this view and asked Moghira, "But what about the other side of this agriculture as a practice of *sumud*?" (Arabic, steadfastness or steadfast perseverance). Sumud has become a Palestinian cultural value that developed a broad significance, but its initial meaning was insistently holding onto the land. The term goes back to the British Mandate, but it was popularized during the 1970s as a description of resistance to Israel's occupation. Throughout the years sumud has developed to include active resistance that contests the occupation and is committed to Palestinian collective rights. Today, the popular usage of *sumud* resembles the indigenous insight that to exist in daily life and to live as a Palestinian with dignity and agency is to resist subordination and erasure and makes one a *samid* (the one who practices *sumud*) too. Whereas the term originally illustrated a temporality of patient waiting, holding, and staying, today it illustrates the Palestinian personal-social vital present existing as a struggle and a manifestation of futurity.[83]

Moghira's response to my question related to the initial meaning of sumud. He said hesitantly:

> Maybe the Zionist project has had enough. . . . Maybe returning the land of al-Ruha symbolizes they won't confiscate more, maybe only in the West Bank, but not here. In recent years, if the state needs land, they compensate immediately, as in the development of Road Six. . . .[84] Surprisingly, it feels like the people's enemy in terms of land appropriation is starting to be the town's municipal council and not the state. Maybe in the Naqab this is different and they [the Bedouins] still feel there like we felt here thirty-forty years ago.

Moghira played down the significance of agriculture as politics both by the state and by Palestinian citizens' own resistance through agrarian work.

The weakening of the sense of sumud as a pressing task in the Triangle and Galilee repeatedly came up in conversations I held with Palestinian agronomy experts that were interviewed in 2013-2014. All of them referred to sumud in its initial significance of steadfast holding to the land. Their narrative was different from accounts that I heard earlier when Palestinian agriculturalists in Israel shared stories of continuing in family agriculture for the sense of sumud as guarding the land against state dispossession. Now, questions of holding to the land were defined in economic terms—agricultural lands are important to hold to because these could be potential market assets for housing. The contemporaneous scarcity of land for the construction of residential housing in Palestinian towns in Israel is so severe that agricultural parcels are potential plots for building new homes. But also the refusal to present conscious political stances and the state as an enemy is what safeguards Moghira in his work and practice, and it might explain his bystander position at the Oasis Grove inauguration. He is interested in agriculture as a scientific, professional practice and a family endeavor, but he does not make stark political declarations. Only after more conversation did Moghira begin talking about experiences in which he saw the resource depriva-tion that Palestinian cultivators in Israel suffer. He said,

> Most of my day I don't think about it, but then sometimes it emerges. . . . For instance, I saw in al-Battuf a man who has an olive parcel below the mountain, and he had brought there a water tank that irrigates his seedlings in drip irrigation. And next to him, there is land of the JNF that has water infrastructure irrigating oaks and carobs. All these trees produce landscapes and sustain the land, but one has resources and infrastructure, and one does not. This stands out and it is painful.

Free Time Endeavors and Challenges

Dr. Hisham Yunis told me that after he retired from the Ministry of Agri-culture, he became involved in a variety of activities aimed at developing Arab agriculture. He worked as the principal investigator with MERC (USAID's Middle East Regional Cooperation Fund) for regional programs of agricultural collaboration between Jordan, the Palestinian Authority, and Israel. He also co-initiated two NGOs for the development of Arab agriculture in Israel. One of these NGOs aimed to unite Arab shepherds into a union similar to an existing Jewish-Israeli shepherds' organization (Hebrew, Agudat Hanokdim) that would better represent the interests of Palestinian shepherds. For decades Palestinian shepherds have been seen unfavorably by the state. They have been accused of overgrazing, deforestation, incursion onto "state land," and more.[85] The irony is that following many decades of accusations, the ecological reality boomer-anged back on the state: currently, there is an ecological insight that Is-rael's forests are too dense, easily enabling forest fires instead of what used to be a better-managed forest through the interface of grazing goats and their shepherds.[86] The organization established by Dr. Yunis had, in 2013, more than one hundred registered Palestinian herders of goats and sheep aiming to work collaboratively to grant its members better veterinary care and guidance. They also were using their collaborative buying power to get better prices for agricultural inputs and instruct their members on improved farm and flock management. Yet, Dr. Yunis was frustrated that they were not reaching their goals. Their members' geographic dispersion from the Naqab/Negev to Galilee did not help to create a thriving professional community.

The second NGO that he worked to establish was meant to represent the interests of Palestinian Arab agriculturalists under one of the largest political umbrellas of agriculturalists in Israel, the Israel Farmers' Federation. At the time of our meeting, Dr. Yunis was extremely frustrated by the many social challenges he encountered while working at the grassroots level within Palestinian society. Societal lack of trust and a lack of social organization seemed to hover over decades of Yunis's career and efforts in the Palestinian society in Israel. But when he worked under the state system, he had more authority. He recalled critical responses to his early work both forty years ago and more recently. In the past, when he went to the villages in his role with the Ministry of Agriculture, people would tell him: "Shame on you, you come here with propaganda for the Jews?" To win people's trust, he told me that he eventually sponsored a program to provide Palestinian agriculturalists with fertilizers so that they could experiment and see the results with their own eyes before paying for it themselves. He commented that showing proof of progress and of state investment allowed him to work with agriculturalists.

According to Dr. Yunis, until today "the 'Arab Sector' has had an individualistic mentality," not a collective one. His use of the term *Arab Sector* indicated a governmental articulation of Palestinian citizens' collectivity. He expressed much anguish that Arabs are not imitating positive endeavors they can see around them in agriculture. Dr. Yunis talked about Palestinian Arabs in Israel at some moments as an insider and at other moments as an outsider: "The Arabs expect all the times that others will solve their problems. But kibbutzniks, if a state official told them he won't sponsor their project, they would say, 'We will pay for it,' and the development project will happen but maybe just a bit later. We are not like this." He spoke with bitterness about the efforts to improve the conditions of Palestinian agriculture and all the internal social obstacles he was encountering.

Nevertheless, this was a frustration of a very active man, determined to continue. It seemed that his various projects, from aiming to achieve political representation for cultivators to implementing best practices of agricultural work, were all centered around building collaboration and overcoming social suspicion and distrust. This was all work that the state in Israel had done for its Jewish agriculturalists for decades. Now, in his retirement from his work with the state, Dr. Hisham Yunis spends his time counteracting the state's rationale through his professional training to achieve contemporary agriculture standards for those that the state has labeled traditional. Dr. Yunis looked favorably on the pragmatist ethos of Jewish-Israelis, without much consideration of the social conditions that enabled kibbutzniks to have such "a mentality." Like Dr. Yunis's criticisms of the lack of social organization in Palestinian agriculture in Israel, other Palestinian Arab employees of the Ministry of Agriculture, whether they are presently working there or worked there in the past, voiced the critique of their society's lack of social organization and bad "mentality." At first, I thought of these comments as a healthy social self-critique, but over time I came to realize the charged significance of such speech.

In Israeli agriculture, being organized as a part of a cooperative is built into the institutional logic, bureaucracy, and regulations. In fact, it is the basis of the Zionist agricultural endeavor since the establishment of kibbutzim and moshavim a hundred years ago. Therefore, while cooperatives are discussed in studies of rural areas as a useful mechanism to overcome some of the challenges of the market economy elsewhere in the world,[87] in Israel, rural cooperatives are the backbone of the Zionist rural settlement project. Consequently, a plethora of legal regulations for the countryside refers to cooperatives as a way of receiving governmental support, such as water allocation for irrigation or land, and much of the governmental investment for the development of agriculture is structured around cooperatives. The cooperative system is considered a unique marker of Israeli agriculture, a social characteristic, and a symbol of pride in the "Israeli agricultural success story." Yet, this is a social organizational system incorporated into the law that excludes not only Palestinian Arab agriculturalists but also Jewish urbanites and private smallholder farms. The cooperative system has served for many years as a legal structure that restricted Palestinian citizens' access to state allocation of water or state subsidies. Moreover, such internal social critiques mask the strong social organization that is encapsulated in the Palestinian family unit and village unit.

What are the implications of this narrative when it is used by the same people who could initiate a change in the discourse? Palestinian Arab experts' ideas about social organization echo historical explanations about Palestinian society as less cohesive than Jewish society because it is contains regional rivalries, the urban-rural divide, and other social divisions such as sectarian, class, and clan.[88] However, Palestinians as colonized people were a target of multiple surveillance systems for decades—by the British, the Palestinian National Movement (and its later internal divisions), and most prominently, by the Israeli surveillance mechanisms encircling Palestinian lives.[89] Being constantly under surveillance erodes a society's sense of sovereignty, trust, and social cohesion.[90] In such a reality, trust becomes a scarce social resource, one that would take years to counter and rebuild. As traditional forms of social solidarity and mutual support are declining in Palestinian society in Israel, the need to create alternative forms of social organizing is on the rise. While Palestinian civil society in Israel has seen a remarkable surge of non-governmental organizations in the last thirty years that have advocated for the minority's rights, still the marginalized populations and the elderly are not sufficiently attended to through these organizations.[91] Palestinian agriculturalists are often among underserved populations in rural and semi-urban areas as well as underserved age groups, such as being 60 and older. Furthermore, while agrarian communities in Israel receive some support through municipal services of the regional councils, such social-economic structures do not exist in Palestinian Arab municipalities, which have been weakened for years due to discrimination in resource allocation.[92] Hence, constructing an alternative sphere to social organization and internal trust relations in Palestinian-led agricultural mobilization is not a simple matter and is closely tied to a continuous history of dispossession and the sort of present times and future horizons that can emerge out of such history. Retired Palestinian agriculture experts chose to intervene in this space but were presented with great social difficulties.

They encounter Palestinian agriculturalists who have experienced a "before" that cannot lead to the same future that the kibbutzniks can imagine with the same "after." If trust is a social component that must be earned over time to mobilize action and communication to allow social and political leadership to emerge and succeed, what social-political imaginaries and experiences have Palestinian agriculturalists had that give them a reason to trust? Dr. Yunis wanted to "time-trick";[93] he attempted to modify, bend, and restructure the times we are living in, erasing a history of deprivation. His counter-hegemonic aims clashed with his perhaps naïve view of trust in authority created by many years of work in the Israeli Ministry of Agriculture. Perhaps this was a timescape of social-agrarian possibilities but one that was shortsighted about its contextual limits.

When Mustafa Natour retired from the Ministry of Agriculture, he began to be involved in NGO activities. In 2001 he became the coordinator of the agriculturalists' project with al-Ahali NGO for community development. The NGO aimed to empower and organize Palestinian Arab society in Israel and to achieve equality with the Jewish society. It was founded by a group of activists mainly of the National Democratic Alliance Party which was headed by public intellectual Azmi Bishara. Bishara, a former Israeli parliament member, coined and advocated the party's agenda of transforming the state of Israel into a state of all its citizens and opposing the idea of Israel as a Jewish state. One of the fascinating aspects of Mustafa's activity with al-Ahali then is his close work with vocal counter-hegemonic social-political forces. Perhaps such a position is not what one might have expected from a veteran employee of the state. It might indicate what a pragmatic, versatile, and determined actor Mustafa has been as he cooperated in his professional life with various social and political forces to achieve his professional and personal goals over many years. According to Mustafa, a central aspect of al-Ahali NGO activities was its project for agrarian development and rural women's empowerment.[94] Its agrarian activities focused on improving efficient irrigation water use, planting olives in marginal soils, especially in the Naqab/Negev region among Bedouin communities, and developing marketing initiatives of olive oil and goat milk as well as empowering rural women to run agrarian businesses such as apiaries and producing natural cosmetics. Such activities affect a population overseen by the state system, a smallholder population that is neglected and de-developed by the state.

A noteworthy element of the NGO's work was its collaboration with the Jordanian Ministry of Environmental Protection to assist West Bank Palestinians whose lands remained west of the Segregation/Separation Barrier and who hence experienced greater obstacles to their livelihoods and significant impoverishment. The NGO assisted in disseminating professional knowledge and agrarian technologies to West Bank agriculturalists too, building solidarity networks across Palestinian political statuses of citizenship/non-citizenship in the settler colonial condition. These activities reflect Mustafa's agrarian imaginary as a timescape beyond political borders, situated in the broader Palestine and the broader Middle East. Mustafa developed these activities with a professional team employed by the NGO as well as a group of professional agriculture experts who volunteered. He worked closely with Dr. Fathi Abd el-Hadi, whom he described as a committed colleague in these activities, devoting significant efforts to the NGO's activity without any reimbursement. At this point, Dr. Fathi was no longer working in the Ministry of Agriculture but mainly in the private sector; however, his involvement in these initiatives highlights the political freedom to act after being employed by the state. Other Palestinian Arab state employees told me that during the Jewish holidays when official state work is paused, they go to the Occupied Palestinian Territories to visit agriculturalists there.[95] Therefore, free-time activities are undertaken not only upon retirement or during weekends but also made possible by Jewish tradition time.

In 2008, Mustafa experienced increasing difficulty with a new al-Ahali management and resigned from the NGO. In 2009 he and Dr. Fathi established a new NGO, al-Hawakir (Arabic, plural of *hakura*, the Palestinian traditional domestic garden), transferring the agrarian activity of al-Ahali to al-Hawakir. They expanded the agrarian activity in the West Bank and developed agricultural education programs for Palestinian schools in Israel, looking to educate and create futurity in Palestinian children's interest in agriculture.

Therefore, after-work endeavors such as Moghira's and the retirement activities of Palestinian agronomists and experts working for the state reveal their practices of resistance to the power structures they experience during their work life. By attending to the free-time practices of these professionals, I reorient the discussion on minority and native professionals' strategies for coping with the state system and point out their entrepreneurship as a mode of resistance that has been made invisible both by the state and scholarly accounts. Free-time activity becomes the balancing food for the soul for these professionals who cannot achieve all their personal and professional goals through work-time occupations.

Claiming Agrarian Timescapes

When I sat with Mustafa Natour to discuss Palestinian Arab agriculture past and present, he began our conversation by letting me know he was born in 1936 in the family orchard. He was playing with his keychain and smiling while telling me this. He then showed me his keychain and the two coins on it: one was a mill and the other, half a mill—the currency used in Palestine during the British Mandate, first coined in 1927. He told me that as a young child, he received half-mill coin from his father, who returned from Nablus after he secured a loan to continue developing this citrus orchard. Mustafa keeps the coins in his keychain as a memory, a materialized object of that time, that he touches every day. Mustafa also continues to cultivate in his house a *hakura* where he cultivates close to twenty fruit and citrus trees, a variety of herbs, and some vegetables for the house. He insists his family calls it the *hakura* rather than a garden. The *hakura*, once a prevalent marker of Palestinian domestic ecology, has now transformed significantly and cannot be afforded by many due to increasing water prices or shrinking urban space and changing priorities for garden style.[96] But Mustafa continues cultivating his *hakura* of urban domestic agriculture with the help of his two granddaughters and one grandson who live in the same private house as Mustafa and his wife, but in the floor above them, maintaining a traditional intergenerational Palestinian family residence and environment.[97] These vignettes shed light on the constant work of entangled memory and timescape practice that is at stake in the mundane domestic sphere as well as the agrarian imaginary and the professional practice that Mustafa maintains. At a later moment in our conversation, when I asked Mustafa to share with me his achievements at his work in the ministry, he said that aside from the instruction work achievements, he is proud of completing his work in the ministry in peaceful relations with the agriculturalists, the agrarian instructors, the agrarian organizations, and state institutions. His comment was illuminating in pointing out the various ways Mustafa has been successful in holding together distinct and competing interests, timescapes, imaginaries, and practices and the way they all peacefully cohabit in his imaginary. This is not an easy task.

Over the three years I conducted fieldwork at the Ministry of Agriculture policy meetings, I often noted how the mainstream discourse is oblivious to Palestinian agriculture. I recall that in one of these meetings a state interlocutor talked with pathos about the contemporary importance of agriculture to the security of Israel's borders, Israeli identity, and the legacy and relevance of Zionist rural areas to societal challenges in twenty-first-century Israel. The two Palestinian professionals in the room did not turn a hair. Then, when I think about Mustafa's perception of his social achievement, I imagine the sort of mental work it must have taken to be a Palestinian actor in this agrarian system for close to forty years. But Mustafa's satisfaction with his career as well as his colleagues' stories reflect the internal renouncing of harsh emotions that a Palestinian agronomist must employ to survive the state system. In a similar vein, I met with other Palestinian professionals who had worked in the state system for fifteen or twenty years but had recently moved to the private sector and did not dwell much on the ironies and pains of being a Palestinian professional in these companies or in the state. Such professionals focused on timescapes of economic success and globalized communities of experts working together. But it seemed to me that for some of these actors, the longer they spent outside the state system, the more politicization became evident in their stories. Then to complement this, once people must peacefully live with their work in the state system, they must also renounce some of the internal war that such positions may entail or find the spaces and times that allow them to achieve such peace.

It is in this context that I wish to revisit the stories about Moghira that I have presented throughout this chapter. For many Palestinians, the olive's deep roots in the land and its process of fruiting after a multiyear growing period are symbolic of sumud. What, then, are the metaphorical and material implications of Palestinian experts planting Barnea olive groves, which represent Jewish-Israeli olive agriculture? What is the significance of Palestinian experts planting a cultivar that emerged from the legacy of colonial agronomy and was developed to create an Israeli olive oil industry but ultimately, I claimed, dispossessed Palestinian olive agriculture, becoming a pioneer for a globalized, industrialized olive agriculture? Moghira reconciles his role in these practices by adopting a professional pragmatic attitude employing temporal multiplicity that does not abide by a single linear order but rather a fluid temporal logic.

His practice, I suggest, represents an indigenous mode of being and doing that does not exclude spaces or varieties because of their identities or politics nor does it represent a hybrid way of "being between worlds." Hybridity has different connotations depending on the context in which it is used. Mark Rifkin notes that in the North American settler colonial context, the term *native hybridity* was often used to characterize mixed-blood native people or those who had been educated in white institutions and spaces. In such settler colonial contexts, then, this term holds a racialized and offensive significance.[98] But in a postcolonial context, the term *hybridity* is used by Homi Bhabha to describe movement between cultural worlds and forms that have not previously had expression in a single cultural context. Hybridity is an ongoing negotiation between cultures and the creation of a new world of meaning.[99] Although Moghira operates within a settler colonial political reality, his practice of planting his reclaimed olive grove with Barnea olives resembles the postcolonial understanding of hybridity. It is a practice that upends our political expectations by spanning multiple cultural contexts and worlds. In this vein, Moghira's agrarian practice challenges the dichotomies between settler and native. His work is polychronic, asserting that science, technology, industrialized forms of agriculture, and a development model that combines an alternative globalization network with a traditional Palestinian economic unit belong to the native expert and are not exclusive to the settler society.

The agrarian sumud that Palestinian experts have adopted is more than holding onto the land and practicing Palestinian agriculture as an inherited legacy. Rather, Moghira's practice can be seen through Bhabha's articulation of the hybrid as the generation of a new world and way of being, rather than a simple means of keeping a foot in each existing world. His creation of a development model that is based on both traditional forms of societal structures (such as the Palestinian family as an economic unit) as well as newer forms of social organization (such as an NGO working in the global sphere) blends the 1948 timescape with a social imaginary of alternative globalization and a sociotechnical imaginary of industrialization.

Instead of the inclination of some social scientists to see such agrarian experts as mere subjects of the Israeli state system and its coercive logics, I suggest understanding their actions as within the broader sense of the term *samidin*. By using their knowledge, expertise, and familiarity with state and social institutions, these experts have developed a plethora of Palestinian activities in order to advance agrarian-economic enterprises that claim resources and contest the practice of Palestinian agrarian de-development by the Israeli state. These activities maintain a Palestinian agriculture that is up to date with Western agronomic techniques (with all its rights and wrongs) and integrated into local and global markets. This resists the marginalization of Palestinian agriculture by the state as "traditional agriculture." However, a gap does exist between the collective political significance of their preservation of Palestinian agrarian practice and the tendency to articulate their role as devoid of politics. This gap hints at what it takes for an indigenous expert to be employed by the state.

Finally, by focusing on Mustafa's story and practices, as well as Dr. Hisham Yunis's and Moghira Younis's narrations and actions, I ask to reconstruct the agency of Palestinian agronomy science experts as the main agents of their own history and not as actors who only had state policy act upon them.[100] What I aimed to show through their stories and practices are the ways Palestinian Arab employees of the ministry hold polychronic ways of knowing, acting, and being in time. Making sense of historical, present, and future time, governing one's time, and deciding how to address time in one's own work are all fundamental questions of agency. Time is a mode of knowledge, a technology of one's imagination, as well as a collective imagination.[101] But the position of the native expert working for the settler state constantly brings together different time horizons.

The Palestinian experts whose stories I introduced have been agents of their own history both in the workplace and in their after-work activities. As such, their involvement in the project of modernization of Palestinian agriculture echoes globally created models of Green Revolution in agriculture, which always occurred under colonial and imperial contexts such as the Green Revolution in Mexico or India. In Israel/Palestine such modernization efforts were usually celebrated as achievements of the settler society and as a proof of the contribution of this project to the local population. Then, while Palestinian expert-scientific training is a challenge to the state's ever-reproducing narrative of the "traditional Arab," Western science expertise is a tool that serves the settler society's narrative.

As such, this chapter showed how Palestinian experts are holding and practicing both hegemonic and counter-hegemonic views in agricultural-environmental imaginaries and practices. But these professionals are also involved in agrarian practices that challenge the assumed division between settler and native. In their practices they allow us to rethink the negotiation and movements between societal categories of difference and the sort of epistemological alliances and possibilities of self-determination that Palestinian Western science experts may have within their native communities and outside them.

Conclusion

In the summer of 2021 and fall of 2022, I went to talk to Mustafa Natour, the veteran agronomist and agrarian economist, as various questions regarding the future of Palestinian agriculture were still haunting my thoughts. When I asked him about his recent activities, he told me that despite the physical difficulty he experiences at the age of eighty-five, he climbs four floors to the school rooftops in Nazareth to instruct educational school teams on agrarian production. He does this as part of Hawakir's program of teaching agrarian cultivation in Palestinian schools, in open fields if available, or on rooftops in Nazareth if schools do not have any land.[1] The goal of this activity is to restore agrarian practice in schools so that students who are descendants of *fellaheen* families can reclaim their roots. This is seen as an activity that can empower students through a hands-on productive and practical experience and provide them with a sense of accomplishment by working with plants. He emphasized that in only three months of work, a cultivation season, the children see results and can harvest the produce to take home with them. They built 70-square-meter greenhouses (approximately 230 square feet) on the rooftops of these schools and carried up long containers that were filled with potting soil, simulating cultivation rows. At one of the schools, they also created an open-air agriculture "field" on the rooftop with containers mimicking a cultivation row in field-based agriculture. They cultivate vegetables such as tomatoes, cucumbers, lettuce, and herbs. Strawberries are cultivated in the rooftop greenhouse of another of the schools. These are popular crops among Palestinian agriculturalists in Israel today. The work in greenhouses represents the top of crop profitability.[2] The agrarian educational program was coordinated with the Ministry of Education, and the Ministry of Agriculture assisted with building the greenhouses in schools.[3] Hawakir's professional staff supported the school teams and instructed in agrarian matters. Mustafa told me that during the pandemic, he communicated with school teams mainly by phone and the analysis of photographs. Although that technique produced good results, he is now back to climbing to rooftops to support the process. His story indicated how important agricultural work was during the pandemic for him and the school.

The image of the old Palestinian agronomist climbing to rooftops to instruct teams in a program for the young generation is striking. Even when there is very little agrarian land left, agriculture remains a vital practice and culture that connects generations, producing food, sustaining life, and connecting to a place. His description highlighted clearly how agriculture is not about a commodity, but about relations with land, people, and time. His story provided a clear image of what survivance means daily, as an action in time: it disrupts a power system through mere everyday practices and actions that do not just stand in a void but are rather imbued with a social-political context of land confiscation and the state's work to de-territorialize Palestinians. Claiming roots on a rooftop following the loss of land seems poetic and perhaps ironic but not tragic. As Mustafa told the story, there was no victimhood, but an active daily practice of creativity and contestation. Mustafa as a retired state agronomist spends his free time teaching about agriculture as a meaningful occupation. It is as if this eighty-five-year-old man engaging his community's educational circles is saying, "Even when we don't have land to cultivate on, we take the time and space to practice agriculture and grow food high up 'in the air.'" Even though this practice is not guided by detailed outspoken ideology, it reaffirms a Palestinian peasantry heritage that is connected to agriculture's past and future, while also challenging the prevailing logic of power.[4]

Mustafa's endeavor and insistence on educating the younger Palestinian generation about agrarian production are unique in the Palestinian-citizens' landscape of agrarian education and the view about the Palestinian future of agriculture. Throughout this book, I have discussed the state's abandonment of Palestinian agriculture. I claim that abandonment is not a by-product of policy, but a policy of intended neglect. Sadly, following many years of state abandonment, Palestinian agriculture is also being neglected on an internal societal level.[5] Palestinian politicians in Israel attend to agriculture mostly with a pragmatic gaze of attending to the needs of an older generation, rather than seeing food production as one of the great challenges of the twenty-first century. Passing on agriculture is not only about national or native sentiments of belonging to the land; it is about revitalizing and regenerating agriculture in the present time, educating to produce food even in conditions of resource scarcity and climatic uncertainty.

We can think about processes in the global agrarian environment in similar ways. Globally, the agrarian workforce is growing older and it is shrinking. Arable land is deteriorating and being depleted while efforts to revitalize agriculture and adapt it to current environmental challenges have not been sufficient. The demographics of arable land access and management continue to be a feature of settler colonial societies at large.[6]

Yet, the challenges of fresh food supply during moments of commodity chain breakdown as occurred with the COVID-19 pandemic have shown the importance of decentralized food production and local cultivation and access. Globally, robots are transforming and optimizing monocultural farming systems while very few such digitization and automation endeavors are geared toward sustaining small-scale and agroecological farming.[7] Technological development in agriculture is geared to saving labor and making agriculture efficient and accurate in its resource use, but such technologies often imagine large-scale users exacerbating social injustice and environmental harm rather than decentralized productivity. In the face of climate change, there are contradicting agrarian rationales: on the one hand, aiming to expand local food sovereignties through increasing the number of active producers, and on the other hand, agricultural efficiency and productivity discourses still rule, prioritizing large-scale agriculture. These two conflicting rationales need to be settled.[8] The current developments of the agrarian sector present a paradox of time—favoring near-future "efficiency" over a longer-term notion of futurity.

The compression of agrarian productivity in smaller spaces is possible only through the compression of time in suitable agrarian technologies, but these continue to favor settler societies and agribusiness models. These various paradoxes of time can be analytically resolved through a timescape approach. I have used *timescape* throughout the book to refer to a landscape of time interweaving diverse temporal elements that would otherwise seem disparate to work together as a mechanism of governance, structural to our understanding of technologies of power operated by settler colonial societies. Previous scholarship on Israel/Palestine treated various elements of time as separate instances present in social life. However, I argue that looking at all these temporal performances together allows us to recognize and conceptualize time as a constitutive power mechanism operated by the settler colonial structure. Space cannot be colonized alone; rather, time must be colonized too, as time and space are entangled. Claiming native time serves the settler society in justifying its existence and in indigenizing. Through discussing agro-environmental policies I show that governed forms of time are used to deprive Palestinian citizens of agrarian resources and practice. The main elements of time that I have discussed throughout the book are the temporal legalities that weave laws, regulations, and time durations and the ways in which these legalities are used to dispossess Palestinians from land. Further, I illustrate the temporal discourse appearing in policies assigning Palestinian agriculturalists to a "traditional" temporal role versus modern, developed, scientific Jewish Israeli agriculture. This form of discourse as it is used by the state facilitates resource deprivation by assuming Palestinian citizens will not accept change.

Throughout this book, the reversed way in which the repressed Palestinian "traditional agriculture" came back into state documents in appreciative discourse without proper financial reimbursements highlights that traditional agriculture is in fact as much about the present and the future as it is about the past. But the Jewish agrarian tradition has had support from the state since its establishment. I have shown that when conflicts between traditional time and market temporality time arise, the state settles these conflicts. Only in 2015 did the state create a legal procedure that enables Palestinian agriculturalists to apply for state subsidies while cultivating land that is not legally theirs, a predicament of the Muslim inheritance tradition in a capitalist society. I have further suggested that what policymakers refer to as "traditional Arab agriculture" should be better understood as underdeveloped agriculture because of state policies. In conjunction with the "traditional" role, the Israeli agrarian imaginary sees the landscapes of contemporary Palestinian smallholders as "biblical landscape." Such an imaginary manifests the erasure of Palestinian smallholders' legacy from agriculture as an official policy while settling time with Jewish-Israeli imaginaries, traditions, and practices. Finally, I have discussed agrarian labor time as an element of the timescape as dispossession. Palestinian agrarian labor is exploited via its compression in time and space, restricted to high-demand periodicities rather than long-term commitments. Further, I have highlighted how dispossession of labor time is manifested through the differential state sponsorship of agrarian labor-saving tools geared to subsidize machines that increase productivity and efficiency based on significant land estates that Palestinian smallholders do not have. These various performances of time allow for the tracing and articulation of time elements and timescape mechanisms as a form of governance that is too often invisible as an apparatus of power. As opposed to the state's timescape, I have illustrated the Palestinian agronomy experts' timescape as a polychronic one that is characterized by stories of survivance and the carrying of traditions and narratives that both resist erasure and produce sovereignty and liberty in the present moment.

To Imagine a Future for a Palestinian Agriculture

When I further asked Mustafa how he sees the future of Palestinian agriculture in Israel, he sighed and asked to quickly analyze the present conditions to ground any future imagination. He said that land is continuing to shrink both because of the inheritance tradition of land division among heirs and because of Palestinian urban and industrial sprawl into agrarian land. Water allocation to Palestinian agriculture is minimal, as water prices in Israel continue to rise. More irrigation water will be possible only with the use of treated wastewater. Given the urban-rural mixing of land usage in Palestinian towns, he did not predict a rise in water allocation to Palestinian agriculture because of infrastructural limitations. Further, he said, "The organizational structure of Palestinian agriculture in Israel is on an individual level, and there are no authentic representatives of Palestinian agriculturalists who can lobby for them and advocate for governmental subsidies". He highlighted that "other economic sectors are more stable than the risk-based occupation of agriculture, which is highly dependent on natural cycles, weather conditions, and the management of periodic phenomena such as pests." All these factors make it difficult for small-scale cultivators (which most Palestinian agriculturalists are) to survive. Finally, he said, "The education and professional level of Palestinian actors in agriculture is low. Those who study agriculture at an academic level do so in order to work in the Ministry of Agriculture or in the private sector; the average practitioner of Palestinian agriculture does not belong to a professional cadre that is able to easily adapt." Therefore, he said, "I can only predict that Palestinian agriculture will go and shrink in its production units and will transition from vegetable and field production to olive groves [considered as low maintenance]. Those who husband animals such as goats, sheep, and pigs will have to serve them feed rather than take them out to graze. More agriculturalists will have to amalgamate many small parcels to have a competitive production unit that can deal with market dynamics." The picture he illustrated was grim although likely realistic if the status quo is maintained and Palestinian agrarian time and space are further compressed. Serving feed instead of taking a herd to graze makes husbandry significantly more expensive, and the practice itself loses its spatiality and temporality. I was not surprised by the future Mustafa saw. I sometimes ponder whether Palestinians in Israel may find themselves taking their children to West Bank villages to see the resilient smallholder agriculture there that survives the Occupation and learn about their roots in an agrarian society facing local and global challenges.[9]

"And what would you wish for Palestinian agriculture in Israel?" I asked him.

He said, "My wishes have to consider a reality that does not support Palestinian agriculture in Israel. It will suffice if the efforts will be in the direction of encouraging cultivation and avoiding the consolidation of land ownership to a small number of landholders in each town. This can make production more efficient, maximize the efficient use of existing resources, and increase labor opportunities, especially for conservative women who avoid traveling outside of their town for work." He claimed, "This would be possible with legislation that granted landholding rights to owners who may lease their land for a longer time of twenty-five years and will support the agriculturalists who lease large terrains for long periods of time and will thus receive professional guidance from the state's research and knowledge extension system." Mustafa's response stayed within the realm of common sense of what could be possible within the foreseeable future of smallholders' agriculture in a capitalist system. The radical move he envisioned was a new legislation that requires lobbying and political will. But other than that, he maintained a pragmatic scale. Indeed, pragmatism is a solid way to survive in a system that has continuously worked against you and your community. Commonly, imagining a positive future indicates well-being. But Palestinians as a collectivity experience a lack of a political horizon and recurring attacks on the mere possibility of experiencing hope.

Mustafa's connection of a future imaginary to the present conditions evokes the question I presented in the introduction about the imaginary as a political force and its potential to create alternative futures. Jews and Palestinians must practice a political imaginary to take history and the present moment into a desirable future rather than the possible future that emerges out of the status quo.

Yet, for the imaginary to act as a liberating agent requires collective training. Norma Musih (following Hannah Arendt) claims that a political imagination is like a muscle that must be repetitively worked. She emphasizes that to cultivate a political imagination, tools and strategies are needed as well as a public space where they can be collectively exercised and experienced.[10] The power of the political imagination is that it makes present that which is absent.[11] Therefore, its generation requires belief, creativity, and a commitment to endure and persevere. While Palestinians and Israelis often feel the existing power dynamic is stable, the political imagination and the agrarian imaginary can become forces of social change. In a conservative manner, Israeli prime minister Benjamin Netanyahu has asserted that the Israeli Palestinian predicament is unsolvable and therefore the only remaining option is to "manage the conflict." His proposed method of "management" was to develop economic initiatives that improve Palestinian quality of life in the West Bank and in Israel but lack any horizon of political change. Such an approach fails to imagine Israelis and Palestinians living in the future in dignity as equals with equal rights who could one day prosper and benefit in this land without continuing suffering and injustice. Yet looking at other moments of change that have occurred in other places in the world shows that a process of reconciliation and decolonization is possible with a political momentum that may emerge at an unexpected point. How can the tools of an agrarian imaginary and a timescape approach illuminate other possible futures for Israel/Palestine? How does looking at the multiple brushstrokes of time in the agrarian landscapes of this place open new horizons? These questions might be addressed by looking at how the climate crisis requires thinking anew about local agrarian practices.

Israel/Palestine is largely dependent on food imports for its population needs. Fruit and vegetables are produced locally, guaranteeing some food security, estimated as approximately 20 percent of the caloric intake of the population.[12] Yet, the rising cost of international trade as experienced during the COVID-19 pandemic and its effect on market prices offer a small glimpse of what can happen under uncertain conditions like climate change (or war). The possibility of rising prices in international trade and the global challenges of food production in a climate crisis clarify that local agriculture cannot be merely a tool for guarding borders or making claims to national belonging. Rather, it must be reframed as a site supporting food security, fresh food provision, and food decentralization in the uncertain time of climate change.[13]

Understanding the need to reframe local agriculture within the lens of the climate crisis is beginning to emerge in climate-aware Ministry of Agriculture circles and in the Jewish Israeli agrarian–rural areas lobby.[14] They are advancing such views in a moment when Zionist-Israeli intensive agriculture is battling for its existence politically and facing constant societal attacks based on an uproar about the rising prices of produce.[15] But their institutional view on agriculture in the context of climate change is similar to the view of the United Nations Food and Agriculture Organization and is prone to see efficiency and productivity as leading factors of agrarian cultivation in the time of climate change. Thus, they are feeding into neoliberal structures of agriculture. Factors such as food decentralization, food accessibility, and agrarian resilience in the smallholding scale are not sufficiently accounted for.[16]

Throughout this book, I have presented alternative views of thinking about local agriculture that do take these factors into consideration. I have discussed how Palestinian smallholders' agriculture has conserved agro-biodiversity, with a return to the study of local cultivars that are more drought resistant and therefore can be more resilient in the face of climate change. This scientific return is important to highlight after the Israeli industrialized olive varieties unintentionally developed agriculture that is less resistant to droughts.[17] Can the agrarian imaginary and a timescape approach illuminate Palestinian agriculture as an upholder of agrarian biodiversity and sustainability that are crucial to support given the conditions of climate change? Who are the actors who will assemble to lead such an agenda in the public sphere? The views of Palestinian agronomy experts on sustainability highlight that there cannot be meaningful sustainability advocacy without working toward resource equity.

The Possibilities and Failures of Sustainability

The agenda of sustainability delivered a new political imagination for the Israeli state that facilitated agroecological discourses and interventions but had limited effect on Palestinian citizens' agriculture.[18] In chapter 1, I discussed the transition of the state agenda regarding Sahl al-Battuf from agricultural modernization to sustainable development. New agro-environmental imaginaries of conservation and politics in Israel emerged, recruiting coalitions of professionals, non-governmental organizations, and state bodies to achieve environmental goals. But while such a coalition of actors furthered the environmental aspects of ecological conservation in al-Battuf, I have shown the ways that environmental considerations were used to further Palestinian citizens' dispossession through multiple mechanisms of time. Both al-Battuf's sustainable development plan and olive groves' landscape-conservation zoning policies acknowledge the environmental contributions of these agricultures but fail to provide Palestinians with any economic benefits while restricting their land use. Instead of the state ecologist's view that Palestinian suspicion of environmental discourses is an improper understanding of the environmental challenge of this time, I suggest that Israeli conceptions of the environment fail to address resource equity, and economic considerations or attend to Palestinian resource sovereignty. To further illustrate this point is what Dr. Fathi Abd el-Hadi told me about sustainable agriculture in February 2013:

> I would say sustainable agriculture is almost traditional agriculture. Minimum interventions and minimum agricultural inputs and too few outcomes. Sustainable agriculture takes us back in time. I work economically with bigger farms, and I want them to have more income. This is an antithesis to sustainable agriculture. . . . I grew up in sustainable agriculture. This is what we used to have in the Arab villages with rain-fed agriculture, which was sustainable agriculture. . . . And I tell you, I saw agriculture for the Arab sector, and I compared it with Jewish agriculture—these are two separate worlds apart.

Sustainability is understood by Palestinian professionals within the context of resource allocation and deprivation, using natural resources alone bearing low profitability, which makes it a condition to resist. Such an understanding of sustainability was echoed in multiple conversations that I held with Palestinian agriculturalists and professionals in Israel. These opinions must be heard beyond their productivist and modernist conclusions as they repeated themselves throughout the interlocutors and conversations of this book. Dr. Yunis, Dr. Abd-el Hadi, Laithi Ghnaim from al-Battuf, and Moghira Younis at the Ministry of Agriculture's olive agriculture Extension Service. All these professionals are active social agents in agriculture and have referred to the sustainability agenda as a project that conserves technological and economic inferiority as well as an unfair means of resource allocation toward Palestinian Arab agriculture in Israel. These professionals wish for viable technological and economic development for Palestinian Arab agriculture. They are not unaware of the economic power of environmental and sustainability discourses. On the contrary, most of these professionals are involved in grassroots economic endeavors that engage environmental work or certification to promote Palestinian Arab agriculture. Their stories highlighted how Palestinian agriculture practitioners and experts see current sustainability discourses in Israel as a tool of domination serving dispossession. State discourses on the conservation of "traditional agriculture" as ecological or sustainable agriculture were received with contempt by these professionals. Such statements highlight the politics of the term *sustainability* and the structure of knowledge that makes such an agenda a public policy in Israel/Palestine and beyond.

Alternatively, technology, access to production resources like land and water, and promoting industrialization and cooperative marketing endeavors are considered better factors for sustainability by these professionals. They are right in many ways. Local history has shown that when land is not productive enough to sustain livelihoods, it is easier for its owners to sell it or abandon it. Sustainable agriculture for Palestinians in Israel is embodied in social and economic rights for people to develop economically and technologically and to achieve fairer resource distribution. Such framing raises several questions: What is the effect of the Israeli state asking Palestinian citizens to collaborate with sustainability agendas without tackling the basic injustice of resource allocation and social equality? Why does sustainable agriculture take Palestinians "back in time" rather than offering a future for Palestinian agriculture? And what is the role of agronomy professionals as mediators between the state and their communities, between agendas of agrarian modernization as a promise for resource allocation to an appreciation of the agroecological and biodiversity contributions of Palestinian agriculture? Finally, what does the sustainability agenda's view on resource deprivation reveal about the potential for managing a broader environmental crisis phenomenon, such as climate change?

Climate change heightens the uncertainties and risks encapsulated in the agrarian practice by revealing agriculturalists' vulnerability. For instance, the Palestinian smallholder is less likely to have agrarian insurance than his Jewish counterpart, given a cost-benefit analysis for a smallholder as well as the regulatory obstacles regarding state support and landholding legalities. Therefore, a smallholder can access limited financial securitization in the future.[19] Already in 2021, the Israeli Insurance Fund for Natural Risks in Agriculture paid Israeli farmers double insurance payments compared to the previous decade given the rise of temperatures and its dramatic effect on fruit yields.[20]

Then what forms of governmental and societal practices can be cultivated in the interface of agriculture, environment, and climate change to foster equality and the continuation of smallholding? As writings in critical agrarian studies have shown, smallholding is a resilient way of ensuring food decentralization in times of crisis.[21] Palestinian smallholding in Israel sustains agro-biodiversity and landscape heritage and sustains local varieties that could have been lost otherwise in Israeli industrialized agriculture. How could these agrarian characteristics and contributions of Palestinian agriculture be leveraged to create political alliances furthering climate adaptation, mitigation as well as societal decolonization in Israel/Palestine?

In the West Bank social organizations, activists and academics have leveraged agroecology and food sovereignty as a vital way of both surviving and sustaining the local economy and local ecology against the settler colonial and capitalist predicament.[22] Such agrarian work and struggle may represent the sort of work that needs to be noticed as a form of unsettling both climate change and time.

Unsettling Time

Finishing writing this book in proximity to another seven-year Jewish calendar cycle of the shmita year allows me to continue to contemplate the ethics of this biblical commandment. Shmita offers a radical social vision of the redistribution of land, as well as the redistribution of wealth and rights. It is a commandment that echoes indigenous notions that the land is not owned by humans but belongs to God. Therefore, it cannot be infinitely exploited, and it needs rest as well as to be shared equally among humans and nonhumans. This commandment as an ideal with its vision of the jubilee year of land redistribution offers a social vision of agrarian reforms and more equal societies.

But to conclude writing this book during shmita also allows me to further observe the interplay of the shmita commandment with the settler colonial state. On January 11, 2022, the Jewish National Fund (JNF/KKL) operated a day of plantations in the Naqab/Negev area that the Bedouin al-Atrash tribe uses for its seasonal agriculture near Yatir forest (in Hebrew/Zionist vocabulary). The purpose of this JNF work is to "control land" and prevent Bedouins from "taking over" state lands. This work was taking place in a year of shmita. JNF justifies its practice by saying that it abides to Jewish law: it employs non-Jewish workers to carry out the planting operation and the plants will be non-fruit-bearing trees that have been cultivated in soil-detached techniques. But this practice circumvents shmita on technical terms while executing a planting operation that is opposed to the biblical rationale of the shmita commandment to let the land rest and let the poor and gentile equally benefit from the land. Only the ultra-Orthodox parties in Israeli Knesset outspokenly opposed this planting operation and claimed it is absolutely forbidden during a year of shmita. In contrast, center-right politicians and religious Zionist Knesset members went for a photo opportunity on this site making statements such as "No one will tell us where and when to plant trees on our own land."[23] In any other case, the authorities in Israel avoid planting trees during a shmita year.[24] The shmita commandment is once again subordinated to the settler colonial state logic.

Yet, what if shmita were used sincerely as a collective time of contemplation of human-to-human equity and human-to-nonhuman equity as the biblical commandment suggests? What might be the effect of collective contemplation about the significance of the practice of shmita in the twenty-first century as a social guideline rather than the settler society's way of claiming its indigeneity? Instead of reinforcing the tradition-modernity divide characteristic of all settler colonial agrarian endeavors,[25] shmita allows for a critical examination of that structure altogether and an ability to imagine a different future.

Jewish communities in the diaspora have started relating to a year of shmita as a time of social and environmental contemplation rooted in Jewish traditional ecological knowledge, inquiring about relations between rest and work, relationship to land, relationship to community, relationship to debt and debt relief as well as to inequality.[26] In Israel/

Palestine only a marginal group of Jewish renewal and environmental activists are doing similar work. A conference they organized in October 2021 explored the relationship between shmita and climate change.[27] Nevertheless, the political imaginary work that is performed in such circles of Jewish renewal does not inquire about the relationship between Jewish traditional knowledge and the indigenous Palestinian people of the land. This imagines Jewish life in Israel/Palestine as detached from a concrete social-political reality and power structure, making these attempts to build on traditional Jewish knowledge complicit in the settler colonial politics of using shmita as a practice of settling time.

Alternatively, when the state is settling time, social forces can engage in practices of freeing time and decolonizing time. The future envisioned currently in Israel/Palestine lies in a pessimist spectrum of sci-fi images advanced by Palestinian artists primarily in the West Bank to short-term Israeli work of "shrinking the conflict."[28] However, thinking with time as an agentive power not only gives hope but provides tools to address the current reality. Jews and Palestinians are going to continue living on this land together whether they like it or not. Then, how do time and timescape provide a tool to resist the current dynamic? How do uses of timescape open new possibilities of seeing and acting?

The American literary critic Frederic Jameson's famous quote "It has become easier to imagine the end of the world than the end of capitalism" requires us to think about structures of power that seem so all-encompassing, penetrating, and absolute that it is easier for society to imagine its absolute collapse than to envision the work needed to be done for a just and vital future.[29] This statement indicates the collective failure of mobilizing political imaginations for change. While globally, capitalism became a total social fact, sociologist Areej Sabbagh-Khoury in a Durkheimian manner claims that in Israel/Palestine, settler colonialism became a total social fact explaining the root of social lives in this land.[30] This ethnography manifests her claim while still discussing the complexities of societal relations (such as class matters within Palestinian society or Jewish subgroups and the settler colonial condition), the dialectic interactions that create social lives, and the slippages that emerge between settler and native. I emphasized that the timescape of settler colonialism contains a dialectic logic that moves between a straightforward capitalist rationale of short-term profit and non-capitalist temporalities that are subsidized by the state for the sake of the settler society's continuity. The future of the settler society is an issue of major anxiety for the Israeli state. But given the short-term concerns of politicians to assure their future seat in the next parliament or government, long-term planning and visions have seldom been a characteristic of Israeli governance. Yet, what if the people demanded accountability for the future and a ministry for the future? How would turning into the future require a rearranging of politics as states and as regions in the face of climate change?

Environmental anthropology has situated climate change in its wide historical context rather than a technical phenomenon that emerges from anthropogenic carbon dioxide emissions (CO_2). It has been emphasized time and again that industrial capitalism and climate change are co-constituted. But, equally, the rise of industrial capitalism cannot be disentangled from colonial practices and ongoing imperial histories of racism and resource extraction.[31] Therefore, attending to climate change and the future of agriculture must be situated within a historically informed analysis that situates the climate predicament in the local context of agri-environmental struggles and possibilities for change. I have shown that the agrarian struggle locally is not defined by its constituents in the contours of experts' climate discourse or in the climate justice movement's articulations.[32] It is not surprising that the perceived futurity of climate change has not penetrated the current survival modes of Palestinian agriculturalists. Therefore, it is our role to observe, ask, and revisit who are the actors who may articulate the local agrarian struggle in the context of global climate change and to what political effects.

Anticorporate farming scholar and activist Vandana Shiva claimed, "When you control food, you control society. But when you control seed, you control life on Earth."[33] Her powerful warning highlights the importance of public involvement and engagement with the agrarian and food system against corporate power and keeping it as open to as many of us as possible. This book asks that the state be placed back in this dynamic, recognizing that food and agriculture dynamics are highly governed by states and not only markets. Following the global land rush of 2008 and with the economic, food supply, and political shocks that the COVID-19 pandemic created, it becomes evident that producing food contributes to food security, social justice, and democratic societies as decentralizing food production empowers people in a radically changing world. But in this present moment, Palestinians in Israel are not fighting collectively for the future of agriculture. Giving up the right to produce food should be reconsidered.

NOTES

Introduction

1. The articulation *Israel/Palestine* allows destabilizing a simplification of Israel and Palestine or understanding them as separate or distinct. I place *Israel* first in this construct only to indicate that this book focuses ethnographically on the 1948 borders of the Israeli state or historic mandatory Palestine excluding Gaza and the West Bank.

2. Kibbutzim are collective communities created as early as 1909 in Palestine/Israel, aiming to create an intentional community functioning internally in the ethos of Zionist socialism. Moshavim were established as cooperative communities also in the early twentieth century. These cooperative rural communities are considered the backbone of the ethos of Israeli rural areas.

3. One such alternative agrarian ancestry periodization could look at the Natufian hunter-gatherer society remnants identified in the woodland of the Mediterranean zone in the Carmel, Galilee, and in the Jordan Valley. These remnants reveal plant cultivation and animal domestication from 10,000 BCE. The Natufians are considered the forefathers of the agrarian revolution and arguably could have been also celebrated proudly through this policy, but they are not. Perhaps because their story has a universal significance rather than a periodization recruited for the legitimization of settler nation history. See Romana Unger-Hamilton, "The Epi-Palaeolithic Southern Levant and the Origins of Cultivation," *Current Anthropology* 30, no. 1 (1989): 88-103; Ofer Bar-Yosef and Richard H. Meadow, "The Origins of Agriculture in the Near East," in *Last Hunters, First Farmers: New Perspectives on the Prehistoric Transition to Agriculture*, ed. T. Douglas Price and Anne Birgitte Gebauer, 39–94 (School of American Research Press, 1995); Tobias Richter et al., "High Resolution AMS Dates from Shubayqa 1, Northeast Jordan Reveal Complex Origins of Late Epipalaeolithic Natufian in the Levant," *Scientific Reports* 7, no. 1 (2017): 1-10.

4. This section was written by a Palestinian Arab geographer from Haifa University who was hired to write it but who was not paid to participate in the large planning process.

5. See Misrad ha-haklaut, ha-rashut le-tikhnun (Ministry of Agriculture, the Planning Authority), *Ha-tokhnit ha-leumit la-haklaut vela-kfar be-Yisrael, Mismakh* #1 (The national protocol of planning policy of agriculture and rural areas in Israel, # 1), August 13, 2013, 67–68. The "traditional landscape" and landscape compounds for preservation were also crystallized in National Master Plan 35, which established Beit Netofa Valley (Sahl al-Battuf) and Mghar's olive groves as landscape conservation areas. Ministry of Interior, Planning Administration, National Master Plan 35, approved on September 6, 2016, https://www.gov.il/he/Departments/General/tama_35_docs.

6. Khaled Furani and Dan Rabinowitz, "The Ethnographic Arriving of Palestine," *Annual Review of Anthropology* 40 (2011): 475–491.

7. Paige West, *From Modern Production to Imagined Primitive: The Social World of Coffee from Papua New Guinea* (Duke University Press, 2012); Frieda Knobloch, *The Culture of Wilderness: Agriculture as Colonization in the American West* (University of North Carolina Press, 1996); Kusum Nair, *In Defense of the Irrational Peasant: Indian Agriculture after the Green Revolution* (University of Chicago Press, 1979); Johannes Fabian, *Time and the Other: How Anthropology Makes Its Object* (Columbia University Press, 1983); Irus Braverman, "*Nof kdumim*: Remaking the Ancient Landscape in East Jerusalem's National Parks," *Environment and Planning E: Nature and Space* 4, no. 1 (2021): 109–134.

8. Rob Nixon, *Slow Violence and the Environmentalism of the Poor* (Harvard University Press, 2011).

9. Virginia Nazarea, *Heirloom Seeds and Their Keepers: Marginality and Memory in the Conservation of Biological Diversity* (University of Arizona Press, 2005); Michael S. Carolan, "Saving Seeds, Saving Culture: A Case Study of a Heritage Seed Bank," *Society and Natural Resources* 20, no. 8 (2007): 739–750; Anne Meneley, "Hope in the Ruins: Seeds, Plants, and Possibilities of Regeneration," *Environment and Planning E: Nature and Space* 4, no. 1 (2021): 158–172.

10. S. Ryan Isakson, "Derivatives for Development? Small-Farmer Vulnerability and the Financialization of Climate Risk Management," *Journal of Agrarian Change* 15, no. 4 (2015): 569–580; Hannah Bradley and Serena Stein, "Climate Opportunism and Values of Change on the Arctic Agricultural Frontier," *Economic Anthropology* 9, no. 2 (2022): 207–222; Emily Reisman and Madeleine Fairbairn, "Agri-food Systems and the Anthropocene," *Annals of the American Association of Geographers* 111, no. 3 (2020): 687–697; Emily Reisman, "Sanitizing Agri-food Tech: COVID-19 and the Politics of Expectation," *The Journal of Peasant Studies* 48, no. 5 (2021): 910–933; Peter Hazell and Panos Varangis, "Best Practices for Subsidizing Agricultural Insurance," *Global Food Security* 25 (2020): 100326; Marcus

Taylor, "Climate-Smart Agriculture: What Is It Good For?," *The Journal of Peasant Studies* 45, no. 1 (2018): 89–107.

11. *OECD-FAO Agricultural Outlook 2018–2027* (OECD Publishing and FAO, 2018), https://doi.org/10.1787/agr_outlook-2018-en; FAORNE, *Regional Overview of Food Insecurity: Near East and North Africa* (FAO, 2016); Jan Selby et al., "Climate Change and the Syrian Civil War Revisited," *Political Geography* 60 (2017): 232–244; Dan Rabinowitz, *The Power of Deserts* (Stanford University Press, 2020); Andrew S. Mathews and Jessica Barnes, "Prognosis: Visions of Environmental Futures," *Journal of the Royal Anthropological Institute* 22, no. S1 (2016): 9–26; Sophia Stamatopoulou-Robbins, "An Uncertain Climate in Risky Times: How Occupation Became Like the Rain in Post-Oslo Palestine," *International Journal of Middle East Studies* 50, no. 3 (2018): 383–404.

12. Saturnino M. Borras Jr. and Jennifer C. Franco, "The Challenge of Locating Land-Based Climate Change Mitigation and Adaptation Politics within a Social Justice Perspective: Towards an Idea of Agrarian Climate Justice," *Third World Quarterly* 39, no. 7 (2018): 1308–1325; Andrew S. Mathews, "Anthropology and the Anthropocene: Criticisms, Experiments, and Collaborations," *Annual Review of Anthropology* 49 (2020): 67–82; Katharine Bradley and Hank Herrera, "Decolonizing Food Justice: Naming, Resisting, and Researching Colonizing Forces in the Movement," *Antipode* 48, no. 1 (2016): 97–114; E. Melanie DuPuis and David Goodman, "Should We Go 'Home' to Eat?: Toward a Reflexive Politics of Localism," *Journal of Rural Studies* 21, no. 3 (2005): 359–371.

13. Muna Dajani, "Danger, Turbines! A Jawlani Cry against Green Energy Colonialism in the Occupied Syrian Golan Heights," London School of Economics Middle East Centre, blog post, May 20, 2020; Muna Dajani, "How Palestine's Climate Apartheid Is Being Depoliticised," *Open Democracy*, February 25, 2022; Kathryn Yusoff, *A Billion Black Anthropocenes or None* (University of Minnesota Press, 2018); Kyle Whyte, "Indigenous Climate Change Studies: Indigenizing Futures, Decolonizing the Anthropocene," *English Language Notes* 55, no. 1 (2017): 153–162; Kyle P. Whyte, "Indigenous Science (Fiction) for the Anthropocene: Ancestral Dystopias and Fantasies of Climate Change Crises," *Environment and Planning E: Nature and Space* 1, no. 1–2 (2018): 224–242; Anna Lowenhaupt Tsing, *The Mushroom at the End of the World* (Princeton University Press, 2015); Gabi Kirk, "Confronting the Twin Crises of Climate Change and Occupation in Palestine," *Arab Studies Journal* 30, no. 2 (2022): 90–95.

14. See "Our Urgent Demand" Greta Thunberg, November 1, 2021, email to the public through the Avaaz advocacy network; or the repetition of "a race against time" as a phrase and as a meaning in Rabinowitz, *The Power of Deserts*.

15. Areej Sabbagh-Koury delineates the relevance of this paradigm and its genealogy in the case of Israel and its Palestinian citizens. Sabbagh-Khoury, "Tracing Settler Colonialism: A Genealogy of a Paradigm in the Sociology of

Knowledge Production in Israel," *Politics & Society* 50, no. 1 (2021), https://doi
.org/10.1177/0032329221999906; Nadim N. Rouhana and Areej Sabbagh-Khoury,
"Settler-Colonial Citizenship: Conceptualizing the Relationship between Israel
and Its Palestinian Citizens," *Settler Colonial Studies* 5, no. 3 (2015): 205-225; Gershon Shafir, *Land, Labor and the Origins of the Israeli-Palestinian Conflict, 1882-1914*,
vol. 20 (University of California Press, 1996); Patrick Wolfe, "Settler Colonialism
and the Elimination of the Native," *Journal of Genocide Research* 8, no. 4 (2006):
387-409; Tom Pessah, "The Distinction of Violence: Representing Lethal Cleansing in Settler Colonial Societies," PhD diss., Department of Sociology, University
of California, Berkeley, 2014.

16. Stuart Banner, "Why Terra Nullius? Anthropology and Property Law in
Early Australia," *Law and History Review* 23, no. 1 (2005): 95-131; Michael Asch,
"From Terra Nullius to Affirmation: Reconciling Aboriginal Rights with the
Canadian Constitution," *Canadian Journal of Law & Society/La Revue Canadienne
Droit et Société* 17, no. 2 (2002): 23-39; Alexandre Kedar, Ahmad Amara, and Oren
Yiftachel, *Emptied Lands: A Legal Geography of Bedouin Rights in the Negev* (Stan-
ford University Press, 2018); Lucy Taylor, "Four Foundations of Settler Colonial
Theory: Four Insights from Argentina," *Settler Colonial Studies* 11, no. 3 (2021):
344-365.

17. Ann Stoler notes that no imperial society is identical to another and so I
extend her analysis to the settler colonial context, too, in noting how the place of
Jews in the Middle East helps us think of the unique aspects of the Zionist story.
Stoler," On Degrees of Imperial Sovereignty," *Public Culture* 18, no. 1 (2006): 125-
46. Lior B. Sternfeld, *Between Iran and Zion* (Stanford University Press, 2020); Orit
Bashkin, *New Babylonians:A History of Jews in Modern Iraq* (Stanford University
Press, 2012); Michelle Campos, *Ottoman Brothers: Muslims, Christians, and Jews in
Early Twentieth-Century Palestine* (Stanford University Press, 2010). Settler colo-
nial societies also include "arrivants," non-European immigrants, who served
the settler colonial society as laboring bodies. The social channeling of Mizrahi
immigrants to blue-collar labor does just that. Jodi Byrd refers to the term *ar-
rivant* based on Caribbean poet and scholar Edward Kamau Braithwaite. Byrd,
The Transit of Empire: Indigenous Critiques of Colonialism (University of Minnesota
Press, 2011).

18. The story of Palestine Jews allows us to examine moving from the cate-
gory of native to the category of settler. See Yuval Evri and Hagar Kotef, "When
Does a Native Become a Settler? (With Apologies to Zreik and Mamdani),"
Constellations: An International Journal of Critical and Democratic Theory, June 15,
2020, https://doi.org/10.1111/1467-8675.12470; Yuval Ben-Bassat, "The Challenges
Facing the First Aliyah Sephardic Ottoman Colonists," *Journal of Israeli History*
35, no. 1 (2016): 3-15; Piergiorgio Di Giminiani, Martin Fonck, and Paolo Perasso,
"Can Natives Be Settlers? Emptiness, Settlement and Indigeneity on the Settler
Colonial Frontier in Chile," *Anthropological Theory* 21, no. 1 (2021): 82-106.

19. The struggle over indigeneity is not the only confusing aspect of settler colonialism in Palestine/Israel although settlers' claiming indigeneity in the nation state is a shared phenomenon of settler colonial societies. In English and Hebrew, the popular use of the term *settlers* usually refers to *Mitnahalim*, Israelis who, in violation of international law, live in the 1967 Occupied Palestinian Territories (OPT). But the settler colonial analysis assigns settlerhood to the whole Jewish-Israeli society that settled in Palestine following the Zionist movement's establishment. Thus, the term *Mityashvim*, which is used in Hebrew mostly to describe Israelis who live in rural areas in the internationally recognized 1949 borders of Israel, is applied to all Israelis. Part of the linguistic effort to legitimize Jewish settlers in the OPT is to name the 1967 settlements Mityashvim too. See Daniel Monterescu and Ariel Handel, "Liquid Indigeneity: Wine, Science, and Colonial Politics in Israel/Palestine," *American Ethnologist* 46, no. 3 (2019): 313–327; Dafna Hirsch, "'Hummus Is Best When It Is Fresh and Made by Arabs': The Gourmetization of Hummus in Israel and the Return of the Repressed Arab," *American Ethnologist* 38, no. 4 (2011): 617–630; Rachel Busbridge, "Israel-Palestine and the Settler Colonial 'Turn': From Interpretation to Decolonization," *Theory, Culture & Society* 35, no. 1 (2018): 91–115.

20. Irus Braverman, *Planted Flags: Trees, Land, and Law in Israel/Palestine* (Cambridge University Press, 2009); Irus Braverman, *Settling Nature: The Conservation Regime in Palestine-Israel* (University of Minnesota Press, 2023); Omar Tesdell, "Wild Wheat to Productive Drylands: Global Scientific Practice and the Agroecological Remaking of Palestine," *Geoforum* 78 (2017): 43–51; Tamar Novick, *Milk and Honey: Technologies of Plenty in the Making of a Holy Land* (MIT Press, 2023).

21. In a recent interview, Lorenzo Veracini details the many ways that the notion of return frames many settler movements: "returning to the land, returning to an authentic consciousness, returning to an invigorating environment, returning to a prerevolutionary world" and addresses the specific geographic cases. Abe Silberstein, "A Logic of Elimination," Conversation, *Jewish Currents*, January 11, 2022, https://jewishcurrents.org/a-logic-of-elimination?mc_cid=4182 2bff36&mc_eid=ada6d7eaad; see also Patricia M. E. Lorcin, "Rome and France in Africa: Recovering Colonial Algeria's Latin Past," *French Historical Studies* 25, no. 2 (2002): 295–329; Diana K. Davis, *Resurrecting the Granary of Rome: Environmental History and French Colonial Expansion in North Africa*, vol. 58 (Ohio University Press, 2007); Will D. Swearingen, "In Pursuit of the Granary of Rome: France's Wheat Policy in Morocco, 1915–1931," *International Journal of Middle East Studies* 17, no. 3 (1985): 347–363.

22. Jon May and Nigel Thrift, eds., *Timespace: Geographies of Temporality*, vol. 13 (Routledge, 2003); Laura Bear, "Time as Technique," *Annual Review of Anthropology* 45 (2016): 487–502.

23. The Zionist movement and later the Israeli state worked toward the set-

tlement and Judaization of space and in parallel, its de-Arabization in multiple forms under different political regimes in the past 150 years. From approximately fifty small Jewish settlements in 1917, one hundred years later there were 1,176 Jewish settlements in this land, some of which are major cities. Oren Yiftachel, *Landed Power: Israel/Palestine between Ethnocracy and Creeping Apartheid* (Resling Press, 2021). Under the settler colonial framework, these seemingly distinct political subjectivities collapse as all Jewish-Israeli citizens share the position of settling the land benefitting racialized privileges vis-à-vis the Palestinians.

24. Rabea Eghbariah, "Israeli Law and the Rule of Colonial Difference," *Journal of Palestine Studies* 51, no. 1 (2022): 73–77; Amos Nadan, *The Palestinian Peasant Economy under the Mandate: A Story of Colonial Bungling*, vol. 37 (Harvard CMES, 2006); Alexandre Kedar, "Majority Time, Minority Time: Land, Nation, and the Law of Adverse Possession in Israel," *Tel Aviv UL Review* 21 (1997): 665; Michael R. Fischbach, *Records of Dispossession: Palestinian Refugee Property and the Arab-Israeli Conflict* (Columbia University Press, 2003). Oren Yiftachel, *Ethnocracy: Land and Identity Politics in Israel/Palestine* (University of Pennsylvania Press, 2006); Kedar, Amara, and Yiftachel, *Emptied Lands*; Mikko Joronen and Mark Griffiths, "The Affective Politics of Precarity: Home Demolitions in Occupied Palestine," *Environment and Planning D: Society and Space* 37, no. 3 (2019): 561–576.

25. Bear, Laura. "Doubt, Conflict, Mediation: The Anthropology of Modern Time," *Journal of the Royal Anthropological Institute* 20 (2014): 3–30.

26. Nixon, *Slow Violence and the Environmentalism of the Poor*.

27. Patrick Wolfe characterizes the settler colonial invasion as a structure and not an event in an article that became canonical in the recent writing on settler colonialism. Wolfe, "Settler Colonialism and the Elimination of the Native." Other researchers of Israel/Palestine have emphasized that the local reality manifests a process: Areej Sabbagh-Khoury, "Tracing Settler Colonialism"; Joyce Dalsheim, *Israel Has a Jewish Problem: Self-Determination as Self-Elimination* (Oxford University Press, USA, 2019).

28. James Clifford, *Returns* (Harvard University Press, 2013); Gerald Vizenor, ed., *Survivance: Narratives of Native Presence* (University of Nebraska Press, 2008); Nick Estes, *Our History Is the Future: Standing Rock versus the Dakota Access Pipeline, and the Long Tradition of Indigenous Resistance* (Verso, 2019). Such literature is growing locally, analyzing a plethora of Palestinian return, resistance, and survival practices through *Sumud* (steadfastness) enacted through arts, culture, agriculture, the environment, and Palestinian knowledge production. See Khaled Furani, *Silencing the Sea: Secular Rhythms in Palestinian Poetry* (Stanford University Press, 2012); Nadeem Karkabi, "Self-Liberated Citizens: Unproductive Pleasures, Loss of Self, and Playful Subjectivities in Palestinian Raves," *Anthropological Quarterly* 93, no. 4 (2020): 679–708; Ali Nijmeh, "Active and Transformative Sumud Among Palestinian Activists in Israel," in *Palestine and Rule of Power*,

71–103 (Palgrave Macmillan, 2019); Anne Meneley, "Resistance Is Fertile!," *Gastronomica: The Journal of Food and Culture* 14, no. 4 (2014): 69–78; Craig Larkin, "Jerusalem's Separation Wall and Global Message Board: Graffiti, Murals, and the Art of Sumud," *The Arab Studies Journal* 22, no. 1 (2014): 134–169; Nadim N. Rouhana and Areej Sabbagh-Khoury, "Memory and the Return of History in a Settler-Colonial Context: The Case of the Palestinians in Israel," *Interventions* 21, no. 4 (2019): 527–550.

29. Anne Meneley, "Resistance Is Fertile!"; Anne Meneley, "Blood, Sweat and Tears in a Bottle of Palestinian Extra-Virgin Olive Oil," *Food, Culture & Society* 14, no. 2 (2011): 275–292; Meneley, "Hope in the Ruins"; Emily McKee, "Divergent Visions: Intersectional Water Advocacy in Palestine," *Environment and Planning E: Nature and Space* 4, no. 1 (2021): 43–64; Caroline Abu-Sada, "Cultivating Dependence: Palestinian Agriculture under the Israeli Occupation," in *The Power of Inclusive Exclusion: Anatomy of Israeli Rule in the Occupied Palestinian Territories*, ed. A. Ophir, M. Givoni, and S. Ḥanafī, 15–30 (Zone Books, 2009).

30. Interview with agronomist Mughira Younis, February 2013. He is a main interlocutor in chapters 3 and 4.

31. Vizenor, *Survivance*; Gerald Robert Vizenor, *Manifest Manners: Narratives on Postindian Survivance* (University of Nebraska Press, 1999). For an elaborate distinction between Gerald Vizenor's notion of survivance versus Jacques Derrida's, see Elizabeth A. Povinelli, "Divergent Survivances," *E-Flux Journal,* no. 121, October 2021, https://www.e-flux.com/journal/121/424069/divergent-survivances/. Other scholars have illustrated spatiotemporalities of survivance and resistance to colonial captivity. See, for instance, Nadeem Karkabi and Aamer Ibraheem, "On Fleeing Colonial Captivity: Fugitive Arts in the Occupied Jawlan," *Identities* 29, no. 5 (2022): 691–710; Omri Grinberg, "Witnessing and Testimony as Event: Israeli NGOs, Palestinian Witnesses, and the Undoing of Human Rights Bureaucracy," *The Cambridge Journal of Anthropology* 39, no. 1 (2021): 93–110; Nayrouz Abu Hatoum, "Decolonizing [in the] Future: Scenes of Palestinian Temporality," *Geografiska Annaler: Series B, Human Geography* 103, no. 1 (August 2021): 1–16.

32. Carol A. Kidron, "Toward an Ethnography of Silence: The Lived Presence of the Past in the Everyday Life of Holocaust Trauma Survivors and Their Descendants in Israel," *Current Anthropology* 50, no. 1 (2009): 5–27; Yehuda C.Goodman and Nissim Mizrachi, "'The Holocaust Does Not Belong to European Jews Alone': The Differential Use of Memory Techniques in Israeli High Schools," *American Ethnologist* 35, no. 1 (2008): 95–114; Jackie Feldman, "Between Yad Vashem and Mt. Herzl: Changing Inscriptions of Sacrifice on Jerusalem's 'Mountain of Memory,'" *Anthropological Quarterly* 80, no. 4 (Fall 2007): 1147–1174; Jackie Feldman, *Above the Death Pits, beneath the Flag: Youth Voyages to Poland and the Performance of Israeli National Identity* (Berghahn Books, 2008).

33. Areej Sabbagh-Khoury, "Tracing Settler Colonialism"; Shay Hazkani, *Dear Palestine: A Social History of the 1948 War* (Stanford University Press, 2021); Bashir Bashir and Amos Goldberg, "Introduction: The Holocaust and the Nakba: A New Syntax of History, Memory, and Political Thought," in *The Holocaust and the Nakba*, 1–42 (Columbia University Press, 2018); Sari Hanafi, "Explaining Spacio-cide in the Palestinian Territory: Colonization, Separation, and State of Exception," *Current Sociology* 61, no. 2 (2013): 190–205. Oren Yiftachel, "Territory as the kernel of the nation: space, time and nationalism in Israel/Palestine." *Geopolitics* 7, no. 2 (2002): 215–248.

34. Areej Sabbagh-Khoury discusses this point in her article "Tracing Settler Colonialism," and the only exception she notes is Afro-Brazilian genocide in Brazil, but I would not call this an act of population settlers; they were "arrivants," according to Jodi Byrd's analysis.

35. Areej Sabbagh-Khoury, "Memory for Forgetfulness: Conceptualizing a Memory Practice of Settler Colonial Disavowal," *Theory and Society* 52, no. 2 (March 2023): 263–29; Noga Kadman, *Erased from Space and Consciousness: Israel and the Depopulated Palestinian Villages of 1948* (Indiana University Press, 2015); Hagar Kotef, *The Colonizing Self: Or, Home and Homelessness in Israel/Palestine* (Duke University Press, 2020).

36. See, for instance, Bashir Bashir and Amos Goldberg, "Deliberating the Holocaust and the Nakba: Disruptive Empathy and Binationalism in Israel/Palestine," *Journal of Genocide Research* 16, no. 1 (2014): 77–99.

37. Estes, *Our History Is the Future*; Dalsheim, *Israel Has a Jewish Problem*.

38. Jill Lepore, *The Whites of Their Eyes* (Princeton University Press, 2011).

39. Mark Rifkin, *Beyond Settler Time* (Duke University Press, 2017).

40. McKee, "Divergent Visions"; Safa Abu-Rabia, "Is Slavery Over? Black and White Arab Bedouin Women in the Naqab (Negev)," in *Struggle and Survival in Palestine/Israel*, 271–288 (University of California Press, 2012); Omri Grinberg, "Constructing Impossibility: Israeli State Discourses about Palestinian Child Labour," *Children & Society* 30, no. 5 (2016): 396–409.

41. Estes, *Our History Is the Future*.

42. Joan Scott, *Gender and the Politics of History* (Columbia University Press, 1988); Evri and Kotef, "When Does a Native Become a Settler?"; Liron Shani, "Predatory Fleas, Sterile Flies, and the Settlers," *Cultural Anthropology* 38, no. 1 (2023): 87–112.

43. See, for instance, Giordano Nanni, "Time, Empire and Resistance in Settler-Colonial Victoria," *Time & Society* 20, no. 1 (2011): 5–33; Emma Kowal, "Time, Indigeneity and White Anti-racism in Australia," *The Australian Journal of Anthropology* 26, no. 1 (2015): 94–111; Yara Sa'di-Ibraheem, "Settler Colonial Temporalities, Ruinations and Neoliberal Urban Renewal: The Case of Suknet Al-Huresh in Jaffa," *GeoJournal* 87, no. 2 (2022): 661–675.

44. Some examples of such work includes Omar Jabary Salamanca et al., "Past Is Present: Settler Colonialism in Palestine." *Settler Colonial Studies* 2, no. 1 (2012): 1–8; Amahl Bishara, "Driving while Palestinian in Israel and the West Bank: The Politics of Disorientation and the Routes of a Subaltern Knowledge," *American Ethnologist* 42, no. 1 (2015): 33–54; Natalia Gutkowski, "Bodies That Count: Administering Multispecies in Palestine/Israel's Borderlands," *Environment and Planning E: Nature and Space* 4, no. 1 (2021): 135–157; Eghbariah, "Israeli Law and the Rule of Colonial Difference"; Irus Braverman, "Wild Legalities: Animals and Settler Colonialism in Palestine/Israel," *PoLAR: Political and Legal Anthropology Review* 44, no.1 (2021): 7–27; Braverman, *Settling Nature.*

45. See, for instance, Shira N. Robinson, *Citizen Strangers: Palestinians and the Birth of Israel's Liberal Settler State* (Stanford University Press, 2013); Noura Erakat, *Justice for Some: Law and the Question of Palestine* (Stanford University Press, 2020); Yael Berda, *Living Emergency: Israel's Permit Regime in the Occupied West Bank*, Stanford Briefs (Stanford University Press, 2017).

46. The term Green Line (or pre-1967 borders) refers to the demarcation on a map that formed the 1949 armistice agreements between the Israeli army and the armies of neighboring Arab countries following the 1948 war. Contemporaneously, to the west of the Green Line is Israel proper, and to its east the West Bank or the Occupied Palestinian Territory.

47. Kedar, Amara, and Yiftachel, *Emptied Lands*; Alexandre Kedar, "The Legal Transformation of Ethnic Geography: Israeli Law and the Palestinian Landholder 1948–1967," *New York University Journal of International Law & Policy* 33 (2001): 923; Ronen Shamir, "Suspended in Space: Bedouins under the Law of Israel." *Law & Society Review* 30, no. 2 (1996): 231–257.

48. Rema Hammami, "Waiting for Godot at Qualandya: Reflections on Queues and Inequality," *Jerusalem Quarterly* 13 (Summer 2001); Nasser Abourahme, "Spatial Collisions and Discordant Temporalities: Everyday Life between Camp and Checkpoint," *International Journal of Urban and Regional Research* 35, no. 2 (2011): 453–61; Bishara, "Driving while Palestinian in Israel and the West Bank"; H. Tawil-Souri, "Checkpoint Time," *qui parle* 26, no. 2 (2017): 383–422; Julie Peteet, "Closure's Temporality: The Cultural Politics of Time and Waiting," *South Atlantic Quarterly* 117, no. 1 (January 2018): 43–64; Hagar Kotef and Amir Merav, "Between Imaginary Lines: Violence and Its Justifications at the Military Checkpoints in Occupied Palestine," *Theory, Culture & Society* 28 (2011): 55–80; Berda, *Living Emergency*; Mikko Joronen, "Spaces of Waiting: Politics of Precarious Recognition in the Occupied West Bank," *Environment and Planning D: Society and Space* 35, no. 6 (2017): 994–1011. Smadar Lavie also notes bureaucratic subordination embodied in "waiting" in social security regimes as experienced by Mizrahi single mothers. Lavie, *Wrapped in the Flag of Israel: Mizrahi Single Mothers and Bureaucratic Torture* (University of Nebraska Press, 2018).

49. Don Handelman, *Nationalism and the Israeli State: Bureaucratic Logic in Public Events* (Berg, 2004); Don Handelman and Lea Shamgar-Handelman, "The Presence of Absence: The Memorialism of National Death in Israel," in *Grasping Land: Space and Place in Contemporary Israeli Discourse and Experience*, ed. Eyal Ben-Ari and Yoram Bilu, SUNY Series in Anthropology and Judaic Studies (SUNY Press, 1997); Nadia Abu El-Haj, *Facts on the Ground: Archaeological Practice and Territorial Self-Fashioning in Israeli Society* (University of Chicago Press, 2008); Anita Shapira, "The Bible and Israeli Identity," *Association for Jewish Studies Review* 28, no. 1 (2004): 11–41; Braverman, "Wild Legalities"; Gabriel Piterberg, *The Returns of Zionism: Myths, Politics and Scholarship in Israel* (Verso, 2008); Nur Masalha, *The Zionist Bible: Biblical Precedent, Colonialism and the Erasure of Memory*, Bible World (Acumen, 2013); Yael Zerubavel, *Recovered Roots: Collective Memory and the Making of Israeli National Tradition* (University of Chicago Press, 1995); Liora R. Halperin, *The Oldest Guard: Forging the Zionist Settler Past* (Stanford University Press, 2021).

50. Limor Samimian-Darash, "A Pre-event Configuration for Biological Threats: Preparedness and the Constitution of Biosecurity Events," *American Ethnologist* 36, no. 3 (2009): 478–491; Limor Samimian-Darash, "Governing Future Potential Biothreats: Toward an Anthropology of Uncertainty," *Current Anthropology* 54, no. 1 (2012): 1–22; Matan Shapiro and Nurit Bird-David, "Routinergency: Domestic Securitization in Contemporary Israel." *Environment and Planning D: Society and Space* 35, no. 4 (2017): 637–655.

51. Rona Sela, "The Genealogy of Colonial Plunder and Erasure—Israel's Control over Palestinian Archives," *Social Semiotics* 28, no. 2 (2018): 201–229; Rona Sela, "Seized in Beirut: The Plundered Archives of the Palestinian Cinema Institution and Cultural Arts Section," *Anthropology of the Middle East* 12, no. 1 (2017): 83–114; Tamir Sorek, *Palestinian Commemoration in Israel: Calendars, Monuments, and Martyrs* (Stanford University Press, 2015); Kadman, *Erased from Space and Consciousness*; Noga Kadman, "Roots Tourism—Whose Roots? The Marginalization of Palestinian Heritage Sites in Official Israeli Tourism Sites," *Téoros: Revue de recherche en tourisme* 29, no. 1 (2010): 55–66.

52. See Brenna Bhandar, *Colonial Lives of Property* (Duke University Press, 2018) and Irus Braverman, *Settling Nature: The Conservation Regime in Palestine-Israel* (University of Minnesota Press, 2023).

53. Barbara Adam, *Timescapes of Modernity: The Environment and Invisible Hazards* (Routledge, 2005).

54. Adam, *Timescapes of Modernity*; Bear, "Time as Technique"; Ulrike Felt, "Of Timescapes and Knowledgescapes," in *New Languages and Landscapes of Higher Education*, ed. Peter Scott, Jim Gallacher, and Gareth Parry, 129–148 (Oxford, 2016); Rob Kitchin, "The Timescape of Smart Cities," *Annals of the American Association of Geographers* 109, no. 3 (2019): 775–790; Kevin Gillan, "Temporality in Social Movement Theory: Vectors and Events in the Neoliberal Timescape," *Social Movement Studies* 19, no. 5–6 (2020): 516–536.

55. The ninth of Av religious fast commemorates the destruction of the First Temple by the Neo-Babylonian Empire and the Second Temple by the Roman Empire in Jerusalem.

56. At the same time, with a few Palestinian attacks during Jewish holidays, the temporality of Jewish holidays has gone hand in hand with closures on the West Bank banning the entry of Palestinian workers to Israel even though the security regime has changed dramatically since the 1990s.

57. Jon May and Nigel Thrift, eds., *Timespace: Geographies of Temporality*, vol. 13 (Routledge, 2003); Bear, "Time as Technique."

58. See, for instance: Bishara, "Driving while Palestinian in Israel and the West Bank"; Yiftachel, *Ethnocracy: Land and Identity Politics in Israel/Palestine*; Kedar, Amara, and Yiftachel, *Emptied Lands*; Thomas Philip Abowd, *Colonial Jerusalem: The Spatial Construction of Identity and Difference in a City of Myth, 1948–2012* (Syracuse University Press, 2014); Maoz Azaryahu and Arnon Golan, "(Re) Naming the Landscape: The Formation of the Hebrew Map of Israel 1949-1960," *Journal of Historical Geography* 27, no. 2 (2001): 178-195; Julie Peteet, *Space and Mobility in Palestine* (Indiana University Press, 2017); Eyal Ben-Ari and Yoram Bilu, eds., *Grasping Land: Space and Place in Contemporary Israeli Discourse and Experience* (SUNY Press, 2012).

59. Ryan Stock and Trevor Birkenholtz, "The Sun and the Scythe: Energy Dispossessions and the Agrarian Question of Labor in Solar Parks," *The Journal of Peasant Studies* 48, no. 5 (2021): 984-1007; Tania Murray Li, "Rendering Land Investible: Five Notes on Time," *Geoforum* 82 (2017): 276-278; Maywa Montenegro de Wit, "Can Agroecology and CRISPR Mix? The Politics of Complementarity and Moving toward Technology Sovereignty," *Agriculture and Human Values* 39, no. 2 (2022): 733-755.

60. See, for instance, the multiple works by Palestinian artists and activists imagining alternative futures. Abu Hatoum, "Decolonizing [in the] Future"; Tiina Järvi, "Demonstrating the Desired Future: Performative Dimensions of Internally Displaced Palestinians' Return Activities," *Geografiska Annaler: Series B, Human Geography* 103, no. 4 (2021): 380-396; Norma Musih, "Bridging Memories: Training the Imagination to Go Visiting in Israel/Palestine," *Visual Studies* (2021): 1-11; Norma Musih, "Between Knowing and Understanding: Israeli Jews and the Memory of the Palestinian Nakba," *Cultural Studies* 37, no. 3 (2023): 396-417.

61. Sheila Jasanoff and Sang-Hyun Kim, eds., *Dreamscapes of Modernity: Sociotechnical Imaginaries and the Fabrication of Power* (University of Chicago Press, 2015); Diana K. Davis, "Introduction: Imperialism, Orientalism, and the Environment in the Middle East," in *Environmental Imaginaries of the Middle East and North Africa*, ed. Diana K. Davis and Edmund Burke (Ohio University Press, 2011); Maureen McNeil et al., "Conceptualizing Imaginaries of Science, Technology, and Society," *The Handbook of Science and Technology Studies*, ed. Ulrike Felt, Rayvon Fouché, Clark A. Miller, and Laurel Smith-Doerr, 435-464 (MIT Press, 2016).

62. Novick, *Milk and Honey*.

63. Paul Kohlbry, "Palestinian Counter-forensics and the Cruel Paradox of Property," *American Ethnologist* 49, no. 3 (2022): 374–386; Ted Swedenburg, *Memories of Revolt: The 1936–1939 Rebellion and the Palestinian National Past* (University of Arkansas Press, 2003); Ted Swedenburg, "The Palestinian Peasant as National Signifier," *Anthropological Quarterly* (1990): 18–30; Nasser Abufarha, "Land of Symbols: Cactus, Poppies, Orange and Olive Trees in Palestine," *Identities: Global Studies in Culture and Power* 15, no. 3 (2008): 343–368; Braverman, *Planted Flags*; Tesdell, "Wild Wheat to Productive Drylands"; Liron Shani, "Of Trees and People: The Changing Entanglement in the Israeli Desert," *Ethnos* 83, no. 4 (2018): 624–644; Shai M. Dromi and Liron Shani, "Love of Land: Nature Protection, Nationalism, and the Struggle over the Establishment of New Communities in Israel," *Rural Sociology* 85, no. 1 (2020): 111–136; Rafi Grosglik, *Globalizing Organic: Nationalism, Neoliberalism, and Alternative Food in Israel* (SUNY University Press, 2021); Meneley, "Hope in the Ruins"; Yuval Ben-Bassat, "Rural Reactions to Zionist Activity in Palestine before and after the Young Turk Revolution of 1908 as Reflected in Petitions to Istanbul," *Middle Eastern Studies* 49, no. 3 (2013): 349–363.

64. The Ottoman Empire ruled Palestine for four hundred years. As a part of this regime, Palestine was not an independent country but a district of the Greater Syria Ottoman government.

65. Beshara Doumani, *Rediscovering Palestine: Merchants and Peasants in Jabal Nablus, 1700–1900* (University of California Press, 1995), 2–8, 131–142. Nahum Karlinsky, *California Dreaming: Ideology, Society, and Technology in the Citrus Industry of Palestine, 1890–1939* (SUNY Press, 2012), 49–50, 80–82; Mark LeVine, "Land, Law and the Planning of Empire: Jaffa and Tel Aviv during the Late Ottoman and Mandate Periods," in *Constituting Modernity: Private Property in the East and West*, ed. Huri İslamoğlu, 100–148 (I. B. Tauris, 2004); Matan Kaminer, "The Agricultural Settlement of the Arabah and the Political Ecology of Zionism," *International Journal of Middle East Studies* (2021): 1–17.

66. Sherene Seikaly, *Men of Capital: Scarcity and Economy in Mandate Palestine* (Stanford University Press, 2015), 8–9; Roger Owen, *The Middle East in the World Economy, 1800–1914* (Methuen, 1981); Nahla Zu'bi, "The Development of Capitalism in Palestine: The Expropriation of the Palestinian Direct Producers," *Journal of Palestine Studies* 13, no. 4 (1984): 88–109.

67. The OLC advanced five main land categories with different sets of rights and duties. Raja Shehadeh, "The Land Law of Palestine: An Analysis of the Definition of State Lands," *Journal of Palestine Studies* 11, no. 2 (1982): 91. The land categories are *mulk, waqf, matrouk, miri*, and *mawat*. The *mulk* category refers to fully owned land and was found mostly in town centers but was rare in Israel/Palestine. *Waqf* land was endowed for religious and community purposes. *Matrouk* land was allocated for public purposes such as roads. *Miri* land category

is discussed in the text. The fifth OLC category, *mawat*, means "dead land" and refers to wasteland that was not possessed by anyone. *Mawat* "is distant from a town or a village so that the loud voice of a person from the extreme inhabited spot cannot be heard." The OLC declared that anyone who would turn these lands into cultivable land with the authorization of a state official could get miri rights in revived *mawat* land.

68. Article 78 of the Ottoman Land Code.

69. Shafir, *Land, Labor and the Origins of the Israeli-Palestinian Conflict*, 31-42; Amos Nadan, "Colonial Misunderstanding of an Efficient Peasant Institution: Land Settlement and Mushā Tenure in Mandate Palestine, 1921-47," *Journal of the Economic and Social History of the Orient* 46, no. 3 (2003): 320-354; Meari Lena. "The Roles of Palestinian Peasant Women: The Case of al-Birweh Village, 1930–1960," in *Displaced at Home: Ethnicity and Gender among Palestinians in Israel*, ed. Rhoda Ann Kanaaneh and Isis Musair (SUNY Press, 2010); John James Moscrop, *Measuring Jerusalem: The Palestine Exploration Fund and British Interests in the Holy Land* (A&C Black, 2000); Kristen Alff, "Levantine Joint-Stock Companies, Trans-Mediterranean Partnerships, and Nineteenth-Century Capitalist Development," *Comparative Studies in Society and History* 60, no. 1 (2018): 150-177.

70. Kenneth W. Stein, *The Land Question in Palestine, 1917-1939* (UNC Press Books, 2017); Roza El-Eini, *Mandated Landscape: British Imperial Rule in Palestine 1929-1948* (Routledge, 2004).

71. Nadan, "Colonial Misunderstanding of an Efficient Peasant Institution."

72. Mahmoud Yazbak, "From Poverty to Revolt: Economic Factors in the Outbreak of the 1936 Rebellion in Palestine," *Middle Eastern Studies* 36, no. 3 (2000): 93-113; Matthew Hughes, *Britain's Pacification of Palestine: The British Army, the Colonial State, and the Arab Revolt, 1936-1939* (Cambridge University Press, 2019).

73. Stein, *The Land Question in Palestine*; Roger Owen, ed., *Studies in the Economic and Social History of Palestine in the Nineteenth and Twentieth Centuries* (Springer, 1982).

74. Naor Ben-Yehoyada, "The Reluctant Seafarers: Fishing, Self-Acculturation and the Stumbling Zionist Colonisation of the Palestine Coast in the Interbellum Period," *Jewish Culture and History* 13, no. 1 (2012): 7-24; Novick, *Milk and Honey*; Karlinsky, *California Dreaming*; Mustafa Kabha and Nahum Karlinsky, *The Lost Orchard: The Palestinian-Arab Citrus Industry, 1850-1950* (Syracuse University Press, 2021).

75. Omar Tesdell, Yusra Othman, and Saher Alkhoury, "Rainfed Agroecosystem Resilience in the Palestinian West Bank, 1918-2017," *Agroecology and Sustainable Food Systems* 43, no. 1 (2019): 21-39; Nadan, *The Palestinian Peasant Economy under the Mandate*; Kusum Nair, *In Defense of the Irrational Peasant: Indian Agriculture after the Green Revolution* (University of Chicago Press, 1979).

76. Salman Abu Sitta records by name 530 Palestinian towns and villages

that were depopulated. He mentions that his atlas lists a total of 674 depopulated localities but not all are not registered by name as they are either uncertain or satellites of other villages. Salman H. Abu Sitta, *Atlas of Palestine, 1917–1966* (Palestine Land Society, 2010), 106–107. In his preface to an earlier attempt to register the Nakba record, Walid Khalidi mentions that in preparing the volume *All That Remains*, researchers mounted a working list of 436 villages though they were able to document according to the criteria set for the book only 418 villages. He also adds that the criteria of documentation chosen for his book defined a core of permanent structures and a named locality distinguishing it from other places. He notes that such categorization excludes semi-nomadic encampments and Bedouin agriculturalists of the Negev. Khalidi, *All That Remains: The Palestinian Villages Occupied and Depopulated by Israel in 1948* (Institute for Palestine Studies, 1992).These comments indicate that the number of destroyed villages is much higher and indeed similar to Abu Sitta's record. Furthermore, it indicates that even among the Palestinians there are those who are even more otherized and colonized—the Bedouins. Safa Aburabia, "Land, Identity and History: new discourse on the Nakba of Bedouin Arabs in the Naqab," in *Naqab Bedouin and Colonialism: New Perspectives*, ed. M. Nasasra, R. Ratcliffe, S. Abu Rabia-Queder, and S. Richter-Devroe, 90–120 (Routledge, 2014).

77. Meron Benvenisti, *Sacred Landscape* (University of California Press, 2001), 146–147.

78. Hillel Cohen, *Good Arabs: The Israeli Security Agencies and the Israeli Arabs, 1948-1967* (University of California Press, 2011).

79. Khalidi, *All That Remains*; Elia Zureik, *The Palestinians in Israel: A Study in Internal Colonialism* (Routledge, 1979), 116.

80. Fischbach, *Records of Dispossession*, 20–27; Irit Ballas, "Chronotopes of Security Legal Regimes," *University of Toronto Law Journal* 73, no. 1 (2022): 88–111.

81. Kedar, Amara, and Yiftachel, *Emptied Lands*; Kedar, "The Legal Transformation of Ethnic Geography"; Ronen Shamir, "Suspended in Space: Bedouins under the Law of Israel." *Law & Society Review* 30, no. 2 (1996): 231–257.

82. Tania Murray Li, "What Is Land? Assembling a Resource for Global Investment," *Transactions of the Institute of British Geographers* 39, no. 4 (2014): 589–602; Li, "Rendering Land Investible."

83. Karl Marx, *Capital: A Critique of Political Economy*, trans. Ben Fowkes, vol.1, Pelican Marx Library (Vintage Books, 1977); Benny Nuriely, "Tsvira Vepikuach: Hamimshal Htsvai Be-Lod, Yuli 1948-Yuli 1949" (Accumulation and control: The Military Regime in Lod July 1948-July 1949), paper given at the Israeli Anthropological Association, May 30, 2013, Van Leer Institute, Jerusalem; Salman Abu Sitta and Terry Rempel, "The ICRC and the Detention of Palestinian Civilians in Israel's 1948 POW/Labor Camps," *Journal of Palestine Studies* 43, no. 4 (2014): 11–38.

84. Elia T. Zureik, "Transformation of Class Structure among the Arabs in Israel: From Peasantry to Proletariat," *Journal of Palestine Studies* 6, no. 1 (1976):

39–66; Henry Rosenfeld, "From Peasantry to Wage Labor and Residual Peasantry: The Transformation of an Arab Village," in *Process and Pattern in Culture*, 211–234 (Routledge, 2017); Yair Bäuml, "Shi'abud Ha-calcala Ha'Aravit be-YIsrael Le-tovat ha-migzar ha-yehudi" (The subjugation of the Arab economy in Israel for the the Jewish sector 1958–1967), *Hamizrah Hahadash—The New Orient Journal*, no. 48 (2009): 101–129; Yair Bäuml, "MAPAI Committee for Arab Affairs—The Steering Committee for Construction of Establishment Policy towards Israeli Arabs, 1958–68," *Middle Eastern Studies* 47, no. 2 (2011): 413–433; Henry Rosenfeld, "Change, Barriers to Change, and Contradictions in the Arab Village Family 1," *American Anthropologist* 70, no. 4 (1968): 732–752.

81. Zureik, "Transformation of Class Structure among the Arabs in Israel"; Rosenfeld "From Peasantry to Wage Labor and Residual Peasantry"; Bäuml, "Shi'abud Hacalcala Ha'Aravit be-YIsrael Le-tovat ha-migzar ha-yehudi"; Bäuml, "MAPAI Committee for Arab Affairs"; Rosenfeld, "Change, Barriers to Change, and Contradictions in the Arab Village Family."

86. Safa Abu-Rabia, "Memory, Belonging and Resistance: The Struggle over Place among the Bedouin-Arabs of the Naqab/Negev," *Remembering, Forgetting and City Builders*, ed. Tovi Fenster and Haim Yacobi, 65–83 (Routledge 2016); Rouhana and Sabbagh-Khoury, "Memory and the Return of History"; Kiven Strohm, "The Sensible Life of Return: Collaborative Experiments in Art and Anthropology in Palestine/Israel," *American Anthropologist* 121, no. 1 (2019): 243–255; Efrat Ben-Ze'ev, "The Politics of Taste and Smell: Palestinian Rites of Return," *The Politics of Food*, ed. Marianne Elisabeth Lien and Brigitte Nerlich, 141–160 (Berg 2004).

87. Rochelle Davis, *Palestinian Village Histories: Geographies of the Displaced* (Stanford University Press, 2010); Diana Allan, *Refugees of the Revolution: Experiences of Palestinian Exile* (Stanford University Press, 2013).

88. Meneley, "Hope in the Ruins"; Strohm, "The Sensible Life of Return."

89. Sorek, *Palestinian Commemoration in Israel*; Rouhana and Sabbagh-Khoury, "Memory and the Return of History."

90. Rashid I. Khalidi, "Observations on the Right of Return," *Journal of Palestine Studies* 21, no. 2 (1992): 29–40; Allan, *Refugees of the Revolution*.

91. Haim Gvati, *A Hundred Years of Settlement: The Story of Jewish Settlement in the Land of Israel*, vol. 1 (Keter, 1985); Itzhak Arnon and Michael Raviv, "From Fellah to Farmer: A Study on Change in Arab Villages," *Publications on Problems of Regional Development* 31 (1980).

92. For such Marxist theorization, see Ṣabrī Jiryis, *The Arabs in Israel* (Monthly Review Press, 1976); Zureik,1976; Ian Lustick, *Arabs in the Jewish State: Israel's Control of a National Minority*, Modern Middle East Series, no. 6 (University of Texas Press, 1980); Baruch Kimmerling, *Immigrants, Settlers, Natives: The Israeli State and Society between Cultural Pluralism and Cultural Wars* (Am Oved, 2004); Shafir, *Land, Labor and the Origins of the Israeli-Palestinian Conflict*.

93. Raja Khalidi, "Sixty Years after the UN Partition Resolution: What Future for the Arab Economy in Israel?," *Journal of Palestine Studies* 37, no. 2 (2008): 6–22.

94. Ahmad H. Sa'Di, "Modernization as an Explanatory Discourse of Zionist-Palestinian Relations," *British Journal of Middle Eastern Studies* 24, no. 1 (1997): 25–48. Seikaly, *Men of Capital*.

95. Ella Shohat, "The Invention of the Mizrahim," *Journal of Palestine Studies* 29, no. 1 (1999): 5–20; Deborah Bernstein and Shlomo Swirski, "The Rapid Economic Development of Israel and the Emergence of the Ethnic Division of Labour," *British Journal of Sociology* (1982): 64–85; Smadar Sharon, "The Dialectic between Modernization and Orientalization: Ethnicity and Work Relations in the 1950s Lakhish Region Project," *Ethnic and Racial Studies* 40, no. 4 (2017): 732–750; Joseph Massad, "Zionism's Internal Others: Israel and the Oriental Jews," *Journal of Palestine Studies* 25, no. 4 (1996): 53–68.

96. Jay O'Brien, "The Calculus of Profit and Labour-Time in Sudanese Peasant Agriculture," *The Journal of Peasant Studies* 14, no. 4 (1987): 454–468; Bhandar, *Colonial Lives of Property*; Henry Bernstein, *Class Dynamics of Agrarian Change*, vol. 1 (Kumarian Press, 2010); Li, Tania Murray. "Centering Labor in the Land Grab Debate," *The Journal of Peasant Studies* 38, no. 2 (2011): 281–298.

97. Aija Lulle, "Temporal Fix, Hierarchies of Work and Post-Socialist Hopes for a Better Way of Life," *Journal of Rural Studies* 84 (2021): 221–229; Lydia Medland, "'There Is No Time': Agri-food Internal Migrant Workers in Morocco's Tomato Industry," *Journal of Rural Studies* 88 (2021): 482–490. A major platform for publications on critical agrarian studies has been the *Journal of Peasant Studies*; its publication history reflects the lack of engagement with Israel/Palestine except for Paul Kohlbry, "To Cover the Land in Green: Rain-Fed Agriculture and Anti-colonial Land Reclamation in Palestine," *The Journal of Peasant Studies* (2022): 1–19.

98. Additionally, these were mostly Palestinian scholars who published such analyses as early as the 1970s and 1980s, and their voices and analyses were not sufficiently echoed. See Zureik, "Transformation of Class Structure among the Arabs in Israel"; Jiryis, *The Arabs in Israel*; Haim Yacobi, "The Moral Geopolitics of Exported Spatial Development: Revisiting Israeli Involvement in Africa," *Geopolitics* 15, no. 3 (2010): 441–461.

99. Nahla Abdo, "Colonial Capitalism and Agrarian Social Structure: Palestine: A Case Study," *Economic and Political Weekly* (1991): 73–84; Henry Rosenfeld, "Processes of Structural Change within the Arab Village Extended Family," *American Anthropologist* 60, no. 6 (1958): 1127–1139; Rosenfeld, "From Peasantry to Wage Labor and Residual Peasantry"; Salim Tamari, "Building Other People's Homes: The Palestinian Peasant's Household and Work in Israel," *Journal of Palestine Studies* 11, no. 1 (1981): 31–66.

100. Wolfe, "Settler Colonialism and the Elimination of the Native." Alternatively, the following works show how important a labor perspective is in analyzing Israeli settler colonialism: Nimrod Ben Zeev, "Toward a History of Dangerous

Work and Racialized Inequalities in Twentieth-Century Palestine/Israel," *Journal of Palestine Studies* 51, no. 4 (2022): 89–96; Nimrod Ben Zeev, "Palestine along the Colour Line: Race, Colonialism, and Construction Labour, 1918–1948," *Ethnic and Racial Studies* 44, no. 12 (2021): 2190–2212; Andrew Ross, *Stone Men: The Palestinians Who Built Israel* (Verso Books, 2021).

101. Marx, *Capital: A Critique of Political Economy*, 340–416, 655–667, 683–692; Edward P. Thompson, "Time, Work-Discipline, and Industrial Capitalism," *Past & Present* 38 (1967): 56–97.

102. Abdo, "Colonial Capitalism and Agrarian Social Structure." The Marxian term *surplus value* refers to the new value created by workers on top of the cost of their own labor.

103. Alan Gallay, *The Indian Slave Trade: The Rise of the English Empire in the American South, 1670–1717* (Yale University Press, 2009), 18–20; Walter Hixson, *American Settler Colonialism: A History* (Springer, 2013); Edward Cavanagh, "Settler Colonialism in South Africa: Land, Labour and Transformation, 1880–2015," in *The Routledge Handbook of the History of Settler Colonialism*, ed. Edward Cavanagh and Lorenzo Veracini, 313–332 (Routledge, 2016).

104. Sheila Ryan, "Israeli Economic Policy in the Occupied Areas: Foundations of a New Imperialism," *MERIP Reports* 24 (1974): 3–28; Halperin, *The Oldest Guard*.

105. Jonathan L. Dekel-Chen, *Farming the Red Land: Jewish Agricultural Colonization and Local Soviet Power, 1924–1941* (Yale University Press, 2008).

106. However, Palestine was not the only place that was considered a locus to fulfill national Zionist aspirations. The World Zionist Organization founded in 1897 did consider other possible locations for a Jewish national collective settlement, such as Cyprus, Argentina, and Uganda. For ideological and practical reasons, these other sites were ruled out by 1905. Emily McKee, *Dwelling in Conflict: Negev Landscapes and the Boundaries of Belonging* (Stanford University Press, 2016), 4.

107. Novick, *Milk and Honey*; Tesdell, "Wild Wheat to Productive Drylands"; Yael Zerubavel, "Memory, the Rebirth of the Native, and the 'Hebrew Bedouin' Identity," *Social Research: An International Quarterly* 75, no. 1 (2008): 315–352; Monterescu and Handel, "Liquid Indigeneity"; Ian McGonigle, "In Vino Veritas? Indigenous Wine and Indigenization in Israeli Settlements," *Anthropology Today* 35, no. 4 (2019): 7–12; Sarah Sallon et al., "Germination, Genetics, and Growth of an Ancient Date Seed," *Science* 320, no. 5882 (2008): 1464–1464; see also the film by Avner Faingulernt: *In the Desert: A Documentray Diptych* (Ruth Films, 2018); Braverman, *Settling Nature*.

108. This mode of economic support is a second feature of Zionism that is unlike other settler colonies. Jewish settlers in Palestine were not backed by a metropole state hoping to expand its markets and its territorial control. Alternatively, the Jewish philanthropists and the Zionist movement were driven

by a national liberation impetus rather than an expectation of a high return on investments. Gershon Shafir, "Settler Citizenship in the Jewish Colonization of Palestine," in *Settler Colonialism in the Twentieth Century: Projects, Practices, Legacies*, ed. Caroline Elkins and Susan Pedersen, 55–72 (Routledge, 2012); Kimmerling, *Immigrants, Settlers, Natives*, 18, 66–67, 124.

109. Shafir, *Land, Labor and the Origins of the Israeli-Palestinian Conflict*, 9.

110. Liora Halperin usefully criticizes these periodizations and the political structure of "firstness" in a settler colonial structure. See Halperin, *The Oldest Guard.*

111. Zu'bi, "The Development of Capitalism in Palestine"; Shafir, *Land, Labor and the Origins of the Israeli-Palestinian Conflict*; Ryan, "Israeli Economic Policy in the Occupied Areas."

112. Daniel Monterescu and Ariel Handel, "Terroir and Territory on the Colonial Frontier: Making New-Old World Wine in the Holy Land," *Comparative Studies in Society and History* 62, no. 2 (2020): 222–261; Matan Kaminer, "Saving the Face of the Arabah: Thai Migrant Workers and the Asymmetries of Community in an Israeli Agricultural Settlement," *American Ethnologist* 49, no. 1 (2022): 118–131.

113. To compare, the Jewish agrarian sector constituted 11.7 percent in 1961 (Ramsees Gharrah, *Arab Society in Israel: Population, Society, Economy* [Van Leer Publication, 2005]) and 0.9 percent in 2015 (CBS, Agricultural Annual Statistical Report 2015 [Central Bureau of Statistics, 2015]).

114. Gharrah, *Arab Society in Israel* (2015).

115. Rassem Khamaisi, "The Rural-to-Urban Transformation of Arab Localities in Israel and Its Planning Challenges," *Horizons in Geography*, no. 81/82 (2012): 122–142.

116. Tamari, "Building Other People's Homes"; Kaminer, "The Agricultural Settlement of the Arabah"; Kaminer, "Saving the Face of the Arabah."

117. Tamari, "Building Other People's Homes"; Emanuel Farjoun, "Palestinian Workers in Israel: A Reserve Army of Labour," *Khamsin, Journal of Revolutionary Socialists of the Middle East* London 7 (1980): 107–143.

118. A more complete discussion on the role of Thai migrant workers is beyond the scope of this book. For more on their role in local agriculture, please see Rebeca Raijman and Adriana Kemp, "Labor Migration, Managing the Ethnonational Conflict, and Client Politics in Israel," in *Transnational Migration to Israel in Global Comparative Context*, ed Sarah S. Willen, 31–50 (Lexington Books, 2007); Rebeca Raijman and Nonna Kushnirovich, *Labor Migrant Recruitment Practices in Israel* (Ruppin Academic Center, 2012); Matan Kaminer, "Giving Them the Slip: Israeli Employers' Strategic Falsification of Pay Slips to Disguise the Violation of Thai Farmworkers' Right to the Minimum Wage," *Journal of Legal Anthropology* 3, no. 2 (2019): 124–127.

119. Only a marginal minority of these migrant workers are employed by Pal-

estinian citizens of Israel (between 0.6 percent and 2 percent). Kurlannder and Kaminer calculated 2 percent based on the Ministry of Interior quotas. My own calculations based on the Ministry of Agriculture's data was 0.6 percent.

120. Manu Vimalassery, Juliana Hu Pegues, and Alyosha Goldstein, "Introduction: On Colonial Unknowing," *Theory & Event* 19, no. 4 (2016), muse.jhu.edu/article/633283; Byrd, *The Transit of Empire*; Edward Kamau Brathwaite, *The Arrivants: A New World Trilogy—Rights of Passage / Islands / Masks* (Oxford University Press, 1988), 11.

121. Similar to the Thai workers' employment, which transformed Israel's agrarian economy and turned it a globally competitive sector in peripheral areas of the country where it was struggling. Yahel Kurlander and Matan Kaminer, "Permanent Workers in the Backyard: Employing Migrant Farmworkers from Thailand in the Israeli Countryside," *Horizons in Geography* 98 (2020): 131–148; in contrast to the Israeli case, see Candace Fujikane, "Introduction: Asian Settler Colonialism in the US Colony of Hawaiʻi," in *Asian Settler Colonialism*, 1–42 (University of Hawaii Press, 2008).

122. Ministry of Agriculture and Rural Development, "Procedure for Funding Machinery and New Technologies, Precision Agriculture and Laborsaving Machines," January 10, 2018.

123. Ha-shomer Ha-tza'ir means in Hebrew "the young guardian." This youth movement was formed in 1913 in Poland and established the first Zionist-socialist communes in Palestine during the 1920s. It set up kibbutzim before and after the state was founded. Although I developed a critical stance on Zionism, many of the important things I have learned in my life I learned in Ha-shomer Ha-tza'ir. I was an active member of this youth movement for approximately twenty years, living in urban or rural communes and working in education and social change. Learning in the youth movement included informal critical education and inquiry, acting and practicing for social solidarity, activism, and friendship and leadership skills. Zionist youth movements had a central role in education in both the Jewish diaspora and in Israel until the 1990s. The 2020 U.S. Democratic presidential candidate Bernie Sanders lived for a short time in one of the kibbutzim of the Ha-shomer Ha-tza'ir movement in his youth.

124. Mapam was the political party that grew from the kibbutzim of Ha-shomer Ha-tza'ir In 1992, this party merged into what is today the Meretz party in the Israeli parliament. In Ha-shomer Ha-tza'ir we were educated about solidarity and "brotherhood between peoples" (Achvat Amim) and about Zionist history that was never taught in school, such as Martin Buber's Brit Shalom—the advocacy for a binational state in Palestine/Israel. In the 1940s, the movement supported a binational state in Palestine/Israel, but the 1948 War ended that support. Hashomer Hatza'ir is understood as a leftist stream of Zionism. During the 1948 War this movement's kibbutzim and army officials sometimes participated in actively expelling Palestinians from their villages but many other times actively

opposed and refused Palestinian expulsion commands. See Tom Pessah, "The Palestinian Villages and Villagers: Between Expulsion and Representation," in *Encounters between History and Anthropology in Studying the Israeli-Palestinian Space*, ed. Dafna Hirsch, 147–175 (Van Leer Institute and Kibbutz Meuchad Publication, 2019); Areej Sabbagh-Khoury, *Colonizing Palestine: The Zionist Left and the Making of Palestinian Nakba* (Stanford University Press, 2023).

125. Fabian, *Time and the Other*; Linda Tuhiwai Smith, *Decolonizing Methodologies: Research and Indigenous Peoples* (Zed Books, 2021); Jean Comaroff and John L. Comaroff, *Of Revelation and Revolution*, Vol. 1: *Christianity, Colonialism, and Consciousness in South Africa* (University of Chicago Press, 2008).

126. Still being in that social position takes a heavy toll on the ability to show one's belonging to a collective, as Andreas Hackl describes so well. Hackl, *The Invisible Palestinians: The Hidden Struggle for Inclusion in Jewish Tel Aviv* (Indiana University Press, 2022).

127. Erica Weiss, "Pseudonyms as Anti-Citation," in Rethinking Pseudonyms in Ethnography, ed. Carole McGranahan and Erica Weiss, American Ethnologist website, December 13, 2021, https://americanethnologist.org/features/collections/rethinking-pseudonyms-in-ethnography/pseudonyms-as-anti-citation.

Chapter 1

Portions of this chapter appear in a previously published article: Natalia Gutkowski, "Governing through Timescape: Israeli Sustainable Agriculture Policy and the Palestinian-Arab Citizens," *International Journal of Middle East Studies* 50, no. 3 (2018). © Cambridge University Press 2018, reprinted with permission.

1. While Sahl al-Battuf is the Arabic name of this site mostly owned by Palestinian citizens, the place is referred to in policy documents from 1990 to 2017 and on maps by its Hebrew name, Bikat Beit Netofa. The Hebrew etymology of *netofa* refers to drops of water, and the Jewish sage Maimonides in his Mishna Torah interpretation (twelfth century) says that this land is very humid and therefore it is called Beit Netofa. I will be moving between the names al-Battuf and Beit Netofa to emphasize the political dynamic between the Arabic local name and the state's official name for the space. Also, in a novel act of recognition of the Palestinian-Arab landholders, the new master plan for 2017–2018 uses both Hebrew and Arabic names. I suggest this was not the state's official decision but rather an initiative of the architects leading the plan. See Arieh Rahamimov and Liora Meron, *Tokhnit Kollelet Le-Bikat Beit Netofa-Sahel al-Batuf* (A comprehensive plan for Beit Netofa Valley-al-Battuf Plain), Ministry of Agriculture, Ministry of Environmental Protection, and Kishon Drainage Authority, January 2017.

2. A dunum (or dunam) is a unit of land area used in territories of the Ottoman Empire representing the amount of land that can be plowed in a day. One dunum is a thousand square meters or 0.25 acre.

3. The data appears in Ministry of Agriculture and Rural Development and

Ministry of Environmental Protection, "Mitve Lekidum Tochnit Koleleanit Lebikat beit netofa" (Outline for master plan for Beit Netofa Valley), January 11, 2012.

4. The regional planning district committees are subdivisions of the national planning authorities under the jurisdiction of the Israeli Ministry of Interior Affairs.

5. Ofer Steinitz, Ministry of Agriculture, interview with the author, June 12, 2012, Beit Dagan, Israel. Steinitz had only a one-year appointment at the Ministry of Agriculture, and he later moved to work at Israel's Nature and Park Authority. His figure has become emblematic of the ecologist hires in the ministry, with their expertise and mode of thinking. This is why I prefer name him "the ecologist."

6. I discussed the agrarian imaginary in the introduction. In discussing agrarian imaginaries, I thread elements of Diana K. Davis and Edmund Burke's discussion on environmental imaginaries in their edited volume *Environmental Imaginaries of the Middle East and North Africa*, 3; and of Jasanoff and Kim, *Dreamscapes of Modernity*.

7. The original plans can be found in the Israel State Archive: ISA-moag-DeputyMinister-000aaas, files from October 1992 to April 1996 of Walid Saedk, the agriculture vice minister who promoted the plan.

8. Itzhak Elazari-Volkani, "Modernizing the Fellah's Farm," *Palestine and Near East Economic Magazine* 8 (1930): 268–270; Arnon and Raviv, "From Fellah to Farmer"; Sa'di, "Modernization as an Explanatory Discourse of Zionist-Palestinian Relations," 82–95.

9. Glenna Anton, "Blind Modernism and Zionist Waterscape: The Huleh Drainage Project," *Jerusalem Quarterly* 35 (2008); Omri Tubi, "Kill Me a Mosquito and I Will Build a State: Political Economy and the Socio-technicalities of Jewish Colonization in Palestine, 1922–1940," *Theory and Society* 50, no. 1 (2021): 97–124; Sandra M. Sufian, *Healing the Land and the Nation: Malaria and the Zionist Project in Palestine, 1920–1947* (University of Chicago Press, 2008).

10. Laithi became in 2020 the municipal director of SHEFA (in Hebrew an acronym for City Improvements), a municipal unit that oversees municipal departments such as environmental management, sanitary care, and landscape planning.

11. In "Timescapes and Agrarian Imaginaries" in the book's introduction, I discuss the term *timescape* as the landscape of time, illustrating multiple layers of time composed into one social reality.

12. Our meetings took place in the summer of 2014 and we have kept in touch ever since.

13. See, for instance, his interviews (in Arabic) for Kul al-Arab News (news of Palestinians in Israel) on February 16, 2021, https://www.alarab.com/Article/983582?fbclid=IwARorGCbF_YZkCUbofoLmaRxhioCvmFtyNcOWzunPcn20Vn YBmiIXQD6Sblo; and for Jordanian television, Roya channel, on March 3, 2021, https://www.youtube.com/watch?v=FzOXIJTngAo.

14. Paige West, "Making the Market: Specialty Coffee, Generational Pitches, and Papua New Guinea," *Antipode* 42, no. 3 (2010): 690–718; Rafi Grosglik, *Globalizing Organic*.

15. Hirokazu Miyazaki, "The Temporalities of the Market," *American Anthropologist* 105, no. 2 (2003): 255–265.

16. Abbie Rosner, "Roasting Green Wheat in Galilee," *Gastronomica* 11, no. 2 (2011): 66–68; see also Alaa Badarna, "Sahl al-Battuf—A Popular Market for Rainfed Produce," June 5, 2020, https://www.alarab.com/Article/949973.

17. Sherene Seikaly, "The Matter of Time," *The American Historical Review* 124, no. 5 (2019): 1681–1688.

18. The villages that resisted during the war, such as 'Eilabun, were partially depopulated by flight and expulsion. In 'Eilabun the inhabitants were allowed back. The only village that was completely destroyed in the area, with its inhabitants fleeing to Lebanon or remaining in the neighboring al-Battuf villages, was Mi'ar, which was conquered in July 1948. See Benny Morris, *The Birth of the Palestinian Refugee Problem Revisited* (Cambridge University Press, 2003), 475. For a discussion of the state's legal mechanisms for appropriating Palestinian land, see Geremy Forman and Alexandre Kedar, "From Arab Land to 'Israel Lands': The Legal Dispossession of the Palestinians Displaced by Israel in the Wake of 1948," *Environment and Planning D: Society and Space* 22, no. 6 (2004): 809–30; Geremy Forman, "Law and the Historical Geography of the Galilee: Israel's Litigatory Advantages during the Special Operation of Land Settlement," *Journal of Historical Geography* 32 (2006): 796–817; and Fischbach, *Records of Dispossession*.

19. Lustick, *Arabs in the Jewish State*, 177.

20. Doumani, *Rediscovering Palestine*; Zureik.*The Palestinians in Israel*. p.115–129; Rosenfeld, "From Peasantry to Wage Labor and Residual Peasantry"; Bäuml, Shi'abud ha-kalkala ha-'Aravit beyisrael letovat ha-migzar ha-yehudi; Forman and Kedar, "From Arab Land to 'Israel Lands.'"

21. Ghazi Falah, "Israeli 'Judaization' Policy in Galilee and Its Impact on Local Arab Urbanization," *Political Geography Quarterly* 8, no. 3 (1989): 229–253.

22. This subsidiary organization oversees the real estate transactions that the JNF cannot legally perform. Its actions and records are not transparent.

23. Nur Masalha, *Catastrophe Remembered: Palestine, Israel and the Internal Refugees: Essays in Memory of Edward W. Said (1935–2003)* (Zed Books, 2005).

24. During those protests, Israeli policemen killed six unarmed Palestinian protesters, wounded one hundred people, and arrested one hundred Palestinians. Khalil Nakhleh, "Yawm al-Ard" (Land Day), in *The Palestinians in Israel: Readings in History, Politics and Society*, ed. Nadim Rouhana and Areej Sabbagh-Khoury, 83 (Mada al-Carmel—Arab Center for Applied Social Research, 2011). Tamir Sorek discusses the politics of the emergence of Land Day as a national day in *Palestinian Commemoration in Israel*.

25. The Arab Center of Alternative Planning provides this data on their web-

site. See https://www.ac-ap.org/en/article/556/Series-of-maps-showing-the-land -confiscations-from-Arab-villages-and-townships-in-different-regions-in-Israel, accessed April 18, 2016.

26. Until the Separation/Segregation Barrier was constructed in 2002 and 2003, the National Water Carrier was the largest infrastructure project built by the state.

27. Lustick, *Arabs in the Jewish State*; Jiryis, *The Arabs in Israel*, 84.

28. Leena Dallasheh, "Troubled Waters: Citizenship and Colonial Zionism in Nazareth," *International Journal of Middle East Studies* 47 (2015): 467–87; Yoav Kislev, *Meshek Hamaim shel Israel* (Israel's water sector), Policy Research for Taub Center for Social Research, 2011; Jan Selby, "Cooperation, Domination and Colonisation: The Israeli-Palestinian Joint Water Committee," *Water Alternatives* 6, no. 1 (2013): 1–24.

29. Nikhil Anand, "Pressure: The Politechnics of Water Supply in Mumbai," *Cultural Anthropology* 26, no. 4 (2011): 542–564; Antina Von Schnitzler, "Citizenship Prepaid: Water, Calculability, and Techno-politics in South Africa," *Journal of Southern African Studies* 34, no. 4 (2008): 899–917.

30. Samer Alatout, "'States' of Scarcity: Water, Space, and Identity Politics in Israel, 1948–59," *Environment and Planning D: Society and Space* 26, no. 6 (2008): 959–982; Walter Lowdermilk, *Palestine: The Land of Promise* (Harper and Brothers, 1944).

31. Muna Dajani, "Thirsty Water Carriers: The Production of Uneven Waterscapes in Sahl al-Battuf," *Contemporary Levant* 5, no. 2 (2020): 97–112.

32. Israel has become a state rich with water resources due to its reliance on desalination since 2015. Still, for Palestinian agriculturalists, irrigation water access is not simple and requires intervention of assisting bodies, although officially, there is water they can receive for agrarian purposes allocated by the Ministry of Agriculture and the Water Authority. The contemporary case of rehabilitation along Wadi Saffurya/Wadi al-Malak (Arabic, Tzipori Stream) shows that.

33. Mahmoud Darwish, *Journal of an Ordinary Grief*, trans. by Ibrahim Muhawi (Archipelago Books, 2010). This excerpt is reprinted with the permission of Archipelago Books.

34. Timothy Mitchell, "Society, Economy, and the State Effect," in *State/Culture: State Formation after the Cultural Turn*, ed. G. Steinmetz (Cornell University Press, 1999), 76–97; Akhil Gupta, "Blurred Boundaries: The Discourse of Corruption, the Culture of Politics, and the Imagined State," in *The Anthropology of the State: A Reader*, ed. Aradhana Sharma and Akhil Gupta, 211–242 (Blackwell, 2006).

35. For more examples of blurred state boundaries in Israel/Palestine, see Michal Kravel-Tovi, *When the State Winks: The Performance of Jewish Conversion in Israel* (Columbia University Press, 2017); Gutkowski, "Bodies That Count"; Uri Ben-Eliezer, "State versus Civil Society? A Non-Binary Model of Domination

through the Example of Israel," *Journal of Historical Sociology* 11, no. 3 (1998): 370–396; Hedva Eyal and Limor Samimian-Darash, "Unintended Securitization: Military, Medical, and Political-Security Discourses in the Humanitarian Treatment of Syrian Casualties in Israel," *Conflict and Society* 5, no. 1 (2019): 55–71.

36. James Ferguson, *The Anti-politics Machine: "Development," Depoliticization and Bureaucratic Power in Lesotho* (CUP Archive, 1990).

37. Dr. Didi Kaplan, interview with the author, Ramat Hanadiv, November 27, 2014.

38. Dr. Didi Kaplan, interview with the author, Bikat Yad Hanadiv, November 27, 2014.

39. Ministry of Interior, Northern District Committee, Minutes, July 9, 2009.

40. Kaplan, interview with the author, Bikat Yad Hanadiv, November 27, 2014.

41. Braverman, "*Nof kdumim*: Remaking the Ancient Landscape in East Jerusalem's National Parks"; Irus Braverman, "Silent Springs: The Nature of Water and Israel's Military Occupation," *Environment and Planning E: Nature and Space* 3, no. 2 (2020): 527–551.

42. Ministry of Environmental Protection and Nature and Park Authority, Minutes, January 12, 2012.

43. Rahamimov and Meron, *Tokhnit Kollelet Le-Bikat Beit Netofa-Sahel al-Battuf*, 141.

44. Ali Shawahneh, interview with the author, Sakhnin, June 22, 2014.

45. Abdellah Hammoudi, *A Season in Mecca: Narrative of a Pilgrimage* (Polity Press, 2006). Javier Auyero, *Patients of the State: The Politics of Waiting in Argentina* (Duke University Press, 2012); Lavie, *Wrapped in the Flag of Israel*.

46. Iftah Sinai, Nature and Parks Authority, interview with the author, Haifa, October 1, 2014.

47. Nayanika Mathur, "The Reign of Terror of the Big Cat: Bureaucracy and the Mediation of Social Times in the Indian Himalaya," *Journal of the Royal Anthropological Institute* 20, no. S1 (2014): 148–165.

48. Author's field notes, January 16, 2014.

49. Stephen Legg, "Beyond the European Province: Foucault and Postcolonialism," in *Space, Knowledge and Power: Foucault and Geography*, ed. Jeremy W. Crampton and Stuart Elden, 265–289 (Routledge, 2007).

50. Handelman, *Nationalism and the Israeli State*; Berda, *Living Emergency*.

51. Colin Hoag, "Assembling Partial Perspectives: Thoughts on the Anthropology of Bureaucracy," *PoLAR: Political and Legal Anthropology Review* 34 (2011): 81–94; Matthew S. Hull, "The File: Agency, Authority, and Autography in an Islamabad Bureaucracy," *Language & Communication* 23 (2003): 287–314.

52. Peteet, *Space and Mobility in Palestine*. Sophia C. Stamatopoulou-Robbins, "Failure to Build: Sewage and the Choppy Temporality of Infrastructure in Palestine," *Environment and Planning E: Nature and Space* 4, no. 1 (2020): 28–42, https://doi.org/10.1177/2514848620908193; Nayrouz Abu Hatoum, "For "A No-State Yet

to Come": Palestinians Urban Place-Making in Kufr Aqab, Jerusalem," *Environment and Planning E: Nature and Space* 4, no. 1 (2020): 85–108, https://doi.org/10.1177/2514848620943877.

53. Darwish here refers to *Waiting for Godot* (1953), the groundbreaking tragicomic play of Theatre of the Absurd playwright Samuel Beckett that brings together two actors who wait during the whole play for Godot, who never shows up. They have not met him before and they are not sure who he is, but they know they need to wait for him for some unclear reason.

54. Richard Baxstrom, "Even Governmentality Begins as an Image: Institutional Planning in Kuala Lumpur," *Focaal* 61 (2011): 61–72, http://dx.doi.org/10.3167/fcl.2011.610105.

55. Sheila Jasanoff, *Science and Public Reason* (Routledge, 2012).

56. A couple examples regarding this reiterative discourse are Ministry of Agriculture and Environmental Protection Ministry Policy for Beit Netofa, January 11, 2012, and March 13, 2014.

57. Laura A. Ogden, *Swamplife: People, Gators, and Mangroves Entangled in the Everglades* (University of Minnesota Press, 2011); Ann Vileisis, *Discovering the Unknown Landscape: A History of America's Wetlands* (Island Press, 1999).

58. Alon Tal, *Pollution in a Promised Land* (University of California Press, 2002), 152; Anton, "Blind Modernism and Zionist Waterscape: The Huleh Drainage Project."

59. The drainage of Huleh Lake is also seen as one of the events that led to the founding of the Israeli environmental movement. In response to the Huleh drainage and its habitat loss, activists established the Society of Protection of Nature in Israel. See Tal, *Pollution in a Promised Land*, 115–118.

60. Sufian, *Healing the Land and the Nation,* 101–136; Tubi, "Kill Me a Mosquito and I Will Build a State."

61. Bishara, "Driving while Palestinian in Israel and the West Bank"; Ronen Shamir, *Current Flow: The Electrification of Palestine* (Stanford University Press: 2013).; Kurtiç Ekin, "Infrastructural Decay: Maintenance Ecologies and Labor in the Çoruh Basin," *Cultural Anthropology* 38, no. 1 (2023): 142–170.

62. Sufian, *Healing the Land and the Nation.*

63. Samer Alatout, "Bringing Abundance into Environmental Politics: Constructing a Zionist Network of Water Abundance, Immigration, and Colonization," *Social Studies of Science* 39 (2009): 363–94.

64. Other infrastructural projects also differentiated populations. See Shamir, *Current Flow*; Dallasheh, "Troubled Waters: Citizenship and Colonial Zionism in Nazareth."

65. Alatout, "Bringing Abundance into Environmental Politics."

66. Munir Hammoudi, testifying before the Knesset Economy Committee on the al-Battuf flooding, April 30, 2013, https://fs.knesset.gov.il//19/Committees/19_ptv_230209.doc.

67. Rabea Eghbariah, "Ma'avak 'Akub Meza'atar: 'Al Tsimhei ha-makhal shel ha-mitbah ha-falastini vehukei Haganat ha-tsomeah ba-din ha-iysraeli," in *Studies in Food Law*, ed. Aeyal Gross and Yofi Tirosh, 497–533. Law, Society, and Culture Series (Tel Aviv University Press, 2017).

68. Tomaz Mastnak, Julia Elyachar, and Tom Boellstorff, "Botanical Decolonization: Rethinking Native Plants," *Environment and Planning D: Society and Space* 32, no. 2 (2014): 363–380; William Cronon, *Changes in the Land: Indians, Colonists, and the Ecology of New England* (Hill and Wang, 2011); Alfred W. Crosby, *Ecological Imperialism* (Cambridge University Press, 2015); Gutkowski, "Bodies That Count."

69. Arturo Escobar, *Territories of Difference: Place, Movements, Life, Redes* (Duke University Press, 2008); Paul Nadasdy, "The Anti-politics of TEK: The Institutionalization of Co-management Discourse and Practice," *Anthropologica* 47, no. 2 (2005): 215–232; Karl Jacoby, *Crimes against Nature: Squatters, Poachers, Thieves, and the Hidden History of American Conservation* (University of California Press, 2014); Shalini Randeria, "Global Designs and Local Lifeworlds: Colonial Legacies of Conservation, Disenfranchisement and Environmental Governance in Postcolonial India," *interventions* 9, no. 1 (2007): 12–30; Emek Shave, *From Territorial Contiguity to Historical Continuity: Asserting Israeli Control through National Parks in East Jerusalem*, 2014; Raja Shehadeh, *Palestinian Walks: Forays into a Vanishing Landscape* (Scribner, 2008).

70. Iftah Sinai and Mimi Ron, "Seker Tsmahim Nedirim Bevikat Beit Netofa" (unpublished survey, 2006) 2–3; Iftah Sinai, Mimi Ron, and Shai Koren, "Seker Tsmahim Nedirim Bevikat Beit Netofa 2004–2011" (unpublished survey, 2012): 5.

71. Author's field notes, January 15, 2013.

72. Author's field notes, January 15, 2013.

73. Michel Foucault, *Madness and Civilization,* trans. R. Howard (Pantheon, 1965); Gaytri Chakravorty Spivak, "Can the Subaltern Speak?," *Die Philosophin* 14, no. 27 (2003): 42–58.

74. Hanadi Hijris, interview with author, June 15, 2014.

75. Michel Foucault, *Power/Knowledge: Selected Interviews and Other Writings, 1972–1977* (Pantheon, 1980); Jasanoff, *Science and Public Reason*; Andrew S. Mathews, *Instituting Nature: Authority, Expertise, and Power in Mexican Forests* (MIT Press, 2011).

76. Fikret Berkes, Johan Colding, and Carl Folke, "Rediscovery of Traditional Ecological Knowledge as Adaptive Management," *Ecological Applications* 10, no. 5 (2000): 1251–1262; Virginia D. Nazarea, "Local Knowledge and Memory in Biodiversity Conservation," *Annual Review of Anthropology* 35 (2006): 317–335.

77. Fabian, *Time and the Other.*

78. Ministry of Agriculture and Ministry of Environmental Protection, "Mitve Lekidum Tochnit Koleleanit Lebikat beit netofa."

79. Ministry of Agriculture and Ministry of Environmental Protection, "Mitve Lekidum Tochnit Koleleanit Lebikat beit netofa."

80. Racheli Einav, "Haim 'Al Pi Govah Hamayim," *Ynet*, August 26, 2009, accessed 7 September 2017, http://www.ynet.co.il/articles/0,7340,L-3767471,00.html.

81. This is a dynamic prevalent not only in the case of Israel/Palestine, but it is also well-documented in scholarship on the Middle East and Western imagination of it. See Edward W. Said, *Orientalism* (Vintage Books, 2003); Khaled Furani and Dan Rabinowitz, "The Ethnographic Arriving of Palestine," *Annual Review of Anthropology* 40 (2011): 475–91; Lara Deeb and Jessica Winegar, *Anthropology's Politics: Disciplining the Middle East* (Stanford University Press, 2015).

82. The author's translation. Kaplan is cited in Haim Shenhar, "Kelim leshinui megamat pituach beiyechidat nof haklait maosrtit—hamikre shel bet netofa" (Tools for changing development in a landscape unit of traditional agriculture—The case of Beit Netofa) (MA thesis, Haifa University, 2005), 29.

83. Beshara B. Doumani, "Rediscovering Ottoman Palestine: Writing Palestinians into History." *Journal of Palestine Studies* 21, no. 2 (1992): 5–28. p. 7–9; Furani and Rabinowitz, "The Ethnographic Arriving of Palestine."

84. Rifkin, *Beyond Settler Time*.

85. Tradition as an explanatory tool obscures political interpretation in anthropological writings as well. See, for example, Talal Asad, "Anthropological Texts and Ideological Problems: An Analysis of Cohen on Arab Villages in Israel," *Economy and Society* 4 (1975): 251–282; and Dan Rabinowitz, "Oriental Othering and National Identity: A Review of Early Israeli Anthropological Studies of Palestinians," *Identities: Global Studies in Culture and Power* 9 (2002): 305–325.

86. Amir Pearlberg, Liron Amdur, and Uri Ramon, *'Ibudim Bney Kayma Shel Karmey Zeitim Bagalil Hama'aravi- Behinat Mishtanim Kalkalim, Hevratim Ve-ecologim, Do" Sofi* (Pearlberg Report, Kibbutz Ein Karmel, Nekudat Hen, 2012).

87. David A. Wesley, *State Practices and Zionist Images: Shaping Economic Development in Arab Towns in Israel* (Berghahn Books, 2006).

88. I spent time with Ali 'Antar in the fields of al-Batuf and interviewed him on June 21, 2014.

89. Piers Blaikie and Harold Brookfield, "Defining and Debating the Problem," *Land Degradation and Society* (Routledge2015; Paul Robinson, "The Trickster Science," in *The Routledge Handbook of Political Ecology*, ed. Tom Perreault, Gavin Bridge, and James McCarthy, 89–101 (Routledge, 2015).

90. Iftah Sinai, interview with author, October 1, 2014.

91. Paul E. Nadasdy, "Wildlife as Renewable Resource: Competing Conceptions of Wildlife, Time and Management in the Yukon," in *Timely Assets: The Politics of Resources and Their Temporalities*, ed. E. E. Ferry and M. E. Limbert, 75–106 (School for Advanced Research Press, 2008).

92. Interview with Laithi, December 11, 2012.

93. Simone Abram, "The Time It Takes: Temporalities of Planning," *Journal of the Royal Anthropological Institute* 20 (2014): 129–147.

94. In al-Battuf, Palestinian citizens echo what Samer Alatout has pointed out as the distinct environmental narratives of Jewish-Israelis and Palestinians. See Alatout, "Towards a Bio-territorial Conception of Power: Territory, Population, and Environmental Narratives in Palestine and Israel," *Political Geography* 25, no. 6 (2006): 601–621.

95. In this way, al-Battuf echoes Diana Davis's critique of lingering environmental imaginaries of the Middle East, such as the case of desertification as an international problem under UNESCO. See Davis, *The Arid Lands: History, Power, Knowledge* (MIT Press, 2016).

96. Abourahme, "Spatial Collisions and Discordant Temporalities"; Berda, *Living Emergency*; Kotef and Amir, "Between Imaginary Lines."

97. George Holmes, "What is a Land Grab? Exploring Green Grabs, Conservation, and Private Protected Areas in Southern Chile," *Journal of Peasant Studies* 41, no. 4 (2014): 547–567; Evangelia Apostolopoulou and William M. Adams, "Neoliberal Capitalism and Conservation in the Post-Crisis Era: The Dialectics of 'Green' and 'Un-green' Grabbing in Greece and the UK," *Antipode* 47, no. 1 (2015): 15–35; Dianne E. Rocheleau, "Networked, Rooted and Territorial: Green Grabbing and Resistance in Chiapas," *Journal of Peasant Studies* 42, no. 3–4 (2015): 695–723; Saturnino M. Borras Jr. et al., "Towards a Better Understanding of Global Land Grabbing: An Editorial Introduction," *The Journal of Peasant Studies* 38, no. 2 (2011): 209–216.

98. The Government of Change Coalition was formed to block Benjamin Netanyahu. This government created an improbable coalition of two blocs: three rightist parties and four center and left parties, which appealed to the bourgeois and intelligentsia. The two blocs, with the support of a moderate conservative Islamist party led by Mansour Abbas, whose aim was to increase investment in Arab-Israeli communities, initially held a bare majority of sixty-one seats in the Knesset. This government was in power from June 13, 2021, until December 29, 2022.

The Ministry of Agriculture announced the funds allocation scheme for Sahel al-Battuf in "Investment Supports for Agriculture in Arab Society Support Procedure," May 8, 2023, https://www.gov.il/BlobFolder/rfp/arab_society_support_procedure_government_decision_550_2023/he/investment_supports_agri_arab_society_support_procedure_government_decision_550_2023.pdf.

99. Authority for Economic Development of Minorities, post on funding for Sahel al-Battuf, Facebook May 15, 2023, https://www.facebook.com/100071464000674/posts/pfbid0ZVgVG127Mvyij5opuo5z6dKHaq1oEVkLAh6j1QDPmgRBR3NyTj5dQ5iFjRX8xavEl/?mibextid=Nif5oz.

As this book went to print, it was reported in Israeli media that the religious right Finance Minister Bezalel Smotrich was threatening to freeze the money allocated to Arab municipalities through Decision 550.

Chapter 2

1. Dunum measurement is defined in chapter 1. This scene was depicted in newspapers: Kobi Nahshoni, "Heter ha-mekhirah yatsa la-derekh" (The sale permit has hit the road), *Ynet*—Yediot Aahronot, September 5, 2007, https://www.ynet.co.il/articles/0,7340,L-3446165,00.html. Another figure for the land sold is available through the contract of the later sabbath year as it appears in Avi Schiff, "Likrat ha-shmitah mokhrim et admot ha-medina le-goy" (Toward shmitah: The state land is sold to a gentile), *Behadrei Haredim*, September 17, 2014, https://tinyurl.com/35pb22wr.

2. Video documentation of this ritual is available from the following shmitah year, when George Shtreichman, a "non-religion assigned" Ukrainian, bought land from the state. See Tiram Sasson, "Tzfu: Kakh Nimkeru Karkaot ha-Medinah Le-Ger-Toshav" (Watch: The sale of the state's land to a resident-non-Jew), *Srugim*, September 23, 2014, https://tinyurl.com/4zrst25b.

3. Although the Israeli state sees the Druze as historically "loyal citizens" and allies, they were also dispossessed of their historical land in the aftermath of the 1948 War. Ramez Eid and Tobias Haller, "Burning Forests, Rising Power: Towards a Constitutionality Process in Mount Carmel Biosphere Reserve," *Human Ecology* 46 (2018): 41–50; Hussein Abu Hussein and Fiona McKay, *Access Denied—Palestinian Land Rights in Israel* (Zed Books, 2003).

4. "Good Arab" is a term colloquially used by Israelis to point out a "loyal" Arab who does not oppose the state or the Zionist project. It is a term with a loaded history. See Cohen, *Good Arabs: The Israeli Security Agencies and the Israeli Arabs*.

5. For more on the origins of the Jewish-Druze alliance, see Laila Parsons, "The Palestinian Druze in the 1947–1949 Arab-Israeli War," *Israel Studies* 2, no. 1 (1997): 72–93.

6. The seventh-year *shviit* in Hebrew is another name for this year in the Jewish calendar.

7. Leviticus 25:1–5. The commandment appears in Exodus 23:10–12, Leviticus, chapter 25; and Deuteronomy, chapters 15 and 21.

8. The shmita biblical commandment also includes debt release, which has also been granted a rabbinical circumvention. Although it is a fascinating theme, a discussion of the radical Jewish commandment of debt release in shmita is beyond the scope of this chapter.

9. The practice of rest during the seventh year is evident today in the sabbatical year for education workers.

10. However, there was historical continuity in practicing shmita. According to the Talmud and Mishnah (major works of Jewish law and its interpretation

from CE 200 to 400) as well as Greek historians, Jews practiced shmita after the destruction of the Temple in CE 70. Roman powers in the land enforced taxation measures and religious restrictions on Jewish rituals, and so the rabbis allowed alleviations in the practice of the commandment until the practice became uncommon. See Shmuel Safrai, "Mitzvat Shevieit Ba-metziut She-leahar Hurban Bait Sheni" (The Seventh Year Commandment in the reality post Temple destruction), in *Shmitah: Mekorot, Hagut, Mehkar*, 117–164 (Misrad Ha-Hinuch Vehatarbut [Ministry of Education and Culture], 1993); Haim Mordecai Schechter, *Hishtalshelut ha-shemitah: mi-tekufat bayit sheni 'ad ha-yom ha-zeh: shemitat karka'ot shemita kesafim tosefet shevi'it* (The evolution of shmitah from the Second Temple until today) (Tel Aviv [no publisher identified], 1966), 27–36.

11. Generally, in Judaism rabbis can issue permits to solve contradictions of Jewish law and everyday conditions. The major rabbinical, scholarly work in favor of the sale permit was articulated by Rabbi Avraham Yitshak Kook in *Shabbat Ha'aretz* (Sabbath of the land) (Jerusalem, 1909). On the significance of this circumvention, see Arye Edrei, "From Orthodoxy to Religious Zionism: Rabbi Kook and the Sabbatical Year Polemic," *Dine Israel: Studies in Halakhah and Jewish Law* 26 (2009): 45–145. There were earlier rabbinical opinions in favor of shmita circumvention through the land sale that had been carried out since 1889, but Kook's writing is considered the most comprehensive explanation and justification of the land sale.

12. Noel Castree, "The Spatio-temporality of Capitalism," *Time & Society* 18, no. 1 (2009): 26–61.

13. Asher Cohen and Bernard Susser, "The 'Sabbatical' Year in Israeli Politics: An Intra-religious and Religious-Secular Conflict from the Nineteenth through the Twenty-First Centuries," *Journal of Church and State* 52, no. 3 (2010): 454–475.

14. Binyamin Brown, "Kdushat Eretz Yisrael Be'rei Pulmus Ha-Shmitah." in Avi'ezer Ravitski, *Erets-Yisra'el ba-hagut ha-Yehudit ba-me'ah ha-'esrim* (Yad Yitshak Ben Tsvi, 2004), 71–103.

15. I interviewed Jamal Medlege several times between 2012 and 2014, and I met him multiple times during participant observations in Ministry of Agriculture meetings between 2012 and 2015.

16. For an expansive reference list on the land sale polemic since Zionism until 1990s, see Menahem Burshtin, *Shemitah: Tadrikh Limudi: Bibliografyah Ketsad Ume-hekhan Li-lemod Ule-lamed 'inyene Shemitah*. Mahad. 3 Murhevet U-me'udkenet. Kefar Darom (Midreshet Ha-Torah yeha-arets, 1993), 97–103; Ze'ev Vitman, *Likrat Shemitah Mamlakhtit Bi-medinat Yisra'el: Hatsa'ah Le-kiyum Mitsvat Ha-shemitah Ba-metsi'ut Ha-hakla'it Ha-modernit* (Makhon Tsomet, 1993); Knesset, Economic Committee, Minutes no. 190, September 11, 2000: The Impact of Shmitah Year on Agriculturalists.

17. Mathur, "The Reign of Terror of the Big Cat."

18. Nick Estes, *Our History Is the Future: Standing Rock versus the Dakota Access*

Pipeline, and the Long Tradition of Indigenous Resistance (Verso, 2019); Rifkin, *Beyond Settler Time*; Audra Simpson, *Mohawk Interruptus: Political Life across the Borders of Settler States* (Duke University Press, 2014).

19. Celia Deane-Drummond, Robin Grove-White, and Bronislaw Szerszynski, "Genetically Modified Theology: The Religious Dimensions of Public Concerns about Agricultural Biotechnology," *Studies in Christian Ethics* 14, no. 2 (2001): 23–41; Tsipy Ivry, "Kosher Medicine and Medicalized Halacha: An Exploration of Triadic Relations among Israeli Rabbis, Doctors, and Infertility Patients," *American Ethnologist* 37, no. 4 (2010): 662–680; Forrest Clingerman and Kevin J. O'Brien, "Playing God: Why Religion Belongs in the Climate Engineering Debate," *Bulletin of the Atomic Scientists* 70, no. 3 (2014): 27–37.

20. "Twenty-five-hundred-year-old texts" refers to the dating of the biblical book of Leviticus. There are controversies about exactly when Leviticus was written. Scholars agree that the book developed over a long period and that it includes evidence of both considerable antiquity and later editing up to the Persian period in fifth and sixth centuries BCE. For further discussion on the matter, see Gordon J. Wenham, *The Book of Leviticus*, The New International Commentary on the Old Testament (Eerdmans, 1979).

21. Leviticus 25:1–5. The text appears in Ministry of Agriculture, Minhelet Ha-hashkaot (Investment Administration), *Nohal Tmikha be-Haklaim Mashbitei Meshakim Beshnat Ha-shmitah Tashah* (Support of agriculturalists who disable agricultural activity in shmitah year tashah), May 15, 2014, http://www.moag.gov .il/yhidotmisrad/hashkaot/nohalim/Pages/shvita_meshakim_nohal.aspx; and Ministry of Agriculture, Minhelet Ha-hashkaot (Investment Administration), *Nohal Tmikha be-Haklaim Mashbitei Meshakim/Mashtelot/Karmey Yaiin Beshnat Ha-shmitah Tashpav 2017-2021* (Support of agriculturalists who disable agricultural activity/nurseries and wine vines in shmitah year tashpav), December 25, 2017, www.moag.gov.il/yhidotmisrad/hashkaot/ . . . /tmicha_shmita.aspx.

22. ISA/ChiefRabbinate/000in2x, Ha-mahlaka le-halakhot ha-tluyot ba'aretz u'vaHaklaut—letter from sixteenth of Elul, Tashi"h, October 7, 1958.

23. See ISA-ChiefRabbinate/000in2x, with letters from October 1954 to October 1966; ISA-ChiefRabbinate/000ie9u, with letters from November 1, 1957, to June 16, 1958; and ISA/ChiefRabbinate/000u8d5, with letters from February 1965 to August 1973.

24. ISA-ChiefRabbinate/000ie9v, letters from June 17 to July 31, 1958,p.71, Nir Oz letter, July 18, 1958. Author's translation, punctuation errors in the original.

25. Today, all kibbutzim collaborate with the land sale arrangement. For instance, in the shmita year 2021–2022 an external subcontractor was hired by the Ministry of Religions and Ministry of Agriculture to arrange all the signatures for the land sale from Jewish agrarian land leaseholders.

26. Michal Kravel-Tovi, *When the State Winks: The Performance of Jewish Conversion in Israel*, Religion, Culture, and Public Life (Columbia University Press, 2017).

27. ISA/ChiefRabbinate/000in2x, p. 441. Author's translation.

28. Hanna Dib Nakkara,. "Israeli Land Seizure under Various Defense and Emergency Regulations," *Journal of Palestine Studies* 14, no. 2 (1985): 13–34; Sabri Jiryis, "The Legal Structure for the Expropriation and Absorption of Arab Lands in Israel," *Journal of Palestine Studies* 2, no. 4 (1973): 82–104; Forman and Kedar, "From Arab Land to 'Israel Lands.'"

29. The amendment is Hok 'iskaot be-mekark'ein (Kium mitzvat shmitah), Tashl"t 1979.

30. Knesset member Haim Drukman, who was at that time a member of the Mafdal Party of religious Zionism, advanced the law. See deliberations on the law in Ma'agar ha-hakika ha-leumi (National legislation database), Hok 'iskaot be-mekark'ein (Kium mitzvat shmitah), Parliament Discussions of July 31, 1979, and August 1, 1979. http://main.knesset.gov.il/Activity/Legislation/Laws/Pages/LawBill.aspx?t=lawsuggestionssearch&lawitemid=148015.

31. Franz Von Benda-Beckmann and Keebet Von Benda-Beckmann, "Places That Come and Go: A Legal Anthropological Perspective on the Temporalities of Space in Plural Legal Orders," in *The Expanding Spaces of Law*, ed. Irus Braverman et al., 34–35 (Stanford University Press, 2014); Shehadeh, "The Land Law of Palestine," 91.

32. Shehadeh, "The Land Law of Palestine," 91; Kedar, Amara, and Yiftachel, *Emptied Lands*, 46–47, 56–59; Braverman, *Planted Flags*, 35–36, 167–168.

33. Geremy Forman, "A Tale of Two Regions: Diffusion of the Israeli '50 Percent Rule' from the Galilee to the Occupied West Bank," *Law & Social Inquiry* 34, no. 3 (2009): 671–711; Braverman, *Planted Flags*, 35–36, 167–168; see also p. 20 for a further discussion.

34. In Turkey fallow land cycles, called "nadas," were used in the cultivation of wheat and barley in rotation with fallow cycles in almost every region due to the limited rainfall. Yet governmental and World Bank development projects aimed to reduce the use of fallow land to increase income for family farms, decrease rural migration, and increase the use of arable land. Nedret Durutan, "Fallow Reduction Activities under Dryland Conditions in Turkey," *Cahiers Options Méditerranéennes* 2, no. 2 (1995): 97–106. N. Durutan et al., "Annual Cropping under Dryland Conditions in Turkey: A Case Study," in *The Role of Legumes in the Farming Systems of the Mediterranean Areas*, ed. A. E. Osman, M. H. Ibrahim, and M. A. Jones, 239–255 (Springer, 1990); Scott Atran, "Hamula Organisation and Masha'a Tenure in Palestine," *Man*, New Series, 21, no. 2 (1986): 271–295, doi:10.2307/2803160.

35. This quote is from a film by and about Keren Hashviis, the fund for partnership with shmita agriculturalists. Although its interviews with Jewish agriculturalists who keep shmita were conducted in the context of promoting donations, they seem sincere. *Keren Hashviis UK Version*, https://www.youtube.com/watch?v=UrrcWD-3evo.

36. Maria Puig de la Bellacasa, "Making Time for Soil: Technoscientific Futurity and the Pace of Care," *Social Studies of Science* 45, no. 5 (2015): 691–716.

37. As opposed to liberal Jewish NGOs such as Hazon and others. David Krantz, "Shmita Revolution: The Reclamation and Reinvention of the Sabbatical Year," *Religions* 7, no. 8 (2016).

38. Mordekhai Shomoron, *Madrikh Shmitah le-gan ha-noi*, Chief Rabbinate to Israel, Shmitah Committee, Makhon ha-torah ve-ha'aretz, Kfar Darom, 1993; an updated edition of this book was published in 2000. Zaks, M., and Makhon Le-ḥeker Ha-ḥakla'ut 'al Pi Ha-Torah. *Liḳrat Shenat Ha-shemiṭah*: Hoveret Hadrakhah La-ḥakla'i. Tel Aviv: Ha-Makhon Le-ḥeker Ha-ḥakla'ut 'al Pi Ha-Torah She-'al Yad Po'ale Agudat Yiśra'el, 1965. In addition to these publications and institutions, the Chief Rabbinate sponsored the ongoing work of institutions that research agriculture according to the Bible, such as the Institute for the Research of Agriculture and the Beit Yosef Institute, representing different religious streams. See ISA/ReligiousAffairs/Minister/00007a2, letter from Gdalia Schreiber, CEO of the Chief Rabbinate, to the Deputy CEO of the Ministry of Religious Affairs, January 6, 2000.

39. Not only ultra-Orthodox Jews devoted themselves to participating in shmita from afar. Liberal Jewish organizations such as Hazon are reclaiming shmita and its social-environmental significance. See David Krantz, "Shmita Revolution." Eviatar Zerubavel discusses the function of the observance of the Sabbath in Jewish people's life as an important tool for the construction of a group identity. Thus, the temporal separation of the holy day in the three monotheistic religions is a way of constructing separate groups. Zerubavel, *Hidden Rhythms: Schedules and Calendars in Social Life* (University of Chicago Press, 1981), 70–72, 109, 120–135.

40. ISA/moag/Minister/000nbao, letter from lawyer Amnon De -Hartoch to Deputy Attorney General Meny Mazuz, October 19, 1995.

41. The whole archival file ISA/moag/Minister/000nbao, December 1994 to June 1996, is dedicated to the claims of the ultra-Orthodox fund versus the Ministry of Agriculture. The deputy attorney general and members of the Knesset intervened in the discussion to assist the post-shmita year indebted fund. Additionally, the Ministry of Religions supported shmita religious seminaries with NIS 7 million in 1994. See Knesset, Minutes of the 245th meeting of the 13th Knesset, Wednesday, July 20, 1994: Budget for shmita observant agriculturalists who cease cultivation.

42. Interview with Yaakov Roth, June 3, 2018.

43. In a state comptroller report about the state's management of shmita in 2007–2008, it was reported that produce prices for consumers who observe kosher le'mehadrin certification were higher (66 percent) than for those who used the kosher certificate of the sale permit: Mevaker Hamedina Do"h Shnati 59Bet Leshnat 2008 Ulehshbonot Shnat Haksafim 2007 (State Comptroller, Annual

Report 59B and for the Finance Year 2007), Jerusalem, 2009, p. 1050. Shilo Elia, "H"kh Levi: Nihul ha-rabanut et ha-shmitah-Koshel" (Parliament Member Levi: The Rabbinate's management of shmita has failed), *Arutz Sheva*, October 8, 2007, https://www.inn.co.il/News/News.aspx/167296.

44. The National Shmita Committee Law (Hebrew, HokVaadat Shmita Mamlakhtit) was promoted by Member of Parliament Rabbi Yitzhak Levi from the Religious-National party (Ihud Le'umi-Mafdal).

45. Ministry of Religious Services and Ministry of Agriculture, *Madrikh shmitah le-haklaim* (A shmita guide for farmers), 2014, 6. This guide reflects a more politically correct writing style than the shmita guide published fourteen years earlier by only the Chief Rabbinate of Israel and the Religions Ministry: ISA/ ReligiousAffairs/DirectorGeneral/0000afm, 27–53.

46. Novick, *Milk and Honey*. Tamar Novick, "Bible, Bees and Boxes: The Creation of 'The Land Flowing with Milk and Honey' in Palestine, 1880–1931," *Food, Culture & Society* 16, no. 2 (2013): 281–299.

47. The Israeli settlements in the Gaza Strip (Gush Katif) mastered this agricultural method in the 1990s after its initial development in the 1950s.

48. The development of hydroponic agriculture in Israel for shmita purposes was done in the 1950s in Kibbutz Hafetz Haim without any soil, only water and nutrients. The development of detached agriculture is a more sophisticated agricultural-halakhic step.

49. See ISA-EconomyPlanning-EconomyPlanning-000mxnm, "Soilless agriculture"; and 17/56 letter from Eliezer Bert of the Institute of Torah and the Land to Yehezkel in the Ministry of Economy.

50. Mordechai Shomron, Gidul yerakot be-matza' menutak ba-shmitah begush katif. Maamarei emunat 'eitekha, Alon1. Kislev, Tashna (December 1994), http://www.daat.ac.il/daat/kitveyet/emunat/01/00110.htm.

51. Ministry of Agriculture, Minhelet Ha-hashkaot (Investment Administration), *Nohal Tmikha be-Haklaim Mashbitei Meshakim Beshnat Ha-shmitah Tashah* (Support of agriculturalists who disable agricultural activity in shmitah year tashah), May 15, 2014, http://www.moag.gov.il/yhidotmisrad/hashkaot/nohalim /Pages/shvita_meshakim_nohal.aspx; and Ministry of Agriculture, Minhelet Ha-hashkaot (Investment Administration), *Nohal Tmikha be-Haklaim Mashbitei Meshakim/Mashtelot/Karmey Yaiin Beshnat Ha-shmitah Tashpav 2017–2021* (Support of agriculturalists who disable agricultural activity/nurseries and wine vines in shmitah year tashpav), December 25, 2017, www.moag.gov.il/yhidotmisrad/hash kaot/ . . . /tmicha_shmita.aspx.

52. This addition to the budget of the Ministry of Agriculture for shmita support occurred six months prior to shmita year through Government Decision no. 1421, March 18, 2007. Ministry of Finance, Budget Proposal, Ministry of Agriculture 2011–2012, State Budget 2011–2012,

53. This new budgetary category was the result of lobbying and political connections. The former head of the Ministry of Agriculture's Planning Authority, Mr. Yerachmiel Goldin, who also served as the ministry's appointee on shmita in 2000 and 2007, became a consultant of the nurseries after he retired from the Ministry of Agriculture.

54. In fact, there were other budgetary categories, but there is not room here to discuss them all. These arrangements include subsidies for storage of wheat and root vegetables from the sixth year to be consumed during the seventh and the sponsorship of Otsar Beit Din. Otsar Beit Din functions as a Jewish law shmita court's storage, which represents the public's access to the agricultural producer and becomes the mediator between the producer and the ultra-Orthodox constituency.

55. Rasmi Daka, interview with the author, June 25, 2014

56. Samir Mu'adi, August 24, 2008, summary of Shmita year of 2007–2008. Civil Administration to the Area of Judea and Samaria. The data on the growth of cultivation among Palestinians in Israel is based on a quote from Yerahmiel Goldin, the Ministry of Agriculture's appointee to Shmita in 2007, that appeared in several sources in the web.

57. Interview with the author, Central District Office of the Ministry of Agriculture, August 5, 2015.

58. Noaman Gnaim, "Kayamut ba-haklaut ha-'aravit betsel ha-'iur: Ezor ha-meshulash ha-katan hehker mikre" (Sustainability in Arab agriculture in light of urbanization: The case of the Small Triangle), PhD diss., Department of Geography and Environment, Bar Ilan University, 2016.

59. Appendix 321 to Government Decision 104 (5.5.2013): Preparations for Shmita Year, prepared by the Minister of Religious Services and the Minister of Agriculture, May 28, 2014. This was the case again in shmita support in 2021.

60. The idea of this economic model is similar to an advanced-study fund prevalent in Israel's unionized labor market (Keren Hishtalmut) or the 401(k) savings plan in the United States.

61. Mevo Horon is a cooperative moshav and a West Bank settlement that was established in 1974 in the Latrun enclave on the land of the 1967-War-destroyed Palestinian village Beit Nuba.

62. I consulted Yaakov Roth in a series of phone interviews and email exchanges between October 2017 and June 2018. I was directed to speak to him since he is considered an expert on current and historic affairs of shmita.

63. In the previous chapter, I noted that the government is not willing to compensate farmers with environmental payment schemes However, it is willing to pay direct religious support schemes.

64. The commandment appears in Exodus 23:10–12, Leviticus 25, and Deuteronomy 15 and 21.

65. The cities in the Triangle are considered urban localities by only population size according to the Israeli Central Bureau of Statistics and not by any other characteristics of urban life.

66. During the mandate, there was the "Big Triangle" of Arabs in the area between Nablus, Tulkarm, and Jenin in the West Bank. The Big Triangle was the area from which Arab rebels rose during the 1936–1939 Arab revolt. Muhammad Hasan Amara, *Politics and Sociolinguistic Reflexes: Palestinian Border Villages*, Studies in Bilingualism, vol. 19 (John Benjamins Publishing, 1999), 4–10; Avi Shlaim, *The Politics of Partition: King Abdullah, the Zionists, and Palestine, 1921–1951* (Columbia University Press, 1990), 290–292, 306.

67. Abner Cohen, *Arab Border-Villages in Israel: A Study of Continuity and Change in Social Organization* (Manchester University Press, 1965), 5.

68. I discuss this issue in the introduction. On this matter in North America, see Cronon, *Changes in the Land*, 67–82.

69. Fischbach, *Records of Dispossession*, 23–25.

70. Adapted from Lustick, *Arabs in the Jewish State*, 179.

71. I use the term *Segregation/Separation Barrier* as I find it the most accurate of the various names given to this infrastructure. I refrain from calling the infrastructure The Wall, because in agrarian areas it is a huge fence bordered by security roads, watchtowers, and surveillance cameras that allow one, in a distorted way, to see the other side.

72. The Green Line (or pre-1967 borders) is the demarcation line established by the 1949 armistice agreements between the Israeli army and the armies of neighboring Arab countries following the 1948 War.

73. Elisabeth Marteau, "Identity, Solidarity and Socio-economic Networks across the Separation Lines: A Study of Relations between Palestinians in Israel and the Occupied Territories," in *Israelis and Palestinians in the Shadows of the Wall: Spaces of Separation and Occupation*, ed. Stephanie Latte Abdallah and Cédric Parizot, Border Regions Series (Ashgate Publishing Company, 2015).

74. Triangle incomes are lower than the incomes of Palestinians in Jewish-Arab mixed cities but higher than farther-flung Palestinian areas. Gharrah, *Arab Society in Israel* (2015), 86, 94–95.

75. Gharrah, *Arab Society in Israel* (2015), 60, 63–65.

76. Author's conversation with Wajeeh, June 14, 2014.

77. Susana Narotzky, "Where Have All the Peasants Gone?," *Annual Review of Anthropology* 45 (2016): 301–318.

78. The kibbutz's name is a pseudonym.

79. Arnon and Raviv, "From Fellah to Farmer," 131.

80. Dan Rabinowitz and Itai Vardi, *Koḥot Meniʿim: Kvish Hotseh Yisrael vehafratat tashtiot leumiot* (Van Leer Institute and Ha-Kibbutz Ha-meuhad, 2010), 110–140.

81. The Green Patrol is an enforcement body operating under Israel's Nature

and Parks Authority but coordinated with the Ministry of Agriculture and other official bodies. Gadi Algazi discusses the Green Patrol as a colonial policing body. Algazi, "Meya'ar geer le'umm khiran: He'arot al ha-teva ha-coloniali ve-shomrav" (From Geer Forest to Umm Khiran: A commentary on colonial nature and its guards), *Teoria Uvikoret* (Theory and criticism) 37 (2010): 232–254.

82. Vizenor, *Manifest Manners*, 1–42.

83. Andreas Hackl, "Immersive Invisibility in the Settler-Colonial City: The Conditional Inclusion of Palestinians in Tel Aviv," *American Ethnologist* 45, no. 3 (2018): 341–353.

84. Sa'id told me that all the company employees are paid by the agricultural operation. His own salary is paid for by the proceeds of renting space for an antenna to a cellular company. He also receives a disability allowance from social security. Sa'id has a generous salary in comparison to the Israeli average.

85. Artemy Magun, "Marx's Theory of Time and the Present Historical Moment," *Rethinking Marxism* 22, no. 1 (2010): 90–1093.

86. Berda, *Living Emergency*.

87. Prime Minister's Office (PMO), Ovdim zarim Be-'anaf há-haklaut (Foreign workers in the agriculture sector), March 6, 2012, http://www.pmo.gov.il/Secretary/GovDecisions/2012/Pages/des4408.aspx.

88. Anne Meneley, "Time in a Bottle: The Uneasy Circulation of Palestinian Olive Oil," *Middle East Report* 248 (2008): 18–23; Abourahme, "Spatial Collisions and Discordant Temporalities."

89. This is my calculation based on Ministry of Agriculture, Reshimat Maasikim Baalei Heiter Lehaasakat Ovdim Zarim (List of employers with permit of to hireing foreign workers), 2011, http://www.moag.gov.il/NR/rdonlyres/F47A218E -5AEB-4A1F-B1BC-0308B2AD2BBC/0/reshimat_ovdim_zarim.xls, retrieved February 28, 2016.

90. Berda, *Living Emergency*.

91. Matan Kaminer, "At the Zero Degree/Below the Minimum: Wage as Sign in Israel's Split Labor Market," *Dialectical Anthropology* 43, no. 3 (2019): 317–332; Kaminer, "Saving the Face of the Arabah."

92. Peter Benson, "El Campo: Faciality and Structural Violence in Farm Labor Camps," *Cultural Anthropology* 23, no. 4 (2008): 589–629.

93. Ministry of Agriculture and Rural Development, Vaadat Bhinat Meshek Mishpahti (Committee for family farms review), 2013.

94. Ministry of Agriculture and Rural Development, Vaadat Bhinat Meshek Mishpaht. The average U.S. farm is 435 acres, or 1,760 dunums. In 2017 Israel's Central Bureau of Statistics (CBS) published an agricultural census, the first it had conducted in twenty years. In that census the average moshav farm cultivates a terrain of 120 dunums while the average Arab agriculture farm is 29 dunums. The report mentions that the data does not provide sufficient coverage on Arab agriculture especially because of the vast number of cultivators in the

olive sector who are not registered in the records and farm only part time. CBS, National Agricultural Census 2017—Preliminary Findings, 2020.

95. For inheritance in the Qur'an, see Surah al-Nisaa 4:11, 4:12, and 4:176.

96. There is also criticism of the Muslim inheritance system on a gender basis as men tend to inherit twice as much property as women, who are often are expected to waive their property rights. Daphna Hacker, "The Gendered Dimensions of Inheritance: Empirical Food for Legal Thought," *Journal of Empirical Legal Studies* 7, no. 2 (2010): 322–354.

97. Noel J. Coulson, *A History of Islamic Law*, Islamic Surveys, 2 (Edinburgh University Press, 1964).

98. David S. Powers, "The Islamic Inheritance System: A Socio-Historical Approach," *Arab Law Quarterly* 8, no. 1 (1993): 13–29.

99. Yasir Billoo, "Change and Authority in Islamic Law: The Islamic Law of Inheritance in Modern Muslim States," *University of Detroit Mercy Law Review* 84 (2007): 637–765.

100. Powers, "The Islamic Inheritance System"; Naila Kabeer, "Resources, Agency, Achievements: Reflections on the Measurement of Women's Empowerment," *Development and Change* 30, no. 3 (1999): 435–464.

101. Ann Black, Hossein Esmaeili, and Nadirsyah Hosen, *Modern Perspectives on Islamic Law* (Edward Elgar, 2013), 195, 200–204.

102. While this regulation helps to keep Jewish-Israeli farms profitable, it can cause havoc within families. A web search for the term *"Ben Mamshich"* (literally, "the son that continues"), which is the term used for the heir of a farm in Hebrew, delivers a long list of lawyers' websites.

103. Black, Esmaeili, and Hosen, *Modern Perspectives on Islamic Law*.

104. Dr. Fathi Abd al-Hadi is a central interlocutor in the next chapter, which discusses olive agriculture.

105. Michael Karayanni, *A Multicultural Entrapment: Religion and State Among the Palestinian-Arabs in Israel* (Cambridge University Press, 2020).

106. Interview with Sara Eyal. May 14, 2014.

107. Ministry of Agriculture, Legal Office, Nohal le-hokhahat zekhuiot bekarka pratit le-tsorkhei tmikha ve-haktasat emtsa'i yetsur (Procedure for proving rights on private land for subsidy and allocation of means of production), March 30, 2015.

108. See Emanuel Farjoun, *Palestinian Workers in Israel: A Reserve Army of Labour* (The Socialist Organization in Israel, 1979) (pamphlet) Tamari, "Building Other People's Homes." Another contemporary example of the hypocrisies around kosher agrarian production and Palestinian agrarian labor can be found in wine production. See Monterescu and Handel, "Terroir and Territory on the Colonial Frontier."

109. Naomi Zeveloff, "Farm to Table Across the Green Line," *Forward*, April 24, 2015, 14–16.

110. Yitshak Halevi-Yarden, "Gush Katif—ha-girsah ha-Yardenit" (Gush Katif—The Jordanian version), August 24,2014, https://www.hidabroot.org/article/73546; Dalia Mazori, "Hava Yisraelit be-Yarden tesapek schorah muzelet ba-shmitah" (An Israeli farm in Jordan will provide cheaper produce in Shmitah), *NRG*, October 10, 2014, https://www.makorrishon.co.il/nrg/online/1/ART2/636/003.html.

111. See more on time grabbing in chapter 3, "The Olive Time Grab."

112. This subsection is based on my phone interview with Hamadeh Ghanem on July 20, 2018. I had tried to reach him for a phone interview for a few weeks, and when I introduced myself and my project, he asked for a short conversation only. This was probably the shortest research conversation I held; it lasted only fifteen minutes.

113. I articulated myself in an Israeli center politics discourse, referring to "minorities" because Ghanem supported the Israeli centrist party of Kadima, which hinted that, in his positions, Druze and Palestinians in Israel are distinctly different.

114. In shmita, the purchaser of the land is a different person in every seven years. In contrast, in the annual temporary state sale of chametz during Passover, the state has been selling to Hussein Jaber from the village of Abu-Ghosh all its bread products for the past twenty years. Chametz is any food that is made from grain that has been allowed to rise (ferment). According to Jewish law chametz items are forbidden to be in the possession of Jews during Passover. In Israel the state enacts a national (symbolic) sale of bread, which then can be stored in the freezers or storage space of individual households until the holiday is over.

115. Mathur, "The Reign of Terror of the Big Cat."

116. In this regard, see Monterescu and Handel, "Liquid Indigeneity"; Monterescu and Handel, "Terroir and Territory on the Colonial Frontier"; McGonigle, "In Vino Veritas?"

117. Estes, *Our History Is the Future*; Rifkin, *Beyond Settler Time*; Simpson, *Mohawk Interruptus*.

118. Wolfe, "Settler Colonialism and the Elimination of the Native."

119. Zerubavel, *Hidden Rhythms*. Joyce Dalsheim, "The Trouble with Christian Time: Thinking in Jewish," paper presented at On Time: Biennial Conference of the Finnish Anthropological Society, Helsinki, Finland, August 28-30, 2019.

120. Erica Weiss and Nissim Mizrachi, "A Time of Peace: Divergent Temporalities in Jewish–Palestinian Peace Initiatives," *HAU: Journal of Ethnographic Theory* 9, no. 3 (2019): 565-578; Raef Zreik, "When Does a Settler Become a Native?(With Apologies to Mamdani)," *Constellations* 23, no. 3 (2016): 351-364.

121. It is a calendar in which Jewish holidays immediately subject West Bank Palestinians to closure policies restricting their movement and freedom.

122. Anika Rice and Zachary Goldberg, "'Harvesting a Participatory Move-

ment': Initial Participatory Action Research with the Jewish Farmer Network," *Journal of Agriculture, Food Systems, and Community Development* 11, no. 1 (2021): 115–136; Adrienne Krone, ""A Shmita Manifesto": A Radical Sabbatical Approach to Jewish Food Reform in the United States," *Scripta Instituti Donneriani Aboensis* 26 (2015): 303–325; Krantz, "Shmita Revolution."

123. Hizky Shoham, "A Tale of Two Cultures: An Outline for a Comparative Cultural Analysis of Israeli and North American Jewry," *Journal of Modern Jewish Studies* 21, no. 1 (2022): 1–20; Jeremy Benstein, "The Sabbatical Paradigm Shift," in *The Spirit of Conscious Capitalism: Contributions of World Religions and Spiritualities*, 133–142 (Springer International Publishing, 2022).

Chapter 3

1. Kibbutz Magal was established in 1953. Like many other kibbutzim in Israel located by the borders, Magal is near the 1949 Green Line ceasefire border that determined the Israel-Jordan border and today neighbors the Palestinian West Bank. In Magal there are three hundred kibbutz members who legally share a cooperative lease for cultivating agricultural lands and seven hundred additional members of the community association (Harhava Kehilatit), who reside in the kibbutz but are not economic members of the cooperative association of the kibbutz.

2. This kibbutz's land belonged to the nearby Palestinian towns until seventy years ago. The land was confiscated during the first decade following the establishment of the state and the major acts of Palestinian land dispossession discussed in the book's introduction. Magal's products often win national and international extra-virgin olive oil awards. A leading Israeli expert of olive oil quality lives in the kibbutz.

3. Palestinian citizens owned approximately 250,000 dunums, mostly rain-fed. Jewish-Israeli agriculturalists owned approximately 90,000 dunums of irrigated olive agriculture, according to Israel's Olive Oil Council and Ministry of Agriculture data. Of the 90,000 dunums of irrigated olive groves, 20,000 are for table olives and not for oil. See Adi Naali, "Review on the Recovery and Sensitivities of the Olive Oil Sector 2016," Israeli Olive Council, https://tinyurl.com/2p97ujkf.

4. The formulation of modern/intensive versus traditional/rain-fed olive agriculture is prevalent in other Mediterranean olive cultures that have gone through industrialization in the last twenty to thirty years.

5. Dimitrios Theodossopoulos, "The Pace of the Work and the Logic of the Harvest: Women, Labour and the Olive Harvest in a Greek Island Community," *Journal of the Royal Anthropological Institute* 5, no. 4 (1999): 611–626.

6. Abufarha, "Land of Symbols: Cactus, Poppies, Orange and Olive Trees in Palestine"; Carol B. Bardenstein, "Trees, Forests, and the Shaping of Palestinian and Israeli Collective Memory," in *Acts of Memory: Cultural Recall in the Present*, ed.

Mieke Bal, Jonathan V. Crewe, and Leo Spitzer, 148–168 (University Press of New England); Braverman, *Planted Flags*.

7. S. Lavee, A. Haskal, and M. Wodner, "Barnea'a New Olive Cultivar from First Breeding Generation," *Olea* 17, no. 12 (1986): 95–99.

8. H. Hartmann, "'Swan Hill': A New Ornamental Fruitless Olive for California," *California Agriculture* 21, no. 1 (1967): 4–5; R. Fernandez-Escobar and G. Martin, "'Swan Hill' as an Ornamental Olive Cultivar," *California Agriculture* 40, no. 11 (1986): 18.

9. Luis Rallo, "Breeding Oil and Table Olives for Mechanical Harvesting in Spain," *HortTechnology* 24, no. 3 (2014): 295–300.

10. Israel supports agricultural research more than most industrialized states. Agricultural research and development play a role in Israeli diplomacy and economics as well as farming. Agricultural training in developing nations for more than sixty years now positively serves Israel's politics and foreign policy, while Israel's main agricultural export is not fresh produce but agriculture research, knowledge, and technologies. See OECD, *Agricultural Policy Monitoring and Evaluation 2015* (OECD Publishing, 2015); Lynn Schler, "Dilemmas of Postcolonial Diplomacy: Zambia, Kenneth Kaunda, and the Middle East Crisis, 1964–73," *The Journal of African History* 59, no. 1 (2018): 97–119; "Israel Farms Morocco," *Israel Business Today* 7, no. 353 (1993): 7; Alexander Keynan and Dany Shoham, "Scientific Cooperation in Agriculture and Medical Research as a Means for Normalizing Relations between Egypt and Israel," *Annals of the New York Academy of Sciences* 866, no. 1 (1998): 182–199; Haim Zaban, *150 Years of Agriculture in Israel* (Maariv Publication, 2012).

11. This view existed since early Zionist agricultural intervention in Palestine in citriculture, and it accelerated in the late 1920s as a response to the political pressure to show greater agricultural productivity in response to the British Mandate's immigration restrictions. This perception of traditional agriculture was accepted among European experts who viewed non-Westerners through a modernization prism. See Karlinsky, *California Dreaming*, 91.

12. Benvenisti, *Sacred Landscape*.

13. Jiryis, *The Arabs in Israel*; Fischbach, *Records of Dispossession*, 35.

14. Shimon Lavee, "Following Olive Footprints in Israel," in *Following Olive Footprints* (Olea europaea L.)—*Cultivation and Culture, Folklore and History, Tradition and Uses*, ed. M. El-Kholy et al., 164–175 (International Society for Horticultural Science, 2012).

15. Lustick, *Arabs in the Jewish State*, 19–20.

16. Moshe Basson, interview with the author, April 4, 2019.

17. Anne Meneley, "The Olive and Imaginaries of the Mediterranean," *History and Anthropology* 31, no. 1 (2020): 66–83; Alexander Koensler and Pietro Meloni, "Dieta mediterranea: Nostalgia o salute?," in *Antropologia dell'alimentazione Produzione, consumo, movimenti sociali*, 140–144 (Carocci Editore, 2019); Richard

Pfeilstetter, "Heritage Entrepreneurship: Agency-Driven Promotion of the Mediterranean Diet in Spain," *International Journal of Heritage Studies* 21, no. 3 (2015): 215–231. Rita Ostan et al., "Inflammaging and Cancer: A Challenge for the Mediterranean Diet," *Nutrients* 7, no. 4 (2015): 2589–2621.

18. Or Simovitch, "Back to the Sources through Imported Models: Transformations in the Value of Olive Oil in Israel," master's thesis, The Open University of Israel, Ra'anana, 2015; Ministry of Agriculture, "Olive Oil—Summary of 2019 and Trends across Time," May 2020, https://www.moag.gov.il/yhidotmisrad/research_economy_strategy/publication/2020/Pages/olive_oil_2019.aspx.

19. Following this search for the right tree, they created in ARO a collection of 150 different olive cultivars that serve as a genetic reservoir, or a germplasm reservoir, for future olive improvements.

20. Rallo, "Breeding Oil and Table Olives for Mechanical Harvesting in Spain."

21. Claude Scudamore Jarvis, *Yesterday and Today in Sinai* (William Blackwood, 1931), 169.

22. Dayid Usishḳin, Lily Singer-Avitz, and Hershel Shanks, "Kadesh-Barnea: In the Bible and on the Ground," *Biblical Archaeology Review* 41, no. 5 (2015): 36–44.

23. Shimon Lavee, "Biennial Bearing in Olive (*Olea europaea*)," *Annales Series Historia Naturalis* 17, no. 1 (2007): 101–112.

24. Lavee, "Following Olive Footprints in Israel."

25. Vera Sergeeva, "Following Olive Footprints in Australia," in *Following Olive Footprints (Olea europaea L.)—Cultivation and Culture, Folklore and History, Tradition and Uses*, ed. M. El-Kholy et al., 32–47 (International Society for Horticultural Science, 2012).

26. Here are some interesting examples of such a project: Tesdell, "Wild Wheat to Productive Drylands"; Londa Schiebinger and Claudia Swan, eds., *Colonial Botany: Science, Commerce, and Politics in the Early Modern World* (University of Pennsylvania Press, 2007); Jill H. Casid, *Sowing Empire: Landscape and Colonization* (University of Minnesota Press, 2005); Richard Drayton, *Nature's Government: Science, Imperial Britain, and the "Improvement" of the World* (Yale University Press, 2000); Mark Fiege, *Irrigated Eden: The Making of an Agricultural Landscape in the American West* (University of Washington Press, 1999).

27. Noah J. Efron, "Zionism and the Eros of Science and Technology," *Zygon* 46, no. 2 (2011): 413–428; Alon Tal, "To Make a Desert Bloom: The Israeli Agricultural Adventure and the Quest for Sustainability," *Agricultural History* 81, no. 2 (2007): 228–257; Derek Jonathan Penslar, *Zionism and Technocracy: The Engineering of Jewish Settlement in Palestine, 1870–1918* (Indiana University Press, 1991).

28. Creating links between the Biblical past and the modern present and solidifying Israel's moral claims to indigeneity also occurs through the "finding" of indigenous wine or the politics of archeology as a source of nation-making and

fact-making on the ground. See Abu el-Haj, *Facts on the Ground*, 5–10; Monterescu and Handel, "Liquid Indigeneity."

29. Jasanoff, *Science and Public Reason*, 5–20.

30. Prior scientific studies had examined the effects of saline water on table olive productivity while the effect of salinity on olive oil varieties such as Barnea was examined later. See I. Klein et al., "Saline Irrigation of cv. Manzanillo and Uovo di Piccione Trees," in *II International Symposium on Olive Growing 356*, ed. S. Lavee and I. Klein, 176–180 (ISHS Acta Horticulturae 356, 1993); M. Cresti et al., "Effect of Salinity on Productivity and Oil Quality of Olive (*Olea europaea L.*) Plants," *Advances in Horticultural Science* 8 (1994): 211–214; Riccardo Gucci and M. Tattini, "Salinity Tolerance in Olive," *Horticultural Reviews* 21 (1997): 177–214; Z. Wiesman, D. Itzhak, and N. Ben Dom, "Optimization of Saline Water Level for Sustainable Barnea Olive and Oil Production in Desert Conditions," *Scientia Horticulturae* 100, no. 1–4 (2004): 257–266, Alon Ben-Gal, "Salinity and Olive: From Physiological Responses to Orchard Management," *Israel Journal of Plant Sciences* 59, no. 1 (2011): 15–28.

31. Jewish National Fund, Negev Growth Plan, 1995. According to Uri Yogev from Kibbutz Revivim in the Negev, the state began the drilling operation in search for oil, but it found a table of saline water in the depth of 700 meters below the ground. Searching how to use this saline water the resilience of olives to high salinity was discovered. Uri Yogev, "Production and Consumption of Olive Oil in Israel," presented at the Conference of Mahon Ha-Tora ve-Haaretz, December 20, 2020, https://www.youtube.com/watch?v=XP927eEwsIU.

32. The Arabah region in southern Israel is an outstanding example of the lifeline that the JNF provides to certain Jewish-Israeli rural communities. See Liron Shani, *The Arava Approach—Anthropology of Nature and (Agri)Culture*, Lamda Scholarship (The Open University of Israel Press and BGI Press, 2021); Kaminer, "The Agricultural Settlement of the Arabah and the Political Ecology of Zionism."

33. Alatout, "Bringing Abundance into Environmental Politics"; Samer Alatout, "Locating the Fragments of the State and Their Limits," *Israel Studies Forum* 23, no. 1 (2008): 40–65.

34. Jessica Barnes, *Cultivating the Nile: The Everyday Politics of Water in Egypt* (Duke University Press, 2014). Ben Orlove and Steven C. Caton, "Water Sustainability: Anthropological Approaches and Prospects," *Annual Review of Anthropology* 39 (2010).

35. Elizabeth Emma Ferry and Mandana E. Limbert, *Timely Assets: The Politics of Resources and Their Temporalities* (School for Advanced Research Press, 2008).

36. I interviewed Dr. Hisham Yunis in 2009 and 2013, and his views on this matter had not changed. The quote is from an interview on December 15, 2009, cited in Natalia Gutkowski, "The Green Line and the Equator: Fair Trade Olive

Oil in Israel and Palestine," master's thesis, School of Environmental Studies and the Department of Sociology and Anthropology, Tel Aviv University, 2010. Additionally, the pattern of Palestinian wastewater resources serving Israeli agriculturalists repeats itself in the transboundary water management dynamic between West Bank Palestinians and Israeli communities within the 1948 borders. See Stamatopoulou-Robbins, *Waste Siege: The Life of Infrastructure in Palestine* (Stanford University Press, 2019), 176–181.

37. Barnes, *Cultivating the Nile*.

38. In chapter 1, I also discussed other factors leading to water inequality in "Timescape of al-Battuf" and in the section on "Ecology as Public Knowledge and as Time." For an explanation about municipal poverty, see Rassem Khamaisi, "Barriers to Developing Employment Zones in the Arab Palestinian Localities in Israel and Their Implications," in *Palestinians in the Israeli Labor Market*, ed. Khattab, Nabil, and Sami Miaari 185–212 (Palgrave Macmillan, 2013). Regarding sewage treatment, see Zafrir Rinat, "Le-shakhnea Haklaim 'Aravim sh-Biyuv ze Tov" (Convince Arab farmers that sewage is good), *Ha'aretz*, January 24, 2014, https://www.haaretz.co.il/news/science/zafrir/.premium-1.2224154; Aviv Lavi, "Ha-yeshuvim Ha-'Aravim: Kol Ha-Likhlukh Yotze Ha-hutsah" (The Arab towns: All the waste is flowing out), *NRG*, November 17, 2013, https://www.makorrishon .co.il/nrg/online/54/ART2/522/670.html.

39. Stamatopoulou-Robbins, "Failure to Build"; Sophia Stamatopoulou-Robbins, *Waste Siege: The Life of Infrastructure in Palestine *, 63.

40. Jasanoff and Kim, *Dreamscapes of Modernity*.

41. Ben-Yehoyada, "The Reluctant Seafarers"; Yitzhak Elazari-Volkani, *The Fellah's Farm* (The Jewish Agency for Palestine, Institute of Agriculture and Natural History, Agricultural Experiment Station, 1930), 7–24. This of course is a pattern seen in other colonial relations. See Frederick Cooper, "Colonizing Time—Work Rhythms and Labor Conflict in Colonial Mombasa," in *Colonialism and Culture*, ed. Nicholas B. Dirks, 209–246 (University of Michigan, 1992).

42. Braverman, *Planted Flags*.

43. Abufarha, "Land of Symbols"; Bardenstein, "Trees, Forests, and the Shaping of Palestinian and Israeli Collective Memory." Yael Zerubavel, "The Forest as a National Icon: Literature, Politics, and the Archaeology of Memory," *Israel Studies* 1, no. 1 (1996): 60–99; Shaul Ephraim Cohen, *The Politics of Planting: Israeli-Palestinian Competition for Control of Land in the Jerusalem Periphery* (University of Chicago Press, 1993).

44. Abu Zinada Ismail, Isaac Jad, Fares F. Jabi, and Hrimat Nader, "Following Olive Footprints in Palestine," in *Following Olive Footprints (Olea europaea L.)- Cultivation and Culture, Folklore And History, Tradition and Uses*, ed. M. El-Kholy et al. 293–308,(International Society for Horticultural Science, 2012).

45. Braverman, *Planted Flags*.

46. Dr. Fathi Abd el-Hadi, interview February 6, 2013. I met him for official

NOTES TO CHAPTER 3   249

and unofficial interviews and conversations during my research's fieldwork over the years, and I developed a great liking and respect for him. It was very tragic and unexpected when he died at the young age of 54 on November 7, 2016, while he was giving a lecture on olive cultivation to students in his hometown of Iksal. Dr. Fathi Abd el-Hadi also had an important role in the "scientization" of olive agriculture in Israel/Palestine. He volunteered with Palestinian NGOs in Israel and the West Bank aiming to introduce Palestinian olive agriculture to the global standards of olive oil quality.

47. Simaan Juman, "Olive Growing in Palestine: A Decolonial Ethnographic Study of Collective Daily-Forms-of-Resistance," *Journal of Occupational Science* 24, no. 4 (2017): 510–523.

48. A similar issue arises with the use of compost because of the Muslim perception of the problem of use of impure materials. See Shlomit Paz, Ofira Ayalon, and Areej Haj, "The Potential Conflict between Traditional Perceptions and Environmental Behavior: Compost Use by Muslim Farmers," *Environment, Development and Sustainability* 15, no. 4 (2013): 967–978.

49. More on this endeavor in chapter 4's introduction and its section "Oasis Grove Agricultural Cooperation Endeavor."

50. This quote is from our meeting in al-Rameh on January 26, 2013.

51. Rifkin, *Beyond Settler Time*.

52. I elaborate more on their initiatives in chapter 4's introduction and its sections "Oasis Grove Agricultural Cooperation Endeavor" and "Free Time Endeavors and Challenges." Abdelmajid Hssein was one of the founding members of the Sindyanna of Galilee NGO. We met several times during my research on fair trade olive oil in agrarian fields at his home in Deir Hanna and at NGO meetings between 2008 and 2010, and later for this research, we met on January 26, 2013, in the high school in Rameh where he teaches.

53. See Lila Abu-Lughod, "Imagining Palestine's Alter-Natives: Settler Colonialism and Museum Politics," *Critical Inquiry* 47, no. 1 (2020): 1–27; Simpson, *Mohawk Interruptus*, 6–7; Rifkin, *Beyond Settler Time*.

54. Interview with Dr. Arnon Dag, Ministry of Agriculture, Beit Dagan, August 22, 2015.

55. Anne Meneley, "Discourses of Distinction in Contemporary Palestinian Extra-Virgin Olive Oil Production," *Food and Foodways* 22, no. 1–2 (2014): 48–64; Natalia Gutkowski, Dafna Disegni, and Dan Rabinowitz, "Fair Trade Olive Oil and its Environmental Impact," *The Journal of Ecology and the Environment* 4, no. 1 (2013): 22–13.

56. Meneley, "Discourses of Distinction in Contemporary Palestinian Extra-Virgin Olive Oil Production."

57. Marcelo Svirsky and Ronnen Ben-Arie, *From Shared Life to Co-resistance in Historic Palestine* (Rowman & Littlefield, 2017).

58. Alexander Koensler, "Reinventing Transparency," *Ethnologia Europaea*

48, no. 1 (2017); Brittany Cook, "The Aesthetic Politics of Taste: Producing Extra Virgin Olive Oil in Jordan," *Geoforum* 92 (2018): 36–44; Emily Reisman, "Protecting Provenance, Abandoning Agriculture? Heritage Products, Industrial Ideals and the Uprooting of a Spanish Turrón," *Journal of Rural Studies* 89 (2022): 45–53.

59. Koensler, "Reinventing Transparency"; Richard Wilk, ed., *Fast Food/Slow Food: The Cultural Economy of the Global Food System* (Rowman Altamira, 2006).

60. Moghira Younis, interview, February 24, 2013, ʿAra.

61. Dan Rabinowitz, "Oriental Nostalgia: When Did the Palestinians Become Israeli Arabs?" *Theory and Criticism* 4 (Winter 1993): 141–151; Gil Eyal, *The Disenchantment of the Orient: Expertise in Arab Affairs and the Israeli State* (Stanford University Press, 2006), 152–184.

62. Thompson, "Time, Work-Discipline, and Industrial Capitalism."

63. Shaul Adler, "Mesika, Hovala, Ihsun Ve-hafakat Shemen Zait Me-zeitim" (Harvest, transportation, storage and oil production of olives) Ha-mahon Le-handasah Ve-pirion Ha-yitsur Ba-haklaut. Beit Dagan. 1965.

64. Theodore Schultz, *Transforming Traditional Agriculture* (Yale University Press, 1964).

65. Cook, "The Aesthetic Politics of Taste."

66. Paige West, *From Modern Production to Imagined Primitive: The Social World of Coffee from Papua New Guinea* (Duke University Press, 2012).

67. Dr. Arnon Dag interview, July 22, 2015, Ministry of Agriculture, Beit Dagan.

68. Avraham Singer, "Tarbut ha-zayit" (Olive Culture), *Ha-sadeh,* December 1997, 20–23; Avraham Singer, *Hatipul Bezeitey Baal* (Care of rain-fed olives) (Ministry of Agriculture, Sheut Hahadracha Vehamiktzoa [Agricultural Extension Services], 1969). Shimon Lavee interview, July 23, 2015.

69. Mathews, *Instituting Nature.*

70. Aboud Touma, "Estimation of Environmental Pollution Potential from Olive Mill Wastewaters in Israel and Potential and Integrated Solutions," paper presented at Olive Mills Management Symposium, Ministry of Agriculture, Beit Dagan, June 12, 2013; S. Shmolewitch, "ʿAkar in Waste Treatment Plants and Its Environmental Pollution, paper presented at Olive Mills Management Symposium, Ministry of Agriculture, Beit Dagan, June 12, 2013.

71. Ministry of Environmental Protection, "Environmental Hazards of Olive Mills—Northern District," January 6, 2008, http://www.sviva.gov.il/YourEnv/NorthCounty/Projects/Documents/OilPressNorth.pdf.

72. Yogev, "Production and Consumption of Olive Oil in Israel," https://www.youtube.com/watch?v=XP927eEwsIU, 15:44–16:00.

73. Israel Olive Oil Council, conclusion of 2022 Harvest Season, https://www.instagram.com/reel/Cn4F8qto8yS/?igshid=MDM4ZDc5MmU=.

74. Marx, *Capital: A Critique of Political Economy*, 340–416, 655–667, 683–692.

75. Thompson, "Time, Work-Discipline, and Industrial Capitalism."

76. According to Professor Shimon Lavee, interview July 23, 2015, Rehovot.

77. Roni Hershkovitz, "'Anaf Shemen Hazait: Skirat Megamot Beitsur Vesahar Olami" (Olive oil: Review of production trends and global trends) (Ministry of Agriculture and Rural Development, Research Economy and Strategy Division, 2016).

78. Moghira Younis, interview, February 24, 2013, 'Ara.

79. Ministry of Agriculture and Rural Development, "Procedure for Funding Machinery and New Technologies, Precision Agriculture and Laborsaving Machines."

80. Arnon Dag et al., "The Effect of Irrigation Level and Harvest Mechanization on Virgin Olive Oil Quality in a Traditional Rain-Fed 'Souri' Olive Orchard Converted to Irrigation," *Journal of the Science of Food and Agriculture* 88, no. 9 (2008): 1524–1528.

81. Motti Kaplan, Naama Ringel, and Liron Amdur, *Haklaut Nofit—Haklaut Bat Kayma* (Agricultural landscapes—sustainable agriculture) (Nekudat Hen Foundation, 2011); Motti Kaplan and Naama Ringel, *Nofei ha-haklaut ha-kedumah be-harey Yehuda* (Landscapes of ancient agriculture in the Judean mountains) (PowerPoint presentation, 2013).

82. Fernand Braudel, "History and the Social Sciences: The Longue Durée," *Review (Fernand Braudel Center)* 32, no. 2 (2009): 171–200; Immanuel Wallerstein, "Braudel on the Longue Durée: Problems of Conceptual Translation," *Review (Fernand Braudel Center)* 32, no. 2 (2009): 155–170.

83. William J. T. Mitchell, "Holy Landscape: Israel, Palestine, and the American Wilderness," *Critical Inquiry* 26, no. 2 (2000): 193–223.

84. David Kaniewski et al., "Primary Domestication and Early Uses of the Emblematic Olive Tree: Palaeobotanical, Historical and Molecular Evidence from the Middle East," *Biological Reviews* 87, no. 4 (2012): 885–899.

85. Kaplan, Ringel, and Amdur, *Haklaut Nofit—Haklaut Bat Kayma*; Motti Kaplan, Naama Ringel, and Haim Zaban, "Monitoring and Supervising National Master Plan 35—A Policy Approach to Agricultural Terrains," (Kaplan Planners and Zenovar Consultancy report submitted to the Planning Administration, 2011); Ministry of Agriculture and Rural Development, "Mismakh Mediniut Haklaut Vekfar—Do"h Shlav Gimel—Hmalatsot" (The protocol for policy of agriculture and the rural areas—stage 3 report— recommendations and instructions for planning), 2013.

86. Ministry of Agriculture, "The National Agricultural Planning Policy Protocol," 2013, 68–69; author's translation.

87. Wolfe, "Settler Colonialism and the Elimination of the Native."

88. Contemporary scientific attempts to date local olive trees or olive terracing go back to the twelfth century. However, scientific evidence does show millennial olive domestication in the region that reach the late Natufian period. See Yuval Gadot et al., "The Formation of a Mediterranean Terraced Landscape:

Mount Eitan, Judean Highlands, Israel," *Journal of Archaeological Science: Reports* 6 (2016): 397–417; Mauro Bernabei, "The Age of the Olive Trees in the Garden of Gethsemane," *Journal of Archaeological Science* 53 (2015): 43–48. Also see Unger-Hamilton, "The Epi-Palaeolithic Southern Levant and the Origins of Cultivation"; Bar-Yosef and Meadow, "The Origins of Agriculture in the Near East."

89. Lila Abu-Lughod, "Return to Half-Ruins: Memory." Postmemory, and Living History in Palestine," in *Nakba: Palestine, 1948, and the Claims of Memory*, ed. Ahmad H. Sa'di and Lila Abu-Lughod, 77–103 (Columbia University Press, 2007); Kotef, *The Colonizing Self*; Kadman, *Erased from Space and Consciousness*; Susan Slyomovics, *The Object of Memory: Arab and Jew Narrate the Palestinian Village* (University of Pennsylvania Press, 1998).

90. See, for instance, the greening policy at European Commission, Common Agricultural Policy 2023–2027, https://agriculture.ec.europa.eu/common-agricultural-policy/income-support/greening_en#howdoesitwork. A similar version of these directions existed for 2015–2020.

91. Roni Hershkovitz, *Tools to Support Agriculture in Israel*, Research Report 65 (Milken Institute Fellows Program, December 2012).

92. Adi Naali, interview, June 24, 2013, Israeli Plant Council, Or Yehuda. Ten years later, the Israeli Ministry of Agriculture had not yet approved an environmental/green payment policy like that in the European Union. Various environmental initiatives in agriculture have been pushing the ministry to adopt such policy but as of this writing, it only experiments with such payments where there are site-specific initiatives, as in the case of the Tzippori Stream/Wadi Mileq.

93. For earlier examples of this phenomenon, see Rassem Khamaisi, "Environmental Policies and Spatial Control: The Case of the Arab Localities Development In Israel," *Arab Studies Quarterly* 28, no. 1 (2006): 33–54; Rassem Khamaisi, "Environmental Spatial Policies and Control of Arab Localities' Development," in *Palestinian and Israeli Environmental Narratives* (York Centre for International and Security Studies, York University, Toronto, 2004).

94. Adi Naali, "Olive Groves Plantation as a Sustainable Solution to Abandoned Agricultural Land," PhD diss., Department of Geography and Environmental Studies, Haifa University, 2009.

95. Hershkovitz, *Tools to Support Agriculture in Israel*; Lavee, "Following Olive Footprints in Israel."

96. Eran Segal et al., "Olive Orchard Irrigation with Reclaimed Wastewater: Agronomic and Environmental Considerations," *Agriculture, Ecosystems & Environment* 140, no. 3–4 (2011): 454–461.

97. Filomena Duarte, Nádia Jones, and Luuk Fleskens, "Traditional Olive Orchards on Sloping Land: Sustainability or Abandonment?," *Journal of Environmental Management* 89, no. 2 (2008): 86–98; Pearlberg, Amdur, and Ramon, *Ibudim Bney Kayma Shel Karmey Zeitim Ba-galil Ha-ma'aravi- Behinat Mishtanim Kalkalim, Hevratim Ve'ecologim, Do" h Sofi*.

98. Gregory A. Gambetta et al., "The Physiology of Drought Stress in Grapevine: Towards an Integrative Definition of Drought Tolerance," *Journal of Experimental Botany* 71, no. 16 (2020): 4658–4676; Oded Barzilai et al., "Productivity versus Drought Adaptation in Olive Leaves: Comparison of Water Relations in a Modern versus a Traditional Cultivar," *Physiologia Plantarum* 173, no. 4 (2021): 2298–2306.

99. Environmental economic analysis would consider whether absorbing urban waste or preventing soil erosion and whether reducing fertilizer use or promoting biodiversity are more environmentally valuable. Environmental-economic evaluations struggle when they try to compare values that are not alike. See Jon Mulberg, "Modernity and Environmental Economics: A Sociological Critique," *Innovation: The European Journal of Social Science Research* 9, no. 4 (1996): 435–447; Robin Grove-White, "The Environmental 'Valuation' Controversy: Observations and Its Recent History and Implications," in *Valuing Nature? Ethics, Economics and the Environment* ed. John Foster (Routledge, 1997), 21–31.

100. Tsing, *The Mushroom at the End of the World*.

101. James Fairhead, Melissa Leach, and Ian Scoones, "Green Grabbing: A New Appropriation of Nature?," *Journal of Peasant Studies* 39, no. 2 (2012): 237–261; Li, "Rendering Land Investible."

102. Prakash Kumar et al., "Roundtable: New Narratives of the Green Revolution," *Agricultural History* 91, no. 3 (2017): 397–422; Patrick Kilby, *The Green Revolution: Narratives of Politics, Technology and Gender* (Routledge, 2019).

103. Braverman, *Planted Flags*.

104. Security was quoted as justification for the uprooting and destruction of olive trees, particularly when it came to the razing of trees on roadsides and next to Israeli settlements where there were cases of Palestinians shooting at or throwing stones at Israeli settlers' cars as well as for the construction of the Separation/Segregation Barrier.

105. Assaf Harel, "Beyond Gush Emunim: On Contemporary Forms of Messianism among Religiously Motivated Settlers in the West Bank," in *Normalizing Occupation*, ed. Allegra, Marco, Ariel Handel, and Erez Maggor, 128–147 (Indiana University Press, 2017) .

106. Meneley, "Time in a Bottle"; Meneley, "Blood, Sweat and Tears in a Bottle of Palestinian Extra-Virgin Olive Oil."

107. Abu-Sada, "Cultivating Dependence"; Kyra Reynolds, "Palestinian Agriculture and the Israeli Separation Barrier: The Mismatch of Biopolitics and Chronopolitics with the Environment and Human Survival," *International Journal of Environmental Studies* 72, no. 2 (2014): 1–19.

108. I refer to "slow violence" as a process of continuous neglect that is an everyday practice of oppression where its victimization is dispersed, making it hidden and difficult to resist. See Nixon, *Slow Violence and the Environmentalism of the Poor*.

109. A first study that is more of a social history is Judith M. Taylor, *The Olive in California: History of an Immigrant Tree* (Ten Speed Press, 2000).

110. Amanda Hilton, "Amara e bella, Bitter and Beautiful: A Praxis of Care in Valuing Sicilian Olive Oil and Landscapes," *Economic Anthropology* 9, no. 2 (2022): 257–269; Andrew S. Mathews, *Trees Are Shape Shifters: How Cultivation, Climate Change, and Disaster Create Landscapes* (Yale University Press, 2022); Sabine Gennai-Schott et al., "Who Remains When Professional Farmers Give Up? Some Insights on Hobby Farming in an Olive Groves-Oriented Terraced Mediterranean Area," *Land* 9, no. 5 (2020): 168.

Chapter 4

1. In chapter 1, "Timescape of Sahl al-Battuf," I discuss the Palestinian commemoration of Land Day. For further scholarly attention to the importance of Land Day in the Palestinian calendar, see Sorek, *Palestinian Commemoration in Israel*.

2. This chapter involves fieldwork and conversations I held over twelve years starting in 2009, when I was writing an MA thesis about fair trade endeavors in Israel/Palestine, until my postdoctoral research in 2022. I have followed Sindyanna of Galilee's activity as a women-led nonprofit NGO engaged in fair trade since 2008. All employees of the NGO have an income a bit higher than minimum wage. The Sindyanna NGO is linked to two other socialist Arab-Jewish organizations in Israel: the Da'am Workers Party, which has never won a seat in the Israeli Parliament, and Ma'an Workers Union, which unites Jewish and Palestinian workers. The Jewish activists who co-founded the NGO are from a group that retreated from Matzpen radical left organization in the late 1970s. Two of the Jewish members of the organization were imprisoned for two years in the late 1980s in an Israeli jail for what was seen by the state as their terrorist collaboration with the Palestinian communist organization, the Democratic Front for the Liberation of Palestine (al-Jabha al-democratiya le-tahrir Falastin). Currently, the Da'am party advocates a one-state solution and an Israeli-Palestinian Green New Deal.

3. Additionally, the NGO's efforts to develop employment opportunities for Palestinian Arab women in Israel—the social group that has the highest unemployment rate in Israel—have been shown to contribute significantly to these women's livelihoods. Nasreen Hadad Haj-Yahya, Izhak Schnell, and Nabil Khattab, "The Exclusion of Young Arab Women from Work, Education and Training in Israel," *Quality & Quantity* 52, no. 1 (2018): 157–173.

4. I spell the company name according to how the family members spell it in English and not according to Arabic transliteration guidelines of IJMES.

5. In chapter 1 I discussed how qur'anic traditions of inheritance pose obstacles in cultivation for Palestinian agriculturalists in "Timescape of Sahl al-Battuf," and in chapter 2 in "The Family Farm's Land, Muslim Inheritance, and the State."

6. One of the critiques of fair trade labeling initiatives is that they are not assisting the most impoverished farmers but rather those that have social mobility, social organization, skills, etc. This argument resonates with this partnership.

7. The settler colonial structure and process of invasion/resistance was discussed in the book's introduction in "Settling Time."

8. Sabbagh-Khoury, *Colonizing Palestine*, 65.

9. A notable figure on the committee was Sheikh Raed Salah, who was then the mayor of Umm al-Fahem and the leader of the Northern Branch of the Islamic Movement.

10. Dunum (or dunam) is a measure of land area used in parts of the former Turkish empire, including Israel/Palestine; it is equal to about 900 square meters, or less than one acre.

11. I had many notes in my fieldwork journal from this event. I thank Yoram Ron for finding his video of this inauguration ceremony for me years later, which allowed me to make an accurate transcription. I thank my Arabic teacher and friend Hiba Qawasmi for helping me improve my translation of Wadia's speech, and I thank Robert Dressler for helping me refine the translation.

12. Sa'di and Abu-Lughod, eds., *Nakba: Palestine, 1948, and the Claims of Memory*; Lital Levy, "Temporalities of Israel/Palestine: Culture and Politics," *Critical Inquiry* 47, no. 4 (2021): 675–698; Abu Hatoum, "Decolonizing [in the] Future."

13. With the failure of the Oslo accord, there are greater expectations of return not as a minor settlement but as an unalienable right of Palestinians. Khalidi, "Observations on the Right of Return"; Allan, *Refugees of the Revolution*.

14. Rouhana and Sabbagh-Khoury, "Memory and the Return of History."

15. While fair trade initiatives in Palestinian olive oil are prevalent in the OPT, in Israel they are rare. See Gutkowski, "The Green Line and the Equator: Local Fair Trade and the Olive Oil Sector"; Meneley, "Blood, Sweat and Tears in a Bottle of Palestinian Extra-Virgin Olive Oil."

16. The NGO's activists also advocate for a one-state solution through its allied party Daam.

17. There is significant scholarly writing on this form of political solidarity in the West Bank through international solidarity tourism but much less writing on Jewish-Palestinian co-resistance and solidarity through this activity although it has been practiced by Jewish activists for decades too. See Anne Meneley, "The Accidental Pilgrims: Olive Pickers in Palestine," *Religion and Society* 5, no. 1 (2014): 186–199; Juman Simaan, "Olive Growing in Palestine: A Decolonial Ethnographic Study of Collective Daily-Forms-of-Resistance," *Journal of Occupational Science* 24, no. 4 (2017): 510–523; Jennifer Lynn Kelly,. "Asymmetrical Itineraries: Militarism, Tourism, and Solidarity in Occupied Palestine," *American Quarterly* 68, no. 3 (2016): 723–745.

18. Irus Braverman, "Uprooting Identities: The Regulation of Olive Trees in

the Occupied West Bank," *PoLAR: Political and Legal Anthropology Review* 32, no. 2 (2009): 237–264; Emily McKee, "Performing Rootedness in the Negev/Naqab: Possibilities and Perils of Competitive Planting," *Antipode* 46, no. 5 (2014): 1172–1189; Cohen, *The Politics of Planting.*

19. On the native mode of being, see Rifkin, *Beyond Settler Time.*

20. With "nonbinary timescape," I allude to indigenous temporalities as resonating with queer temporalities, ones that refuse to be defined or that may be different things at the same time. See Karen Barad, *Meeting the Universe Halfway* (Duke University Press, 2007); J. Jack Halberstam and Judith Halberstam, *In a Queer Time and Place: Transgender Bodies, Subcultural Lives* (NYU Press, 2005); C. Heike Schotten, "To Exist Is to Resist: Palestine and the Question of Queer Theory," *Journal of Palestine Studies* 47, no. 3 (2018): 13–28. Regarding situatedness, see Donna Haraway, "Situated Knowledges: The Science Question in Feminism and the Privilege of Partial Perspective," *Feminist Studies* 14, no. 3 (1988): 575–599.

21. Julie Lahn, "Being Indigenous in the Bureaucracy: Narratives of Work and Exit," *International Indigenous Policy Journal* 9, no. 1 (2018); Sarah A. Radcliffe and Andrew J. Webb, "Subaltern Bureaucrats and Postcolonial Rule: Indigenous Professional Registers of Engagement with the Chilean State," *Comparative Studies in Society and History* 57, no. 1 (2015): 248–273; Celeste Watkins-Hayes, "Race, Respect, and Red Tape: Inside the Black Box of Racially Representative Bureaucracies," *Journal of Public Administration Research and Theory* 21, no.2 (2011): i233–i251. Only recently, with the rise and influence of a Palestinian citizens' upper-middle class, scholars have begun to attend to the challenges Palestinian professionals face in the Israeli state. On Palestinians in the creative industries, see Amal Jamal and Noa Lavie, "Subaltern Agency in the Cultural Industries: Palestinian Creative Labor in the Israeli Series Fauda," *International Journal of Communication* 14 (2020): 19; Liora Gvion, "Why Can't Palestinian Chefs Penetrate the Boundaries of Upscale Dining in Israel?," *Ethnicities* 19, no. 6 (2019): 1082–1100. On Palestinians in the health professions and medicine, see Sarab Abu-Rabia-Queder, "The Biopolitics of Declassing Palestinian Professional Women in a Settler-Colonial Context," *Current Sociology* 67, no. 1 (2019): 141–158; Guy Shalev, "Medicine and the Politics of Neutrality: The Professional and Political Lives of Palestinian Physicians in Israel" (PhD diss., University of North Carolina, Chapel Hill, 2018). On Palestinians in the private sector, see Hackl, "Immersive Invisibility in the Settler-Colonial City: The Conditional Inclusion of Palestinians in Tel Aviv."

22. Michael Lipsky, *Street-Level Bureaucracy: Dilemmas of the Individual in Public Service* (Russell Sage Foundation, 2010).

23. Julie Rose, *Free Time* (Princeton: Princeton University Press, 2016).

24. For similar efforts, see Jeannie Lynn Sowers, *Environmental Politics in Egypt: Activists, Experts, and the State,* Routledge Studies in Middle Eastern Politics 50 (Routledge, 2013); Jeannie Lynn Sowers, "Remapping the Nation, Critiquing the State in Egypt," in *Environmental Imaginaries of the Middle East and North*

Africa, ed. Diana K. Davis and Edmund Burke, 158-191, Ohio University Press Series in Ecology and History (Ohio University Press, 2011); Kim TallBear, "Feminist, Queer, and Indigenous Thinking as an Antidote to Masculinist Objectivity and Binary Thinking in Biological Anthropology," *American Anthropologist* 121, no. 2 (2019): 494-496.

25. See, for instance, Kareem Rabie, *Palestine Is Throwing a Party and the Whole World Is Invited: Capital and State Building in the West Bank* (Duke University Press, 2021); Seikaly, *Men of Capital*; Stamatopoulou-Robbins, *Waste Siege*; Hackl, *The Invisible Palestinians*.

26. Khalil Nakhleh, "Anthropological and Sociological Studies on the Arabs in Israel: A Critique," *Journal of Palestine Studies* 6, no. 4 (1977): 41-70; Furani and Rabinowitz, "The Ethnographic Arriving of Palestine." Alternatives to these narratives that engage with Palestinian expertise and experts can be found in recent publications such as Tesdell, "Wild Wheat to Productive Drylands"; Omar Tesdell, "Territoriality and the Technics of Drylands Science in Palestine and North America," *International Journal of Middle East Studies* 47, no. 3 (2015): 570-573; and Stamatopoulou-Robbins, "An Uncertain Climate In Risky Times."

27. Joseph S. Cotter, *Troubled Harvest: Agronomy and Revolution in Mexico, 1880-2002* (Greenwood Publishing Group, 2003); Jenny Springer, "State Power and Agricultural Transformation in Tamil Nadu," in *Agrarian Environments: Resources, Representations, and Rule in India*, ed. Agrawal Arun and Kalyanakrishnan Sivaramakrishnan, 86-106 (Duke University Press, 2000); Max Ajl, "Delinking, Food Sovereignty, and Populist Agronomy: Notes on an Intellectual History of the Peasant Path in the Global South," *Review of African Political Economy* 45, no. 155 (2018): 64-84.

28. Mark Rifkin in *Beyond Settler Time* discusses how literature and film allow native people to explore the horizons and possibilities of indigenous self-determination. Nayrouz Abu Hatoum also recently explored Palestinians' narrations of their future through artistic expression. See Abu Hatoum, "Decolonizing [in the] Future."

29. On the JNF pine forests as political tools in the landscape see Braverman, *Planted Flags*; Kadman, *Erased from Space and Consciousness*.

30. I have written in chapter 3about the techno-scientific transformation of the olive sector in Israel/Palestine and the implications of the new "Zionist" cultivar Barnea versus the Palestinian varieties for society and spatio-temporal politics.

31. Until Israel dismantled the military regime enforced on Palestinians in Israel, water allocations and governmental tractor allocations also had to be approved by the military governor of the region, according to Mustafa Natour.

32. Beshara Doumani notes the payment for olive oil ahead of time was prevalent in olive oil producing regions in Palestine during the nineteenth century. *Salam* (advance purchase) contracts between moneylenders and peasants put

the power mostly in the hands of the moneylenders, who were more familiar with market fluctuations. Doumani adds that advance payments for commodities were prevalent in Islamic law for many centuries. The Hanafi school of jurisprudence posits that the capital be advanced at the time the contract is drafted and that the specificities of the produce are agreed upon along with the date and place of delivery and whether the commodity was grown on irrigated or rain-fed land. See Doumani, *Rediscovering Palestine*, 135–140. When Israel was established, one of its ways of dominating the Palestinians citizens was through the control of olive oil prices and detention of Palestinians who refused to sell the olive oil to state actors in those prices. See Jeffrey D. Reger, "Olive Cultivation in the Galilee, 1948–1955: Hegemony and Resistance," *Journal of Palestine Studies* 46, no. 4 (2017): 28–45.

33. Thompson, "Time, Work-Discipline, and Industrial Capitalism."

34. Even though this is a case of a legal agreement of sublease and not sale, I highlight that the sale of Arab land to Jews was considered treasonous as early as the Ottoman period. See more on the historical context of Arab land sales and collaboration (in the derogatory meaning) in Cohen, *Good Arabs*, 97–101; Hillel Cohen, *Army of Shadows: Palestinian Collaboration with Zionism, 1917–1948* (University of California Press, 2008).

35. The NGO has won many local and international olive oil competitions in recent years. For instance, in 2021, it won a silver award in the New York International Olive Oil Competition (NYIOOC). Wasim Shahzad, "Israeli Producers Celebrate Record Year at World Competition," Olive Oil Times, June 24, 2021, https://www.oliveoiltimes.com/competitions/israeli-producers-celebrate-record-year-at-world-competition/95583.

36. Palestinian cultivators' approaches to market temporality are approached in each of this book's chapters. Market incongruency is discussed especially in chapters 1 and 3.

37. Michael K. Goodman, "Reading Fair Trade: Political Ecological Imaginary and the Moral Economy of Fair Trade Foods," *Political Geography* 23, no. 7 (2004): 891–915.

38. Moghira's comment also highlights common marketing as a Palestinian practice rather than a Zionist cooperative one.

39. For instance, efforts such as the "Nakba Law" (officially the Budget Foundations Law) passed in March 2011 and penalties for actions that are seen as "rejecting the existence of the State of Israel as a Jewish and democratic state" or "commemorating Independence Day or the day of the establishment of the state as a day of mourning." The law essentially seeks to target Palestinian citizens of Israel who commemorate the Nakba. For other examples see Sorek, *Palestinian Commemoration in Israel*. The governmental policies to reorder native peoples' memories and to align them with settler accounts is also discussed in Rifkin, *Beyond Settler Time*; Vizenor, *Manifest Manners*.

40. Rosemary Sayigh, *The Palestinians: From Peasants to Revolutionaries* (Zed Books, [1979] 2013).

41. Swedenburg, "The Palestinian Peasant as National Signifier."

42. Davis, *Palestinian Village Histories*, 24; Sayigh, *The Palestinians: From Peasants to Revolutionaries.*

43. Sayigh, *The Palestinians: From Peasants to Revolutionaries.*

44. Palestinian agriculturalists ask for loans for agrarian investment mainly from family members instead of banks or the state because of the difficulties of proving legal ownership of the land they cultivate.

45. In chapter 3 in "Contesting 'Traditional' Palestinian Olive Trees," I described the endeavor in Iksal developed by Dr. Fathi Abd al-Hadi.

46. While Jewish cultivators lament this too, their agriculture is usually organized in larger units, which facilitates investing in private instruction.

47. The scarcity of Palestinian organic olive oil certification and the lack of interest in it as an economic venue for the development of Palestinian agriculture in Israel is highlighted through the prominent parallel process of organic certification taking place on the West Bank with the support of international fair trade organizations and Palestinian agricultural development cooperatives. Additionally, one could make a claim that Palestinian Arab olive oil being sold internally through Palestinian community's social relations without reaching market bar-coding is a way of contesting the Israeli state's taxation system. However, I do not think this is the case, as I elaborated in chapter 3 in "'Unscientific and Non-commoditized Olives.'"

48. Jasanoff and Kim. *Dreamscapes of Modernity*, 22.

49. Nisreen Mazzawi and Amalia Saʾar, "The ḥawākīr of Nazareth: The History and Contemporary Face of a Cultural Ecological Institution," *International Journal of Middle East Studies* 50, no. 3 (2018): 537–556.

50. Sir Ellis Kadoorie established during the British Mandate one Jewish agricultural school in Mount Tabor and one in Tul Karm, Palestine, which was recognized in 2007 as a technical university. See Roza I. M. el-Eini, "British Agricultural-Educational Institutions in Mandate Palestine and Their Impress on the Rural Landscape," *Middle Eastern Studies* 35, no. 1 (1999): 98–114; and Tamar Novick and Dubnov M. Arie, "The Unknown History of the Palestinian School Funded by an Iraqi Jew," +972 *Magazine*, February 25, 2017, https://972mag.com/the-unknown-history-of-the-palestinian-school-funded-by-an-iraqi-jew/125443/.

51. See Cohen, *Good Arabs*, 12. Interestingly, the narratives told by the Palestinian graduates of these schools from the 1940s and 1950s talked about complete integration and the respect that they received in these schools with only rare incidents of discrimination. According to the school's current website, Kadoorie today also accepts a multicultural student body and brings together Arab and Jewish students of various ethnic backgrounds. Such a statement of diversity and multiculturalism is unusual for Israeli schools.

52. The military rule that Israel imposed on the Palestinian citizens between 1948 and 1966 restricted their movement, political organization, and access to means of livelihood.

53. I say this to distinguish between Hisham Yunis's 1948 war- and military regime–stricken generation and the emergence of their grandsons—a new sociological generation of Palestinians in Israel, born since the late 1970s, which Dan Rabinowitz and Khaula Abu Baker label the Stand-Tall Generation. According to them, the representatives and leaders of this new generation, many of them women, display a new assertive voice, abrasive style, and self-determination that is far removed from the political experience of Hisham Yunis's generation. Rabinowitz and Abu Baker, *Coffins on Our Shoulders: The Experience of the Palestinian Citizens of Israel* (University of California Press. 2005).

54. Gharrah, *Arab Society in Israel* (2018), 71.

55. In 2014, 55 percent of Palestinian academics in Israel with a bachelor's or advanced degree worked in the education system and 21 percent in the medical professions. In comparison, 32 percent and 11 percent, respectively, of the Jewish academically educated labor force participates in these fields. See Gharrah, *Arab Society in Israel*, 48.

56. In the United States there is also a noticeable enrollment decline in colleges of agriculture, particularly of agronomy majors. This trend is affected by demographic tendencies such as the declines in college-age rural populations and economic trends that make a career in agriculture less attractive to the younger generation. Dennis L. McCallister, Donald J. Lee, and Stephen C. Mason, "Student Numbers in Agronomy and Crop Science in the United States: History, Current Status, and Possible Actions," *NACTA Journal* (2005): 24–29.

57. These include Prof. Abed Gera, head of the Plant Protection Services and vice chief scientist of the Ministry of Agriculture, who was appointed to his influential positions in 2015, and Dr. Omar Zidan, vice manager of Shaham, the Extension Service for instruction for agriculturalists, and head of the Council for Plant Breeders Rights, who retired from the Ministry of Agriculture in 2016 after forty-eight years. Zidan is also a graduate of the Zionist schools of agriculture; he studied in Mikveh Israel School.

58. Publicly, the state declares it is aiming to reduce this underrepresentation. Amir Parger, *Fair Representation in the State Service: The Arab Society* (Hebrew), The Knesset Research and Information Center, August 4, 2020, https://fs.knesset.gov.il/globaldocs/MMM/01e6da30-93ba-ea11-8116-00155d0af32a/2_01e6da30-93ba-ea11-8116-00155d0af32a_11_16234.pdf.

59. Sabbagh-Khoury, A. "Tracing Settler Colonialism."

60. See Hackl, "Immersive Invisibility in the Settler-Colonial City"; Shalev, "Medicine and the Politics of Neutrality."

61. Kim TallBear, "Indigenous Bioscientists Constitute Knowledges across Cultures of Expertise and Tradition," in *RE: MINDINGS: Co-Constituting Indige-*

nous/Academic/Artistic Knowledges, ed. J. Gärdebo, M. Öhman, and H. Maryuama, Uppsala Multiethnic Papers 55 (The Hugo Valentin Centre, Uppsala University, Uppsala, 2014).

62. Edward W. Said, *The Question of Palestine* (Vintage, 1992), 19.

63. Other scholars have discussed how events of violence in Israel/Palestine affect Palestinian citizens' professional lives. Gvion, "Why Can't Palestinian Chefs Penetrate the Boundaries of Upscale Dining in Israel?"; Guy Shalev, "Conditional Heroes: On Palestinian Doctors during the War against Covid-19," *Israeli Sociology*, no. 2 (2021): 63–73, https://www.jstor.org/stable/27006639.

64. Abu-Rabia-Queder discusses this issue, focusing on intersectional vulnerability experienced by Bedouin women professionals who are affected by such fears in the interface of space and mobility in a patriarchal context. However, she does not address the time waste and temporal subordination that these professionals now need to spend on their commute to their workplace. Abu-Rabia-Queder, "The Biopolitics of Declassing Palestinian Professional Women in a Settler-Colonial Context."

65. In this vein, we can contrast the erasures and forgetfulness that Palestinians need to employ in order to survive their social reality with the erasures that settlers constantly employ. See Kotef, *The Colonizing Self.*

66. In chapter 3 in the section "Unscientific and Non-commoditized Olives," I discuss the benefits that Moghira sees to working with Jewish olive cultivators.

67. Joseph Cotter sees a similar pattern among Mexican agronomists who had more in common with U.S. imperial agronomy in Mexico than with the campesino classes they aimed to serve. For them as well, the issue of spaces to conduct agrarian research was fundamental for professional development. Cotter, *Troubled Harvest.*

68. Stamatopoulou-Robbins, *Waste Siege*, 55. On professionalism and class formation, see Ajantha Subramanian, *The Caste of Merit: Engineering Education in India* (Harvard University Press, 2019); Yasemin İpek, "Bala wāsṭa: Aspirant Professionals, Class-Making, and Moral Narratives of Social Mobility in Lebanon," *Journal of the Royal Anthropological Institute* 28, no. 3 (2022): 746–768.

69. Doumani, *Rediscovering Palestine*, 165–181; Alff, "Levantine Joint-Stock Companies, Trans-Mediterranean Partnerships, and Nineteenth-Century Capitalist Development" (Alff mentions the possessions in Palestine on p. 157); Seikaly, *Men of Capital.*

70. Cotter, *Troubled Harvest*, 325; Ajantha Subramanian, "Making Merit: The Indian Institutes of Technology and the Social Life of Caste," *Comparative Studies in Society and History* 57, no. 2 (2015): 291–322.

71. For example, in chapter 3, I refer to a case where Moghira Younis was successful for a short while in shifting return on investment for pneumatic harvesters, a smaller-scale technology that serves Palestinian Arab cultivators and smallholders' cultivation of olive trees.

72. For a similar example of how surveillance consciousness lingers for Palestinians in their employment in state institutions such as education, see Muzna Awayed-Bishara, Hadar Netz, and Tommaso Milani, "Translanguaging in a context of colonized education: The case of EFL classrooms for arabic speakers in Israel," *Applied Linguistics* 43, no. 6 (2022): 1051–1072.

73. Khalidi, "Sixty Years after the UN Partition Resolution"; Arnon and Raviv, "From Fellah to Farmer"; Gvati, *A Hundred Years of Settlement*; Sa'di, "Modernization as an Explanatory Discourse of Zionist-Palestinian Relations."

74. Walid Haj Yahia (publicly known as Walid Sadik) was a classmate of Mustafa Natour from their childhood in Taybe. Sadik was elected to his role as a Meretz Party candidate, a leftist Zionist party. For more on the Palestinian collective narrative about the Rabin government as a golden era of Palestinian citizens–state relations, see Sorek, *Palestinian Commemoration in Israel*, ch. 11, "Latent Nostalgia for Yitzhak Rabin."

75. Tesdell, Othman, and Alkhoury, "Rainfed Agroecosystem Resilience in the Palestinian West Bank, 1918–2017"; Reisman and Fairbairn, "Agri-food Systems and the Anthropocene"; Akram-Lodhi, A. Haroon. "The Ties That Bind? Agroecology and the Agrarian Question in the Twenty-First Century," *The Journal of Peasant Studies* 48, no. 4 (2021): 687–714.

76. Sara Roy, "The Gaza Strip: A Case of Economic De-development," *Journal of Palestine Studies* 17, no. 1 (1987): 56–88.

77. Seikaly, *Men of Capital*, 3.

78. See Ministry of Agriculture, Planning Authority, The Jewish Agency, and The Zionist Histadrut, *Hasefer Hayarok II—Mediniut Le-haklaut Ve-lakfar BeIsrael* (The Green Book II—Policy for agriculture and the rural areas), June 1996, 4. In other policy plans there was no mention of Palestinian citizens' agriculture at all and at times also no reference to private Jewish landholders' agriculture, as if local agriculture was practiced only by Jews in cooperative communities. See Ministry of Agriculture, Planning Authority, The Jewish Agency, and The Zionist Histadrut, *Hasefer Hayarok: Mediniut shikum upituach ha-haklaut betkufat mashber ve-alyia Hamonit 1990-1995* (The Green Book: Agrarian recovery and development in the time of crisis and massive immigration 1990-1995), January 1991; Ministry of Agriculture, Planning Authority, The Jewish Agency, and The Zionist Histadrut, *Hasefer Hayarok: Kavei Mediniut La-haklaut Ve-lakfar BeIsrael 2000-2005* (The Green Book: Policy guidelines for agriculture and rural areas in Israel), July 1999; Ministry of Agriculture, Planning Authority, The Jewish Agency, and The Zionist Histadrut, *Tochnit shesh shanim Lepitauch Ha-haklaut Ve-haityashvut 1980-1985, Sikum Hamimzaim Veprograma operativitit* (A six-year plan for the development of agriculture and settlement 1980-1985: Summary of findings and an operative plan), November 1980.

79. To contextualize the common Palestinian view toward Palestinians who serve in the Israeli military, see Rhoda Kanaaneh, "Boys or Men? Duped or

"Made"? Palestinian Soldiers in the Israeli Military," *American Ethnologist* 32, no. 2 (2005): 260–275.

80. Palestinian Arab citizens' highest representation in public service is in the medical system, where they constitute 25 percent of the physician workforce, 27 percent of x-ray technicians, and 30 percent of nurses. Parger, "Fair Representation in the State Service." Regarding Shalev, see Guy Shalev, "Helsinki in Zion: Hospital Ethics Committees and Political Gatekeeping in Israel/Palestine," *American Anthropologist* 124, no. 4 (2022): 688–702. In a similar vein, Yael Assor shows how objectivity is recruited as a moral virtue by female bureaucrats in the Israeli national medical committee. Assor, "'Objectivity' as a Bureaucratic Virtue: Cultivating Unemotionality in an Israeli Medical Committee," *American Ethnologist* 48, no. 1 (2021): 105–119.

81. Vizenor, *Manifest Manners*, vii.

82. Rabie, *Palestine Is Throwing a Party and the Whole World Is Invited*, 57, 61.

83. Jamal Raji Nassar and Roger Heacock, eds. *Intifada: Palestine at the Crossroads* (Greenwood Publishing Group, 1990), 28; Alexandra Rijke and Toine Van Teeffelenm "To Exist Is to Resist: Sumud, Heroism, and the Everyday," *Jerusalem Quarterly* 59 (2014): 86; Levy, "Temporalities of Israel/Palestine: Culture and Politics"; Lori Allen, "Getting By the Occupation: How Violence Became Normal during the Second Palestinian Intifada," *Cultural Anthropology* 23, no. 3 (2008): 453–487.

84. The Trans-Israel Highway—Road Six (Hebrew, Hotseh Israel) was constructed in the early 2000s to connect Israel's north and south. The highway failed to deliver economic development for the Triangle region and exacerbated ethno-national inequality. The company and the state did pay compensation for land or exchanged land. But scholars showed that where the highway was routed through agrarian areas, Jewish cooperative settlements received greater compensation than Palestinian private landowners did. See Dan Rabinowitz and Itai Vardi, *Kohot Meni'im, Kvish Hotseh Israel Vehafratat Tashtiot Ezrahiot* (Driving forces: Trans-Israel Highway and the privatization of civil infrastructures) (Hakibbutz Hameuchad, 2010). This difference was a classic case of environmental injustice where different modes of land ownership, different social-agrarian organization, and different political intervention disadvantaged Palestinian citizens.

85 Noam Seligman, "The Environmental Legacy of the Fellaheen and the Bedouin in Palestine," in *Between Ruin and Restoration: An Environmental History of Israel*, ed. Daniel E. Orenstein, Char Miller, and Alon Tal (University of Pittsburgh Press, 2013); Novick, *Milk and Honey*.

86. Forest fires during the November 2016 brought about unprecedented statements from the chief scientist of the Nature and Parks Authority such as "there are too many trees in Israel" and "we need to have more grazing in the forests." See Nir Hasson, "Adama Harukha 'ad Ha-ofek" (Scorched land until the

horizon), *Ha'aretz*, November 28, 2016, http://www.haaretz.co.il/news/science/
.premium-1.3135320.

87. Vladislav Valentinov, "Why Are Cooperatives Important in Agriculture? An Organizational Economics Perspective," *Journal of institutional economics* 3, no. 1 (2007): 55–69; Gerald F. Ortmann and Robert P. King, "Agricultural Cooperatives I: History, Theory and Problems," *Agrekon* 46, no. 1 (2007): 40–68.

88. Sayigh, *The Palestinians: From Peasants to Revolutionaries*; Doumani, *Rediscovering Palestine*.

89. Hillel Cohen, "The Matrix of Surveillance in Times of National Conflict: The Israeli–Palestinian Case." in *Surveillance and Control in Israel/Palestine*, ed. Elia Zureik, David Lyon, and Yasmeen Abu-Laban, 123–136 (Routledge, 2010); Ariel Handel and Hilla Dayan, "Multilayered Surveillance in Israel/Palestine: Dialectics of Inclusive Exclusion," *Surveillance & Society* 15, no. 3/4 (2017): 471–476; Helga Tawil-Souri, "Colored Identity: The Politics and Materiality of ID Cards in Palestine/Israel," *Social Text* 29, no. 2 (2011): 67–97.

90. Abdalhadi Alijla, "Political Division and Social Destruction: Generalized Trust in Palestine," *Contemporary Arab Affairs* 12, no. 2 (2019): 81–104; Abdalhadi Alijla, *Trust in Divided Societies: State, Institutions and Governance in Lebanon, Syria and Palestine* (Bloomsbury Publishing, 2020).

91. Amal Jamal, "The Counter-Hegemonic Role of Civil Society: Palestinian-Arab NGOs in Israel," *Citizenship Studies* 12, no. 3 (2008): 283–306; Amal Jamal, "The Arab Leadership in Israel: Ascendance and Fragmentation," *Journal of Palestine Studies* 35, no. 2 (2006): 6–22.

92. Jamal, "The Arab Leadership in Israel."

93. Roxana Moroşanu and Felix Ringel. "Time-Tricking: A General Introduction," *The Cambridge Journal of Anthropology* 34, no. 1 (2016): 17–21; Felix Ringel, "Can Time Be Tricked? A Theoretical Introduction," *The Cambridge Journal of Anthropology* 34, no. 1 (2016): 22–31.

94. Sponsored by the Ford Foundation, the New Israel Fund, the United States Department of Agriculture Research Fund, and other European funds.

95. Dr. Omar Zidan also told me of such activities.

96. Mazzawi and Sa'ar, "The ḥawākīr of Nazareth."

97. This residential structure is a traditional intergenerational housing unit, once prevalent in the Palestinian society and nowadays not always available because of shrinking space in Palestinian localities in Israel.

98. Rifkin, *Beyond Settler Time*, 193n5, 204n147.

99. Homi K. Bhabha, *The Location of Culture* (Routledge, [1994] 2012), 19–37.

100. I should also say that I chose to focus on these stories as representing the world of some of these professionals, but in my research, I talked to a few more actors whose stories make some similar contributions and points.

101. Carol J. Greenhouse, *A Moment's Notice: Time Politics across Cultures* (Cornell University Press, 1996); Bear, "Time as Technique."

Conclusion

1. Rooftop agriculture is becoming increasingly popular in urban environments globally and in Palestine's urban and semi-rural spheres too because of their ever-shrinking land spaces and the need to make more fresh food available for both low-income and high-income households. See, for instance, Amahl Bishara et al., "The Multifaceted Outcomes of Community-Engaged Water Quality Management in a Palestinian Refugee Camp," *Environment and Planning E: Nature and Space* 4, no. 1 (2021): 65–84. Additional examples include the community center Sinisla in East Jerusalem and Sindyanna of Galilee's program of training Palestinian Arab women in Israel to produce food in hydroponic gardens on their rooftops. For the global phenomenon, see Kathrin Specht and Esther Sanyé-Mengual, "Risks in Urban Rooftop Agriculture: Assessing Stakeholders' Perceptions to Ensure Efficient Policymaking," *Environmental Science & Policy* 69 (2017): 13–21; Elisa Appolloni et al., "The Global Rise of Urban Rooftop Agriculture: A Review of Worldwide Cases," *Journal of Cleaner Production* (2021): 126556; Kathrin Specht, Kristin Reynolds, and Esther Sanyé-Mengual, "Community and Social Justice Aspects of Rooftop Agriculture," in *Rooftop Urban Agriculture*, ed. Francesco Orsini et al., 277–290 (Springer, 2017).

2. There is a consistent increase in profitability among the various subsectors of crops. The least profitable are field crops; then vegetable cultivation in fields, flowers, and orchards offers middling profits; and the most profitable are vegetables and herbs in greenhouses.

3. The institutional/national support of agricultural education in the school system dates to Zionist settlement in Palestine in the pre-state days when the national Zionist institutions funded the establishment of agricultural schools that would train Jewish youth in agricultural science and practice along with their regular studies. They hoped to cultivate the next generation of farmers. Also, the British government, which sought to improve the level of agriculture in the country, participated in funding some of the schools without much effect on Palestinian agriculture. After the establishment of the state, in the 1950s it funded the creation of another thirty youth villages (*kfarei noar*) dedicated to agricultural education along with the absorption of Jewish immigrants. Aside from the agrarian schools, farms were established in urban areas to facilitate agrarian education in schools. Since the early 2000s agrarian education in Israel has been managed under the Administration of Rural Settlements Education (Minhal Le-Hinuch Hityashvuti). See Amin Khalaf and Dotan Halevy, "Foreigners in Their Own Country: The Arab Students of Mikveh Israel School 1870–1939," *Zmanim* 135 (2016): 82–99. Estie Yankelevitch, "Agricultural Education in Agricultural High Schools in Palestine, 1870–1948" (PhD diss., University of Haifa, 2004).

4. Mikko Joronen shows how fundamental this form of resistance is in the Palestinian struggle in the West Bank. See Joronen, "'Refusing to Be a Victim, Refusing to Be an Enemy': Form-of-Life as Resistance in the Palestinian Strug-

gle against Settler Colonialism," *Political Geography* 56 (2017): 91–100. Nir Barak claimed that urban gardening contributes to ecological and citizen resilience aligning and serving multiple political goals across countries. Nir Barak, "Ecological City-zenship," *Environmental Politics* 29, no. 3 (2020): 479–499.

5. These choices are understandable in the context of the poverty of Palestinian municipalities in Israel, which receive 70 percent their income from residential taxes rather than industrial zone incomes or business taxes according to CBS (Israeli Central Bureau of Statistics), Local Authorities in Israel—2018 (CBS, July 26, 2020); and Ministry for Social Equality, *The Implementation Status of Decision 922*, June 21, 2021.

6. Sarah Rotz, "'They Took Our Beads, It Was a Fair Trade, Get Over It': Settler Colonial Logics, Racial Hierarchies and Material Dominance in Canadian Agriculture," *Geoforum* 82 (2017): 158–169.

7. Lenora Ditzler and Clemens Driessen, "Automating Agroecology: How to Design a Farming Robot without a Monocultural Mindset?," *Journal of Agricultural and Environmental Ethics* 35, no. 1 (2022): 1–31; Miguel A. Altieri, Clara I. Nicholls, and Rene Montalba, "Technological Approaches to Sustainable Agriculture at a Crossroads: An Agroecological Perspective," *Sustainability* 9, no. 3 (2017): 349–362.

8. Borras and Franco, "The Challenge of Locating Land-Based Climate Change Mitigation and Adaptation Politics within a Social Justice Perspective."

9. Tesdell, Othman, and Alkhoury, "Rainfed Agroecosystem Resilience in the Palestinian West Bank, 1918–2017."

10. Musih, "Bridging Memories."

11. Hannah Arendt relies on Kant's understanding of the imagination. Arendt, *Lectures on Kant's Political Philosophy* (University of Chicago Press, 1989), 80.

12. Chicken, turkey, and most milk products are produced and consumed locally too but they are based on imported grains. The main imports are grains, sugar, and vegetable oils. See Israel's food import dependency ratio in State of Israel, Central Bureau of Statistics, *Food Provision Balance* (Maazan Aspakat Hamazon), February 2022, 17–18, table 11. Liron Amdur, *National Food Security in Israel* (Yesodot Research Institute, 2022).

13. This approach needs to be accompanied by emergency food reservoirs too. See Tsach Ben-Yehuda, *Authority for Food Emergency—Review of the Local Conditions and a Global Comparative View* (Knesset Research and Information Center, August 12, 2015), https://fs.knesset.gov.il/globaldocs/MMM/90c28d55-f7f7-e411 -80c8-00155d010977/2_90c28d55-f7f7-e411-80c8-00155d010977_11_8712.pdf.

14. See Amdur, *National Food Security in Israel*; Gidon Toperoff et al., "Sustainable Nutrition and Food Security in Israel: Quantitative Data Based on Crop Cultivation," *Ecology and the Environment* 4, no. 9 (2018): 18–27.

15. Nir Kipnis, "Perhaps You Should Grow Eggs Instead of Fighting for Their Quotas?," *Walla* February 9, 2022, https://finance.walla.co.il/item/3487963.

16. Borras and Franco, "The Challenge of Locating Land-Based Climate Change Mitigation and Adaptation Politics within a Social Justice Perspective."

17. Barzilai et al., "Productivity versus Drought Adaptation in Olive Leaves: Comparison of Water Relations in a Modern versus a Traditional Cultivar"; Yizhar Tugendhaft et al., "Drought Tolerance of Three Olive Cultivars Alternatively Selected for Rain Fed or Intensive Cultivation," *Scientia Horticulturae* 199 (2016): 158–162.

18. Avi Perevolotski, *Agriculture and Ecology—Can Harmony Be Found? Perspectives on Agroecology from Israel and Abroad* (Agricultural Research Organization, Volcani Center, December 2019).

19. Hazell and Varangis, "Best Practices for Subsidizing Agricultural Insurance"; J. U. Chikaire, A. R. Tijjani, and K. A. Abdullahi, "The Perception of Rural Farmers of Agricultural Insurance as a Way of Mitigation against Climate Change Variability in Imo State, Nigeria," *International Journal of Agricultural Policy and Research* 4, no. 2 (2016): 17–21.

20. Lee Yaron, "Once the Winter Used to Be in November, Now It Is Only in January: Apricots and Peaches Are Disappearing and It's Only the Beginning," *Haaretz*, January 18, 2022, https://www.haaretz.co.il/nature/climate/.premium .HIGHLIGHT-MAGAZINE-1.10532860.

21. Stephen R. Gliessman, *Agroecology: The Ecology of Sustainable Food Systems* (CRC Press, 2014).

22. Meneley, "Resistance Is Fertile"; Meneley, "Hope in the Ruins."

23. See Likkud Party Twitter with a picture of thirteen of its Knesset members in this desert site on January 11, 2022, https://twitter.com/likud_party/status /1480897073792888832?lang=ar-x-fm.

24. Nir Hasson et al., "Even the Climate Crisis Does Not Postpone the Shmita Year in Municipal Authorities and Institutions," *Haaretz*, September 1, 2021, https://www.haaretz.co.il/nature/.premium-1.10169938.

25. Knobloch, *The Culture of Wilderness*; Douglas Cazaux Sackman, *Orange Empire: California and the Fruits of Eden* (University of California Press, 2005); Allaine Cerwonka, *Native to the Nation: Disciplining Landscapes and Bodies in Australia* (University of Minnesota Press, 2004); Lauren Kepkiewicz and Bryan Dale, "Keeping 'Our' Land: Property, Agriculture and Tensions between Indigenous and Settler Visions of Food Sovereignty in Canada," *The Journal of Peasant Studies* 46, no. 5 (2019): 983–1002; Zoe Matties, "Unsettling Settler Food Movements: Food Sovereignty and Decolonization in Canada," *Cuizine: The Journal of Canadian Food Cultures/Cuizine: Revue des cultures culinaires au Canada* 7, no. 2 (2016).

26. See "Smita Project," Hazon: The Jewish Lab for Sustainability, https:// hazon.org/shmita-project/overview/; Krantz, "Shmita Revolution"; Steven E. Silvern, "The Jewish Food Movement: A Sustainable and Just Vision for Place, Identity, and Environment," in *Religion, Sustainability, and Place*, ed. Steven E.Silvern and Edward H. Davis, 327–354 (Palgrave Macmillan, 2021).

27. What Does Shmita Have to Do with Climate Change?, Annual Conference for Sustainability and Community, Jerusalem Botanical Garden, October 17, 2021. The conference was organized by the Heschel Center for Sustainability, The Masorti Movement, and Jerusalem Municipality.

28. Layla AlAmmar, "Palestinian Postmemory: Melancholia and the Absent Subject in Larissa Sansour's *In Vitro,* Saleem Haddad's 'Song of the Birds,' and Adania Shibli's *Touch,*" *Journal of Literature and Trauma Studies* 8, no. 1 (2019): 1–23; Abu Hatoum, "Decolonizing [in the] Future:"; Hoda El Shakry, "Palestine and the Aesthetics of the Future Impossible," *Interventions* 23, no. 5 (2021): 669–690. On shrinking the conflict, see the website of Shrinking the Conflict at https://www.tzimzum.org.il/eng/.

29. Fredric Jameson, *The Seeds of Time* (Columbia University Press, 1994) , xii.

30. Areej Sabbagh-Khoury, "Sociology of Complexity or Sociology of Complicity? Urban Settler Colonialism in East Jerusalem," lecture presented at the 53rd Annual Conference of the Israeli Sociological Association, Hebrew University of Jerusalem, February 9, 2022.

31. Yusoff, *A Billion Black Anthropocenes or None*; Whyte, "Indigenous Climate Change Studies"; Mathews, "Anthropology and the Anthropocene."

32. Borras and Franco, "The Challenge of Locating Land-Based Climate Change Mitigation and Adaptation Politics within a Social Justice Perspective"; Saturnino M. Borras Jr., Ian Scoones, Amita Baviskar, Marc Edelman, Nancy Lee Peluso, and Wendy Wolford, "Climate Change and Agrarian Struggles: An Invitation to Contribute to a JPS Forum," *The Journal of Peasant Studies* 49, no. 1 (2022): 1–28.

33. Camila Beckett and James Beckett, dirs., *The Seeds of Vandana Shiva,* December 2022, https://vandanashivamovie.com/.

BIBLIOGRAPHY

Abdo, Nahla. "Colonial Capitalism and Agrarian Social Structure: Palestine: A Case Study." *Economic and Political Weekly* 26, no. 30 (July 27, 1991): 73–84.

Abourahme, Nasser. "Spatial Collisions and Discordant Temporalities: Everyday Life between Camp and Checkpoint," *International Journal of Urban and Regional Research* 35, no. 2 (2011): 453–461.

Abowd, Thomas Philip. *Colonial Jerusalem: The Spatial Construction of Identity and Difference in a City of Myth, 1948–2012.* Syracuse University Press, 2014.

Abram, Simone. "The Time It Takes: Temporalities of Planning." *Journal of the Royal Anthropological Institute* 20 (2014): 129–147.

Abufarha, Nasser. "Land of Symbols: Cactus, Poppies, Orange and Olive Trees in Palestine." *Identities-Global Studies in Culture and Power* 15, no. 3 (2008): 343–68.

Abu-Rabia, Safa. " Is Slavery Over? Black and White Arab Bedouin Women in the Naqab (Negev)." In *Struggle and Survival in Palestine/Israel*, 271–288. University of California Press, 2012.

———. "Land, Identity and History: New Discourse on the Nakba of Bedouin Arabs in the Naqab." In *Naqab Bedouin and Colonialism: New Perspectives*, edited by M. Nasasra, R. Ratcliffe, S. Abu Rabia-Queder, and S. Richter-Devroe, 90–120. Routledge, 2014.

———. "Memory, Belonging and Resistance: The Struggle over Place among the Bedouin-Arabs of the Naqab/Negev." In *Remembering, Forgetting and City Builders*, edited by Tovi Fenster and Haim Yacobi, 65–83. Routledge, 2016.

Abu-Rabia-Queder, Sarab. "The Biopolitics of Declassing Palestinian Professional Women in a Settler-Colonial Context." *Current Sociology* 67, no. 1 (2019): 141–158.

Abu El-Haj, Nadia. *Facts on the Ground: Archaeological Practice and Territorial Self-Fashioning in Israeli Society.* University of Chicago Press, 2008.

Abu Hatoum, Nayrouz. "Decolonizing [in the] Future: Scenes of Palestinian Temporality." *Geografiska Annaler: Series B, Human Geography* 103, no. 1 (August 2021): 1–16.

———. "For 'A No-State Yet to Come': Palestinians Urban Place-Making in Kufr Aqab, Jerusalem." *Environment and Planning E: Nature and Space* 4, no. 1 (2020): 85–108. https://doi.org/10.1177/2514848620943877.

Abu-Lughod, Lila. "Imagining Palestine's Alter-Natives: Settler Colonialism and Museum Politics." *Critical Inquiry* 47, no. 1 (2020): 1–27.

———. "Return to Half-Ruins: Memory, Postmemory and Living History in Palestine." In *Nakba: Palestine, 1948, and the Claims of Memory*, edited by Ahmad H. Sa'di and Lila Abu-Lughod, 77–103. Columbia University Press, 2007.

Abu-Sada, Caroline. "Cultivating Dependence: Palestinian Agriculture under the Israeli Occupation." In *The Power of Inclusive Exclusion: Anatomy of Israeli Rule in the Occupied Territories*, edited by Ophir Adi, Michal Givoni, and Sari Hanafi, 413–433. Princeton University Press, 2009.

Abu Sitta, Salman H. *Atlas of Palestine, 1917–1966*. Palestine Land Society, 2010.

Abu Sitta, Salman H., and Terry Rempel. "The ICRC and the Detention of Palestinian Civilians in Israel's 1948 POW/Labor Camps." *Journal of Palestine Studies* 43, no. 4 (2014): 11–38.

Abu Zinada, Ismail, Isaac Jad, Fares F. Jabi, and Hrimat Nader. "Following Olive Footprints in Palestine." In *Following Olive Footprints* (Olea europaea L.)*: Cultivation and Culture, Folklore and History, Tradition and Uses*, edited by M. El-Kholy, D. Avanzato, J. M. Caballero, K. Chartzoulakis, F. Vita Serman, and E. Perry. 293–308, International Society for Horticultural Science, 2012.

Adam, Barbara. *Timescapes of Modernity: The Environment and Invisible Hazards*. Routledge. 2014.

Ajl, Max. "Delinking, Food Sovereignty, and Populist Agronomy: Notes on an Intellectual History of the Peasant Path in the Global South." *Review of African Political Economy* 45, no. 155 (2018): 64–84.

Akram-Lodhi, A. Haroon. "The Ties That Bind? Agroecology and the Agrarian Question in the Twenty-First Century." *The Journal of Peasant Studies* 48, no. 4 (2021): 687–714.

AlAmmar, Layla. "Palestinian Postmemory: Melancholia and the Absent Subject in Larissa Sansour's *In Vitro*, Saleem Haddad's 'Song of the Birds,' and Adania Shibli's *Touch*." *Journal of Literature and Trauma Studies* 8, no. 1 (2019): 1–23.

Alatout, Samer. "Bringing Abundance into Environmental Politics: Constructing a Zionist Network of Water Abundance, Immigration, and Colonization," *Social Studies of Science* 39 (2009): 363–94.

———. "Locating the Fragments of the State and Their Limits." *Israel Studies Forum* 23, no. 1 (2008): 40–65.

———. " 'States' of Scarcity: Water, Space, and Identity Politics in Israel, 1948–59." *Environment and Planning D: Society and Space* 26, no. 6 (2008): 959–982.

———. "Towards a Bio-territorial Conception of Power: Territory, Population, and Environmental Narratives in Palestine and Israel." *Political Geography* 25, no. 6 (2006): 601–621.

Alff, Kristen. "Levantine Joint-Stock Companies, Trans-Mediterranean Partnerships, and Nineteenth-Century Capitalist Development." *Comparative Studies in Society and History* 60, no. 1 (2018): 150–177.

Allan, Diana. *Refugees of the Revolution: Experiences of Palestinian Exile.* Stanford University Press, 2013.

Allen, Lori. "Getting By the Occupation: How Violence Became Normal during the Second Palestinian Intifada." *Cultural Anthropology* 23, no. 3 (2008): 453–487.

Algazi, Gadi. "Meya'ar geer le'umm khiran: He'arot al ha-teva ha-coloniali ve-shomrav" (From Geer Forest to Umm Khiran: A commentary on the colonial nature and its guards). *Teoria Uvikoret* (Theory and criticism) 37 (2010): 232–254.

Alijla, Abdalhadi. "Political Division and Social Destruction: Generalized Trust in Palestine." *Contemporary Arab Affairs* 12, no. 2 (2019): 81–104.

———. *Trust in Divided Societies: State, Institutions and Governance in Lebanon, Syria and Palestine.* Bloomsbury Publishing, 2020.

Altieri, Miguel A., Clara I. Nicholls, and Rene Montalba. "Technological Approaches to Sustainable Agriculture at a Crossroads: An Agroecological Perspective." *Sustainability* 9, no. 3 (2017): 349.

Amara, Muhammad Hasan. *Politics and Sociolinguistic Reflexes: Palestinian Border Villages.* Studies in Bilingualism, vol. 19. John Benjamins Publishing, 1999.

Amdur, Liron. *National Food Security in Israel.* Yesodot Research Institute, 2022.

Anand, Nikhil. "Pressure: The Politechnics of Water Supply in Mumbai." *Cultural Anthropology* 26, no. 4 (2011): 542–564.

Anton, Glenna. "Blind Modernism and Zionist Waterscape: The Huleh Drainage Project." *Jerusalem Quarterly* 35 (2008).

Appolloni, Elisa, Francesco Orsini, Kathrin Specht, Susanne Thomaier, Esther Sanyé-Mengual, Giuseppina Pennisi, and Giorgio Gianquinto. "The Global Rise of Urban Rooftop Agriculture: A Review of Worldwide Cases." *Journal of Cleaner Production* 296 (May 10, 2021). https://doi.org/10.1016/j.jclepro.2021.126556.

Apostolopoulou, Evangelia, and William M. Adams. "Neoliberal Capitalism and Conservation in the Post-Crisis Era: The Dialectics of 'Green' and 'Un-green' Grabbing in Greece and the UK." *Antipode* 47, no. 1 (2015): 15–35.

Arendt, Hannah. *Lectures on Kant's Political Philosophy.* University of Chicago Press, 1989.

Arnon, Itzhak, and Raviv, Michael. "From Fellah to Farmer: A Study on Change in Arab Villages." *Publications on Problems of Regional Development* 31 (1980): 3–70.

Asad, Talal. "Anthropological Texts and Ideological Problems: An Analysis of Cohen on Arab Villages in Israel." *Economy and Society* 4 (1975): 251–282.

Asch, Michael. "From Terra Nullius to Affirmation: Reconciling Aboriginal Rights with the Canadian Constitution." *Canadian Journal of Law & Society/La Revue Canadienne Droit et Société* 17, no. 2 (2002): 23–39.

Assor, Yael. " 'Objectivity' as a Bureaucratic Virtue: Cultivating Unemotionality in an Israeli Medical Committee." *American Ethnologist* 48, no. 1 (2021): 105–119.

Atran, Scott. "Hamula Organisation and Masha'a Tenure in Palestine." *Man*, New Series, 21, no. 2 (1986): 271–95. doi:10.2307/2803160.

Auyero, Javier. *Patients of the State: The Politics of Waiting in Argentina*. Duke University Press, 2012.

Awayed-Bishara, Muzna, Hadar Netz, and Tommaso Milani. "Translanguaging in a Context of Colonized Education: The Case of EFL Classrooms for Arabic Speakers in Israel." *Applied Linguistics* 43, no. 6 (2022): 1051–1072.

Azaryahu, Maoz, and Arnon Golan. "(Re)Naming the Landscape: The Formation of the Hebrew Map of Israel 1949–1960." *Journal of Historical Geography* 27, no. 2 (2001):178–195.

Badarna, Alaa. "Sahl al-Battuf—A Popular Market for Rainfed Produce." June 5, 2020. Retrieved March 1, 2021. https://www.alarab.com/Article/949973.

Ballas, Irit. "Chronotopes of Security Legal Regimes." *University of Toronto Law Journal* 73, no. 1 (2022): 88–111.

Banner, Stuart. "Why Terra Nullius? Anthropology and Property Law in Early Australia." *Law and History Review* 23, no. 1 (2005): 95–131.

Bar-Yosef, Ofer, and Richard H. Meadow. "The Origins of Agriculture in the Near East." In *Last Hunters, First Farmers: New Perspectives on the Prehistoric Transition to Agriculture*, edited by T. Douglas Price and Anne Birgitte Gebauer, 39–94. School of American Research Press, 1995.

Barad, Karen. *Meeting the Universe Halfway*. Duke University Press, 2007.

Barak, Nir. "Ecological City-zenship." *Environmental Politics* 29, no. 3 (2020): 479–499.

Barakat, Rana. "Writing/Righting Palestine Studies: Settler Colonialism, Indigenous Sovereignty and Resisting the Ghost(s) of History." *Settler Colonial Studies* 8, no. 3 (2018): 349–363.

Bardenstein, Carol B. "Trees, Forests, and the Shaping of Palestinian and Israeli Collective Memory." In *Acts of Memory: Cultural Recall in the Present*, edited by Bal, Mieke, Jonathan V. Crewe and Leo Spitzer, 148–168. University Press of New England,1999.

Barnes, Jessica. *Cultivating the Nile: The Everyday Politics of Water in Egypt*. Duke University Press, 2014.

Barzilai, Oded, May Avraham, Yonatan Sorek, Hanita Zemach, Arnon Dag, and Uri Hochberg. "Productivity versus Drought Adaptation in Olive Leaves: Comparison of Water Relations in a Modern versus a Traditional Cultivar." *Physiologia Plantarum* 173, no. 4 (2021): 2298–2306.

Bashir, Bashir, and Amos Goldberg. "Deliberating the Holocaust and the Nakba:

Disruptive Empathy and Binationalism in Israel/Palestine." *Journal of Genocide Research* 16, no. 1 (2014): 77–99.

———. "Introduction: The Holocaust and the Nakba: A New Syntax of History, Memory, and Political Thought." In *The Holocaust and the Nakba*, 1–42. Columbia University Press, 2018.

Bashkin, Orit. *New Babylonians: A History of Jews in Modern Iraq.* Stanford University Press, 2012.

Bäuml, Yair. "MAPAI Committee for Arab Affairs—The Steering Committee for Construction of Establishment Policy towards Israeli Arabs, 1958–68." *Middle Eastern Studies* 47, no. 2 (2011): 413–433.

———. "Shi'abud ha-calcala ha-'aravit beYIsrael Le-tovat ha-migzar ha-yehudi" (The subjugation of the Arab economy in Israel for the Jewish sector 1958–1967). *Hamizrah Hahadash—The New Orient Journal* 48 (2009): 101–129.

Baxstrom, Richard. "Even Governmentality Begins as an Image: Institutional Planning in Kuala Lumpur." *Focaal* 61 (2011): 61–72. http://dx.doi.org/10.3167/fcl.2011.610105.

Bear, Laura. "Doubt, Conflict, Mediation: The Anthropology of Modern Time." *Journal of the Royal Anthropological Institute* 20 (2014): 3–30.

———. "Time as Technique." *Annual Review of Anthropology* 45 (2016): 487–502.

Ben-Ari, Eyal, and Yoram Bilu, eds. *Grasping Land: Space and Place in Contemporary Israeli Discourse and Experience.* SUNY Press, 2012.

Ben-Bassat, Yuval. "The Challenges Facing the First Aliyah Sephardic Ottoman Colonists." *Journal of Israeli History* 35, no. 1 (2016): 3–15.

———. "Rural Reactions to Zionist Activity in Palestine before and after the Young Turk Revolution of 1908 as Reflected in Petitions to Istanbul." *Middle Eastern Studies* 49, no. 3 (2013): 349–363.

Ben-Eliezer, Uri. "State versus Civil Society? A Non-Binary Model of Domination through the Example of Israel." *Journal of Historical Sociology* 11, no. 3 (1998): 370–396.

Ben-Gal, Alon. "Salinity and Olive: From Physiological Responses to Orchard Management." *Israel Journal of Plant Sciences* 59, no. 1 (2011): 15–28.

Ben-Yehoyada, Naor. "The Reluctant Seafarers: Fishing, Self-Acculturation and the Stumbling Zionist Colonisation of the Palestine Coast in the Interbellum Period." *Jewish Culture and History* 13, no. 1 (2012): 7–24.

Ben-Ze'ev, Efrat. "The Politics of Taste and Smell: Palestinian Rites of Return." *The Politics of Food*, edited by Marianne Elisabeth Lien and Brigitte Nerlich, 141–160. Berg, 2004.

Ben Zeev, Nimrod. "Palestine along the Colour Line: Race, Colonialism, and Construction Labour, 1918–1948." *Ethnic and Racial Studies* 44, no. 12 (2021): 2190–2212.

———. "Toward a History of Dangerous Work and Racialized Inequalities in Twentieth-Century Palestine/Israel." *Journal of Palestine Studies* 51, no. 4 (2022): 89–96.

Bernabei, Mauro. "The Age of the Olive Trees in the Garden of Gethsemane." *Journal of Archaeological Science* 53 (2015): 43–48.

Bernstein, Deborah, and Shlomo Swirski. "The Rapid Economic Development of Israel and the Emergence of the Ethnic Division of Labour." *British Journal of Sociology* 33, no. 1 (1982): 64–85.

Benson, Peter. "El Campo: Faciality and Structural Violence in Farm Labor Camps." *Cultural Anthropology* 23, no. 4 (2008): 589–629.

Benstein, Jeremy. "The Sabbatical Paradigm Shift." In *The Spirit of Conscious Capitalism: Contributions of World Religions and Spiritualities*, edited by Michel Dion and Moses Pava, 133–142. Springer International Publishing, 2022.

Benvenisti, Meron. *Sacred Landscape: The Buried History of the Holy Land since 1948*. University of California Press, 2000.

Berda, Yael. *Living Emergency: Israel's Permit Regime in the Occupied West Bank*. Stanford Briefs. Stanford University Press, 2017.

Berkes, Fikret, Johan Colding, and Carl Folke. "Rediscovery of Traditional Ecological Knowledge as Adaptive Management." *Ecological Applications* 10, no. 5 (2000): 1251–1262.

Bernstein, Henry. *Class Dynamics of Agrarian Change*. Vol. 1. Kumarian Press, 2010.

Bhabha, Homi K. *The Location of Culture*. Routledge, (1994) 2012.

Bhandar, Brenna. *Colonial Lives of Property*. Duke University Press, 2018.

Billoo, Yasir. "Change and Authority in Islamic Law: The Islamic Law of Inheritance in Modern Muslim States." *University of Detroit Mercy Law Review* 84 (2007): 637–765.

Bishara, Amahl. "Driving while Palestinian in Israel and the West Bank: The Politics of Disorientation and the Routes of a Subaltern Knowledge." *American Ethnologist* 42 (2015): 33–54.

Bishara, Amahl, Nidal Al-Azraq, Shatha Alazzeh, and John L. Durant. "The Multifaceted Outcomes of Community-Engaged Water Quality Management in a Palestinian Refugee Camp." *Environment and Planning E: Nature and Space* 4, no. 1 (2021): 65–84.

Black, Ann, Hossein Esmaeili, and Nadirsyah Hosen. *Modern Perspectives on Islamic Law*. Edward Elgar, 2013.

Blaikie, Piers, and Harold Brookfield. "Defining and Debating the Problem." *Land Degradation and Society*. Routledge 1987.

Borras, Saturnino M., Jr., and Jennifer C. Franco. "The Challenge of Locating Land-Based Climate Change Mitigation and Adaptation Politics within a Social Justice Perspective: Towards an Idea of Agrarian Climate Justice." *Third World Quarterly* 39, no. 7 (2018): 1308–1325.

Borras, Saturnino M., Jr., Ruth Hall, Ian Scoones, Ben White, and Wendy Wolford. "Towards a Better Understanding of Global Land Grabbing: An Editorial Introduction." *The Journal of Peasant Studies* 38, no. 2 (2011): 209–216.

Borras, Saturnino M., Jr., Ian Scoones, Amita Baviskar, Marc Edelman, Nancy

Lee Peluso, and Wendy Wolford, "Climate Change and Agrarian Struggles: An Invitation to Contribute to a JPS Forum," *The Journal of Peasant Studies* 49, no. 1 (2022): 1–28.

Bradley, Hannah, and Serena Stein. "Climate Opportunism and Values of Change on the Arctic Agricultural Frontier." *Economic Anthropology* 9, no. 2 (2022): 207–222.

Bradley, Katharine, and Hank Herrera. "Decolonizing Food Justice: Naming, Resisting, and Researching Colonizing Forces in the Movement." *Antipode* 48, no. 1 (2016): 97–114.

Brathwaite, Edward Kamau. *The Arrivants: A New World Trilogy—Rights of Passage / Islands / Masks*. Oxford University Press, 1988.

Braudel, Fernand. "History and the Social Sciences: The Longue Durée." Translated by Immanuel Wallerstein. *Review (Fernand Braudel Center)* 32, no. 2 (2009): 171–200. http://www.jstor.org/stable/40647704.

Braverman, Irus. "*Nof kdumim*: Remaking the Ancient Landscape in East Jerusalem's National Parks." *Environment and Planning E: Nature and Space* 4, no. 1 (2019): 109–134. https://doi.org/10.1177/2514848619889594.

———. *Planted Flags: Trees, Land, and Law in Israel/Palestine*. Cambridge Studies in Law and Society. Cambridge University Press, 2009.

———. *Settling Nature: The Conservation Regime in Palestine-Israel*. University of Minnesota Press, 2023.

———. "Silent Springs: The Nature of Water and Israel's Military Occupation." *Environment and Planning E: Nature and Space* 3, no. 2 (2020): 527–551.

———. "Uprooting Identities: The Regulation of Olive Trees in the Occupied West Bank." *PoLAR: Political and Legal Anthropology Review* 32, no. 2 (2009): 237–264.

———. "Wild Legalities: Animals and Settler Colonialism in Palestine/Israel." *PoLAR: Political and Legal Anthropology Review* 44, no. 1 (May 2021): 7–27.

Brown, Binyamin. "Kdushat Eretz Yisrael Be'rei Pulmus Ha-Shmita." In Avi'ezer Ravitski, *Erets-Yisra'el ba-hagut ha-Yehudit ba-me'ah ha-'esrim*, 71–103. Yad Yitshak Ben Tsvi, 2004.

Burshtin, Menaḥem. *Shemiṭah: Tadrikh Limudi: Bibliografyah Ketsad Ume-hekhan Li-lemod Ule-lamed 'inyene Shemiṭah*. Mahad. 3 Murḥevet U-me'udkenet. Kefar Darom: Midreshet Ha-Torah ye-Ha-aretz, 1993.

Busbridge, Rachel. "Israel-Palestine and the Settler Colonial 'Turn': From Interpretation to Decolonization." *Theory, Culture & Society* 35, no. 1 (2018): 91–115.

———. "Messianic Time, Settler Colonial Technology and the Elision of Palestinian Presence in Jerusalem's Historic Basin." *Political Geography* 79 (2020): 102158

Byrd, Jodi A. *The Transit of Empire: Indigenous Critiques of Colonialism*. University of Minnesota Press, 2011.

Campos, Michelle. *Ottoman Brothers: Muslims, Christians, and Jews in Early Twentieth-Century Palestine*. Stanford University Press, 2010.

Carolan, Michael S. "Saving Seeds, Saving Culture: A Case Study of a Heritage Seed Bank." *Society and Natural Resources* 20, no. 8 (2007): 739–750.

Casid, Jill H. *Sowing Empire: Landscape and Colonization.* University of Minnesota Press, 2005.

Castree, Noel. "The Spatio-temporality of Capitalism." *Time & Society* 18, no. 1 (2009): 26–61.

Cavanagh, Edward. "Settler Colonialism in South Africa: Land, Labour and Transformation, 1880–2015." In *The Routledge Handbook of the History of Settler Colonialism,* edited by Edward Cavanagh and Lorenzo Veracini, 313–332. Routledge, 2016.

Cerwonka, Allaine. *Native to the Nation: Disciplining Landscapes and Bodies in Australia.* Borderlines, vol. 21. University of Minnesota Press, 2004.

Chikaire, J. U., A. R. Tijjani, and K. A. Abdullahi. "The Perception of Rural Farmers of Agricultural Insurance as a Way of Mitigation against Climate Change Variability in Imo State, Nigeria." *International Journal of Agricultural Policy and Research* 4, no. 2 (2016): 17–21.

Clifford, James. *Returns.* Harvard University Press, 2013.

Clingerman, Forrest, and Kevin J. O'Brien. "Playing God: Why Religion Belongs in the Climate Engineering Debate." *Bulletin of the Atomic Scientists* 70, no. 3 (2014): 27–37.

Cohen, Abner. *Arab Border-Villages in Israel: A Study of Continuity and Change in Social Organization.* Manchester University Press, 1965.

Cohen, Asher, and Bernard Susser. "The 'Sabbatical' Year in Israeli Politics: An Intra-religious and Religious-Secular Conflict from the Nineteenth through the Twenty-First Centuries." *Journal of Church and State* 52, no. 3 (2010): 454–475.

Cohen, Hillel. *Army of Shadows: Palestinian Collaboration with Zionism, 1917–1948.* University of California Press, 2008.

———. *Good Arabs: The Israeli Security Agencies and the Israeli Arabs, 1948–1967.* University of California Press, 2011.

———. "The Matrix of Surveillance in Times of National Conflict: The Israeli-Palestinian Case." In *Surveillance and Control in Israel/Palestine,* edited by Elia Zureik, David Lyon, and Yasmeen Abu-Laban, 123–136. Routledge, 2010.

Cohen, Shaul Ephraim. *The Politics of Planting: Israeli-Palestinian Competition for Control of Land in the Jerusalem Periphery.* Geography Research Paper, no. 236. University of Chicago Press, 1993.

Comaroff, Jean, and John L. Comaroff. *Of Revelation and Revolution.* Vol. 1: *Christianity, Colonialism, and Consciousness in South Africa.* University of Chicago Press, 2008.

Cook, Brittany. "The Aesthetic Politics of Taste: Producing Extra Virgin Olive Oil in Jordan." *Geoforum* 92 (2018): 36–44.

Cooper, Frederick. "Colonizing Time—Work Rhythms and Labor Conflict in Colonial Mombasa." In *Colonialism and Culture*, edited by Nicholas B. Dirks, 209–246. University of Michigan Press, 1992.

Cotter, Joseph S. *Troubled Harvest: Agronomy and Revolution in Mexico, 1880–2002*. Contributions in Latin American Studies, no. 22. Greenwood Publishing Group, 2003

Coulson, Noel J. *A History of Islamic Law*. Islamic Surveys, 2. Edinburgh University Press, 1964.

Cresti, M., A. Cimato, M. Tattini, and F. Ciampolini. "Effect of Salinity on Productivity and Oil Quality of Olive (*Olea europaea* L.)." *Advances in Horticultural Science* 8 (1994): 211–214.

Cronon, William. *Changes in the Land: Indians, Colonists, and the Ecology of New England*. Hill and Wang, 2011.

Crosby, Alfred W. *Ecological Imperialism*. Cambridge University Press, 2015.

Dag, Arnon, Alon Ben-Gal, Uri Yermiyahu, Loai Basheer, Yogev Nir, and Zohar Kerem. "The Effect of Irrigation Level and Harvest Mechanization on Virgin Olive Oil Quality in a Traditional Rain-Fed 'Souri' Olive Orchard Converted to Irrigation." *Journal of the Science of Food and Agriculture* 88, no. 9 (2008): 1524–1528.

Dajani, Muna. "Danger, Turbines! A Jawlani Cry against Green Energy Colonialism in the Occupied Syrian Golan Heights." London School of Economics Middle East Centre, blog post, May 20, 2020. https://blogs.lse.ac.uk/mec/2020/05/04/danger-turbines-a-jawlani-cry-against-green-energy-colonialism-in-the-occupied-syrian-golan-heights/.

———. "How Palestine's Climate Apartheid Is Being Depoliticised." *openDemocracy*, February 25, 2022. https://www.opendemocracy.net/en/north-africa-west-asia/how-palestines-climate-apartheid-is-being-depoliticised/.

———. "Thirsty Water Carriers: The Production of Uneven Waterscapes in Sahl al-Battuf." *Contemporary Levant* 5, no. 2 (2020): 97–112.

Dallasheh, Leena. "Troubled Waters: Citizenship and Colonial Zionism in Nazareth." *International Journal of Middle East Studies* 47 (2015): 467–487.

Dalsheim, Joyce. *Israel Has a Jewish Problem: Self-Determination as Self-Elimination*. Oxford University Press, USA, 2019.

———. "The Trouble with Christian Time: Thinking in Jewish." Paper presented at On Time: Biennial Conference of the Finnish Anthropological Society, Helsinki, Finland, August 28–30, 2019.

Davis, Diana K. *The Arid Lands: History, Power, Knowledge*. MIT Press, 2016.

———. *Resurrecting the Granary of Rome: Environmental History and French Colonial Expansion in North Africa*. Series in Ecology and History, vol. 58. Ohio University Press, 2007.

Davis, Diana K., and Edmund Burke, eds. *Environmental Imaginaries of the Middle East and North Africa*. Ohio University Press Series in Ecology and History. Ohio University Press, 2011.

Davis, Rochelle. *Palestinian Village Histories: Geographies of the Displaced*. Stanford University Press, 2010. https://doi.org/10.1515/9780804777186.

Deane-Drummond, Celia, Robin Grove-White, and Bronislaw Szerszynski. "Genetically Modified Theology: The Religious Dimensions of Public Concerns about Agricultural Biotechnology." *Studies in Christian Ethics* 14, no. 2 (2001): 23–41.

Deeb, Lara, and Jessica Winegar, *Anthropology's Politics: Disciplining the Middle East*. Stanford University Press, 2015.

Degani, Arnon. "Israel Is a Settler Colonial State—and That's OK." *Haaretz*, September 13, 2016.

Dekel-Chen, Jonathan L. *Farming the Red Land: Jewish Agricultural Colonization and Local Soviet Power, 1924–1941*. Yale University Press, 2008.

Ditzler, Lenora, and Clemens Driessen. "Automating Agroecology: How to Design a Farming Robot without a Monocultural Mindset?" *Journal of Agricultural and Environmental Ethics* 35, no. 1 (2022): 1–31

Dixon, Marion. "The Land Grab, Finance Capital, and Food Regime Restructuring: The Case of Egypt." *Review of African Political Economy* 41, no. 140 (2014): 232–248

Doumani, Beshara. "Rediscovering Ottoman Palestine: Writing Palestinians into History." *Journal of Palestine Studies* 21, no. 2 (1992): 5–28.

———. *Rediscovering Palestine: Merchants and Peasants in Jabal Nablus, 1700–1900*. University of California Press, 1995.

Drayton, Richard. *Nature's Government: Science, Imperial Britain, and the "Improvement" of the World*. Yale University Press, 2000.

Dromi, Shai M., and Liron Shani. "Love of Land: Nature Protection, Nationalism, and the Struggle over the Establishment of New Communities in Israel." *Rural Sociology* 85, no. 1 (2020): 111–136.

Duarte, Filomena, Nádia Jones, and Luuk Fleskens. "Traditional Olive Orchards on Sloping Land: Sustainability or Abandonment?" *Journal of Environmental Management* 89, no. 2 (2008): 86–98.

DuPuis, E. Melanie, and David Goodman. "Should We Go "Home" to Eat?: Toward a Reflexive Politics of Localism." *Journal of Rural Studies* 21, no. 3 (2005): 359–371.

Durutan, Nedret. "Fallow Reduction Activities under Dryland Conditions in Turkey." *Cahiers Options Méditerranéennes* 2, no. 2 (1995): 97–106.

Durutan, Nedret, K. Meyveci, M. Karaca, M. Avci, and H. Eyuboglu. "Annual Cropping under Dryland Conditions in Turkey: A Case Study." In *The Role of Legumes in the Farming Systems of the Mediterranean Areas*, edited by A. E. Osman, M. H. Ibrahim, and M. A. Jones, 239–255. Springer, 1990.

Edrei, Arye. "From Orthodoxy to Religious Zionism: Rabbi Kook and the Sabbatical Year Polemic." *Dine Israel: Studies in Halakhah and Jewish Law* 26 (2009): 45–145.

Efron, Noah J. "Zionism and the Eros of Science and Technology." *Zygon* 46, no. 2 (2011): 413–428.

Eghbariah, Rabea. "Israeli Law and the Rule of Colonial Difference." *Journal of Palestine Studies* 51, no. 1 (2021): 73–77.

———. "Ma'avak 'Akub Meza'atar: 'Al Tsimhei ha-makhal shel ha-mitbah ha-falastini vehukei Haganat ha-tsomeah ba-din ha-iysraeli" (The criminalization of Za'atar and Akkoub: On edible plants in Palestinian cuisine and Israeli plant protection law). In *Studies in Food Law*, edited by Aeyal Gross and Yofi Tirosh, 497–533. Law, Society, and Culture Series. Tel Aviv University Press, 2017.

Eid, Ramez, and Tobias Haller. "Burning Forests, Rising Power: Towards a Constitutionality Process in Mount Carmel Biosphere Reserve." *Human Ecology* 46 (2018): 41–50.

Elazari-Volkani, Isaac. *The Fellah's Farm*. The Jewish Agency for Palestine, Institute of Agriculture and Natural History, Agricultural Experiment Station, 1930.

———. "Modernizing the Fellah's Farm." *Palestine and Near East Economic Magazine* 8 (1930): 268–270.

El-Eini, Roza I. M. "British Agricultural-Educational Institutions in Mandate Palestine and Their Impress on the Rural Landscape." *Middle Eastern Studies* 35, no. 1 (1999): 98–114.

———. *Mandated Landscape: British Imperial Rule in Palestine 1929–1948*. Routledge, 2004.

Elia, Shilo. "H"kh Levi: Nihul ha-rabanut et ha-shmitah-Koshel" (Parliament Member Levi: The Rabbinate's management of shmita has failed). *Arutz Sheva*, October 8, 2007. Retrieved June 12, 2018. https://www.inn.co.il/News/News.aspx/167296.

El-Kholy, M., D. Avanzato, J. M. Caballero, K. Chartzoulakis, F. Vita Serman, and E. Perry. *Following Olive Footprints* (Olea europaea L.)—*Cultivation and Culture, Folklore and History, Tradition and Uses*. International Society for Horticultural Science, 2012.

El Shakry, Hoda. "Palestine and the Aesthetics of the Future Impossible." *Interventions* 23, no. 5 (2021): 669–690.

Erakat, Noura. *Justice for Some: Law and the Question of Palestine*. Stanford University Press, 2020.

Escobar, Arturo. *Territories of Difference: Place, Movements, Life, Redes*. Duke University Press, 2008.

Estes, Nick. *Our History Is the Future: Standing Rock versus the Dakota Access Pipeline, and the Long Tradition of Indigenous Resistance*. Verso, 2019.

Evri, Yuval, and Hagar Kotef. "When Does a Native Become a Settler? (With Apologies to Zreik and Mamdani)." *Constellations: An International Journal of Critical and Democratic Theory*, June 15, 2020. https://doi.org/10.1111/1467-8675.12470.

European Commission. "The Common Agricultural Policy 2023-27." https://agriculture.ec.europa.eu/common-agricultural-policy/cap-overview/cap-2023-27_en.

Eyal, Gil. *The Disenchantment of the Orient: Expertise in Arab Affairs and the Israeli State*. Stanford University Press, 2006.

Eyal, Hedva, and Limor Samimian-Darash. "Unintended Securitization: Military, Medical, and Political-Security Discourses in the Humanitarian Treatment of Syrian Casualties in Israel." *Conflict and Society* 5, no. 1 (2019): 55-71.

Fabian, Johannes. *Time and the Other: How Anthropology Makes Its Object*. Columbia University Press, 2014.

Faingulernt, Avner, writer, director, cinematographer. *In the Desert: A Documentary Diptych*. Ruth Films, 2018.

Fairhead, James, Melissa Leach, and Ian Scoones. "Green Grabbing: A New Appropriation of Nature?" *Journal of Peasant Studies* 39, no. 2 (2012); 237-261.

Falah, Ghazi. "Israeli 'Judaization' Policy in Galilee and Its Impact on Local Arab Urbanization." *Political Geography Quarterly* 8, no. 3 (1989): 229-253.

Farjoun, Emanuel. "Palestinian Workers in Israel: A Reserve Army of Labour." *Khamsin, Journal of Revolutionary Socialists of the Middle East* 7 (1980): 107-143.

———. *Palestinian Workers in Israel: A Reserve Army of Labour*. Pamphlet. The Socialist Organization in Israel, 1979.

Feldman, Jackie. *Above the Death Pits, beneath the Flag: Youth Voyages to Poland and the Performance of Israeli National Identity*. Berghahn Books, 2008.

———. "Between Yad Vashem and Mt. Herzl: Changing Inscriptions of Sacrifice on Jerusalem's 'Mountain of Memory.'" *Anthropological Quarterly* 80, no. 4 (Fall 2007): 1147-1174.

Ferguson, James. *The Anti-politics Machine: "Development," Depoliticization and Bureaucratic Power in Lesotho*. CUP Archive, 1990.

Fernandez-Escobar, Ricardo, and G. Martin. "'Swan Hill' as an Ornamental Olive Cultivar." *California Agriculture* 40, no. 11 (1986): 18.

Ferry, Elizabeth Emma, and Mandana E. Limbert. *Timely Assets: The Politics of Resources and Their Temporalities*. School for Advanced Research Press, 2008.

Fiege, Mark. *Irrigated Eden: The Making of an Agricultural Landscape in the American West*. University of Washington Press, 1999.

Fischbach, Michael R. *Records of Dispossession: Palestinian Refugee Property and the Arab Israeli Conflict*. Institute for Palestine Studies Series. Columbia University Press, 2003.

Forman, Geremy. "Law and the Historical Geography of the Galilee: Israel's Litigatory Advantages during the Special Operation of Land Settlement." *Journal of Historical Geography* 32 (2006): 796-817.

———. "A Tale of Two Regions: Diffusion of the Israeli '50 Percent Rule' from the Galilee to the Occupied West Bank." *Law & Social Inquiry* 34, no. 3 (2009): 671-711.

Forman, Geremy, and Alexandre Kedar. "From Arab Land to 'Israel Lands': The Legal Dispossession of the Palestinians Displaced by Israel in the Wake of 1948." *Environment and Planning D: Society and Space* 22, no. 6 (2004): 809–830.

Foucault, Michel. *Madness and Civilization.* Translated by R. Howard. Pantheon, 1965.

———. *Power/Knowledge: Selected Interviews and Other Writings, 1972–1977.* Pantheon, 1980.

Fujikane, Candace. "Introduction: Asian Settler Colonialism in the US Colony of Hawai'i." In *Asian Settler Colonialism: From Local Governance to the Habits of Everyday Life in Hawaii,* 1–42. University of Hawaii Press, 2008.

Furani, Khaled. *Silencing the Sea: Secular Rhythms in Palestinian Poetry.* Stanford University Press, 2012.

Furani, Khaled, and Dan Rabinowitz. "The Ethnographic Arriving of Palestine." *Annual Review of Anthropology* 40 (2011): 475–491.

Gadot, Yuval, Uri Davidovich, Gideon Avni, Yoav Avni, Michal Piasetzky, Gala Faershtein, Dan Golan, and Naomi Porat. "The Formation of a Mediterranean Terraced Landscape: Mount Eitan, Judean Highlands, Israel." *Journal of Archaeological Science: Reports* 6 (2016): 397–417.

Gallay, Alan. *The Indian Slave Trade: The Rise of the English Empire in the American South, 1670–1717.* Yale University Press, 2009.

Gambetta, Gregory A., Jose Carlos Herrera, Silvina Dayer, Quishuo Feng, Uri Hochberg, and Simone D. Castellarin. "The Physiology of Drought Stress in Grapevine: Towards an Integrative Definition of Drought Tolerance." *Journal of Experimental Botany* 71, no. 16 (2020): 4658–4676.

Gennai-Schott, Sabine, Tiziana Sabbatini, Davide Rizzo, and Elisa Marraccini. "Who Remains When Professional Farmers Give Up? Some Insights on Hobby Farming in an Olive Groves-Oriented Terraced Mediterranean Area." *Land* 9, no. 5 (2020): 168. doi:10.3390/land9050168.

Gharrah, Ramsees. *Arab Society in Israel: Population, Society, Economy.* Van Leer Publication, 2005.

———. *Arab Society in Israel: Population, Society, Economy.* Van Leer Publication, 2015.

———. *Arab Society in Israel: Population, Society, Economy.* Van Leer Publication, 2018.

Gilad, Efrat. ""The Child Needs Milk and Milk Needs a Market" The Politics of Nutrition in the Interwar Yishuv." *Gastronomica: The Journal for Food Studies* 21, no. 1 (2021): 7–16.

Gillan, Kevin. "Temporality in Social Movement Theory: Vectors and Events in the Neoliberal Timescape." *Social Movement Studies* 19, no. 5–6 (2020): 516–536.

Giminiani, Piergiorgio Di, Martin Fonck, and Paolo Perasso. "Can Natives Be Settlers? Emptiness, Settlement and Indigeneity on the Settler Colonial Frontier in Chile." *Anthropological Theory* 21, no. 1 (2021): 82–106.

Gliessman, Stephen R. *Agroecology: The Ecology of Sustainable Food Systems.* CRC Press, 2014.

Gnaim, Noaman. "Kayamut ba-haklaut ha-ʿaravit betsel ha-ʿiur: Ezor ha-meshulash ha-katan hehker mikre" (Sustainability in Arab agriculture in light of urbanization: The case of the Small Triangle). PhD diss., Department of Geography and Environment, Bar Ilan University, 2016.

Goodman, Michael K. "Reading Fair Trade: Political Ecological Imaginary and the Moral Economy of Fair Trade Foods." *Political Geography* 23, no. 7 (2004): 891–915.

Goodman, Yehuda C., and Nissim Mizrachi. " 'The Holocaust Does Not Belong to European Jews Alone': The Differential Use of Memory Techniques in Israeli High Schools." *American Ethnologist* 35, no. 1 (2008): 95–114.

Greenhouse, Carol J. *A Moment's Notice: Time Politics across Cultures.* Cornell University Press, 1996.

Grinberg, Omri. "Constructing Impossibility: Israeli State Discourses about Palestinian Child Labour." *Children & Society* 30, no. 5 (2016): 396–409.

———. "Witnessing and Testimony as Event: Israeli NGOs, Palestinian Witnesses, and the Undoing of Human Rights Bureaucracy." *The Cambridge Journal of Anthropology* 39, no. 1 (2021): 93–110.

Grosglik, Rafi. *Globalizing Organic: Nationalism, Neoliberalism, and Alternative Food in Israel.* SUNY Press, 2021.

———. "Post-national Organic: Globalization and the Field of Organic Food in Israel." In *Re-Thinking Organic Food and Farming in a Changing World*, edited by Bernhard Freyer, and R. James Bingen, 141–155. Springer, 2015.

Grosglik, Rafi, Ariel Handel, and Daniel Monterescu. "Soil, Territory, Land: The Spatial Politics of Settler Organic Farming in the West Bank, Israel/Palestine." *Environment and Planning D: Society and Space* 39, no. 5 (2021): 906–924.

Grove-White, Robin. "The Environmental 'Valuation' Controversy: Observations and Its Recent History and Implications." In *Valuing Nature? Ethics, Economics and the Environment*, edited by John Foster, 21–31. Routledge, 1997.

Gucci, R., and M. Tattini. "Salinity Tolerance in Olive." *Horticultural Reviews*, edited by J. Janick, 177–214. Oxford, 2010.

Gupta, Akhil. "Blurred Boundaries: The Discourse of Corruption, the Culture of Politics, and the Imagined State." In *The Anthropology of the State: A Reader*, edited by Aradhana Sharma and Akhil Gupta, 211–242. Blackwell, 2006.

Gutkowski, Natalia. "Bodies That Count: Administering Multispecies in Palestine/Israel's Borderlands." *Environment and Planning E: Nature and Space* 4, no. 1 (2020): 135–157. https://doi.org/10.1177/2514848620901445.

———. "Governing through Timescape: Israeli Sustainable Agriculture Policy and the Palestinian-Arab Citizens." *International Journal of Middle East Studies* 50, no. 3 (2018): 471–492.

———. "The Green Line and the Equator: Fair Trade Olive Oil in Israel and Palestine." Master's thesis, School of Environmental Studies and the Department of Sociology and Anthropology, Tel Aviv University, 2010.

Gutkowski, Natalia, Dafna Disegni, and Dan Rabinowitz. "Fair Trade Olive Oil and Its Environmental Impact." *The Journal of Ecology and the Environment* 4, no. 1 (2013): 22–13.

Gvati, Haim. *A Hundred Years of Settlement: The Story of Jewish Settlement in the Land of Israel.* Keter, 1985.

Gvion, Liora. "Why Can't Palestinian Chefs Penetrate the Boundaries of Upscale Dining in Israel?" *Ethnicities* 19, no. 6 (2019): 1082–1100.

Hacker, Daphna. "The Gendered Dimensions of Inheritance: Empirical Food for Legal Thought." *Journal of Empirical Legal Studies* 7, no. 2 (2010): 322–354.

Hackl, Andreas. "Immersive Invisibility in the Settler-Colonial City: The Conditional Inclusion of Palestinians in Tel Aviv." *American Ethnologist* 45, no. 3 (2018): 341–353.

———. *The Invisible Palestinians: The Hidden Struggle for Inclusion in Jewish Tel Aviv.* Indiana University Press, 2022.

Halberstam, J. Jack, and Judith Halberstam. *In a Queer Time and Place: Transgender Bodies, Subcultural Lives.* Sexual Cultures Series, vol. 3. NYU Press, 2005.

Halevi-Yarden, Yitshak. "Gush Katif—ha-girsah ha-Yardenit" (Gush Katif—The Jordanian version). Hidabroot website, August 24, 2014. Retrieved July 1, 2018. https://www.hidabroot.org/article/73546.

Halperin, Liora R. *The Oldest Guard: Forging the Zionist Settler Past.* Stanford University Press, 2021.

Haj-Yahya, Nasreen Hadad, Izhak Schnell, and Nabil Khattab. "The Exclusion of Young Arab Women from Work, Education and Training in Israel." *Quality & Quantity* 52, no. 1 (2018): 157–173.

Hammami, Rema. "Waiting for Godot at Qualandya: Reflections on Queues and Inequality." *Jerusalem Quarterly* 13 (Summer 2001).

Hammoudi, Abdellah. *A Season in Mecca: Narrative of a Pilgrimage.* Polity Press, 2006.

Hanafi, Sari. "Explaining Spacio-cide in the Palestinian Territory: Colonization, Separation, and State of Exception." *Current Sociology* 61, no. 2 (2013): 190–205.

Handel, Ariel, and Hilla Dayan. "Multilayered Surveillance in Israel/Palestine: Dialectics of Inclusive Exclusion." *Surveillance & Society* 15, no. 3/4 (2017): 471–476.

Handelman, Don. *Nationalism and the Israeli State: Bureaucratic Logic in Public Events.* Berg, 2004.

Handelman, Don, and Lea Shamgar-Handelman. "The Presence of Absence: The Memorialism of National Death in Israel." In *Grasping Land: Space and Place in Contemporary Israeli Discourse and Experience,* edited by Eyal Ben-Ari and Yoram Bilu. SUNY Series in Anthropology and Judaic Studies. SUNY Press, 1997.

Haraway, Donna. "Situated Knowledges: The Science Question in Feminism and the Privilege of Partial Perspective." *Feminist Studies* 14, no. 3 (1988): 575–599.

Harel, Assaf. "Beyond Gush Emunim: On Contemporary Forms of Messianism among Religiously Motivated Settlers in the West Bank." In *Normalizing Occupation: The Politics of Everyday Life in the West Bank Settlements*, edited by Ariel Handel, Marco Allegra, and Erez Maggor, 128–147. Indiana University Press, 2017.

Harrigan, Jane. *The Political Economy of Arab Food Sovereignty.* Springer, 2014.

Hartmann, H. "'Swan Hill': A New Ornamental Fruitless Olive for California." *California Agriculture* 21, no. 1 (1967): 4–5.

Hasson, Nir. "Adama Harukha 'ad Ha-ofek" (Scorched land until the horizon). *Ha'aretz*, November 28, 2016. http://www.haaretz.co.il/news/science/.premium-1.3135320.

Hasson, Nir, Ran Shimoni, Adi Hashmonai Almog Ben-Zichri, and Naama Riva. "Even the Climate Crisis Does Not Postpone the Shmita Year in Municipal Authorities and Institutions." *Haaretz*, September 1, 2021. Retrieved February 14, 2022. https://www.haaretz.co.il/nature/.premium-1.10169938.

Hazkani, Shay. *Dear Palestine: A Social History of the 1948 War.* Stanford University Press, 2021.

Hazell, Peter, and Panos Varangis. "Best Practices for Subsidizing Agricultural Insurance." *Global Food Security* 25 (2020): 100326.

Hershkovitz, Roni. *Tools to Support Agriculture in Israel.* Research Report 65. Milken Institute Fellows Program, December 2012.

Hilton, Amanda. "Amara e bella, Bitter and Beautiful: A Praxis of Care in Valuing Sicilian Olive Oil and Landscapes." *Economic Anthropology* 9, no. 2 (2022): 257–269.

Hirsch, Dafna. "'Hummus Is Best When It Is Fresh and Made by Arabs': The Gourmetization of Hummus in Israel and the Return of the Repressed Arab." *American Ethnologist* 38, no. 4 (2011): 617–630.

———. "Urban Food Venues as Contact Zones between Arabs and Jews during the British Mandate Period." In *Making Levantine Cuisine: Modern Foodways of the Eastern Mediterranean*, edited by Anny Gaul, Graham Auman Pitts, and Vicki Valosik, 91–114. University of Texas Press, 2021.

Hixson, Walter. *American Settler Colonialism: A History.* Springer, 2013.

Hoag, Colin. "Assembling Partial Perspectives: Thoughts on the Anthropology of Bureaucracy." *PoLAR: Political and Legal Anthropology Review* 34 (2011): 81–94.

Holmes, George. "What Is a Land Grab? Exploring Green Grabs, Conservation, and Private Protected Areas in Southern Chile." *Journal of Peasant Studies* 41, no. 4 (2014): 547–567.

Hughes, Matthew. *Britain's Pacification of Palestine: The British Army, the Colonial State, and the Arab Revolt, 1936–1939.* Cambridge University Press, 2019.

Hull, Matthew S. "The File: Agency, Authority, and Autography in an Islamabad Bureaucracy," *Language & Communication* 23 (2003): 287–314.

Hussein, Hussein Abu, and Fiona McKay. *Access Denied—Palestinian Land Rights in Israel.* Zed Books, 2003.

İpek, Yasemin. "Bala wāsṭa: Aspirant Professionals, Class-Making, and Moral Narratives of Social Mobility in Lebanon," *Journal of the Royal Anthropological Institute* 28, no. 3 (2022): 746–768.

Isakson, S. Ryan. "Derivatives for Development? Small-Farmer Vulnerability and the Financialization of Climate Risk Management." *Journal of Agrarian Change* 15, no. 4 (2015): 569–580.

"Israel Farms Morocco." *Israel Business Today* 7, no. 353 (1993): 7.

Ivry, Tsipy. "Kosher Medicine and Medicalized Halacha: An Exploration of Tri-adic Relations among Israeli Rabbis, Doctors, and Infertility Patients." *American Ethnologist* 37, no. 4 (2010): 662–680.

Jacoby, Karl. *Crimes against Nature: Squatters, Poachers, Thieves, and the Hidden History of American Conservation.* University of California Press, 2014.

Jamal, Amal. "The Arab Leadership in Israel: Ascendance and Fragmentation." *Journal of Palestine Studies* 35, no. 2 (2006): 6–22.

———. "The Counter-Hegemonic Role of Civil Society: Palestinian-Arab NGOs in Israel." *Citizenship Studies* 12, no. 3 (2008): 283–306.

Jamal, Amal, and Noa Lavie. "Subaltern Agency in the Cultural Industries: Palestinian Creative Labor in the Israeli Series Fauda." *International Journal of Communication* 14 (2020): 19.

Jameson, Fredric. *The Seeds of Time.* Columbia University Press, 1996.

Järvi, Tiina. "Demonstrating the Desired Future: Performative Dimensions of Internally Displaced Palestinians' Return Activities." *Geografiska Annaler: Series B, Human Geography* 103, no. 4 (2021): 38–396.

Jarvis, Claude Scudamore. *Yesterday and Today in Sinai.* William Blackwood & Sons, 1931.

Jasanoff, Sheila. *Science and Public Reason.* Routledge, 2012.

Jasanoff, Sheila, and Sang-Hyun Kim, eds. *Dreamscapes of Modernity: Sociotechnical Imaginaries and the Fabrication of Power.* University of Chicago Press, 2015.

Jiryis, Ṣabrī. *The Arabs in Israel.* Monthly Review Press, 1976.

———. "The Legal Structure for the Expropriation and Absorption of Arab Lands in Israel," *Journal of Palestine Studies* 2, no. 4 (1973): 82–104

Joronen, Mikko. "'Refusing to Be a Victim, Refusing to Be an Enemy': Form-of-Life as Resistance in the Palestinian Struggle against Settler Colonialism." *Political Geography* 56 (2017): 91–100.

———. "Spaces of Waiting: Politics of Precarious Recognition in the Occupied West Bank." *Environment and Planning D: Society and Space* 35, no. 6 (2017): 994–1011.

Joronen, Mikko, and Mark Griffiths. "The Affective Politics of Precarity: Home Demolitions in Occupied Palestine." *Environment and Planning D: Society and Space* 37, no. 3 (2019): 561–576.

Johnson, Andrew, A. Holland, and A. Johnson. *Needs, Fears and Fantasies.* Chapman & Hall, 1998.

Kabha, Mustafa, and Nahum Karlinsky. *The Lost Orchard: The Palestinian-Arab Citrus Industry, 1850–1950.* Syracuse University Press, 2021.

Kabeer, Naila. "Resources, Agency, Achievements: Reflections on the Measurement of Women's Empowerment." *Development and Change* 30, no. 3 (1999): 435–464.

Kadman, Noga. *Erased from Space and Consciousness: Israel and the Depopulated Palestinian Villages of 1948.* Indiana University Press, 2015.

———. "Roots Tourism—Whose Roots? The Marginalization of Palestinian Heritage Sites in Official Israeli Tourism Sites." *Téoros: Revue de recherche en tourisme* 29, no. 1 (2010): 55–66.

Kaminer, Matan. "The Agricultural Settlement of the Arabah and the Political Ecology of Zionism." *International Journal of Middle East Studies* (2021): 1–17.

———. "At the Zero Degree/Below the Minimum: Wage as Sign in Israel's Split Labor Market." *Dialectical Anthropology* 43, no. 3 (2019): 317–332.

———. "By the Sweat of Other Brows: Thai Migrant Labor and the Transformation of Israeli Settler Agriculture." PhD diss., University of Michigan, 2019.

———. "Giving Them the Slip: Israeli Employers' Strategic Falsification of Pay Slips to Disguise the Violation of Thai Farmworkers' Right to the Minimum Wage." *Journal of Legal Anthropology* 3, no. 2 (2019): 124–127.

———. "Saving the Face of the Arabah: Thai Migrant Workers and the Asymmetries of Community in an Israeli Agricultural Settlement." *American Ethnologist* 49, no.1 (February 2022):118–131.

Kanaaneh, Rhoda. "Boys or Men? Duped or "Made"? Palestinian Soldiers in the Israeli Military." *American Ethnologist* 32, no. 2 (2005): 260–275.

Kaniewski, David, Elise Van Campo, Tom Boiy, Jean-Frédéric Terral, Bouchaïb Khadari, and Guillaume Besnard. "Primary Domestication and Early Uses of the Emblematic Olive Tree: Palaeobotanical, Historical and Molecular Evidence from the Middle East." *Biological Reviews* 87, no. 4 (2012): 885–899.

Kaplan, Motti, and Naama Ringel. *Nofei ha-haklaut ha-kedumah be-harey Yehuda* (Landscapes of ancient agriculture in the Judean mountains). PowerPoint presentation, 2013.

Kaplan, Motti, Naama Ringel, and Liron Amdur. *Haklaut Nofit—Haklaut Bat Kayma* (Agricultural landscapes—Sustainable agriculture). Nekudat Hen Foundation. 2011.

Kaplan, Motti, Naama Ringel, and Haim Zaban. *Monitoring and Supervising National Master Plan 35—A Policy Approach to Agricultural Terrains.* Kaplan

Planners and Zenovar Consultancy report submitted to the Planning Administration, 2011.

Karayanni, Michael. *A Multicultural Entrapment: Religion and State among the Palestinian-Arabs in Israel.* Cambridge University Press, 2020.

Karlinsky, Nahum. *California Dreaming: Ideology, Society, and Technology in the Citrus Industry of Palestine, 1890–1939.* SUNY Press, 2012.

Karkabi, Nadeem. "Self-Liberated Citizens: Unproductive Pleasures, Loss of Self, and Playful Subjectivities in Palestinian Raves." *Anthropological Quarterly* 93, no. 4 (2020): 679–708.

Karkabi, Nadeem, and Aamer Ibraheem. "On Fleeing Colonial Captivity: Fugitive Arts in the Occupied Jawlan." *Identities* 29, no. 5 (2022): 691–710.

Kedar, Alexandre. "The Legal Transformation of Ethnic Geography: Israeli Law and the Palestinian Landholder 1948–1967." *NYU Journal of International Law and Politics* 33 (2001): 923.

———. "Majority Time, Minority Time: Land, Nation, and the Law of Adverse Possession in Israel." *Tel Aviv University Law Review* 21 (1997): 665.

Kedar, Alexandre, Ahmad Amara, and Oren Yiftachel. *Emptied Lands: A Legal Geography of Bedouin Rights in the Negev.* Stanford University Press, 2018.

Kelly, Jennifer Lynn. "Asymmetrical Itineraries: Militarism, Tourism, and Solidarity in Occupied Palestine." *American Quarterly* 68, no. 3 (2016): 723–745.

Kepkiewicz, Lauren, and Bryan Dale. "Keeping 'Our' Land: Property, Agriculture and Tensions between Indigenous and Settler Visions of Food Sovereignty in Canada." *The Journal of Peasant Studies* 46, no. 5 (2019): 983–1002.

Keynan, Alexander, and Dany Shoham. "Scientific Cooperation in Agriculture and Medical Research as a Means for Normalizing Relations between Egypt and Israel." *Annals of the New York Academy of Sciences* 866, no. 1 (1998): 182–199.

Khalaf, Amin, and Dotan Halevy, "Foreigners in Their Own Country: The Arab Students of Mikveh Israel School 1870-1939." *Zmanim* 135 (2016): 82–99.

Khalidi, Raja. "Sixty Years after the UN Partition Resolution: What Future for the Arab Economy in Israel?" *Journal of Palestine Studies* 37, no. 2 (2008): 6–22.

Khalidi, Rashid I. "Observations on the Right of Return." *Journal of Palestine Studies* 21, no. 2 (1992): 29–40.

Khalidi, Walid. *All That Remains: The Palestinian Villages Occupied and Depopulated by Israel in 1948.* Institute for Palestine Studies, 1992.

Khamaisi, Rassem. "Barriers to Developing Employment Zones in the Arab Palestinian Localities in Israel and Their Implications." In *Palestinians in the Israeli Labor Market*, edited by Nabil Khattab and Sami Miaari, 185–212. Palgrave Macmillan, 2013.

———. "Between Man and Land: Distinctive Proprietary Engineering." In *Conditional Citizenship: On Citizenship, Equality and Offensive Legislation*, edited by S. Ozacky-Lazar and Y. Jabareen, 243–272, Pardes Publications, 2016.

———. "Environmental Policies and Spatial Control: The Case of the Arab Localities Development in Israel." *Arab Studies Quarterly* 28, no. 1 (2006): 33–54.

———. "Environmental Spatial Policies and Control of Arab Localities' Development." In *Palestinian and Israeli Environmental Narratives*, Edited by Stuart Schoenfeld. York Centre for International and Security Studies, York University, 2004.

———. "The Rural-to-Urban Transformation of Arab Localities in Israel and Its Planning Challenges." *Horizons in Geography*, no. 81–82 (2012): 122–142.

Kidron, Carol A. "Toward an Ethnography of Silence: The Lived Presence of the Past in the Everyday Life of Holocaust Trauma Survivors and Their Descendants in Israel." *Current Anthropology* 50, no. 1 (2009): 5–27.

Kilby, Patrick. *The Green Revolution: Narratives of Politics, Technology and Gender.* Routledge, 2019.

Kimmerling, Baruch. *Immigrants, Settlers, Natives: The Israeli State and Society between Cultural Pluralism and Cultural Wars.* Am Oved, 2004.

Kipnis, Nir. "Perhaps You Should Grow Eggs Instead of Fighting for Their Quotas?" *Walla*, February 9, 2022. Retrieved February 16, 2022. https://finance.walla.co.il/item/3487963.

Kirk, Gabi. "Confronting the Twin Crises of Climate Change and Occupation in Palestine." *Arab Studies Journal* 30, no. 2 (2022): 90–95.

Kislev, Yoav. *Meshek Ha-maim shelYisrael* (Israel's water sector). Policy Research for Taub Center for Social Research, 2011.

Kitchin, Rob. "The Timescape of Smart Cities." *Annals of the American Association of Geographers* 109, no. 3 (2019): 775–790.

Klein, I., Y. Ben-Tal, S. Lavee, Y. De Malach, and I. David. "Saline Irrigation of cv. Manzanillo and Uovo di Piccione Trees." In *II International Symposium on Olive Growing*, edited by S. Lavee and I. Klein, 176–180. ISHS Acta Horticulturae 356, 1993.

Knobloch, Frieda. *The Culture of Wilderness: Agriculture as Colonization in the American West.* University of North Carolina Press, 1996.

Koensler, Alexander. "Reinventing Transparency." *Ethnologia Europaea* 48, no. 1 (2017).

Koensler, Alexander, and Pietro Meloni. "Dieta mediterranea: nostalgia o salute?" In *Antropologia dell'alimentazione: Produzione, consumo, movimenti sociali*, 140–144. Carocci Editore, 2019.

Kohlbry, Paul. "Palestinian Counter-forensics and the Cruel Paradox of Property." *American Ethnologist* 49, no. 3 (2022): 374–386.

———. "To Cover the Land in Green: Rain-Fed Agriculture and Anti-colonial Land Reclamation in Palestine." *The Journal of Peasant Studies* (2022): 1–19. doi:10.1080/03066150.2022.2120807.

Kotef, Hagar. *The Colonizing Self: Or, Home and Homelessness in Israel/Palestine.* Duke University Press, 2020.

Kotef, Hagar, and Merav Amir. "Between Imaginary Lines: Violence and Its Justifications at the Military Checkpoints in Occupied Palestine." *Theory, Culture & Society* 28 (2011): 55–80.

Kook, Avraham Yitzhak. *Shabbat Ha'aretz* (Sabbath of the land). Jerusalem, 1909.

Krantz, David. "Shmita Revolution: The Reclamation and Reinvention of the Sabbatical Year." *Religions* 7, no. 8 (2016): 100–131.

Kravel-Tovi, Michal. *When the State Winks: The Performance of Jewish Conversion in Israel.* Religion, Culture, and Public Life. Columbia University Press, 2017.

Krone, Adrienne. "'A Shmita Manifesto': A Radical Sabbatical Approach to Jewish Food Reform in the United States." *Scripta Instituti Donneriani Aboensis* 26 (2015): 303–325.

Kumar, Prakash, Timothy Lorek, Tore C. Olsson, Nicole Sackley, Sigrid Schmalzer, and Gabriela Soto Laveaga. "Roundtable: New Narratives of the Green Revolution." *Agricultural History* 91, no. 3 (2017): 397–422.

Kurlander, Yahel, and Matan Kaminer. "Permanent Workers in the Backyard: Employing Migrant Farmworkers from Thailand in the Israeli Countryside." *Horizons in Geography* 98 (2020): 131–148.

Kurtiç, Ekin. "Infrastructural Decay: Maintenance Ecologies and Labor in the Çoruh Basin." *Cultural Anthropology* 38, no. 1 (2023): 142–170.

Laforge, Julia M. L., Bryan Dale, Charles Z. Levkoe, and Faris Ahmed. "The Future of Agroecology in Canada: Embracing the Politics of Food Sovereignty." *Journal of Rural Studies* 81 (2021): 194–202.

Lahn, Julie. "Being Indigenous in the Bureaucracy: Narratives of Work and Exit." *International Indigenous Policy Journal* 9, no. 1 (2018).

Larkin, Craig. "Jerusalem's Separation Wall and Global Message Board: Graffiti, Murals, and the Art of Sumud." *The Arab Studies Journal* 22, no. 1 (2014): 134–169.

Lavee, Shimon. "Biennial Bearing in Olive (*Olea europaea*)." In *Annales Series Historia Naturalis* 17, no. 1 (2007): 101–112.

———. "Following Olive Footprints in Israel." In *Following Olive Footprints* (Olea europaea L.)*—Cultivation and Culture, Folklore and History, Tradition and Uses,* edited by M. El-Kholy, D. Avanzato, J. M. Caballero, K. Chartzoulakis, F. Vita Serman, and E. Perry. 164–175 International Society for Horticultural Science, 2012.

Lavee, Shimon, A. Haskal, and M. Wodner. "Barnea'a New Olive Cultivar from First Breeding Generation." *Olea* 17, no. 12 (1986): 95–99.

Lavi, Aviv. "Ha-yeshuvim Ha-ʿAravim: Kol Ha-Likhlukh Yotze Ha-hutsah" (The Arab towns: All the waste is flowing out). *NRG*, November 17, 2013. Retrieved August 1, 2018. https://www.makorrishon.co.il/nrg/online/54/ART2/522/670.html.

Lavie, Smadar. *Wrapped in the Flag of Israel: Mizrahi Single Mothers and Bureaucratic Torture* Berghahn Books, 2014.

Legg, Stephen. "Beyond the European Province: Foucault and Postcolonialism." In *Space, Knowledge and Power: Foucault and Geography*, edited by Jeremy W. Crampton and Stuart Elden, 265–289. Routledge, 2007.

Lepore, Jill. *The Whites of Their Eyes*. Princeton University Press, 2011.

Levy, Lital. "Temporalities of Israel/Palestine: Culture and Politics." *Critical Inquiry* 47, no. 4 (2021): 675–698.

LeVine, Mark. "Land, Law and the Planning of Empire: Jaffa and Tel Aviv during the Late Ottoman and Mandate Periods." In *Constituting Modernity: Private Property in the East and West*, edited by Huri İslamoğlu, 100–148. I. B. Tauris, 2004.

Li, Tania Murray. "Centering Labor in the Land Grab Debate." *The Journal of Peasant Studies* 38, no. 2 (2011): 281–298.

———. "Rendering Land Investible: Five Notes on Time." *Geoforum* 82 (2017): 276–278.

———. "What Is Land? Assembling a Resource for Global Investment." *Transactions of the Institute of British Geographers* 39, no. 4 (2014): 589–602.

Lipsky, Michael. *Street-Level Bureaucracy: Dilemmas of the Individual in Public Service*. Russell Sage Foundation, 2010.

Lorcin, Patricia M. E. "Rome and France in Africa: Recovering Colonial Algeria's Latin Past." *French Historical Studies* 25, no. 2 (2002): 295–329.

Lowdermilk, Walter. *Palestine: The Land of Promise*. Harper and Brothers, 1944.

Lulle, Aija. "Temporal Fix, Hierarchies of Work and Post-socialist Hopes for a Better Way of Life." *Journal of Rural Studies* 84 (2021): 221–229.

Lustick, Ian. *Arabs in the Jewish State: Israel's Control of a National Minority*. Modern Middle East Series, no. 6. University of Texas Press, 1980.

Magun, Artemy. "Marx's Theory of Time and the Present Historical Moment." *Rethinking Marxism* 22, no. 1 (2010): 90–1093.

Marteau, Elisabeth. "Identity, Solidarity and Socio-economic Networks across the Separation Lines: A Study of Relations between Palestinians in Israel and the Occupied Territories." In *Israelis and Palestinians in the Shadows of the Wall: Spaces of Separation and Occupation*, edited by Stephanie Latte Abdallah and Cédric Parizot. Border Regions Series. Ashgate Publishing Company, 2015.

Matties, Zoe. "Unsettling Settler Food Movements: Food Sovereignty and Decolonization in Canada." *Cuizine: The Journal of Canadian Food Cultures/Cuizine: Revue des cultures culinaires au Canada* 7, no. 2 (2016). https://doi.org/10.7202/1038478ar.

Marx, Karl. *Capital: A Critique of Political Economy*. Translated by Ben Fowkes. Pelican Marx Library, vol. 1. Vintage Books, 1977.

Mathews, Andrew S. "Anthropology and the Anthropocene: Criticisms, Experiments, and Collaborations." *Annual Review of Anthropology* 49 (2020): 67–82.

———. *Instituting Nature: Authority, Expertise, and Power in Mexican Forests*. MIT Press, 2011.

———. *Trees Are Shape Shifters: How Cultivation, Climate Change, and Disaster Create Landscapes*. Yale University Press, 2022.

Mathews, Andrew S., and Jessica Barnes. "Prognosis: Visions of Environmental Futures." *Journal of the Royal Anthropological Institute* 22, no. S1 (2016): 9–26.

Mathur, Nayanika. "The Reign of Terror of the Big Cat: Bureaucracy and the Mediation of Social Times in the Indian Himalaya." *Journal of the Royal Anthropological Institute* 20, no. S1 (2014): 148–165.

Masalha, Nur. *Catastrophe Remembered: Palestine, Israel and the Internal Refugees: Essays in Memory of Edward W. Said (1935–2003)*. Zed Books, 2005.

———. *The Zionist Bible: Biblical Precedent, Colonialism, and the Erasure of Memory*. Bible World. Acumen, 2013.

Massad, Joseph. "Zionism's Internal Others: Israel and the Oriental Jews." *Journal of Palestine Studies* 25, no. 4 (1996): 53–68.

Mastnak, Tomaz, Julia Elyachar, and Tom Boellstorff. "Botanical Decolonization: Rethinking Native Plants." *Environment and Planning D: Society and Space* 32, no. 2 (2014): 363–380.

May, Jon, and Nigel Thrift, eds. *Timespace: Geographies of Temporality*. Critical Geographies, vol. 13. Routledge, 2003.

Mazori, Dalia. "Hava Yisraelit be-Yarden tesapek schorah muzelet ba-shmitah" (An Israeli farm in Jordan will provide cheaper produce in Shmitah). *NRG*, October 10, 2014. Retrieved July 1, 2018. https://www.makorrishon.co.il/nrg/online/1/ART2/636/003.html.

Mazzawi, Nisreen, and Amalia Sa'ar. "The ḥawākīr of Nazareth: The History and Contemporary Face of a Cultural Ecological Institution." *International Journal of Middle East Studies* 50, no. 3 (2018): 537–556.

McCallister, Dennis L., Donald J. Lee, and Stephen C. Mason. "Student Numbers in Agronomy and Crop Science in the United States: History, Current Status, and Possible Actions." *NACTA Journal* 49, no.3 (2005): 24–29.

McGonigle, Ian. "In Vino Veritas? Indigenous Wine and Indigenization in Israeli Settlements." *Anthropology Today* 35, no. 4 (2019): 7–12.

McKee, Emily. "Divergent Visions: Intersectional Water Advocacy in Palestine." *Environment and Planning E: Nature and Space* 4, no. 1 (2021): 43–64.

———. *Dwelling in Conflict: Negev Landscapes and the Boundaries of Belonging*. Stanford, California: Stanford University Press, 2016.

———. "Performing Rootedness in the Negev/Naqab: Possibilities and Perils of Competitive Planting." *Antipode* 46, no. 5 (2014): 1172–1189.

McMichael, Philip. "The Land Grab and Corporate Food Regime Restructuring." *The Journal of Peasant Studies* 39, no. 3–4 (2012): 681–701.

McNeil, Maureen, Michael Arribas-Ayllon, Joan Haran, Adrian Mackenzie, and Richard Tutton. "Conceptualizing Imaginaries of Science, Technology, and Society." In *The Handbook of Science and Technology Studies*, edited by Ulrike

Felt, Rayvon Fouché, Clark A. Miller, and Laurel Smith-Doerr, 435–464. MIT Press, 2016.

Meari, Lena. "The Roles of Palestinian Peasant Women: The Case of al-Birweh Village, 1930–1960." In *Displaced at Home: Ethnicity and Gender among Palestinians in Israel*, edited by Rhoda Ann Kanaaneh and Isis Nusair. 119–132. SUNY Press, 2010.

Medland, Lydia. "'There Is No Time': Agri-food Internal Migrant Workers in Morocco's Tomato Industry." *Journal of Rural Studies* 88 (2021): 482–490.

Meneley, Anne. "Blood, Sweat and Tears in a Bottle of Palestinian Extra-Virgin Olive Oil." *Food, Culture, & Society* 14, no. 2 (2011): 275–292.

———. "Discourses of Distinction in Contemporary Palestinian Extra-Virgin Olive Oil Production." *Food and Foodways* 22, no. 1–2 (2014): 48–64.

———. "Hope in the Ruins: Seeds, Plants, and Possibilities of Regeneration." *Environment and Planning E: Nature and Space* 4, no. 1 (2021): 158–172.

———. "The Olive and Imaginaries of the Mediterranean." *History and Anthropology* 31, no. 1 (2020): 66–83.

———. "Resistance Is Fertile!" *Gastronomica: The Journal of Food and Culture* 14, no. 4 (2014): 69–78.

———. "The Accidental Pilgrims: Olive Pickers in Palestine." *Religion and Society* 5, no. 1 (2014): 186–199.

———. "Time in a Bottle: The Uneasy Circulation of Palestinian Olive Oil." *Middle East Report* 248 (2008): 18–23.

Mitchell, Timothy. "Society, Economy, and the State Effect." In *State/Culture: State Formation after the Cultural Turn*, edited by G. Steinmetz, 76–97. Cornell University Press, 1999.

Mitchell, William J. T. "Holy Landscape: Israel, Palestine, and the American Wilderness." *Critical Inquiry* 26, no. 2 (2000): 193–223.

Miyazaki, Hirokazu. "The Temporalities of the Market." *American Anthropologist* 105, no. 2 (2003): 255–265.

Montenegro de Wit, Maywa. "Can Agroecology and CRISPR Mix? The Politics of Complementarity and Moving toward Technology Sovereignty." *Agriculture and Human Values* 39, no. 2 (2022): 733–755.

———. "What Grows from a Pandemic? Toward an Abolitionist Agroecology." *The Journal of Peasant Studies* 48, no. 1 (2021): 99–136.

Monterescu, Daniel, and Ariel Handel. "Liquid Indigeneity: Wine, Science, and Colonial Politics in Israel/Palestine." *American Ethnologist* 46, no. 3 (2019): 313–327.

———. "Terroir and Territory on the Colonial Frontier: Making New-Old World Wine in the Holy Land." *Comparative Studies in Society and History* 62, no. 2 (2020): 222–261.

Morris, Benny. *The Birth of the Palestinian Refugee Problem Revisited*. Cambridge University Press, 2003.

———. *Leidata Shel Behayat Haplitim Haphaletiniim, 1947–1949* (The birth of the Palestinian refugee problem, 1947–1949). Am Oved, 1991.

Moroșanu, Roxana, and Felix Ringel. "Time-Tricking: A General Introduction." *The Cambridge Journal of Anthropology* 34, no. 1 (2016): 17–21.

Moscrop, John James. *Measuring Jerusalem: The Palestine Exploration Fund and British Interests in the Holy Land.* A & C Black, 2000.

Mulberg, Jon. "Modernity and Environmental Economics: A Sociological Critique." *Innovation: The European Journal of Social Science Research* 9, no. 4 (1996): 435–447.

Musih, Norma. "Between knowing and understanding: Israeli Jews and the memory of the Palestinian Nakba." *Cultural Studies* 37, no. 3 (2023): 396–417.

———. "Bridging Memories: Training the Imagination to Go Visiting in Israel/Palestine." *Visual Studies* (2021): 1–11. doi:10.1080/1472586X.2021.1979899.

Naali, Adi. "Olive Groves Plantation as a Sustainable Solution to Abandoned Agricultural Land." PhD diss., Department of Geography and Environmental Studies, Haifa University, 2009.

Nadan, Amos. "Colonial Misunderstanding of an Efficient Peasant Institution: Land Settlement and Mushā Tenure in Mandate Palestine, 1921–47." *Journal of the Economic and Social History of the Orient* 46, no. 3 (2003): 320–354.

———. *The Palestinian Peasant Economy under the Mandate: A Story of Colonial Bungling.* Harvard Center for Middle East Studies, Harvard University Press, 2006.

Nadasdy, Paul. "The Anti-politics of TEK: The Institutionalization of Co-management Discourse and Practice." *Anthropologica* 47, no. 2 (2005): 215–232.

———. "Wildlife as Renewable Resource: Competing Conceptions of Wildlife, Time and Management in the Yukon." In *Timely Assets: The Politics of Resources and Their Temporalities*, edited by E. E. Ferry and M. E. Limbert, 75–106. School for Advanced Research Press, 2008.

Nahshoni, Kobi. "Heter ha-mekhirah yatsa la-derekh" (The sale permit has hit the road). *Ynet*–Yediot Aahronot, September 5, 2007. Retrieved May 30, 2018. https://www.ynet.co.il/articles/0,7340,L-3446165,00.html.

Nair, Kusum. *In Defense of the Irrational Peasant: Indian Agriculture after the Green Revolution.* University of Chicago Press, 1979.

Nakhleh, Khalil. "Anthropological and Sociological Studies on the Arabs in Israel: A Critique." *Journal of Palestine Studies* 6, no. 4 (1977): 41–70.

———. "Yawm al-Ard" (Land Day). In *The Palestinians in Israel: Readings in History, Politics and Society*, edited by Nadim Rouhana and Areej Sabbagh-Khoury, 83–89. Mada al-Carmel—Arab Center for Applied Social Research, 2011.

Narotzky, Susana. "Where Have All the Peasants Gone?" *Annual Review of Anthropology* 45 (2016): 301–318.

Nanni, Giordano. "Time, Empire and Resistance in Settler-Colonial Victoria." *Time & Society* 20, no. 1 (2011): 5–33.

Nassar, Jamal Raji, and Roger Heacock, eds. *Intifada: Palestine at the crossroads.* Greenwood Publishing Group, 1990.

Nazarea, Virginia D. *Heirloom Seeds and Their Keepers: Marginality and Memory in the Conservation of Biological Diversity.* University of Arizona Press, 2005.

———. "Local Knowledge and Memory in Biodiversity Conservation." *Annual Review of Anthropology* 35 (2006): 317–335.

Nijmeh, Ali. "Active and Transformative Sumud Among Palestinian Activists in Israel." In *Palestine and Rule of Power*, edited by Alaa Tartir and Timothy Seidel, 71–103. Palgrave Macmillan, 2019.

Nixon, Rob. *Slow Violence and the Environmentalism of the Poor.* Harvard University Press, 2011.

Novick, Tamar. "Bible, Bees and Boxes: The Creation of 'The Land Flowing with Milk and Honey' in Palestine, 1880–1931." *Food, Culture & Society* 16, no. 2 (2013): 281–299.

———. *Milk and Honey: Technologies of Plenty in the Making of a Holy Land, 1880–1960.* MIT Press, 2023.

Novick, Tamar, and Dubnov M. Arie. "The Unknown History of the Palestinian School Funded by an Iraqi Jew." +972 *Magazine*, February 25, 2017. https://972 mag.com/the-unknown-history-of-the-palestinian-school-funded-by-an-iraqi -jew/125443/.

Nuriely, Benny. "Tsvira Vepikuach: Hamimshal Htsvai Be-Lod, Yuli 1948–Yuli 1949" (Accumulation and control: The military regime in Lod, July 1948–July 1949). Paper presented at the Israeli Anthropological Association, Van Leer Institute, Jerusalem, May 30, 2013.

O'Brien, Jay. "The Calculus of Profit and Labour-Time in Sudanese Peasant Agriculture." *The Journal of Peasant Studies* 14, no. 4 (1987): 454–468.

Ogden, Laura A. *Swamplife: People, Gators, and Mangroves Entangled in the Everglades.* University of Minnesota Press, 2011.

Orlove, Ben, and Steven C. Caton. "Water Sustainability: Anthropological Approaches and Prospects." *Annual Review of Anthropology* 39 (2010): 401–415.

Ortmann, Gerald F., and Robert P. King. "Agricultural Cooperatives I: History, Theory and Problems." *Agrekon* 46, no. 1 (2007): 40–68.

Ostan, Rita, Catia Lanzarini, Elisa Pini, Maria Scurti, Dario Vianello, Claudia Bertarelli, Cristina Fabbri et al. "Inflammaging and Cancer: A Challenge for the Mediterranean Diet." *Nutrients* 7, no. 4 (2015): 2589–2621.

Owen, Roger, ed. *Studies in the Economic and Social History of Palestine in the Nineteenth and Twentieth Centuries.* Springer, 1982.

Parsons, Laila. "The Palestinian Druze in the 1947–1949 Arab-Israeli War." *Israel Studies* 2, no. 1 (1997): 72–93.

Paz, Shlomit, Ofira Ayalon, and Areej Haj. "The Potential Conflict between Traditional Perceptions and Environmental Behavior: Compost Use by Muslim Farmers." *Environment, Development and Sustainability* 15, no. 4 (2013): 967–978.

Pearlberg, Amir, Liron Amdur, and Uri Ramon. *'Ibudim Bney Kayma Shel Karmey Zeitim Bagalil Ha-ma'aravi- Behinat Mishtanim Kalkalim, Hevratim Veecologim, Do"h Sofi.* Pearlberg Report, Kibbutz Ein Karmel, Nekudat Hen, 2012.

Penslar, Derek Jonathan. *Zionism and Technocracy: The Engineering of Jewish Settlement in Palestine, 1870–1918.* Indiana University Press, 1991.

Peteet, Julie. "Closure's Temporality: The Cultural Politics of Time and Waiting." *South Atlantic Quarterly* 117, no. 1 (January 2018): 43–64.

———. *Space and Mobility in Palestine.* Indiana University Press, 2017.

Perevolotski Avi. *Agriculture and Ecology—Can Harmony Be Found? Perspectives on Agroecology from Israel and Abroad.* Agricultural Research Organization, Volcani Center, December 2019.

Pessah, Tom. "The Distinction of Violence: Representing Lethal Cleansing in Settler Colonial Societies." PhD diss., Department of Sociology, University of California, Berkley, 2014.

———. "The Palestinian Villages and Villagers: Between Expulsion and Representation." In *Encounters between History and Anthropology in Studying the Israeli-Palestinian Space*, edited by Dafna Hirsch, 147–175. Van Leer Institute and Kibbutz Meuchad Publication, 2019.

Pfeilstetter, Richard. "Heritage Entrepreneurship: Agency-Driven Promotion of the Mediterranean Diet in Spain." *International Journal of Heritage Studies* 21, no. 3 (2015): 215–231.

Piterberg, Gabriel. *The Returns of Zionism: Myths, Politics and Scholarship in Israel.* Verso, 2008.

Porat, Naomi, Uri Davidovich, Yoav Avni, Gideon Avni, and Yuval Gadot. "Using OSL Measurements to Decipher Soil History in Archaeological Terraces, Judean Highlands, Israel." *Land Degradation & Development* 29, no. 3 (2018): 643–650.

Povinelli, Elizabeth A. "Divergent Survivances." *E-flux Journal* no. 121 (October 2021). https://www.e-flux.com/journal/121/424069/divergent-survivances/.

———. *Labor's Lot: The Power, History, and Culture of Aboriginal Action.* University of Chicago Press, 1993.

Powers, David S. "The Islamic Inheritance System: A Socio-Historical Approach." *Arab Law Quarterly* 8, no. 1 (1993): 13–29.

Puig de la Bellacasa, Maria. "Making Time for Soil: Technoscientific Futurity and the Pace of Care." *Social Studies of Science* 45, no. 5 (2015): 691–716.

Rabie, Kareem. *Palestine Is Throwing a Party and the Whole World Is Invited: Capital and State Building in the West Bank.* Duke University Press, 2021.

Rabinowitz, Dan. "Oriental Othering and National Identity: A Review of Early Israeli Anthropological Studies of Palestinians." *Identities: Global Studies in Culture and Power* 9 (2002): 305–325.

———. *The Power of Deserts.* Stanford University Press, 2020.

———."Oriental Nostalgia: When Did the Palestinians Become Israeli Arabs?" *Theory and Criticism* 4 (Winter 1993): 141–151.

Rabinowitz, Dan, and Khaula Abu Baker. *Coffins on Our Shoulders: The Experience of the Palestinian Citizens of Israel*. University of California Press, 2005.

Rabinowitz, Dan, and Itai Yardi. *Koḥot Meni'im. Kvish Hotseh Yisrael ve-hafratat tashtiot leumiot*. Van Leer Institute and Ha-Kibbutz Ha-meuhad, 2010.

Radcliffe, Sarah A., and Andrew J. Webb. "Subaltern Bureaucrats and Postcolonial Rule: Indigenous Professional Registers of Engagement with the Chilean State." *Comparative Studies in Society and History* 57, no. 1 (2015): 248–273.

Raijman, Rebeca, and Adriana Kemp. "Labor Migration, Managing the Ethnonational Conflict, and Client Politics in Israel." *Transnational Migration to Israel in Global Comparative Context,* edited by Sarah S. Willen, 31–50. Lexington Books, 2007.

Raijman, Rebeca, and Nonna Kushnirovich. *Labor Migrant Recruitment Practices in Israel*. Ruppin Academic Center, 2012.

Rallo, Luis. "Breeding Oil and Table Olives for Mechanical Harvesting in Spain." *HortTechnology* 24, no. 3 (2014): 295–300.

Randeria, Shalini. "Global Designs and Local Lifeworlds: Colonial Legacies of Conservation, Disenfranchisement and Environmental Governance in Postcolonial India." *interventions* 9, no. 1 (2007): 12–30.

Reger, Jeffrey D. "Olive Cultivation in the Galilee, 1948–1955: Hegemony and Resistance." *Journal of Palestine Studies* 46, no. 4 (2017): 28–45.

Reisman, Emily. "Protecting Provenance, Abandoning Agriculture? Heritage Products, Industrial Ideals and the Uprooting of a Spanish Turrón." *Journal of Rural Studies* 89 (2022): 45–53.

———. "Sanitizing Agri-food Tech: COVID-19 and the Politics of Expectation." *The Journal of Peasant Studies* 48, no. 5 (2021): 910–933.

Reisman, Emily, and Madeleine Fairbairn. "Agri-food Systems and the Anthropocene." *Annals of the American Association of Geographers* 111, no. 3 (2020): 687–697.

Reynolds, Kyra. "Palestinian Agriculture and the Israeli Separation Barrier: The Mismatch of Biopolitics and Chronopolitics with the Environment and Human Survival." *International Journal of Environmental Studies* 72, no. 2 (2014): 1–19.

Rice, Anika, and Zachary Goldberg. "'Harvesting a Participatory Movement': Initial Participatory Action Research with the Jewish Farmer Network." *Journal of Agriculture, Food Systems, and Community Development* 11, no. 1 (2021): 115–136.

Richter, Tobias, Amaia Arranz-Otaegui, Lisa Yeomans, and Elisabetta Boaretto. "High Resolution AMS Dates from Shubayqa 1, Northeast Jordan Reveal Complex Origins of Late Epipalaeolithic Natufian in the Levant." *Scientific Reports* 7, no. 1 (2017): 1–10.

Rifkin, Mark. *Beyond Settler Time: Temporal Sovereignty and Indigenous Self-Determination*. Duke University Press, 2017.

Rijke, Alexandra, and Toine Van Teeffelen. "To Exist Is to Resist: Sumud, Heroism, and the Everyday." *Jerusalem Quarterly* 59 (2014): 86.

Rinat, Zafrir. "Le-shakhnea Haklaim 'Aravim sh-Biyuv ze Tov'" (Convince Arab farmers that sewage is good). *Ha'aretz*, January 24, 2014. Retrieved August 1, 2018. https://www.haaretz.co.il/news/science/zafrir/.premium-1.2224154.

Ringel, Felix. "Can Time Be Tricked? A Theoretical Introduction." *The Cambridge Journal of Anthropology* 34, no. 1 (2016): 22–31.

Robinson, Paul. "The Trickster Science." In *The Routledge Handbook of Political Ecology*, edited by Tom Perreault, Gavin Bridge, and James McCarthy, 89–101. Routledge, 2015.

Robinson, Shira N. *Citizen Strangers: Palestinians and the Birth of Israel's Liberal Settler State*. Stanford University Press, 2013.

Rocheleau, Dianne E. "Networked, Rooted and Territorial: Green Grabbing and Resistance in Chiapas." *Journal of Peasant Studies* 42, no. 3–4 (2015): 695–723.

Rose, Julie. *Free Time*. Princeton University Press, 2016.

Rosenfeld, Henry. "Change, Barriers to Change, and Contradictions in the Arab Village Family ." *American Anthropologist* 70, no. 4 (1968): 732–752.

———. "From Peasantry to Wage Labor and Residual Peasantry: The Transformation of an Arab Village in Israel." In *Process and Pattern in Culture*, edited by Robert Alan Manners and Julian Haynes Steward, 211–34. Routledge, (1964) 2017.

———. "Processes of Structural Change within the Arab Village Extended Family." *American Anthropologist* 60, no. 6 (1958): 1127–1139.

Rosner, Abbie. "Roasting Green Wheat in Galilee." *Gastronomica* 11, no. 2 (2011): 66–68.

Ross, Andrew. *Stone Men: The Palestinians Who Built Israel*. Verso Books, 2021.

Rotz, Sarah. " 'They Took Our Beads, It Was a Fair Trade, Get Over It': Settler Colonial Logics, Racial Hierarchies and Material Dominance in Canadian Agriculture." *Geoforum* 82 (2017): 158–169.

Rotz, Sarah, Evan Gravely, Ian Mosby, Emily Duncan, Elizabeth Finnis, Mervyn Horgan, Joseph LeBlanc et al. "Automated Pastures and the Digital Divide: How Agricultural Technologies Are Shaping Labour and Rural Communities." *Journal of Rural Studies* 68 (2019): 112–122.

Rouhana, Nadim N., and Areej Sabbagh-Khoury. "Memory and the Return of History in a Settler-Colonial Context: The Case of the Palestinians in Israel." *Interventions* 21, no. 4 (2019): 527–550.

———. "Settler-Colonial Citizenship: Conceptualizing the Relationship between Israel and Its Palestinian Citizens." *Settler Colonial Studies* 5, no. 3 (2015): 205–225.

Roy, Sara. "The Gaza Strip: A Case of Economic De-development." *Journal of Palestine Studies* 17, no. 1 (1987): 56–88.

Ryan, Sheila. "Israeli Economic Policy in the Occupied Areas: Foundations of a New Imperialism." *MERIP Reports* 24 (1974): 3–28.

Sabbagh-Khoury, Areej. *Colonizing Palestine: The Zionist Left and the Making of Palestinian Nakba*. Stanford University Press, 2023.

———. "Memory for Forgetfulness: Conceptualizing a Memory Practice of Settler Colonial Disavowal." *Theory and Society* 52, no. 2 (March 2023): 263–292.

———."Sociology of Complexity or Sociology of Complicity? Urban Settler Colonialism in East Jerusalem." Lecture presented at 53rd Annual Conference of the Israeli Sociological Association, Hebrew University of Jerusalem, February 9, 2022.

———. "Tracing Settler Colonialism: A Genealogy of a Paradigm in the Sociology of Knowledge Production in Israel." *Politics & Society* 50, no. 1 (2021): 44–83. https://doi.org/10.1177/0032329221999906.

Sackman, Douglas Cazaux. *Orange Empire: California and the Fruits of Eden*. University of California Press, 2005.

Sa'di, Ahmad H. "Modernization as an Explanatory Discourse of Zionist-Palestinian Relations." *British Journal of Middle Eastern Studies* 24 (1997): 25–48.

Sa'di, Ahmad H., and Lila Abu-Lughod, eds. *Nakba: Palestine, 1948, and the Claims of Memory*. Columbia University Press, 2007.

Sa'di-Ibraheem, Yara. "Jaffa's Times: Temporalities of Dispossession and the Advent of Natives' Reclaimed Time." *Time & Society* 29, no. 2 (2020): 340–361.

———. "Settler Colonial Temporalities, Ruinations and Neoliberal Urban Renewal: The Case of Suknet Al-Huresh in Jaffa." *GeoJournal* 87, no. 2 (2022): 661–675.

Safrai, Shmuel. "Mitzvat Shevieit Ba-metziut She-leahar Hurban Bait Sheni" (The Seventh Year Commandment in the reality post Temple destruction). In *Shmitah: Mekorot, Hagut, Mehkar*, 117–164. Misrad Ha-Hinuch Veha-tarbut (Ministry of Education and Culture), 1993.

Said, Edward W. *Orientalism*. Vintage Books, 2003.

———. *The Question of Palestine*. Vintage, 1992.

Salamanca, Omar Jabary, Mezna Qato, Kareem Rabie, and Sobhi Samour. "Past Is Present: Settler Colonialism in Palestine." *Settler Colonial Studies* 2, no. 1 (2012): 1–8.

Sallon, Sarah, Elaine Solowey, Yuval Cohen, Raia Korchinsky, Markus Egli, Ivan Woodhatch, Orit Simchoni, and Mordechai Kislev. "Germination, Genetics, and Growth of an Ancient Date Seed." *Science* 320, no. 5882 (2008): 1464–1464.

Samimian-Darash, Limor. "Governing Future Potential Biothreats: Toward an Anthropology of Uncertainty." *Current Anthropology* 54, no. 1 (2012): 1–22.

———. "A Pre-event Configuration for Biological Threats: Preparedness and the Constitution of Biosecurity Events." *American Ethnologist* 36, no. 3 (2009): 478–491.

Sasson, Tiram. "Tzfu: Kakh Nimkeru Karkaot ha-Medinah Le-Ger-Toshav" (Watch: The sale of the state's land to a resident-non-Jew), *Srugim*, September 23, 2014. Retrieved June 7, 2018. https://tinyurl.com/4zrst25b.

Sayigh, Rosemary. *The Palestinians: From Peasants to Revolutionaries*. Zed Books, (1979) 2013.

Scaramelli, Caterina. *How to Make a Wetland: Water and Moral Ecology in Turkey*. Stanford University Press, 2021.

Schechter, Haim Mordecai. *Hishtalshelut ha-shemitah: mi-tekufat bayit sheni 'ad ha-yom ha-zeh: shemitat karka'ot shemita kesafim tosefet shevi'it* (The evolution of shmitah from the Second Temple until today). Tel Aviv: publisher not identified, 1966.

Schiff, Avi. "Likrat ha-shmitah mokhrim et admot ha-medina le-goy" (Toward shmitah: The state land is sold to a gentile). *Behadrei Haredim*, September 17, 2014. Retrieved June 7, 2018. https://tinyurl.com/35pb22wr.

Schotten, C. Heike. "To Exist Is to Resist: Palestine and the Question of Queer Theory." *Journal of Palestine Studies* 47, no. 3 (2018): 13–28.

Sela, Rona. "The Genealogy of Colonial Plunder and Erasure—Israel's Control over Palestinian Archives." *Social Semiotics* 28, no. 2 (2018): 201–229.

———. "Seized in Beirut: The Plundered Archives of the Palestinian Cinema Institution and Cultural Arts Section." *Anthropology of the Middle East* 12, no. 1 (2017): 83–114.

Shapiro, Matan, and Nurit Bird-David. "Routinergency: Domestic Securitization in Contemporary Israel." *Environment and Planning D: Society and Space* 35, no. 4 (2017): 637–655.

Schiebinger, Londa, and Claudia Swan, eds. *Colonial Botany: Science, Commerce, and Politics in the Early Modern World*. University of Pennsylvania Press, 2007.

Schler, Lynn. "Dilemmas of Postcolonial Diplomacy: Zambisharabia, Kenneth Kaunda, and the Middle East Crisis, 1964–73." *The Journal of African History* 59, no. 1 (2018): 97–119.

Schultz, Theodore. *Transforming Traditional Agriculture*. Yale University Press, 1964.

Scott, Joan Wallach. *Gender and the Politics of History*. Columbia University Press, 1988.

Segal, Eran, Arnon Dag, Alon Ben-Gal, Isaac Zipori, Ran Erel, Shoshana Suryano, and Uri Yermiyahu. "Olive Orchard Irrigation with Reclaimed Wastewater: Agronomic and Environmental Considerations." *Agriculture, Ecosystems & Environment* 140, no. 3–4 (2011): 454–461.

Seikaly, Sherene. "The Matter of Time." *The American Historical Review* 124, no. 5 (2019): 1681–1688.

———. *Men of Capital: Scarcity and Economy in Mandate Palestine*. Stanford University Press, 2015.

Selby, Jan. "Cooperation, Domination and Colonisation: The Israeli-Palestinian Joint Water Committee." *Water Alternatives* 6, no. 1 (2013): 1–24.

Selby, Jan, Omar S. Dahi, Christiane Fröhlich, and Mike Hulme. "Climate Change and the Syrian Civil War Revisited." *Political Geography* 60 (2017): 232–244.

Seligman, Noam. "The Environmental Legacy of the Fellaheen and the Bedouin in Palestine." In *Between Ruin and Restoration: an Environmental History of Israel*, edited by Daniel E. Orenstein, Char Miller, and Alon Tal, 29–52. University of Pittsburgh Press, 2013.

Sergeeva, Vera. "Following Olive Footprints in Australia." In *Following Olive Footprints* (Olea europaea L.)—*Cultivation and Culture, Folklore and History, Tradition and Uses*, edited by M. El-Kholy, D. Avanzato, J. M. Caballero, K. Chartzoulakis, F. Vita Serman, and E. Perry, 32–47. International Society for Horticultural Science, 2012.

Shafir, Gershon. *Land, Labor and the Origins of the Israeli-Palestinian Conflict, 1882–1914*. University of California Press, 1996.

———. "Settler Citizenship in the Jewish Colonization of Palestine." In *Settler Colonialism in the Twentieth Century: Projects, Practices, Legacies*, edited by Caroline Elkins and Susan Pedersen, 55–72. Routledge, 2012.

Shalev, Guy. "Conditional Heroes: On Palestinian Doctors during the War against Covid-19." *Israeli Sociology*, no. 2 (2021): 63–73. https://www.jstor.org/stable/27006639.

———. "Helsinki in Zion: Hospital Ethics Committees and Political Gatekeeping in Israel/Palestine." *American Anthropologist* 124, no. 4 (2022): 688–702.

———. "Medicine and the Politics of Neutrality: The Professional and Political Lives of Palestinian Physicians in Israel." PhD diss., University of North Carolina, Chapel Hill, 2018.

Shamir, Ronen. *Current Flow: The Electrification of Palestine*. Stanford University Press, 2013.

———. "Suspended in Space: Bedouins under the Law of Israel." *Law & Society Review* 30, no. 2 (1996): 231–257.

Shani, Liron. *The Arava Approach—Anthropology of Nature and (Agri)Culture*. Lamda Scholarship, The Open University of Israel Press, and BGI Press, 2021.

———. "Liquid Distinctions: Negotiating Boundaries between Agriculture and the Environment in the Israeli Desert." *Anthropological Quarterly* 91, no. 3 (2018): 1075–1103.

———. "Of Trees and People: The Changing Entanglement in the Israeli Desert." *Ethnos* 83, no. 4 (2018): 624–644.

———. "Predatory Fleas, Sterile Flies, and the Settlers." *Cultural Anthropology* 38, no. 1 (2023): 87–112.

Shapira, Anita. "The Bible and Israeli Identity." *AJS Review* 28, no. 1 (2004): 11–41.

Sharon, Smadar. "The Dialectic between Modernization and Orientalization: Ethnicity and Work Relations in the 1950s Lakhish Region Project." *Ethnic and Racial Studies* 40, no. 4 (2017): 732–750.

Shlaim, Avi. *The Politics of Partition: King Abdullah, the Zionists, and Palestine, 1921–1951*. Columbia University Press, 1990.

Shehadeh, Raja. "The Land Law of Palestine: An Analysis of the Definition of State Lands." *Journal of Palestine Studies* 11, no. 2 (1982): 82–99.

———. *Palestinian Walks: Forays into a Vanishing Landscape*. Scribner, 2008.

Shohat, Ella. "The Invention of the Mizrahim." *Journal of Palestine Studies* 29, no. 1 (1999): 5–20.

Shoham, Hizky. "A Tale of Two Cultures: An Outline for a Comparative Cultural Analysis of Israeli and North American Jewry." *Journal of Modern Jewish Studies* 21, no. 1 (2022): 1–20.

Shomron, Mordechai. "Gidul yerakot be-matza' menutak ba-shmitah be-gush katif." *Maamarei emunat 'eitekha*, 'Alon 1. Kislev, Tashna (December 1994). http://www.daat.ac.il/daat/kitveyet/emunat/01/00110.htm.

Silvern, Steven E. "The Jewish Food Movement: A Sustainable and Just Vision for Place, Identity, and Environment." In *Religion, Sustainability, and Place*, edited by Silvern, Steven E., and Edward H. Davis 327–354. Palgrave Macmillan, 2021.

Simaan, Juman. "Olive Growing in Palestine: A Decolonial Ethnographic Study of Collective Daily-Forms-of-Resistance." *Journal of Occupational Science* 24, no. 4 (2017): 510–523.

Simpson, Audra. *Mohawk Interruptus: Political Life across the Borders of Settler States*. Duke University Press, 2014.

Simovitch, Or. "Back to the Sources through Imported Models: Transformations in the Value of Olive Oil in Israel." Master's thesis, Open University of Israel, Ra'anana, 2015.

Singer, Avraham. *Hatipul Bezeitey Baal* (Care of rain-fed olives). Ministry of Agriculture Sherut Hahadracha Vehamiktzoa (Agricultural Extension Service), 1969.

———. "Tarbut ha-zayit" (Olive culture). *Ha-sadeh*, December 1997, 20–23.

Slyomovics, Susan. *The Object of Memory: Arab and Jew Narrate the Palestinian Village*. University of Pennsylvania Press, 1998.

Smith, Linda Tuhiwai. *Decolonizing Methodologies: Research and Indigenous Peoples*. Zed Books, 2021

Sorek, Tamir. *Palestinian Commemoration in Israel: Calendars, Monuments, and Martyrs*. Stanford University Press, 2015.

Sowers, Jeannie Lynn. *Environmental Politics in Egypt: Activists, Experts, and the State*. Routledge Studies in Middle Eastern Politics, 50. Routledge, 2013.

———. "Remapping the Nation, Critiquing the State in Egypt." In *Environmental Imaginaries of the Middle East and North Africa*, edited by Diana K. Davis and Edmund Burke, 158–191. Ohio University Press, 2011.

Specht, Kathrin, and Esther Sanyé-Mengual. "Risks in Urban Rooftop Agriculture: Assessing Stakeholders' Perceptions to Ensure Efficient Policymaking." *Environmental Science & Policy* 69 (2017): 13–21.

Specht, Kathrin, Kristin Reynolds, and Esther Sanyé-Mengual. "Community and Social Justice Aspects of Rooftop Agriculture." In *Rooftop Urban Agriculture*, edited by Francesco Orsini, Marielle Dubbeling, Henk de Zeeuv, and Giorgio Gianquinto, 277-290. Springer, 2017.

Spivak, Gayatri Chakravorty. "Can the Subaltern Speak?" *Die Philosophin* 14, no. 27 (2003): 42-58.

Springer, Jenny. "State Power and Agricultural Transformation in Tamil Nadu." In *Agrarian Environments: Resources, Representations, and Rule in India*, edited by Arun Agrawal and Kalyanakrishnan Sivaramakrishnan, 86-106. Duke University Press, 2000.

Stamatopoulou-Robbins, Sophia C. "Failure to Build: Sewage and the Choppy Temporality of Infrastructure in Palestine." *Environment and Planning E: Nature and Space* 4, no. 1 (2020): 28-42. https://doi.org/10.1177/2514848620908193.

———. "An Uncertain Climate in Risky Times: How Occupation Became Like the Rain in Post-Oslo Palestine." *International Journal of Middle East Studies* 50, no. 3 (2018): 383-404.

———. *Waste Siege: The Life of Infrastructure in Palestine*. Stanford University Press, 2019.

Stein, Kenneth W. *The Land Question in Palestine, 1917-1939*. UNC Press Books, 2017.

Sternfeld, Lior B. *Between Iran and Zion*. Stanford University Press, 2020.

Stock, Ryan, and Trevor Birkenholtz. "The Sun and the Scythe: Energy Dispossessions and the Agrarian Question of Labor in Solar Parks." *The Journal of Peasant Studies* 48, no. 5 (2021): 984-1007.

Stoler, Ann Laura. "On Degrees of Imperial Sovereignty." *Public Culture* 18, no. 1 (2006): 125-146.

Strohm, Kiven. "The Sensible Life of Return: Collaborative Experiments in Art and Anthropology in Palestine/Israel." *American Anthropologist* 121, no. 1 (2019): 243-255.

Subramanian, Ajantha. *The Caste of Merit: Engineering Education in India*. Harvard University Press, 2019.

———. "Making Merit: The Indian Institutes of Technology and the Social Life of Caste." *Comparative Studies in Society and History* 57, no. 2 (2015): 291-322.

Sufian, Sandra M. *Healing the Land and the Nation: Malaria and the Zionist Project in Palestine, 1920-1947*. University of Chicago Press, 2008.

Swearingen, Will D. "In Pursuit of the Granary of Rome: France's Wheat Policy in Morocco, 1915-1931." *International Journal of Middle East Studies* 17, no. 3 (1985): 347-363.

Swedenburg, Ted. *Memories of Revolt: The 1936-1939 Rebellion and the Palestinian National Past*. University of Arkansas Press, 2003.

———. "The Palestinian Peasant as National Signifier." *Anthropological Quarterly* 63, no. 1, (1990): 18-30.

Svirsky, Marcelo, and Ronnen Ben-Arie. *From Shared Life to Co-resistance in Historic Palestine*. Rowman & Littlefield, 2017.

Tal, Alon. *Pollution in a Promised Land*. University of California Press, 2002.

———. "To Make a Desert Bloom: The Israeli Agricultural Adventure and the Quest for Sustainability." *Agricultural History* 81, no. 2 (2007): 228–257.

TallBear, Kim. "Feminist, Queer, and Indigenous Thinking as an Antidote to Masculinist Objectivity and Binary Thinking in Biological Anthropology." *American Anthropologist* 121, no. 2 (2019): 494–496.

———. "Indigenous Bioscientists Constitute Knowledges across Cultures of Expertise and Tradition." In *RE: MINDINGS: Co-Constituting Indigenous/Academic/Artistic Knowledges*, edited by J. Gärdebo, M. Öhman, and H. Maryuama. Uppsala Multiethnic Papers 55. Hugo Valentin Centre, Uppsala University, 2014.

Tamari, Salim. "Building Other People's Homes: The Palestinian Peasant's Household and Work in Israel." *Journal of Palestine Studies* 11, no. 1 (1981): 31–66.

Taylor, Judith M. *The Olive in California: History of an Immigrant Tree*. Ten Speed Press, 2000.

Taylor, Marcus. "Climate-Smart Agriculture: What Is It Good For?" *The Journal of Peasant Studies* 45, no. 1 (2018): 89–107.

Taylor, Lucy. "Four Foundations of Settler Colonial Theory: Four Insights from Argentina." *Settler Colonial Studies* 11, no. 3 (2021): 344–365.

Tawil-Souri, Helga. "Checkpoint Time." *qui parle* 26, no. 2 (2017): 383–422.

———. "Colored Identity: The Politics and Materiality of ID Cards in Palestine/Israel." *Social Text* 29, no. 2 (2011): 67–97.

Tesdell, Omar. "Territoriality and the Technics of Drylands Science in Palestine and North America." *International Journal of Middle East Studies* 47, no. 3 (2015): 570–573.

———. "Wild Wheat to Productive Drylands: Global Scientific Practice and the Agroecological Remaking of Palestine." *Geoforum* 78 (2017): 43–51.

Tesdell, Omar, Yusra Othman, and Saher Alkhoury. "Rainfed Agroecosystem Resilience in the Palestinian West Bank, 1918–2017." *Agroecology and Sustainable Food Systems* 43, no. 1 (2019): 21–39.

Theodossopoulos, Dimitrios. "The Pace of the Work and the Logic of the Harvest: Women, Labour and the Olive Harvest in a Greek Island Community." *Journal of the Royal Anthropological Institute* 5, no. 4 (1999): 611–626.

Thompson, Edward P. "Time, Work-Discipline, and Industrial Capitalism." *Past & Present* 38 (1967): 56–97.

Toperoff, Gidon, Tzafrir Grinhut, Yael Kahal, Anat Lowengart, and Hanan Bazak. "Sustainable Nutrition and Food Security in Israel: Quantitative Data Based on Crop Cultivation." *Ecology and the Environment* 4, no. 9 (2018): 18–27.

Tsing, Anna Lowenhaupt. *The Mushroom at the End of the World*. Princeton University Press, 2015.

Tubi, Omri. "Kill Me a Mosquito and I Will Build a State: Political Economy and the Socio-technicalities of Jewish Colonization in Palestine, 1922–1940." *Theory and Society* 50, no. 1 (2021): 97–124.

Tugendhaft, Yizhar, Amir Eppel, Zohar Kerem, Oz Barazani, Alon Ben-Gal, Joachim W. Kadereit, and Arnon Dag. "Drought Tolerance of Three Olive Cultivars Alternatively Selected for Rain Fed or Intensive Cultivation." *Scientia Horticulturae* 199 (2016): 158–162.

Ulrike Felt, "Of Timescapes and Knowledgescapes," In *New Languages and Landscapes of Higher Education*, edited by Peter Scott, Jim Gallacher, and Gareth Parry, 129–148. Oxford 2016.

Unger-Hamilton, Romana. "The Epi-Palaeolithic Southern Levant and the Origins of Cultivation." *Current Anthropology* 30, no. 1 (1989): 88–103.

Usishkin, David, Lily Singer-Avitz, and Hershel Shanks. "Kadesh-Barnea: In the Bible and on the Ground." *Biblical Archaeology Review* 41, no. 5 (2015): 36–44.

Valentinov, Vladislav. "Why Are Cooperatives Important in Agriculture? An Organizational Economics Perspective." *Journal of Institutional Economics* 3, no. 1 (2007): 55–69.

Vileisis, Ann. *Discovering the Unknown Landscape: A History of America's Wetlands.* Island Press, 1999.

Vimalassery, Manu, Juliana Hu Pegues, and Alyosha Goldstein. "Introduction: On Colonial Unknowing." *Theory & Event* 19, no. 4 (2016). muse.jhu.edu/article /633283.

Vitman, Ze'ev. *Likrat Shemitah Mamlakhtit Bi-medinat Yiśra'el: Hatsa'ah Le-kiyum Mitsvat Ha-shemitah Ba-metsi'ut Ha-ḥakla'it Ha-modernit.* Makhon Tsomet, 1993.

Vizenor, Gerald, ed. *Survivance: Narratives of Native Presence.* University of Nebraska Press, 2008.

Vizenor, Gerald Robert. *Manifest Manners: Postindian Warriors of Survivance.* University Press of New England, 1994.

Von Benda-Beckmann, Franz, and Keebet von Benda-Beckmann. "Places That Come and Go: A Legal Anthropological Perspective on the Temporalities of Space in Plural Legal Orders." In *The Expanding Spaces of Law*, edited by Irus Braverman, Nicholas K. Blomley, David Delaney, and Alexandre Kedar, 30–52. Stanford University Press, 2014.

Von Schnitzler, Antina. "Citizenship Prepaid: Water, Calculability, and Techno-politics in South Africa." *Journal of Southern African Studies* 34, no. 4 (2008): 899–917.

Wallerstein, Immanuel. "Braudel on the Longue Durée: Problems of Conceptual Translation." *Review (Fernand Braudel Center)* 32, no. 2 (2009): 155–170.

Watkins-Hayes, Celeste. "Race, Respect, and Red Tape: Inside the Black Box of Racially Representative Bureaucracies." *Journal of Public Administration Research and Theory* 21, no. 2 (2011): i233-i251.

Wenham, Gordon J. *The Book of Leviticus*. The New International Commentary on the Old Testament. Eerdmans, 1979.

Weiss, Erica. "Pseudonyms as Anti-Citation." In *Rethinking Pseudonyms in Ethnography*, edited by Carole McGranahan and Erica Weiss. American Ethnologist website, December 13, 2021. https://americanethnologist.org/features/collections/rethinking-pseudonyms-in-ethnography/pseudonyms-as-anti-citation.

Weiss, Erica, and Nissim Mizrachi. "A Time of Peace: Divergent Temporalities in Jewish–Palestinian Peace Initiatives." *HAU: Journal of Ethnographic Theory* 9, no. 3 (2019): 565–578.

Wesley, David A. *State Practices and Zionist Images: Shaping Economic Development in Arab Towns in Israel*. Berghahn Books, 2006.

West, Paige. *From Modern Production to Imagined Primitive: The Social World of Coffee from Papua New Guinea*. Duke University Press, 2012.

———. "Making the Market: Specialty Coffee, Generational Pitches, and Papua New Guinea." *Antipode* 42, no. 3 (2010): 690–718.

Whyte, Kyle. "Indigenous Climate Change Studies: Indigenizing Futures, Decolonizing the Anthropocene." *English Language Notes* 55, no. 1 (2017): 153–162.

———. "Indigenous Science (Fiction) for the Anthropocene: Ancestral Dystopias and Fantasies of Climate Change Crises." *Environment and Planning E: Nature and Space* 1, no. 1-2 (2018): 224–242.

Wiesman, Z. D. Itzhak, and N. Ben Dom. "Optimization of Saline Water Level for Sustainable Barnea Olive and Oil Production in Desert Conditions." *Scientia Horticulturae* 100, no. 1-4 (2004): 257–266,

Wilk, Richard, ed. *Fast Food/Slow Food: The Cultural Economy of the Global Food System*. Rowman Altamira, 2006.

Woertz, Eckart. "Arab Food, Water, and the Big Landgrab That Wasn't." *Brown Journal of World Affairs* 18 (2011): 119–132.

Wolf, Eric R. *Europe and the People without History*. University of California Press, 2010.

Wolfe, Patrick. "Settler Colonialism and the Elimination of the Native." *Journal of Genocide Research* 8, no. 4 (2006): 387–409.

Yacobi, Haim. "The Moral Geopolitics of Exported Spatial Development: Revisiting Israeli Involvement in Africa." *Geopolitics* 15, no. 3 (2010): 441–461.

Yankelevitch, Estie. "Agricultural Education in Agricultural High Schools in Palestine, 1870–1948." PhD diss., University of Haifa, 2004.

Yaron, Lee. "Once the Winter Used to Be in November, Now It Is Only in January: Apricots and Peaches Are Disappearing and It's Only the Beginning." *Haaretz*, January 18, 2022. Retrieved, February 1, 2022. https://www.haaretz.co.il/nature/climate/.premium.HIGHLIGHT-MAGAZINE-1.10532860.

Yazbak, Mahmoud. "From Poverty to Revolt: Economic Factors in the Outbreak of the 1936 Rebellion in Palestine." *Middle Eastern Studies* 36, no. 3 (2000): 93–113.

Yiftachel, Oren. *Ethnocracy: Land and Identity Politics in Israel/Palestine.* University of Pennsylvania Press, 2006.

———. *Landed Power: Israel/Palestine between Ethnocracy and Creeping Apartheid.* Resling Press, 2021.

———. "Territory as the kernel of the nation: space, time and nationalism in Israel/Palestine." *Geopolitics* 7, no. 2 (2002): 215–248.

Yusoff, Kathryn. *A Billion Black Anthropocenes or None.* University of Minnesota Press, 2018.

Zaban, Haim. *150 Years of Agriculture in Israel.* Maariv Publication, 2012.

Zaks, M., and Makhon Le-ḥeḳer Ha-ḥaḳlaʾut ʿal Pi Ha-Torah. *Liḳrat Shenat Ha-shemiṭah 5726* (Toward shmita year 5726). Hoveret Hadrakhah La-ḥaḳlaʾi (Agricultural instruction booklet). Ha-Makhon Le-ḥeḳer Ha-ḥaḳlaʾut ʿal Pi Ha-Torah She-ʿal Yad Poʿale Agudat Yiśraʾel, 1965.

Zerubavel, Eviatar. *Hidden Rhythms: Schedules and Calendars in Social Life.* University of Chicago Press, 1981.

Zerubavel, Yael. "The Forest as a National Icon: Literature, Politics, and the Archaeology of Memory." *Israel Studies* 1, no. 1 (1996): 60–99.

———. "Memory, the Rebirth of the Native, and the 'Hebrew Bedouin' Identity." *Social Research: An International Quarterly* 75, no. 1 (2008).

———. *Recovered Roots: Collective Memory and the Making of Israeli National Tradition.* University of Chicago Press, 1995.

Zeveloff, Naomi. "Farm to Table across the Green Line." *Forward,* April 24, 2015, 14–16.

Zoomers, Annelies. "Globalisation and the Foreignisation of Space: Seven Processes Driving the Current Global Land Grab." *The Journal of Peasant Studies* 37, no. 2 (2010): 429–447.

Zreik, Raef. "When Does a Settler Become a Native? (With Apologies to Mamdani)." *Constellations* 23, no. 3 (2016): 351–364.

Zu'bi, Nahla. "The Development of Capitalism in Palestine: The Expropriation of the Palestinian Direct Producers." *Journal of Palestine Studies* 13, no. 4 (1984): 88–109.

Zureik, Elia. *The Palestinians in Israel: A Study in Internal Colonialism.* Routledge, 1979.

———. "Transformation of Class Structure among the Arabs in Israel: From Peasantry to Proletariat." *Journal of Palestine Studies* 6, no. 1 (1976): 39–66.

Governmental and Intergovernmental Reports, Documents, and Minutes

Aboud, Touma. "Estimation of Environmental Pollution Potential from Olive Mill Wastewaters in Israel and Potential and Integrated Solutions." Paper presented at Olive Mills Management Symposium, Ministry of Agriculture, Beit Dagan, June 12, 2013.

Adler, Shaul. *Mesika, Hovala, Ihsun Ve-hafakat Shemen Zait Me-zeitim* (Harvest, transportation, storage, and oil production of olives). Ha-mahon Le-handasah Ve-pirion Ha-yitsur Ba-haklaut. 1965.

Ben-Yehuda, Tsach. *Authority for Food Emergency—Review of the Local Conditions and a Global Comparative View.* Knesset Research and Information Center, August 12, 2015. https://fs.knesset.gov.il/globaldocs/MMM/90c28d55-f7f7-e411-80c8-00 155d010977/2_90c28d55-f7f7-e411-80c8-00155d010977_11_8712.pdf .

CBS (Central Bureau of Statistics), National Agricultural Census 2017—Preliminary Findings. CBS, State of Israel, January 16, 2020.

———. Local Authorities in Israel—2018. CBS, State of Israel, July 26, 2020.

FAORNE. *Regional Overview of Food Insecurity: Near East and North Africa.* FAO, 2016.

Hershkovitz, Roni. *'Anaf Shemen Hazait: Skirat Megamot Beitsur Vesahar Olami* (Olive oil: Review of production trends and global trends). Ministry of Agriculture and Rural Development, Research Economy and Strategy Division, 2016.

Hok 'iskaot be-mekark'ei (Kium mitzvat shmitah) (Law of land transactions] Implementing shmita]). Knesset, 1979. https://main.knesset.gov.il/activity/ legislation/laws/pages/LawBill.aspx?t=LawReshumot&lawitemid=148015.

Israel Olive Oil Council. *Summary of 2022 Harvest Season.* https://www.instagram .com/reel/Cn4F8qto8yS/?igshid=MDM4ZDc5MmU%3D.

Jewish National Fund/Keren Kayemet LeIsrael. *Negev shel Tzmicha* (Negev growth plan). 1995.

Knesset. "Budget for Shmitah Observant Agriculturalists Who Cease Cultivation." In Minutes of the 245th meeting of the 13th Knesset, Wednesday, July 20, 1994. https://main.knesset.gov.il/activity/plenum/pages/SessionItem .aspx?itemID=437367.

Knesset, Economy Committee. Minutes no. 190 from meeting convened on September 11, 2000: The Impact of Shmitah Year on Agriculturalists. https://fs .knesset.gov.il//15/Committees/15_ptv_494858.docx.

———. Al-Battuf Flooding, April 30, 2013. https://fs.knesset.gov.il//19/Committees /19_ptv_230209.doc.

Ma'agar ha-hakika ha-leumi (National legislation database). Hok 'iskaot be-mekark'ein (Kium mitzvat shmitah). Parliament discussions of July 31, 1979, and August 1, 1979. http://main.knesset.gov.il/Activity/Legislation/Laws/ Pages/LawBill.aspx?t=lawsuggestionssearch&lawitemid=148015.

Mevaker Hamedina Do"h Shnati 59Bet Leshnat 2008 Ulehshbonot Shnat Haksafim 2007 (State Comptroller, annual report 59B for the fiscal year 2007). Jerusalem, 2009.

Minister of Religious Services and the Minister of Agriculture. Government Decision 104 (5.5.2013), Appendix 321—Preparations for Shmitah Year, May 28, 2014.

Ministry of Agriculture. Budget Proposal, Ministry of Agriculture 2011–2012. In State Budget 2011–2012, Ministry of Finance.

———. *The National Agricultural Planning Policy Protocol*, 2013.

———. *Olive Oil—Summary of 2019 and Trends across Time*, May 2020.

———. *Reshimat Maasikim Baalei Heiter Lehaasakat Ovdim Zarim* (List of employers with permit to hire foreign workers), 2011. Retrieved February 28, 2016. http://www.moag.gov.il/NR/rdonlyres/F47A218E-5AEB-4A1F-B1BC -0308B2AD2BBC/0/reshimat_ovdim_zarim.xls.

Ministry of Agriculture, Legal Office. *Nohal le-hokhahat zekhuiot be-karka pratit le-tsorkhei tmikha ve-haktasat emtsa'i yetsur* (Procedure for proving rights on private land for subsidy and allocation of means of production), March 30, 2015.

Ministry of Agriculture, Minhelet Ha-hashkaot (Investment Administration). *Nohal Tmikha be-Haklaim Mashbitei Meshakim Beshnat Ha-shmita Tashah* (Support of agriculturalists who disable agricultural activity in shmitah year tashah), May 15, 2014. Retrieved March 6, 2018. http://www.moag.gov.il/ yhidotmisrad/hashkaot/nohalim/Pages/shvita_meshakim_nohal.aspx.

Ministry of Agriculture, Minhelet Ha-hashkaot (Investment Administration). *Nohal Tmikha be-Haklaim Mashbitei Meshakim/Mashtelot/Karmey Yaiin Beshnat Ha-shmitah Tashpav 2017-2021* (Support of agriculturalists who disable agricultural activity/nurseries and wine vines in shmitah year tashpav), December 25, 2017. Retrieved March 6, 2018. www.moag.gov.il/yhidotmisrad/hashkaot/ . . . /tmicha_shmita.aspx.

Ministry of Agriculture, Planning Authority, the Jewish Agency and the Zionist Histadrut. *Hasefer Hayarok: Kavei Mediniut La-haklaut Ve-lakfar BeIsrael 2000–2005* (The Green Book: Policy guidelines for agriculture and rural areas in Israel), July 1999.

———. *Hasefer Hayarok: Mediniut shikum upituach ha-haklaut betkufat mashber ve-alyia Hamonit 1990–1995* (The Green Book: Agrarian recovery and development in the time of crisis and massive immigration 1990–1995), January 1991.

———. *Hasefer Hayarok II: Mediniut La-haklaut Ve-lakfar BeIsrael* (The Green Book II: Policy for agriculture and the rural areas), June 1996.

———. *Tochnit shesh shanim Le-pitauch Ha-haklaut Ve-haityashvut 1980–1985, Sikum Ha-mimzaim Ve-programa operativitit* (A six-year plan for the development of agriculture and settlement 1980-1985: Summary of findings and an operative plan), November 1980.

Ministry of Agriculture and Rural Development. *Mismakh Mediniut Haklaut Vekfar—Do"h Shlav Gimel—Hmalatsot* (The protocol for policy of agriculture and the rural areas—stage 3 report—recommendations and instructions for planning), 2013.

———. *Procedure for Funding Machinery and New Technologies, Precision Agriculture and Laborsaving Machines*, January 10, 2018. Retrieved April 23, 2018. http:

//www.moag.gov.il/yhidotmisrad/hashkaot/nohalim/Documents/nohal_
tmicha_100118.pdf.

———. *Vaadat Bhinat Meshek Mishpahti* (Committee for family farms review),
2013.

Ministry of Agriculture and Rural Development, Planning Authority (Misrad
ha-haklaut, ha-rashut le-tikhnun). *Ha-tokhnit ha-leumit la-haklaut vela-kfar be-
Yisrael, Mismakh #1* (The national protocol of planning policy of agriculture
and rural areas in Israel, # 1), August 13, 2013.

Ministry of Agriculture and Rural Development and Ministry of Environmental Protection. *Mitve Lekidum Tochnit Koleleanit LeBikat Beit Netofa* (Outline for
master plan for Beit Netofa Valley), January 11, 2012.

———. *Tochnit* Beit Netofa, March 13, 2014.

Ministry of Environmental Protection and Nature and Park Authority. Minutes,
January 12, 2012.

Ministry of Interior, Northern District Committee. Minutes, July 9, 2009.

Ministry of Interior, Planning Administration. National Master Plan 35, approved on September 6, 2016.

Ministry of Religious Services and Ministry of Agriculture. *Madrikh shmitah le-
haklaim* (A shmitah guide for farmers), 2014.

Ministry for Social Equality. *The Implementation Status of Decision 922*, June 21, 2021.

Mu'adi, Samir. *Summary of Shmita Year of 2007–2008.* Civil Administration to the
Area of Judea and Samaria, August 24, 2008.

Naali, Adi. "Review on the Recovery and Sensitivities of the Olive Oil Sector
2016," Israeli Olive Council, https://tinyurl.com/2p97ujkf

Organization for Economic Cooperation and Development (OECD). *Agricultural
Policy Monitoring and Evaluation 2015.* OECD Publishing, 2015. https://www
.oecd-ilibrary.org/agriculture-and-food/agricultural-policy-monitoring-and
-evaluation-2015_agr_pol-2015-en.

OECD-FAO Agricultural Outlook 2018–2027. OECD Publishing and FAO, 2018.
https://doi.org/10.1787/agr_outlook-2018-en.

Parger, Amir. *Fair Representation in the State Service: The Arab Society.* (Hebrew).
The Knesset Research and Information Center, August 4, 2020. https://fs
.knesset.gov.il/globaldocs/MMM/01e6da30-93ba-ea11-8116-00155d0af32a/2_
01e6da30-93ba-ea11-8116-00155d0af32a_11_16234.pdf.

Prime Minister's Office. *Ovdim zarim Be-'anaf há-haklaut* (Foreign workers in the
agriculture sector), March 6, 2012. Retrieved on February 19, 2016. http://
www.pmo.gov.il/Secretary/GovDecisions/2012/Pages/des4408.aspx.

Rahamimov, Arieh, and Meron Liora. *Tokhnit Kollelet Le-Bikat Beit Netofa-Sahel al-
Batuf* (A comprehensive plan for Beit Netofa Valley-al-Batuf Plain). Ministry
of Agriculture, Ministry of Environmental Protection, and Kishon Drainage
Authority, January 2017.

Shmolewitch, S. "'Akar in Waste Treatment Plants and Its Environmental Pollution." Paper presented at Olive Mills Management Symposium, Ministry of
Agriculture, Beit Dagan, June 12, 2013.

Shomoron, Mordekhai. *Madrikh Shmitah le-gan ha-noi*. Chief Rabbinate to Israel,
The Shmitah Committee, Makhon ha-torah ve-ha'aretz, Kfar Darom, 1993.

Sinai, Iftah, and Mimi Ron. "Seker Tsmahim Nedirim Bevikat Beit Netofa." Unpublished survey, 2006.

Sinai, Iftah, Mimi Ron, and Shai Koren, "Seker Tsmahim Nedirim Bevikat Beit
Netofa 2004–2011." Unpublished survey, 2012.

State of Israel, Central Bureau of Statistics. *Food Provision Balance* (Maazan Aspakat Hamazon), February 2022.

Israel State Archive (ISA)

ISA-ChiefRabbinate/000in2x, with letters from October 1954 to October 1966.

ISA/ChiefRabbinate/000in2x. Ha-mahlaka le-halakhot ha-tluyot ba'aretz
u'vaHaklaut (The Department for Jewish Laws Pertaining to the Land and
Agriculture).

ISA-ChiefRabbinate/000ie9u, with letters from November 1, 1957, to June 16,
1958.

ISA/ChiefRabbinate/000u8d5, with letters from February 1965 to August 1973.

ISA-ChiefRabbinate/000ie9v, with letters from June 17 to July 31, 1958.

ISA-EconomyPlanning-EconomyPlanning-000mxnm shmita December 1990.

ISA-moag-DeputyMinister-000aaas, October 1992 to April 1996.

ISA/moag/Minister/000nbao, December 1994 to June 1996.

ISA/moag/Minister/000nbao. Letter from lawyer Amnon De-Hartoch to Deputy
Attorney General Meny Mazuz, October 19, 1995.

ISA/ReligiousAffairs/DirectorGeneral/000oafm.

ISA/ReligiousAffairs/Minister/00007a2. Letter from Gdalia Schreiber, CEO of
the Chief Rabbinate, to the Deputy CEO of the Ministry of Religious Affairs,
January 6, 2000.

NGO Reports and References

The Arab Center for Alternative Planning. http://www.ac-ap.org/heb/?mod=
articles&ID=628.

Emek Shave. *From Territorial Contiguity to Historical Continuity: Asserting Israeli
Control through National Parks in East Jerusalem*, 2014.

Keren Hashviis. UK version of video, no name, no date. Retrieved July 10, 2018.
https://www.youtube.com/watch?v=UrrcWD-3evo.

INDEX

Page numbers in italics denote tables and figures. Endnotes are indicated by "n" followed by the endnote number.

The authorized representative in the EU for product safety and compliance is:
Mare Nostrum Group
B.V Doelen 72
4831 GR Breda
The Netherlands